HEAVEN
AND HELL

A new translation into modern English of the unique major work by the West's most remarkable philosopher and theologian

HEAVEN AND HELL

EMANUEL SWEDENBORG

translated by
GEORGE F. DOLE

SWEDENBORG FOUNDATION, INC.
NEW YORK

HEAVEN AND HELL

58th printing, 1990

First published in Latin, London, 1758
First English translation, U.S.A., 1812
First Dole translation, 1976
Revised Dole translation, 1979
1st Large Print edition—1982
Third Dole edition 1984

ISBN: 0-87785-167-0

Library of Congress Catalog Card Number: 81-52785

Cover design Nancy Crompton

Printed in the United States of America

Swedenborg Foundation, Inc.
139 East 23rd Street
New York, New York 10010

TABLE OF CONTENTS

5

PART II   THE WORLD OF SPIRITS

PART III   HELL

INTRODUCTION

There is a paradox involved in the basic quality of human existence. Our hands touch solid objects, our eyes see shapes and colors, our everyday horizons are narrow; yet there are times when the soul seems to stand on hilltops and to glimpse immense vistas of meaning. This feeling is not confined to saints or poets or philosophers—we all have it at certain moments of happiness and relaxation. It seems somehow *realer* than the trivialities of everyday existence. And this is the paradox. For surely "reality" means this world of solid objects that surround us, and the things they tell us about on television news? The poet replies, "No, these things are not 'realer' than the mystical vision; they are only *more close-up*." And he continues to try to find his way back to the hilltops. Many of the finest poets and artists of the 19th century died of exhaustion and despair at being unable to find them again.

Until the seventeenth century, European civilization was essentially Christian—which meant that man had a clear idea of the meaning of human existence. There was a heaven above and a hell beneath, and man was suspended somewhere between the two, able to glimpse heaven or sink into hell. That meant, essentially, that there was a greater "Meaning" behind the trivial meanings of his everyday existence, and he felt that everything he did had an invisible significance, which would become clear when he reached the After Life.

Science not only destroyed the religious myths, but also their deeper meanings. If man believes in nothing but the material world, he becomes a victim of the narrowness of his own consciousness. He is trapped in triviality. Religion gave man a *reason* for trying to reach the stars—for creating the magnificent spires and arches of Gothic cathedrals, the great masses of the medieval composers, the stained glass of Chartres, the mosaics of Michelangelo. Where there is a distance between heaven and earth there is also a great vault in which the spirit can soar. When heaven descends to earth, poetry has to crawl on its hands and knees.

Swedenborg belonged to an age of faith, when the majority of people believed in angels and devils; now, the new German critics insisted that the Bible was merely a piece of imaginative fiction, and that Jesus never existed. Intellectual men began to look back on the "age of faith" with nostalgia. Many of them—like Carlyle, Tennyson, Emerson, Melville—were men of religious feelings who were totally unable to accept traditional Christianity; they felt stranded in an emotional wasteland. In 1850, Emerson produced a long essay on Swedenborg in his *Representative Men*, treating him as one of the great mystical giants: "One of the . . . mastodons of literature he is not to be measured by whole colleges of ordinary scholars. . . . Our books are false by being fragmentary. . . . But Swedenborg is systematic and respective of the world in every sentence . . . his faculties work with astronomic punctuality, and this admirable writing is pure from all pertness or egoism." But he goes on to warn that to understand Swedenborg "requires almost a genius equal to his own."

At the age of fourteen, I was an ardent admirer of Emerson; I had expected his essays to be stuffy, and was amazed to discover that they were clear, shrewd, and imbued with a kind of heroic individualism. *Representative Men* impressed me even more; so when I saw the old Everyman edition of *True Christian Religion* in a Leicester bookshop, I saved up two weeks' pocket money and bought it. The disappointment was immense. It seemed to consist almost entirely of quotations from the scriptures, and long discussions of their precise meaning. That seemed to me a sheer waste of time. The Bible might be an extraordinary historical and religious document; but I was convinced that it was "inspired" only in the same sense as Shakespeare's plays or Dante's *Divine Comedy*. So it seemed pointless to discuss its words as if they were mathematical propositions from which you could prove something.

And then there were those incredible sections called "Memorabilia," in which Swedenborg described his discussions with angels. Most of them read like parables; but apparently Swedenborg insisted that they had actually taken place. At which point, I decided that Swedenborg was a man whose brain had addled through too much brooding on religion—like the religious nuts who came to our front door with tracts and gramophones. I pushed the book into a corner of the bookcase, and forgot about it.

Two years later, I discovered the poetry of William Blake, and began to read everything I could find about him. It seemed that in spite of the hostile remarks about Swedenborg, Blake had been strongly influenced by him. That was interesting, for Blake seemed to possess a healthy and skeptical intellect—not unlike that of Bernard Shaw. I borrowed Cyriel Sigstedt's *The Swedenborg Epic** from the library, and was startled to discover that Swedenborg began life as a scientist and engineer, and that everyone who met him agreed that he was a polite, logical man with a kindly manner and a sense of humor. And then there were those baffling stories of his second sight. About to sit down to dinner in Gothenburg, Swedenborg turned pale and told the company that a great fire had just broken out in Stockholm,

---

* *The Swedenborg Epic* (New York, Bookman Associates, 1952)

three hundred miles away. Two hours later, he said: "Thank heavens, the fire is now under control. It had almost reached my doorstep." Two days later, a letter arrived from Stockholm confirming everything he had said. That, of course, is "second sight," and many people possess it. The same might be said for the story of how he helped Madame Marteville, the widow of the Dutch ambassador, who had received a bill from a silversmith, although she was convinced that her husband had paid it; a few days later, Swedenborg told her that the receipted bill could be found in a secret drawer of a certain bureau. The bill was found where he had described it. Swedenborg claimed he had obtained the information direct from the deceased ambassador in the spirit world. He made the same claim about a message from the deceased brother of the Queen of Sweden; when Swedenborg described to her the contents of the last letter she had sent to her brother, the queen exclaimed "No one but God knows this secret."

Medieval culture was based on saints and visionaries; modern culture is based on Freud, Darwin and Marx. We envy Dante and Fra Angelico for having a heaven to soar into. And we recognize that men like Pascal, Blake, Swedenborg were attempting to reassert the basic reality of heaven, and so to create the conditions in which the spirit could soar. Our materialistic philosophy has made us slaves of the trivial. Yet how could Swedenborg and Blake begin to undermine this materialism? Only by asserting the solid *reality* of the visionary world. Blake said he saw a tree full of angels. Possibly he was lying—or exaggerating. But what of a man who says, "No, it is just a tree." Is he not lying too? Perhaps Blake's angels are closer to the truth. . . .

The argument is fair; but it begs the question of Swedenborg's visions. He insisted that he was *not* exaggerating or telling lies, or speaking in parables. Yet in another book he describes the inhabitants of the moon, Mars and Venus (admittedly, their spiritual inhabitants; not solid creatures). Which brings us back to the problem that baffled his contemporaries. Was he a genuine visionary, a God-inspired prophet? Or was he suffering from delusions?

Of one thing there can be no doubt: Swedenborg's contemporaries were in no position to answer that question. For there were only two possible schools of thought: scientists, who would dismiss the whole thing as superstition, and orthodox Christians who would admit that, in theory at any rate, there was no reason why a "chosen vessel" should not be taken on a circular tour of heaven.

In the late 19th century, science would begin to admit a third possibility: that the mind contains unexplored depths in which the visions might have originated. Freud's interpretation of that possibility would have been wholly negative: that the visions were basically some form of mental illness or compensation mechanism. But his ex-disciple Carl Jung suggested altogether more interesting possibilities. The subconscious mind is not a cellar filled with decaying rubbish and repressed passions. In fact, we make a mistake in thinking of the subconscious as something "inside" us. Perhaps the truth may be that we are inside *it*, like fishes in the sea. This "sea" contains many universal symbols, or archetypes, which are common to us all. What Jung was asserting was that there are things in the mind that have an *independent existence,* just like the objects around us in the material world. Jung developed a technique called "active imagination" that enabled him to descend into his own mind and hold conversations with "imaginary" beings. There was a character whom he called Philemon, and Jung says, "In my fantasies I held conversations with him, and he said things which I had not consciously thought. *For I observed clearly that it was he who spoke, not I."* [My italics.]

In 1953, the writer Aldous Huxley experimented with the drug mescaline sulphate, which produced the effect of intensifying his perception of reality, and making him aware that when we think we are "seeing" the world, we are actually perceiving it through a thick mental blanket of our own concepts and desires. And in a book whose title—*Heaven and Hell*—seems to be a deliberate evocation of Swedenborg, he stated, "Like the earth of a hundred years ago, our mind still has its darkest Africas, its unmapped Borneos and Amazonian basins." And he went on to say that these unexplored continents of the mind contain creatures as strange and improbable as the giraffe and duckbilled platypus.

These observations, while they leave certain basic questions unanswered, nevertheless enable us to understand that the words "vision" and "reality" are not mutually exclusive. Shaw was hinting at the same thing when he made his Joan of Arc say that God speaks to us through the imagination. He was using the word "imagination" in Blake's sense. ("Vision or Imagination is a Representation of what Eternally Exists. . .")

The same point is made very clearly in an important recent work, *Essay on the Origin of Thought* by Jurij Moskvitin*—a Danish philosopher. He began by observing that when he lay with his eyes half-closed in the sunlight, looking at the sky through his eyelashes, he became aware of a fascinating spectrum of colors, and of geometric patterns. Gradually, he accustomed himself to "focusing" these patterns at will, and concluded that they were made up of "dancing sparks." Further observation convinced him that the sparks were not really independent; they were prominent parts of certain "smoke-like forms." He explains this with a useful image,

---

* Moskvitin, Jurij, *Essay on the Origin of Thought*. (Ohio University Press, 1974).

saying that if you look at the sea in the sunlight, the breaking waves seem to be tipped with light, but that if you stare hard, these "sparks" are seen to be part of rings and nets that move over the water. He goes on to say that the smoke-like forms "became the elements of waking dreams, forming persons, landscapes, strange mathematical forms . . ." It struck him that much religious art seems to contain perceptions of these forms. "The actual experience is like a Rorschach test—always interpreted according to what a man has in his mind. . . . This is the derivation of all ghosts, elves and demons."

Moskvitin is perhaps not as clear as he might be—and much of the book is impossibly abstract—but the basic meaning seems clear. We are inclined to think of our perception as a kind of mirror, merely reflecting the reality around us. You are like a man looking through a reflecting telescope; light travels from that book to the mirror, and is reflected down to "you," looking through the eyepiece. Moskvitin is saying that in perception, we "project" some kind of magic element from *behind* the eyes: the world is not reflected in a mirror, but in something more like the moving surface of the sea, and we *infer* the reality through a skill developed over a lifetime. (Moskvitin mentions, as a parallel, how the satin draperies in a Dutch painting, or a realistic-looking wine glass, are actually seen, on closer inspection, to be a few careless strokes of colored paint, *suggesting* rather than depicting.)

And in his book on Swedenborg, *The Presence of Other Worlds,** Dr. Wilson Van Dusen advances suggestions about Swedenborg's visions that are based on his own experience of meditation and "hypnagogic states" (i.e. states that exist on the borderline of sleeping and waking). Most

* Wilson Van Dusen, *The Presence of Other Worlds*. (New York: Harper & Row, 1974).

of us observe such states briefly, then fall asleep. Van Dusen insists that it is possible to remain awake, observing "mental processes occur spontaneously." Like Jung, he notes that, "There is enough self-awareness in the hypnagogic state to remember, record and even talk to inner processes."

And now, I think, we may say that we are getting altogether closer to the reality of Swedenborg's visionary experiences—or at least, to their basic mechanisms. Moskvitin comments that, "What I felt to be 'me' and my thoughts were actually the things to be observed." That is to say when a man becomes practiced in this kind of observation he somehow withdraws *behind* his thoughts, feelings and impressions, no longer assuming that they are part of himself. It is as if, in our "normal" state, we imagined that our clothes were a part of our bodies, and had to learn to observe the sensations in the skin to recognize that clothes are quite separate from the rest of us.

Beyond the hypnagogic state lies the trance state, in which the "naked self," so to speak, learns to descend into the inner world without falling asleep. Consciousness is intensified, but bodily awareness is lost.

And at this point, we must admit that it is difficult to follow Swedenborg—or Van Dusen—any further. Were the angels and devils seen by Swedenborg real beings? Or were they "Rorschach blots" transformed by Swedenborg's subconscious? Or by Jung's racial unconscious? Although we certainly know more about these inner states than Swedenborg's contemporaries, we still have only half the answer, or perhaps even less. Jung believed that Philemon was, in fact, a "wiser self," representing superior insight. Other modern psychologists have made use of the concept of the "superconscious mind." For if the mind has its subconscious "cellar," may it not also have a superconscious "attic," a part of the mind that possesses deeper insight and higher knowledge than the "everyday self"? Many water diviners believe that their dowsing rods respond to the knowledge of the superconscious mind; this seems to be confirmed by the fact that a good dowser can divine for *anything*, simply by "tuning in." If he is dowsing for oil or iron ore, his rod will ignore water. And so it seems probable, at least, that Swedenborg's angels were, like Philemon, representatives of his higher self, and that his visions of heaven and hell were symbolic representations of real inner states encountered by the soul after death. (According to Swedenborg, the world after death consists entirely of inner states, and has no external space and time like our world.)

At the same time, we must admit that it *is* possible that these angels were, in fact, higher beings, and not "symbols" created by the mind. Van Dusen states flatly that "these inner states raise the issue of the presence of other spiritual beings interacting in our lives." Novels like *The Exorcist* have certainly popularized the possibility that demonic forces might exist independent of the human mind. And when we begin to examine recorded cases of "possession," we again become aware of the ambiguities that are concealed by our clear, scientific concepts. Jung began his career as a psychologist by observing a female cousin who seemed to possess two completely distinct personalities. Psychologists who have studied cases of dual—and even multiple—personalities conclude that there are strange ways in which the self can split into several mutually independent personalities. This seems to suggest that we are dealing simply with a Freudian problem of repression. But then, how do we explain how "possessed" people occasionally speak in languages of which they have no knowledge—for example, Latin?

An experience recorded by the "paranormal" researcher

Alan Vaughan may help to throw light on one aspect of
Swedenborg's powers. At the beginning of *Patterns of
Prophecy*, he explains how he became interested in the
power of foreseeing the future. Experimenting alone with
a Ouija board, Vaughan found himself "possessed" by a
neurotic woman, whose "voice" somehow got inside his
head. Experimenting with another friend, Vaughan suddenly
experienced a second presence inside his head—this time
a benevolent presence, which made him write out a message:
"Each of us has a spirit while living. Do not meddle with
the spirits of the dead." Suddenly, a third presence seemed
to rise inside him with a flood of energy, driving out both
the other two. In this moment of "dispossession," Vaughan
experienced a tremendous elation and well-being, and realized that he could read other people's minds, and see into
the future "through some kind of extended awareness."
The experience led to his interest in prophetic dreams.

Quite obviously, we stand on the borderline of a new
domain of knowledge, and we know as little of it as Marco
Polo knew of China, or the earliest explorers of Africa. One
thing seems clear: there are mental states in which we can
glimpse vistas of knowledge that remain concealed from us
in "everyday consciousness." Our great mistake lies in
supposing that the kind of "knowledge" we acquire slowly
over a lifetime is real, ultimate knowledge. We are probably
like blind men, born into a world in which we have to find
our way around by the sense of touch—and by the use of
walking sticks, scientific extensions of sensory knowledge.
Like the citizens of Wells' country of the blind, we take it
as a law of nature that only certain forms of knowledge are
possible (for example, that you cannot know when a man
is approaching until he is close enough to hear). Vaughan's
sudden glimpse of a power to read other people's minds and
see into the future seems to be the equivalent of "sight"
in our blind men.

We know that Swedenborg always possessed unusual intellectual powers, and a remarkable ability to concentrate for long periods. We know that he went through great spiritual crises in his sixth decade, and it seems probable that his frantic struggles led to the activation of this "new faculty." Books like *Divine Providence* and *Divine Love and Wisdom* were not written in some confused state of religious mania, but in a strange state of visionary clarity that led him to write at top speed to try to convey everything he saw. He lived in a religious age; his father was a bishop; he had studied the Bible since childhood. It was therefore natural that his visions expressed themselves in terms of the Bible. If he had been brought up on the works of Shakespeare or Dante, no doubt his ideas would have expressed themselves in the form of gigantic commentaries on the Tragedies or the *Divine Comedy*. The chief obstacle to the modern understanding of Swedenborg is that few of us can take the Bible for granted in the way that our great-grandfathers did. This is a sad reflection on the modern age; and it means that if anyone is anxious to reach some understanding of Swedenborg's strange mystical vision, he will have to take the trouble to become acquainted with this vital part of our literary heritage.

For the beginner, patience is certainly necessary; originally written in Latin, by a man whose previous works had all been scientific treatises, their style makes an initial impression of dullness. Once you have grown accustomed to his habit of mind, they are readable enough, and a good modern translation makes a considerable difference. It quickly dawned on me that I was mistaken about one thing. Swedenborg is no cranky religious messiah, demanding total credence and allegiance. He admits that he is an intellectual, who prefers to be understood rather than believed. One of the Memorabilia in his *True Christian Religion* describes his encounter (in the spirit world, of course), with a preacher whose religious obscurities are punctuated with the statement that it is important to "keep our reason in subjection to faith." This view makes Swedenborg see red. Swedenborg tells the priest that there is no point in talking about "mysteries" unless you are prepared to try and *look inside them* and try to understand them. The priest is furious, and the congregation make their way home contentedly, "intoxicated with paradoxes, bewildered with verbiage and enveloped in darkness."

This very quickly becomes plain as you read Swedenborg: he is obsessed with making himself clear. No one ever cared less about trying to impress with tricks of style or poetic images. Compared to some of the Catholic saints—Theresa of Avila, for example—he seems to be almost a rationalist.

Heaven and Hell has always been Swedenborg's most popular book because it can be read with a minimum of such preparation. Yet even this book has its pitfalls. Emerson said of it: "A vampire sits in the seat of the prophet, and turns with gloomy appetite to the images of pain. Indeed, a bird does not more readily weave its nest . . . than this seer of the souls substructs a new hell and pit, each more abominable than the last . . . Except Rabelais and Dean Swift, nobody ever had such science of filth and corruption." This makes Swedenborg sound like an old fashioned hellfire preacher. Yet the Swedish genius Strindberg, passing through a severe psychological crisis that brought him to the brink of madness, found sanity in *Heaven and Hell*, recognizing that Swedenborg had described the succession of mental states and decisions that had brought him to the brink of his own private hell. Strindberg became increasingly convinced that Swedenborg was a visionary genius who had foreseen the spiritual torments of the twentieth century. Strindberg himself foretold them with extraordinary clarity, even though he died before the first world war.

When the psychologist William James passed through a crisis of depression and panic anxiety, he used Swedenborg's term "vastation" to describe the state. And this was natural enough since his own father, Henry James, Sr., had been brought back from the brink of mental and physical breakdown by the discovery of Swedenborg's works. The breakdown had come upon him suddenly and without warning, one day after eating a comfortable dinner, sitting idly at the table and feeling rather pleased with himself. "Suddenly—in a lightning flash, as it were—fear came upon me, and trembling, which made all my bones to shake. To all appearances it was a perfectly insane and abject terror, without ostensible cause, and only to be accounted for, to my perplexed imagination, by some damned shape squatting invisible to me within the precincts of the room, and raying out from his fetid personality influences fatal to life. . . ."

The depression and terror continued for two years, until a woman friend told him that he was suffering from what Swedenborg called "vastation," and that it could well be the gateway to some inward transformation. James was so ill that he was not allowed to read; nevertheless, he bought two volumes of Swedenborg and kept them by his bed, dipping into them for a few sentences at a time. Finally, he began to read avidly. "I read from the first with palpitating interest. My heart divined, even before my intelligence was prepared to do justice to the books, the unequalled amount of truth to be found in them. Imagine a fever patient, sufficiently restored of his malady to think of something besides himself, suddenly transported where the free airs of heaven blow upon him, and the sound of running water refreshes his jaded sense; and you have a feeble image of my delight in reading. . . ." James became convinced that the cause of all his suffering had been "the profound unconscious death I bore about in my . . . selfhood."

Swedenborg's crises had brought him close to insanity; this is undoubtedly why he possesses such extraordinary power to bring peace to tormented souls like Strindberg and James. "One thunderstorm followed another. My enduring these storms was a matter of brute strength. Others have been shattered by them—Nietzsche and Hölderlin, and many others. But there was a demoniac strength in me, and from the beginning there was no doubt in my mind that I must find the meaning of what I was experiencing . . ." This is not Swedenborg speaking—as the reference to Nietzsche and Hölderlin must have made plain—but Jung. Yet no one who has read both Jung and Swedenborg can doubt that it was the mystic, not the psychologist, who ventured furthest into the depths of this alien world that lies inside us.

Heaven and Hell is the best introduction to Swedenborg because it has the quality of a compressed image of all his theological works. His writings amount to fifty or so heavy volumes, and their range is immense—from a study of the human brain to a study of the Pentateuch that is longer than the Old Testament itself. The books represent a spiritual journey through an unmapped continent; there are vast forests, underground rivers, burning mountains. Emerson was right to classify Swedenborg with Plato, Shakespeare, Goethe. He is not ultimately unknowable; but complete understanding would cost years of effort. A book like this can at least offer a glimpse of the unmapped continent; but it can give no idea of its size.

Colin Wilson
Cornwall, 1978

TRANSLATOR'S PREFACE

There have been at least nineteen distinct translations or revisions of translations of Swedenborg's *Heaven and Hell* in English since 1778, the most recent being the 1958 revision by Doris Harley of the 1900 translation by J. C. Ager. The impetus for the present version, then, does not come from any fear of the work's unavailability. Rather, it comes from the conviction that the directness and simplicity of the Latin text is an integral part of its design, and has been consistently obscured in English translations by the choice of a heavily Latinate style.

The present effort, then, is not an attempt at "popularization." In fact, several distinctions are here consistently observed which are consistently ignored in other versions. The translator's task has been seen as finding an English style, both in vocabulary and syntax, comparable to that of the Latin. This has involved such steps as finding equivalent syntactic devices rather than adopting classical ones, and "translating" the punctuation as consciously and consistently as possible.

The first draft and typescript were done with virtually no reference to other translations, primarily to avoid reacting to the opinions of others. A draft portion of the manuscript was submitted to a number of other translators before final revision. Mr. John Chadwick responded most helpfully; I have adopted most of his suggestions and have tried to locate the kinds of faults he observed elsewhere, and to correct them. The final revisions, which uncovered many further errors, involved a line by line comparison with the Harley version mentioned above.

For purposes of the present edition, Swedenborg's copious references to his *Arcana Coelestia* have been omitted. Bibliographical information on other works referred to may be found at the back of the book. Biblical quotations are translated directly from Swedenborg's Latin.

Swedenborg numbered each section. This numbering is uniform in all editions and has been retained in the margins. The subsection numbers are from J. F. Pott's *The Swedenborg Concordance*.

The new reader will note that these numbers are invaluable in giving consistency to references in a work that has appeared in so many editions.

No translation can present all the dimensions of its original, in this sense, a "Standard Edition" is not to be desired. It is my hope that the present version will stand beside others, and will at least suggest a clarity and concreteness of thought in the original that has usually been obscured. I may hope also that it will provoke constructive discussion in the small circle of translators of Swedenborg. The person who translates alone cannot hope to find optimum solutions to every problem, and I trust that better work will emerge in the course of time with the exchange of ideas and information.

Finally, I would like to express my gratitude to many people whose interest has encouraged me—they do not know how helpful they have been—and particularly to the Swedenborg Foundation for its consistent and cheerful support.

G. F. Dole
Sharon, Mass.
March 1975

AUTHOR'S PREFACE

1. In *Matthew* 24, the Lord is talking to His disciples about the end of the age, or the last time of the church. In concluding His predictions about the church's successive states of love and faith, He says,

> Immediately after the misery of those days the sun will be darkened and the moon will not give her light, and the stars will fall from heaven, and the powers of the heavens will be shaken. And then the sign of the Son of man will appear in heaven, and then all the tribes of the earth will mourn; and they will see the Son of man coming in the clouds of heaven with power and great glory. And He will send His angels with a trumpet and a great voice, and they will gather together His elect from the four winds, from one end of the heavens to the other. (Matthew 24:29-31.)

People who take these words literally can only believe that all these things are going to happen literally, just as described, in some final time called the Last Judgment. That is, the sun and moon will become dark, the stars will fall from heaven, the sign of the Lord will appear in heaven, and He Himself will appear in the clouds, along with the angels with trumpets. Beyond this even, according to predictions elsewhere, they believe the whole visible world is going to perish, and then a new heaven and a new earth will emerge.

There are many people in the church today who think this way. But such people do not know the arcana[1] underlying the very details of the Word. For in the very details of the Word there is an inner meaning, one that deals not with

---

[1]Arcana (sg. arcanum), "things which lie hidden."

natural, earthly matters like those in the literal sense, but with spiritual and heavenly matters.

This holds true not just for groups of words, but even for each single word. For the Word was composed using pure correspondences for the very purpose of having an inner meaning in every detail. The nature of this meaning can be ascertained from all the statements and explanations of it in *Arcana Coelestia*. A collection of these may be found in the exegesis of *The White Horse described in Revelation*.

This is the sense in which we should understand what the Lord said about His coming in the clouds in the passage cited above. There, the sun which will be darkened refers to the Lord in respect to love, the moon to the Lord in respect to faith. The stars refer to insights of what is good and true (or of love and faith), the sign of the Son of man in heaven to Divine truth becoming visible, and the coming of the Lord in the clouds of heaven with power and glory to His presence in the Word and to revelation. The clouds refer to the literal meaning of the Word, the glory to the Word's inner meaning, and the angels with trumpet and loud voice to heaven, where Divine truth comes from.

On this basis we can determine what these words of the Lord would have us understand, namely that the Lord is going to open the Word in respect to its inner meaning at the end of the church, when there is no more love and therefore no faith; and that he is going to uncover arcana of heaven. The arcana which are uncovered in the pages that now follow have to do with heaven and hell, and accordingly with man's life after death.

Today's churchman knows almost nothing about heaven, hell, or his own life after death, even though this is all described in the Word. It has gone so far that even many people born in the church deny these things and ask in their hearts, "Has anyone come back and told us?"

To prevent so negative an attitude (which is particularly prevalent among people with much worldly wisdom) from infecting and corrupting people of simple heart and simple faith, it has been made possible for me to be right with angels and to talk with them person to person. I have also been allowed to see what heaven is like and then what hell is like; this has been going on for thirteen years. So now I may describe heaven and hell from what I have seen and heard, hoping for the enlightenment of ignorance and the dispersion of disbelief by this means. The reason for the occurrence today of such direct revelation is that this is what ''the Lord's coming'' means.

1.

THE LORD IS HEAVEN'S GOD

2. We need first to know who the God of heaven is, since the rest depends on this. Throughout the whole of heaven, no one is recognized as God except the Lord. They say there, just as He Himself taught, that

> He is one with the Father; that the Father is in Him and He in the Father; that anyone who sees Him sees the Father; and that everything holy comes from Him.
>
> (John 10:30, 38; 14:9-11; 16:13-15)

I have quite often talked with angels about this, and they have invariably said that in heaven they are quite incapable of dividing the Divine in three. This is because they both know and perceive that the Divine is one and is one in the Lord. They have further said that church people coming from the world with the idea of three "Divines" cannot be let into heaven, since their thought wanders from one to another, and since in heaven they may not think "three" and say "one."

This is because everyone in heaven speaks from his thought, for they have thought-speech there, or vocal thought. So there is no possibility of accepting people who in the world divided the Divine in three, adopting a separate idea of each and not unifying and centering their concept in the Lord. Actually, there occurs in heaven a communication of all thoughts, so that if someone were to arrive who thought "three" and said "one," he would be recognized and repelled instantly.

However, it is essential to know that people who have not separated what is true from what is good (or faith from love) all accept the heavenly concept of the Lord when they are taught in the other life—the concept, that is, that the Lord is the God of the universe. It is quite different with people who have separated faith from life, that is, who have not lived by the principles of a true faith.

3. Church people who deny the Lord, recognizing only the Father, and who let themselves harden in this kind of faith, are outside of heaven. And since there occurs among them no inflow from heaven, where only the Lord is worshipped, step by step they lose the ability to think the truth about anything. Eventually they become like mutes or speak sluggishly, and wander about with their arms dangling loose as though they were powerless at the joints.

People who deny the Divine side of the Lord and recognize only His Human side, like Socinians, are likewise outside of heaven. They are moved forward a bit toward the right and let down deep, so becoming completely separated from everyone else from Christendom.

As for people who claim to believe in an invisible Divine called the Reality of the Universe, the source of all that exists, but who cast aside any belief about the Lord, they are shown to believe in no God at all. This is because an invisible Divine is for them like nature in first principles, which is no fit subject for faith and love because it is no fit subject for thought. They are sent off to be with people called naturalists.

Things work out differently for people born outside the church, called Gentiles; but more on this below.

4. Little children, who make up a third of heaven, all are led at first into a recognition and belief that the Lord is their own Father, and later into a recognition and belief that He is the Lord of everyone and therefore God of heaven and earth. We will show later that little children mature in heaven, and develop to angelic intelligence and wisdom by means of insights.

5. People from the church should have no uncertainty about the Lord's being the God of heaven, since He Himself has taught that everything of the Father's is His (Matthew 11:27, John 16:25, 17:2) and that He owns all power in heaven and on earth (Matthew 28:18). He said "in heaven and on earth" because heaven's ruler also rules earth, the one being dependent on the other. Ruling heaven and earth means receiving from Him everything good, which is the property of love, and everything true, which is the property of faith. This means all intelligence and wisdom, and therefore all happiness; in a word, it is receiving eternal life.

The Lord taught this as well when He said,

Whoever believes in the Son has eternal life; but whoever does not believe in the Son will not see life.   (John 3:36)

and elsewhere,

I am the resurrection and the life, whoever believes in Me, even though he die, will yet live; and whoever lives and believes in Me shall not die forever.   (John 11:25-26)

and elsewhere,

I am the way, the truth, and the life.   (John 14:6)

6. There are particular spirits who, during their life on earth, had made much of the Father, having no concept of the Lord except as just another man. So they did not believe that He was the God of heaven. Because of this, they were allowed to travel about wherever they wanted and ask whether there was some heaven that did not belong to the Lord. They asked here and there for some days, but they found no such place.

They were of the type that thought heaven's happiness lay in glory and authority. Since they could not get what they craved and were told that heaven does not consist of things like these, they felt resentful. They wanted a heaven where they could have authority over others and could rival the kind of glory that exists in the world.

2.

THE LORD'S DIVINE MAKES HEAVEN

7. The angels collectively are called heaven, since they make it up. But in the last analysis it is the Divine from the Lord, flowing into angels and accepted by them, that makes heaven overall and in every part. The Divine coming from the Lord is the good content of love and the true content of faith. So to the extent that people accept what is good and true from the Lord, they are angels, and are heaven.

8. Absolutely everyone in heaven knows and believes and even perceives that he neither intends nor does anything good nor thinks nor believes anything true on his own, but that his ability comes from the Divine, which means that it is from the Lord. He also sees that anything good or true from himself is not really good or true because it contains no life from the Lord. In fact, the angels of the inmost heaven see this clearly and feel the inflow. To the extent that they accept it, it seems to them that they are in heaven; for the measure of their acceptance is the measure of their involvement in love and faith and in the light of intelligence and wisdom, and the measure of their resultant heavenly joy.

Granted, then, that all these things do come from the Lord's Divine, and that heaven, for the angels, is within them, it is clearly the Lord's Divine that makes heaven, and not the angels—not by reason of anything that really belongs to them.

This is why heaven is called "the Lord's home" and "His throne" in the Word, and why people in heaven are said to be "in the Lord." More will be said below about just how the Divine emanates from the Lord and fills heaven.

9. Because of their wisdom, angels go a step further. Not only, they say, is everything good and true from the Lord, even all of life is from Him. They support this with the principle that nothing can emerge from itself; everything needs some antecedent. So all things emerge from a First, which they call the very Being of all life. Things endure in the same manner, since enduring is constant emergence. If anything is not kept in constant connection with the First by means of something in between, it will promptly decay and utterly disintegrate.

[2] Further, they say that there is only one fountain of life. Man's life is one of its brooks, which would trickle away if it did not stay constantly supplied from its fountain.

Further still, they say that nothing comes from that only fountain of life, the Lord, that is not Divinely good and Divinely true. These influence every particular individual according to the way he accepts them. People who accept them with belief and life find heaven in them. But people who cast them aside or stifle them transform them into hell; for by transforming the good into the evil and the true into the false, they transform life into death.

The angels also support the principle that all life is from the Lord as follows: everything in the universe goes back to the good and the true. Man's voluntary life—the life of his love—goes back to the good, and man's intellectual life—the life of his belief—goes back to the true. So if everything good and true comes from above, so does all of life.

[3] Because angels do believe this, they shrug off any expressions of gratitude for good they have done. They are insulted and go away if anyone credits them with goodness. They are amazed that anyone would believe he is wise on

his own or does good on his own. They do not call it "good" when someone does good for his own sake, for this comes from the person himself. They call it good from the Lord when someone does what is good for its own sake. Such "good," they say, is what makes heaven, because such "good" is the Lord.

10. There are spirits who, while they still lived on earth, had convinced themselves that their good deeds and true beliefs came from themselves, or who took credit for them. This is the belief of all people who associate merit with good works and claim righteousness for themselves. They are not accepted in heaven. The angels shun them. They see them as senseless and as thieves—senseless because they are always looking at themselves and not at the Divine, and thieves because they steal from the Lord what belongs to Him. Such attitudes go against heaven's faith that it is the Lord's Divine among the angels that makes heaven.

11. The Lord also teaches that people in heaven and in the church are in Him, and He in them, when He says,

Stay in Me, and I in you. As the branch cannot bear fruit by itself, unless it stays in the vine, neither can you, unless you stay in Me. I am the vine, you are the branches. Whoever stays in Me, and I in him, bears much fruit; for without Me you cannot do anything. (John 15:4-5)

12. On this basis we can ascertain that the Lord dwells in what belongs to Him among the angels of heaven. We can also see that the Lord is all there is to heaven, because the good from the Lord is the Lord among the angels. For whatever is from Him is Himself. It is the good from the Lord, then, that is heaven to angels, not anything that belongs to them.

3.

THE LORD'S DIVINE IN HEAVEN IS LOVE FOR HIM AND CHARITY TOWARD ONE'S NEIGHBOR

13. In heaven, the Divine that emanates from the Lord is called "the Divine-True," for a reason which will be discussed below. This Divine-True flows into heaven from the Lord out of His Divine Love. Divine Love and its resulting Divine-True relate to each other like the sun's fire, and its resulting light in the world. The love is like the sun's fire, and the resulting truth like light from the sun. By reason of this correspondence, then, fire refers to love and light to the truth that comes from it.

We can determine from this the nature of the Divine-Truth that comes from the Lord's Divine Love. Essentially, it is the Divine-Good yoked to the Divine-True. Because it is yoked, it makes all elements of heaven live, just as in this world the sun's warmth yoked to its light makes all the elements of the world bear fruit in spring and summertime. It is different when warmth is not yoked to the light, when the light is therefore cold. Then everything is numbed and lies dead.

The Divine-Good, which we have compared to warmth, is for angels the good content of love. The Divine-True, which is like light, is the means and source of the good content of that love.

14. The reason the formative Divine in heaven is love is that love is a spiritual bond. It joins angels to the Lord, and joins them to each other. It actually joins them in a way that makes them a "one" in the Lord's sight.

Further, Love is the very Being of everyone's life. It is therefore the source of life for angel and man alike. Anybody can know that man's central vitality comes from love if he weighs the facts that love's presence warms him, love's absence chills him, and love's total removal means his death. But he should also realize that everyone's love is of the same quality as his life.

15. In heaven, there are two distinct loves—love for the Lord and love toward the neighbor. Love for the Lord dwells in the inmost or third heaven; love toward the neighbor dwells in the second or intermediate heaven. Each comes from the Lord, and each makes a heaven. In heaven's open light, the way these two loves differ and the way they connect is clear, but it is quite hard to see this on earth. In heaven, "loving the Lord" is not understood to mean loving Him in His role, but loving the good that comes from Him. Loving the good means intending and doing what is good, out of love. "Loving the neighbor" is not understood to mean loving a companion in his role, but loving what is true that comes from the Word. Loving what is true means intending and doing what is true. We can see from this that these loves differ the way the good and true differ, and associate the way the good associates with the true. But this will not fit comfortably into the concepts of a person who does not realize what love, the good, and the neighbor are.

16. I have talked a number of times with angels about this. They were amazed, they said, that church people do not know that loving the Lord and loving the neighbor mean loving what is good and what is true and doing them intentionally. Yet they might well realize that a person shows love by voluntarily doing what someone else wants. So he is loved in return, and becomes yoked to the other. This does not happen by loving someone and not doing what he wants, which intrinsically is "not-loving."

They might also realize that the good which comes from the Lord is a likeness of Him because He is within it. People are likenesses of Him when they make the good and the true part of their lives by intention and act—intending is loving to do. The Lord teaches the truth of this in the Word, saying,

> Whoever holds my commandments and does them is the one who loves Me; . . . and I will love him, and will make a home with him. (John 14:21, 23)

and elsewhere,

> If you do my commandments, you will stay in my love. (John 15: 10, 12)

17. All the evidence in heaven bears witness to the fact that the Divine which emanates from the Lord, influences angels, and makes heaven, is love. All the people who are there are actual models of love and charity. They look bewilderingly beautiful; love radiates from their faces, their speech, and every detail of their lives.

Further, there are spiritual spheres of life which emanate from each angel and spirit and envelop him. By means of these spheres, one can tell sometimes even at a distance what they are like in affections of love, because these spheres flow out from each individual's life of affection and its resultant thought, or from his love's life and its resultant faith.

The spheres projected by angels are so full of love that they move the very depth of life of people about them. They have reached my own perceptions a number of times, and have moved me to these depths.

I have also been able to see that love is the source of angels' life because in the other life everyone turns in the direction of his love. People who are involved in a love for the Lord and in a love toward the neighbor always turn toward the Lord. People who are, conversely, involved in a love of self always turn away from the Lord. This applies to their every bodily "move," for in the other life spatial intervals are arranged according to people's more inward state. So are their major regions, for they do not have the kind of boundaries we have on earth. Rather, their boundaries depend on the direction people are facing. Actually it is not angels who turn toward the Lord, but the Lord who turns them toward Himself if they love to do things that stem from Him. But this will be further discussed below, in dealing with the major regions in the other life.

18. The reason why the Lord's Divine in heaven is love is that love is the vessel of everything heavenly—that is, of peace, intelligence, wisdom, and happiness. For love accepts any and all things suitable to it; it wants them, seeks them out, and soaks them in gladly, so to speak, from a desire constantly to be enriched and fulfilled with them. Man does know this, since his own love, you might say, surveys the contents of his memory and pulls out everything agreeable. It gathers these things and arranges them in and beneath itself—in itself so that they may really belong to it, and beneath itself so that they may be of service to it. But it casts off and banishes other things, which are not agreeable.

I have been able to see very clearly indeed, in people who have been raised into heaven, that love has a complete power to accept suitable truths, and has a longing to bond them to itself. Even though such people were of simple mind on earth, they reached angelic wisdom and heavenly happiness when they were among angels. This was because they loved the good and the true for their own sakes, and rooted them in their lives; this is how they were enabled to accept heaven and everything inexpressible there.

Conversely, people involved in love of self and the world have no ability to accept these truths; they turn them away, they cast them aside. At their first touch and inflow these people run away and join people in hell who are involved in similar loves.

There were some spirits doubtful about love's possession of such characteristics, who wanted to know whether this was true. So with certain hindrances temporarily removed, they were assigned to a state of heavenly love. Then they were brought forward some distance to the location of an angelic heaven. They talked with me from there, saying they had sensed a happiness too inward to render in words, and were severely troubled at the prospect of returning to their former condition. Others too were raised into heaven; and as they were taken further in or up they came into intelligence and wisdom, so that they could grasp things that had been quite beyond them.

We can see, then, that love emanating from the Lord is the vessel of heaven and of everything there.

19. The inclusion of all Divine truths in love for the Lord and love toward the neighbor can be supported by what the Lord Himself said about this pair of loves:

> You shall love . . . your God with your whole heart and your whole soul . . .: This is the greatest and first commandment; the second, which is similar, is that you love your neighbor as yourself. On these two commandments hang the Law and the Prophets.(Matthew 22:37-40)

''The Law and the Prophets'' are the whole Word—therefore all Divine Truth.

4.

HEAVEN IS DIVIDED INTO TWO KINGDOMS

20. Since there is infinite diversity in heaven—no one community or even angel is quite like another—heaven is divided overall, regionally, and locally. Overall, it is divided into two kingdoms, regionally into three heavens, and locally into countless communities, the details of which will be discussed below. The term "kingdoms" is used because heaven is called "the kingdom of God."

21. Some angels accept the Divine that emanates from the Lord more inwardly, some less inwardly. The ones who accept more inwardly are called "celestial [or heavenly] angels"; the ones who accept less inwardly are called "spiritual angels." On this basis heaven is divided into two kingdoms, one called "the celestial kingdom" and one called "the spiritual kingdom."

22. Since the angels who make up the celestial kingdom accept the Lord's Divine more inwardly, they are called more inward angels and also higher angels. So the heavens they make up are called the more inward and higher heavens. The reason for speaking of them as "higher" and "lower" is that more inward and more outward things are given these names.

23. The love the inhabitants of the celestial kingdom are involved in is called "celestial love"; the love the inhabitants of the spiritual kingdom are involved in is called "spiritual love." Celestial love is love for the Lord; and spiritual love is charity toward the neighbor.

Further, since everything good is a matter of love (for

what a person loves is, to him, good), the "good" of the first kingdom is called "celestial" and the "good" of the other "spiritual." This enables us to see just how these two kingdoms are differentiated —obviously, in the same way as the good quality of love for the Lord is differentiated from the good quality of charity toward the neighbor. Since the former "good" is a more inward one and the former love is a more inward one, celestial angels are more inward angels, and are called "higher."

24. Further still, the celestial kingdom is called the Lord's priestly kingdom—in the Word, "His dwelling"; while the spiritual kingdom is called His royal kingdom—in the Word, "His throne." Also, the Lord on earth was called "Jesus" from His celestial Divine and "the Christ" from His spiritual Divine.

25. The angels in the Lord's celestial kingdom are vastly superior in wisdom and glory to the angels in the spiritual kingdom. This is because they accept the Lord's Divine more inwardly and are involved in a love for Him, and are therefore nearer Him and more closely joined to Him. These angels are like this because they did and do accept Divine truths directly into life, not, like the spiritual ones, by the route of memory and thinking. Accordingly they have such truths written in their hearts; they grasp them and virtually see them in themselves. They do no calculating about them, as to whether they are true or not. They are the kind of people described in *Jeremiah:*

> I will put my law in their mind, and will write it in their heart. No longer will anyone teach his friend or brother saying, "know Jehovah"; . . . they will know me, from the least of them to the greatest of them.   (Jeremiah 31:33-34)

In *Isaiah* (54:13) they are called "taught by Jehovah." The Lord Himself teaches in *John* (6:45-46) that the people taught by Jehovah are the ones taught by the Lord.

26. It has been stated above that they have more wisdom and glory than others because they did and do accept Divine truths directly into life. The moment they hear them, they intend and do them. They do not store them up in memory and then ponder whether they are true. Angels like this know instantly, by an inflow from the Lord, whether the "truth" they hear is true. The Lord actually flows directly into a person's intending and indirectly, through his intending, into his thinking. In other words, the Lord flows directly into what is good, and indirectly, through what is good, into what is true. For the term "good" applies to what belongs to the intention and its consequent acting, while the term "true" applies to what belongs to the memory and its consequent thinking.

In addition, everything true is converted to something good and rooted in love as soon as it enters the intention. But as long as something true is in the memory and consequent thought, it does not become good; it does not live, nor is it adopted by the individual. For a person is a person by virtue of his intention and his resulting understanding, not from understanding apart from intention.

27. Since this distinction exists between angels of the celestial kingdom and angels of the spiritual kingdom, they do not live together or socialize with each other. There occurs only some communication through intermediate angelic communities called "celestial-spiritual." It is through these that the celestial kingdom flows into the spiritual. This is how heaven makes a one even though it is divided into two kingdoms. The Lord always furnishes intermediate angels of this sort, as agents of communication and connection.

28. For now, we ignore the details, since in much of what follows we will be discussing the angels of one kingdom or the other.

5.

THERE ARE THREE HEAVENS

29. There are three heavens quite distinct from each other—an inmost or third heaven, an intermediate or second, and an outmost or first. They follow each other and are interdependent—just like the top of a person, called his head, his middle or body, and his extremities or feet—or like the top, middle, and bottom of a house. The Divine that comes forth and down from the Lord is similar in design, so by requirement of design, heaven has three parts.

30. The more inward reaches of a person, too, the regions of his inner and outer mind, are arranged in a similar design. He has an inmost, an intermediate, and an extremity, because when he was created the whole Divine design was transcribed into him. Indeed he was fashioned as a Divine design in a form, and was therefore fashioned as a heaven in its smallest image.

As a result, the individual is in touch with the heavens as far as his more inward reaches are concerned. He arrives among angels, too, after death—angels of the inmost or intermediate or outmost heaven depending on his own acceptance of what is Divinely good and true from the Lord during his life on earth.

31. The Divine which flows in from the Lord and is accepted in the third or inmost heaven is called celestial, so the angels there are called celestial angels. The Divine which flows in from the Lord and is accepted in the second or intermediate heaven is called spiritual, so the angels there are called spiritual angels.

But the Divine which flows in from the Lord and is accepted in the outmost or first heaven is called natural. However, since the "naturalness" of that heaven—unlike the "naturalness" of the world—contains something spiritual and celestial, the heaven is called "celestial-natural" and "spiritual-natural," and so are its angels. The ones who accept an inflow from the intermediate or second heaven (the spiritual heaven) are called spiritual-natural, and the ones who accept an inflow from the third or inmost heaven (the celestial heaven) are called celestial-natural. Spiritual-natural and celestial-natural angels are distinguishable, but they make one unbroken heaven because they are on one distinct level.

32. There is an "inner" and an "outer" to each heaven. People in the "inner" are called inner angels, and people in the "outer" are called "outer" angels. The outer and the inner in the heavens—in each heaven, that is—are arranged like the capacity to intend and its capacity to discern in man. The inner is like the capacity to intend; the outer is like its capacity to discern. Every capacity to intend has its own capacity to discern. One without the other is impossible. The capacity to intend is like a flame, and the capacity to discern like the light that comes from it.

33. It is worth realizing fully that the more inward elements of angels determine which heaven they will be in. As more inward elements are more open to the Lord, they are in a more inward heaven. There are three levels of the more inward elements of everyone, angel, spirit, or man. People whose third level has been opened are in the inmost heaven; people whose second, or just whose first has been opened, are in the intermediate heaven or the outmost one.

These more inward elements get opened by the acceptance of what is Divinely good and Divinely true. People who are moved by Divine truths and let them right into life (that is, into intention and action) are in the inmost or third heaven, located there according to their acceptance of the good as a result of their affection for the true. Others, who do not let these truths right into life, let them instead into their memory and consequent understanding, and from there intend and do them. They are in the intermediate or second heaven. Then there are people who live upright lives and believe in a Divine Being, but do not much care about learning. They are in the outmost or first heaven.

This enables us to conclude that the states of the more inward elements make heaven, heaven being within everyone and not outside him. This is what the Lord is teaching when He says,

> The kingdom of God does not come with observation, nor will people say, "look, here it is" or "look, there it is." Look—you have the kingdom of God within you.
>
> (Luke 17:20-21)

34. All perfection increases as one moves inward and decreases as one moves outward. For more inward things are nearer the Divine and are intrinsically more pure, while more outward things are farther from the Divine and intrinsically more crude.

Angelic perfection lies in intelligence, wisdom, love—in everything good and every resultant happiness. It does not lie in happiness alone, for happiness without the rest is superficial, not inward. Since for angels of the inmost heaven the more inward elements are opened on the third level, their perfection vastly exceeds the perfection of angels in the intermediate heaven, whose more inward elements are opened on the second level. The perfection of angels of the intermediate heaven exceeds the perfection of angels in the outmost heaven to a similar degree.

35. This distinctiveness means that an angel of one heaven cannot have access to angels of another heaven. That is, no one from a lower heaven can ascend, and no one from a higher heaven can descend. Anyone who ascends from a lower heaven is gripped by a tension to the point of pain. He cannot see people there, much less talk with them. And anyone who descends from a higher heaven loses his wisdom, stammers, and falls prey to despair.

There were some people from the outmost heaven who had not yet been taught that heaven is made up of angels' more inward elements, who believed they could reach a higher heavenly happiness if only they reached those angels' heaven. They were granted access to them; but while they were there, even though there was a great throng, wherever they looked they saw no one. As outsiders, their more inward reaches were not open to the same level as those of the angels who lived there, and consequently neither was their sight. Shortly, they were gripped by heart pains so severe that they hardly knew whether they were alive or not. On account of this, they abruptly transferred themselves back to the heaven they came from, delighted to get back among their own folk and vowing never again to long for anything higher than what suited their own life.

I have also seen some people lowered from a higher heaven, so losing their wisdom that they even forgot what their own heaven was like.

But when (as often happens) the Lord raises people from a lower heaven to a higher one to see the glory there, it is different. In such cases they are prepared first, and they are attended by mediating angels who serve as agents of communication.

We can see from this that these three heavens are quite distinct from each other.

36. People in the same heaven can associate with anyone there. Still, the pleasures of associating vary depending on the likeness of the kinds of good they are involved in; but more on this in subsequent sections.

37. However, even though the heavens are so different that the angels of one cannot share fellowship with angels of another, still the Lord joins all the heavens together by means of a direct and an indrect flow. The direct inflow is from Himself into all the heavens, and the indirect is from one heaven into another. In this way, He makes the three heavens one, so bound together from the first to the outmost that nothing unconnected exists. Anything that is not tied in with the first by something in between does not endure, but disintegrates and becomes nothing.

38. No one can grasp how the heavens are divided, or even what the inner and outer person are, if he does not know the arrangement of the Divine design in levels. The only idea many people in this world have about inner and outer or higher and lower levels, is a rough idea of something uninterrupted, or something that goes along without a break from purer to more crude. But inner and outer things are arranged as distinct, not as continuous.

Levels are of two kinds. There are continuous levels and noncontinuous levels. With continuous levels, it is like the lessening of light from blazing to dark, or the lessening of sight from things in the light to things in the shade, or like levels of air purity from bottom to top. These levels are assigned spatial units.

[2] Levels which are not continuous, but are distinct, are marked off rather as "leading" and "following," like cause and effect or like producer and product. Anyone who looks carefully will see that there are these levels in every single thing in the whole world, levels of production and composition with one thing obviously resulting from another, a third from that, and so on and on.

[3] The person who does not get a good grasp of these levels has no way of knowing the distinctions between the heavens, between man's inner and outer powers, between

the spiritual world and the natural world, or between man's spirit and his body. As a result, he cannot understand the nature or the source of correspondences and representations or the nature of inflow.

Sense-oriented people do not grasp these distinctions. They take them to be matters of rising and falling on the pattern of continuous levels. Consequently, they have no way of visualizing the spiritual except as a kind of purer natural. So they stay outside, a long, long way from understanding.

39. Lastly, let me mention a particular arcanum about the angels of the three heavens. This is something that has not occurred to anyone before, because no one has yet understood levels.

It is this: every single angel and every single person has an inmost or highest level, or something inmost and highest, where the Lord's Divine flows in first or most directly. From this center the Lord arranges other relatively inward elements that, according to levels of their inward design, follow in sequence. We may call this inmost or highest level the Lord's entryway to angel and man, His very home within them.

It is by this "something inmost or highest" that man is man and is differentiated from non-rational animals, since they do not possess it. This is why man, unlike animals, can as to his more inward reaches or what belongs to his inner and outer mind, be raised by the Lord toward Himself. Man can believe in Him, be moved by love for Him, and so can see Him. As a result also, man can accept intelligence and wisdom and can talk from rational processes. This is also the source of man's living to eternity.

But it does not come openly to the attention of any angel just what the Lord arranges and takes care of at his center, since this is above his thought and beyond his wisdom.

40. These, then, are some general features of the three heavens. There is more to be said later about each heaven in particular.

6.

THE HEAVENS ARE MADE UP OF COUNTLESS COMMUNITIES

41. The angels of any particular heaven are not all together in the same place, but are divided into larger and smaller communities. This is done according to the variations of the good outcome of the love and faith they are involved in. People involved in similar good form a single community. Types of the good occur in heaven in infinite variety, and each single angel is his own good, so to speak.

42. Further, the distances between angelic communities in the heavens are like the general and specific differences between types of the good. For in the spiritual world, the only source of distances is the varieties of the states of the more inward elements—in heaven therefore varieties on the states of love. People who differ greatly are far apart; people who differ slightly are not far apart; and likeness brings unity.

43. Within a given community, all the individuals are distinguished from each other in a similar way. The more perfect ones are in the central region—that is, those who are outstanding in goodness and thus in love, wisdom, and discernment. The less outstanding ones are around the outside, at distances proportional to lessening levels of perfection. It is arranged the way light decreases from a center toward the periphery. The people at the center are in the greatest light, those toward the fringes progressively in less.

44. People are borne by their own natures, as it were, toward those who are like them. With people like themselves, they feel as though they were with their own family, as though they were at home; while with others they feel as though they were with foreigners, as though they were abroad. When they are with people like themselves, they are in their free condition, and as a result are involved in everything that is pleasant about life.

45. We can see from this that the good joins all people together in the heavens and that they are distinguished by its quality. Still, it is not the angels who do this joining—it is the Lord, the source of the good. He Himself leads them, attaches them, distinguishes them, and keeps them in a free condition to the extent that they are involved in something good. In this way He keeps each one involved in the life of his love, his faith, his discernment and wisdom, and therefore in happiness.

46. Further, the very same way people on earth recognize their family members, relatives, and friends, all angels involved in like good recognize each other, even though they may never have seen each other before. This is because there are no kinds of family or relationship or friendship in the other life except spiritual ones, that is, ones that belong to love and faith.

I could see this a number of times when I was in the spirit, taken out of the body and therefore into fellowship with angels. At such times I seemed to have known some of them from infancy, while others I seemed not to have known at all. The ones I seemed to have known from infancy were the ones in a state like that of my own spirit; the unknown ones were in an unlike state.

47. Facially, the people who make up a single angelic community all look alike in general, but not in details. One can get some idea of this "resemblance in general" and "variety in detail" from things in this world, such as the following: we realize that every nationality has a certain general likeness about the face and eyes by which one can recognize it and tell it from a different nationality. This is even more true of telling one family from another. But it is far more complete in the heavens because there, all the more inward affections are visible and radiate from a person's face, faces there being the very outward form and picture of these affections. In heaven, there is no way to have a face different from one's affections.

As a demonstration of the way this general resemblance is varied in detail in the individuals of a single community, there was a face like an angel's that appeared to me. This was varied according to affections from the good and the true such as occur within members of a single community. These variations lasted quite a while; and I noticed that the same general face stayed all the way through like a background, and that the other appearances were simple offshoots or developments from it. So there were shown through this face the affections of the whole community, the sources of the differences in looks of the people there. For as already stated, angelic faces are forms of their more inward elements, and therefore forms of the affections that belong to love and faith.

48. As a further result, an angel of outstanding wisdom sees instantly what another angel is like from his face. It is impossible there for anyone to conceal what lies within him with his expression and to pretend, and quite impossible to lie or to take someone in by cleverness and hypocrisy.

It does sometimes happen that hypocrites sneak into some communities, hypocrites trained to conceal what lies within them and to arrange their outward appearance to resemble the particular good the members of that community are involved in—to disguise themselves as angels of light. But they cannot stay around very long, because they begin to feel pain inside, to feel tortured, to turn blue in the face, and almost to die. These changes stem from their incompatibility with the life that is flowing in and working. So they suddenly dive back into the hell where people of their sort live, and are not eager to climb up again. These are the ones meant by the man who was discovered among the diners and guests, who did not have on a wedding garment and who was thrown out into the darkness (Matthew 22:11ff).

49. All the communities of heaven are in touch with each other, but not through an open interchange, since few people go from their own community to another. For leaving a community is like leaving oneself or one's life and moving to another one that does not fit in the same way. Instead, they are all in touch through the outreach of spheres that come from each one's life.

A "life's sphere" is a sphere that belongs to affections of love and faith. It spreads out into surrounding communities far and wide—farther and wider as the affections are more inward and perfect. Angels have discernment and wisdom proportional to this outreach. People in the inmost heaven, particularly the ones at its center, have an outreach into the whole heaven. This results in a communication of everyone in heaven with each individual, and of each individual with everyone.

But this outreach needs to be dealt with more fully below in connection with a treatment of the heavenly form that determines the arrangement of the heavenly form that determines the arrangement of angelic communities (it will also come up in connection with the Wisdom and Discernment of Angels), since the whole outreach of affections and thoughts moves according to this form.

50. It was stated above that there are larger and smaller communities in the heavens. The larger ones are made up of tens of thousands of people, the smaller ones of thousands, and the smallest of several hundred.

There are also some people who live apart, home by home, so to speak, and family by family. Spread out as they are, they are still arranged like the people in communities. That is, the wisest of them are in the center, and the simpler toward the borders. These people are more closely under the Lord's Divine guidance, and are the best of angels.

7.

EACH COMMUNITY IS A HEAVEN IN A SMALLER FORM, AND EACH ANGEL A HEAVEN IN THE SMALLEST FORM.

51. The reason each community is a heaven in a smaller form, and each angel a heaven in the smallest form, is that the good outcome of love and faith is what makes heaven, and because this "good" is within every community of heaven and within every angel of a community. Regardless of the fact that this "good" is everywhere diverse and varied, it is still the good of heaven. The difference is just that heaven is of one kind in one place and of another kind in another place.

So a person raised into a community of heaven is described as having come into heaven, and the people there are described as being in heaven, each in his own. Everyone who is in the other life is familiar with this. So people located outside a heaven or below it, when they see a group of angels from a distance, say that heaven is there—and also over there. It is rather like the situation of governors, officials, and administrators in a single royal palace or court. Even though they live apart from each other in their own houses, or each in his own apartment, one higher and one lower, they are nevertheless in a single palace or court, with each one being involved in his own particular function in the king's service.

This clarifies what is meant by the Lord's statement that "in his Father's house are many mansions (John 14:2)," and by "the dwellings of heaven" and the "heavens of heaven" in the Prophets.

52. I have been able to find confirmation for the proposition that each community is a heaven in smaller form in this: there is in any particular community a heavenly form or pattern which is like the pattern of the whole heaven. In the middle of the whole heaven live those who stand out above the rest. Round about, all the way to the boundaries, live the ones who are less outstanding, in ever diminishing series (see the statement in the preceding chapter, n. 43).

There is additional confirmation in the fact that the Lord guides all the people who are in the whole heaven as though they were a single angel. He does the same with those in each community. From time to time, therefore, a whole angelic community may appear as a unit in the form of an angel, a sight which the Lord has in fact let me see.

Further, when the Lord appears in the midst of angels, He does not seem to be attended by a throng, but as one Person in an angelic form. This is why in the Word the Lord is called an angel, as also is a whole community. Michael, Gabriel, and Raphael are nothing but angelic communities, given their names by reason of their functions.

53. Just as a whole community is a heaven in smaller form, an angel is a heaven in the smallest form. For heaven is not outside an angel, but within him. Actually, his more inward elements, which belong to his mind, are arranged in the form of heaven precisely so that they can accept all the elements of heaven that are outside him. These the angel accepts according to the quality of the good that is in him from the Lord. So an angel, too, is a heaven.

54. There is no real point in saying that heaven is outside anyone—it is within him. For every angel accepts the heaven outside himself which accords with the heaven inside himself. So we can see how mistaken a person is if he believes that getting into heaven means simply being raised up among angels, no matter what he is like in regard to his more inward life—that heaven, then, is granted to people by direct mercy. For quite the contrary, unless heaven is in a person, nothing of the heaven outside flows in and is accepted.

There are many spirits who hold this opinion. Because of their belief therefore, they have been brought up into heaven. But once there, on account of the opposition of their inner life to the life the angels are involved in, they began to lose their intellectual sight until they became like fools. Emotionally, they were tormented to the point that they carried on like madmen.

In short, people who live badly and come into heaven gasp for breath and writhe like fish out of water, in the air, or like animals in a vacuum chamber, with only the ether left once the air has been extracted.

This may serve to demonstrate that heaven is within a person and not outside him.

55. Since all people accept the heaven outside them in accordance with the quality of the heaven within them, they accept the Lord in the same way; for the Lord's Divine is what makes heaven. This is why the Lord, when He presents Himself in a particular community, takes on an appearance that accords with the quality of the good which that community is involved in. So He does not look the same in one community as in another. Not that this difference is in the Lord—it is in the people who see Him from their own "good" and therefore according to it. They are moved by the sight of Him according to the quality of their love. People who love Him deeply are deeply moved; people who love Him less are less moved. Evil people, who are outside heaven, are tormented by His presence.

When the Lord appears in a particular community, He takes on the appearance of an angel, but He is distinguished from the others by the Divine which shines through.

56. Further, heaven is where the Lord is recognized,

believed, and loved. The diversity of His worship, arising out of the diversity of the good from one community to another, does not do any damage, but rather works to advantage, since it is a source of heaven's perfection. It is hard to get across this fact—that this is a source of heaven's perfection—without marshaling up tried and true maxims from the world of learning and setting forth with them how a "one" which is complete is formed from differing elements.

Every "one" comes into being from differing elements, for a "one" which is not from differing elements is not really anything. It has no form, and therefore no quality. But given a "one" that does come into being from differing elements, which each perfectly formed element in proper turn joining another like a congenial friend, it does have a perfect quality. Now heaven is a "one" made up of different elements arranged in the most perfect form, for the heavenly form is of all forms the most perfect.

We can see from all beauty, charm, and delight that move the senses and the passions that this is the source of all perfection. These do in fact come into being and flow only from the concord and harmony of many elements which agree and accord, whether manifesting themselves all at once in an orderly arrangement, or following each other in a sequence. This does not happen from a "one" without many elements. So it is said that variety is pleasing; and its attraction is known to be in proportion to its quality.

This offers a kind of mirror-view of how perfection results from differing elements, even in heaven. For the things that happen in the material world do offer a kind of mirror-view of things in the spiritual world.

57. Much the same can be said about the church as has been said about heaven, since the church is the Lord's heaven on earth. There are many of these, too, each one called a church; and each one is a church to the extent that the good outcome of love and faith does the governing within it. Here again, the Lord makes a one out of different elements—one church out of many.

Much the same can also be said about the churchman in specific as has been said about the church in general. It can be said that the church is within the individual and not outside him, and that any person at all is a church in whom the Lord is effectively present in the good outcome of love and faith.

Even the statements about an angel with heaven within him can be virtually repeated about a person with the church within him.

We can say that he is a church in its smallest form in the same way that an angel is a heaven in its smallest form; and even more, we can say that a person with the church within him is a heaven just as an angel is. People, after all, are created to enter heaven and become angels. So the person who possesses what is good from the Lord is an angel-man.

It may be worth noting what man has in common with angels, and what he has besides. In common with angels, man's more inward elements are patterned after heaven and he becomes a true likeness of heaven to the extent that he is involved in the good of love and faith. Besides what the angel has, man has the formation of his more outward elements on the pattern of this world, and also the subordination and service of this "world of his" to heaven so far as he is involved in what is good. Then he has also the Lord's effective presence with him on both levels, just as if he were in his heaven. In fact, the Lord is in His Divine order on both levels, for God is order.

58. Lastly, it is worth noting that the person who has heaven in himself has heaven not only in the major or general aspects of himself, but even in his smallest and most particular aspects. Also, the smallest aspects reflect an image of the largest. This stems from the fact that each individual is his own love, that his actual quality is determined by his ruling love. Whatever rules in a person flows into his particular aspects, arranges them, and introduces its own likeness everywhere.

Love for the Lord is what rules in heaven, because there the Lord is loved more than everything. As a result, the Lord is there the all in all, flows into each and all things, arranges them, clothes them with His own likeness, and so works things out that it is heaven where He is.

An angel, then, is a heaven in its smallest form, a community is the same in a larger form, and all the communities taken together are the same in largest form.

On the Lord's Divine constituting heaven and His being the all in all, (see above, nn. 7-12).

8.

HEAVEN, IF GRASPED AS A SINGLE ENTITY, REFLECTS A SINGLE PERSON

59. It is an arcanum still unknown in the world that heaven reflects a single person if it is grasped as a single entity, but in the heavens this is common knowledge. Knowing this even as to specifics and details is a specialty of the understanding of angels there. Many things follow from it, things which cannot be crisply and clearly conceptualized without this as their pervasive first principle. Since angels know that all the heavens, including all their communities, reflect a single person, they actually call heaven "the Greatest and Divine Man." The term "Divine" is used because the Lord's Divine makes heaven (see above, nn. 7-12).

60. People without a proper idea of spiritual and celestial things cannot grasp the arrangement and connection of spiritual and celestial things in this pattern and likeness. They think that earthly, material elements, the ingredients of the lowest level of a person, really constitute him, that without these elements a person would not be a person. They should however realize that a person is not a person by virtue of these elements, but by virtue of his ability to discern what is true and to intend what is good. These are the spiritual and celestial elements that constitute a person.

People do after all know that a person's quality is the quality of his discernment and his intention. We can also recognize that a person's earthly body has been constructed to work for these inner powers in the world, and appropriately to do useful tasks for him in the outmost sphere of nature. So the body does not start anything on its own—it is rather started up, quite compliant to the promptings of discernment and intention. It even follows that what a person thinks, he speaks with his tongue and mouth, that what he intends, he does with his body and limbs; so that discernment and intention are the "doers," while the body by itself is not so at all.

We can then see that abilities to discern and intend make a person human. And they are in a form like his, since they do initiate action in the minutest parts of his body, like an "inside" within an "outside." It is on their account, then, that man is called "internal" and "spiritual." Heaven is such a person in the greatest and most complete form.

61. This is the kind of idea angels have of man. Under no circumstances do they watch what a person is doing with his body. Instead, they watch the intention from which the body is behaving. They call this the real person—this and such discernment as is in unison with the intention.

62. Actually, angels do not see heaven as a single whole in a form like this, for the totality of heaven does not come under any single angel's view. From time to time, though, they do see outlying communities made up of many thousand angels, as one and as in this form. From a community as a sample, they infer what heaven is overall. For in the most perfect form, the greater units are arranged like the smaller sections, and the sections like the greater units. The difference, simply, is like the difference between larger and smaller instances of similar things. So they say that the whole heaven is like this in the Lord's view, because the Divine sees everything from the very center and highest point.

63. Heaven being like this, it is governed by the Lord as though it were one person—like a unit therefore. True, a person is made up of countless different components, both overall and in his parts. Overall, he is made up of members, organs, and viscera, secondarily of chains of fibers, nerves, and blood vessels—of members within members, then, and of parts within parts. Still when a person acts, he acts as a unit. Heaven is like this, under the Lord's authority and guidance.

64. The reason so many different things in man act as a unit is that there is not a single thing involved that does not do something for the larger whole and fulfill a function. The whole fulfills a function for its parts and the parts fulfill functions for the whole. For the whole comprises parts, and the parts constitute the whole. So they take care for each other, keep each other in view, and are assembled into the kind of form in which each and every element reflects the whole and its "good." This is the reason they act as a unit.

[2] Groups in the heavens are like this. People there are bound together in this kind of form according to their useful functions. So people who do not fulfill some function for the community are thrown out of heaven because their nature is different.

Fulfilling a useful function is intending well toward others for the sake of the common good. Not fulfilling a useful function is intending well toward others not for the sake of the common good, but for one's own sake. People who love themselves supremely fall in the latter category; people who love the Lord supremely fall in the former.

This is why the people in heaven act as a unit—not from themselves, but from the Lord. They view Him, in fact, as the only Source; they view His kingdom as the larger whole to which they must attend. This is the intent of the Lord's words,

> Seek the kingdom of God first, and its righteousness, and everything will be added to you. (Matthew 6:33).

"Seeking its righteousness" is seeking its good.

[3] People on earth who love their country's good more

than their own, and their neighbor's good as much as their own, are the ones who in the other life love and seek the Lord's kingdom. For there the Lord's kingdom takes the place of the nation. And people who like to do good for others not for their own sakes but for the sake of the good, are the ones who love the neighbor, for the good *is* the neighbor. All people of this quality are in the "Greatest Man"—that is, in heaven.

65. Since the whole heaven does reflect a single person, even being the Divine Spiritual Person in greatest form (even in shape), heaven is divided into members and parts the way a person is, and these parts have similar names. Angels actually know what member one community or another is in. They say that this community is in some member or district of the head, that one in some member or district of the chest, that one in some member or district of the loins, and so on.

In general, the highest or third heaven makes up the head as far as the neck, the middle or second heaven the torso as far as the loins or knees. The lowest or first heaven makes up the feet right to the soles and also the arms right to the fingers. For despite being at the sides, the arms and hands are lowest things of people. All this again shows why there are three heavens.

66. Spirits who are below heaven are utterly amazed when they hear and see that heaven is underneath as well as above. They have actually the same belief and notion as people in the world, that heaven is overhead only. They do not really know that arrangement of the heavens is like the arrangement of the members and organs and viscera in a person, with some higher up and some lower down. Nor do they realize that it is like the arrangement of the parts within each member or organ or viscus, with some inside and some outside. As a result, they are confused about heaven.

67. This material about heaven as the Greatest Man has been brought in because without an introductory awareness of it, there is no way of grasping things yet to be said about heaven. There is no possibility of having a clear concept of heaven's form, of the Lord's bond with heaven, of heaven's bond with the individual, of the inflow of the spiritual world into the natural, no possibility whatsoever of a clear concept of correspondences, which we must discuss below in their proper place. So the material above has been prefaced in order to shed light on these matters.

9.

EACH COMMUNITY IN THE HEAVENS REFLECTS A SINGLE PERSON

68. A number of times, I have been given to see that each community of heaven reflects a single person, and is in the likeness of a person. There was a community infiltrated by a number of people who knew how to put on the guise of angels of light—hypocrites. As they were weeded out from the angels, the entire community looked first like a hazy unit, then gradually took a human form rather vaguely, and finally in full light looked like a person.

The people in that person, making it up, were the ones who were involved in the good of that community. The other ones, not in the person or making it up, were the hypocrites. The latter were thrown out, the former kept; and so the separation was accomplished.

People are hypocrites who speak in a good manner and act well too, but who are looking out for themselves when you get right down to details. They talk like angels about the Lord and heaven and love and the heavenly life, they even act well in order to seem really to be the way they talk. But their thinking is something else. They believe nothing, they intend good to no one but themselves. Whatever good they do is for their own sakes; if it is at all for others, it is for appearances' sake and therefore for themselves.

69. The appearance of an entire angelic community as a unit in human form when the Lord makes Himself effectively present, is something I have in fact been given to see.

There once appeared, upward and toward the East, something like a bright white cloud taking on a rosy glow, with small stars around it. This cloud descended, and as it did, it gradually brightened until it had a visible, completely human form. The small stars around the cloud were angels, who looked like that because of a light from the Lord.

70. It is most important to realize that, although all the members of a heavenly community look like a person when they are seen together as a unit, still one community is not the same kind of person as another. They can be told apart like the faces of members of a family. The reason is the one mentioned above (n. 47), that they differ according to the differences of the good the members are involved in, the good that shapes them. The most perfect and human beautiful form is the one presented by communities in the inmost or highest heaven, particularly those in the center.

71. It is worth noting that the more people there are in a community, and the more they act as one, the more perfect its human form is. For as already explained (n. 56), variety arranged in heavenly form constitutes perfection, and variety occurs when there are many elements.

Each heavenly community increases numerically every day. As it increases, it becomes more perfect. It is not just the community whose perfection is advanced in this way, but heaven itself overall, since the communities make up heaven.

Seeing that heaven is perfected by increasing numbers, how obviously wrong are people who believe heaven may be closed by being filled to capacity! Actually, it is just the other way around—it will never be closed, and greater and greater fullness makes it more perfect. So there is nothing angels like better than the arrival of new angel-guests.

72. The appearance of each community in human likeness (seen all together and as a unit) stems from all heaven's having this likeness, as was pointed out in the last chapter. In the most perfect form, like the form of heaven, there is a resemblance of the parts to the whole, of the smaller to the largest. Heaven's smaller elements, its parts, are the communities of which it is composed (on these being heavens in smaller form, see above, nn. 51-58).

The constancy of this resemblance stems from the fact that in the heavens everyone's good elements come from one love, and therefore from one source. The one love which gives rise to everyone's good elements there is love for the Lord, from the Lord. This is why the whole heaven is a likeness of Him in general, each community the same less generally, and each angel the same in particular. The reader may refer to what has already been said on this subject (n. 58).

10.

EACH ANGEL IS THEREFORE IN A PERFECT HUMAN FORM

73. We have shown in the last two chapters that heaven, taken as a single whole, reflects a single person, and so does each community in heaven. The reasons there cited converge on the conclusion that every angel also reflects a single person. As heaven is a person in greatest form and a community of heaven is a person in a lesser one, so an angel is a person in least form. For in the most perfect form (which heaven's form is), there is a resemblance to the whole in the part, and a resemblance to the part in the whole.

The reason for this is that heaven is a commonwealth, actually sharing everything it has with each person there, and each member receives everything he has from the commonwealth. An angel is a recipient entity and therefore a heaven in smallest form, as was explained in its own chapter above.

Man too, to the extent that he accepts heaven, is also a recipient entity, a heaven, and an angel (see above, n. 57). In *Revelation,* this is described as follows:

> He measured the wall of the holy Jerusalem, a hundred and forty-four cubits, the measure of a man—that is, of the angel.
>
> (Revelation 21:17)

Here "Jerusalem" is the Lord's church, and in a more important sense, heaven. "The wall" is the truth which protects against the assault of false and evil elements. "A hundred and forty-four" is everything good and true taken together. "The measure" is its quality; "a man" is one who has within him all these elements in general and individually—one who therefore has heaven within; and since an angel is a person by virtue of the elements mentioned, the passage reads, "the measure of a man—that is, of the angel."

This is the spiritual meaning of the words. Without this meaning, who would discern that the wall of the holy Jerusalem is the measure of a man—that is, of the angel?

74. Now on to some evidence. As for angels being human forms, or people, this I have seen thousands of times. I have actually talked with them person to person, sometimes with one, sometimes with several in a group, without seeing anything about their form to distinguish them from man. From time to time I have marvelled at their being the way they are; and to forestall any claim that this is delusion or hallucination, I have been allowed to see them while I was fully awake, that is, while I was aware with all my physical senses and in a state of clear perception.

I have often told angels how people in Christendom are in such blind ignorance about angels and spirits that they believe them to be minds without form, or nothing but thoughts, which could not be conceptualized except the way one might conceptualize an ether containing something living. And since they predicate of angels nothing human but thought, they believe they cannot see because they have no eyes, cannot hear because they have no ears, and cannot talk because they have no mouth or tongue.

[2] The response of angels has been that they know that many people on earth hold this kind of belief, and that it is prevalent among intellectuals and—which surprises them—the clergy. In fact, they say the reason is that intellectuals, the vanguard, the first to rule out any real concept of angels and spirits, have done their thinking on these matters on the basis of sensory data proper to the outer person. If people think on this basis and not from an inner

light or the universally inborn general concept, all they can
do is form notions like these. For the outer person's sensory
organs receive material only from the realm of nature. They
receive nothing higher, and therefore nothing about the spiritual world. A false kind of thought about angels branches
out from this vanguard, these people who serve as leaders,
to others who do not think for themselves but rather follow
their leaders. Anyone who begins by thinking like someone
else and making up his mind, and only later looks at things
with his own intelligence, has a hard time changing his
mind. So most of them are content to reinforce their borrowed opinions.

[3] The angels went on to say that people of simple faith
and heart are not caught up in this concept of angels. They
are involved rather in an idea of angels as being rather like
people of heaven—this because they have not let erudition
extinguish something planted in them from heaven, and do
not recognize anything that has no form. This is why the
angels carved or painted in churches are invariably represented as people.

On the subject of this "something planted in them from
heaven," angels identified it as the Divine flowing in and
working in people involved in the good of faith and life.

75. On the basis of all my experience, covering to date
many years, I can say, I can insist that angels are completely
people in form. They do have faces, eyes, ears, chests,
arms, hands, and feet. They do see each other, hear each
other, and talk with each other. In short, nothing proper to
man whatever is missing, except that they are not clothed
with a material body.

I have seen them in their own light, many times brighter
than earth's noon, and everything about their faces was
crisper and clearer in that light than the faces of people on
earth appear. I have even been given to see an angel of the

inmost heaven. He had a more brilliant and radiant face than the angels of lower heavens. I looked at him carefully, and he had a human form in all perfection.

76. It should however be noted that angels are not visible to men through men's physical senses, only rather through the eyes of the spirit within man. For this is in the spiritual world, while everything physical is in the natural world. Like sees like because it is made of like material. Further, the body's organ of sight, the eye, is so crude that it cannot even see the smaller elements of nature except through a lens, as everyone knows. So it is still less able to see things above the realm of nature like the things in the spiritual world. However, these things are visible to man when he is withdrawn from physical sight and his spirit's sight is opened. This happens in a moment if it is the Lord's good pleasure that they be visible. At such times, it seems to the person exactly as though he were seeing these things with his physical eyes. This is also the way Abraham, Lot, Manoah, and the Prophets saw angels; this is the way the Lord's disciples saw Him after the Resurrection. It is how I have seen angels.

Because the prophets saw in this manner they were called "seers" and "people whose eyes were opened" (I Samuel 9:9, Numbers 24:3). Bringing about such sight is called "opening the eyes," as happened to Elisha's servant, of whom we read,

> In prayer, Elisha said, "Jehovah, open his eyes, please, so that he may see." And once Jehovah had opened the servant's eyes, he saw that behold, the mountain was full of horses and chariots of fire round about Elisha.   (II Kings 6:17)

77. Some honest spirits I talked with on this subject were heartsick at the existence of this kind of ignorance in the church about the condition of heaven and about spirits and angels. They maintained indignantly that I ought to go right back with the message that they were not formless minds, not ethereal gases, but people to a T, that they could see and hear and feel just as well as people on earth.

11.

HEAVEN AS A WHOLE AND IN ITS PARTS REFLECTS A PERSON BECAUSE IT STEMS FROM THE LORD'S DIVINE HUMAN

78. It follows as a conclusion from what has been said and explained in the foregoing chapters, that heaven as a whole and in its parts reflects a person because it stems from the Lord's Divine Human. In the foregoing chapters, we have pointed out the following:

I.   the Lord is the God of heaven;

II.   the Lord's Divine makes heaven;

III.   Heaven is made up of countless communities, each community being a heaven in lesser form and each angel a heaven in least form;

IV.   the whole heaven, taken as one whole, reflects a single person;

V.   each community in the heavens reflects a single person;

VI.   each angel is therefore in a perfect human form.

All these propositions lead to the conclusion that the Divine, since it does makes heaven, is Human in form. The identity of this with the Lord's Divine Human can be seen more clearly from propositions extracted and assembled from the *Arcana Coelestia* (cf. Appendix I), since these are condensed. One can see from these selections that the Lord's Human is Divine, and not—as is believed within the church—that His Human is not Divine. This can also be seen from *The Doctrine of the Holy Jerusalem* toward the end, where it deals with the Lord.

79. A great deal of evidence has demonstrated the truth of this to me; some will be cited in what immediately follows.

All the angels in heaven see the Divine in Human form exclusively. Remarkably, people in the higher heavens cannot think about the Divine in any other way. They are guided into this unavoidable way of thinking both by the Divine itself which flows into them and by the form of heaven according to which their thoughts reach out about them. For every thought angels have has an outreach into heaven, and they have discernment and wisdom proportional to that outreach. This is why everyone there acknowledges the Lord, inasmuch as the Divine Human exists only in Him.

This is not just something told me by angels. It is something I have been given to perceive when raised into a more inward sphere of heaven.

We can then see that the wiser angels are, the more clearly they perceive this. This is also why the Lord appears to them. The Lord actually appears in a Divine Angelic form—which is a human form—to people who acknowledge and believe in a visible Divine, but not to people who believe in an invisible Divine. The former have the ability to see their Divine; the latter do not.

80. Because angels do not perceive an invisible Divine (which they call a formless Divine), but perceive a visible Divine in human form, it is natural for them to say that the Lord alone is Person, and that they themselves are people by reason of Him—also that each of them is a person to the extent that he accepts the Lord.

They understand "accepting the Lord" to mean accepting the good and the true that come from Him, because the Lord is within His "good" and within his "true." This they call wisdom and discernment. According to them, everyone knows that discernment and wisdom constitute a person, and not just a face without them.

The truth of this can be seen in angels of the inner heavens. Being involved in what is good and true from the Lord (and therefore in wisdom and discernment), they are in the loveliest and most perfect human form. Angels of lower heavens are less perfect and lovely in form.

It is the other way around in hell. People there, in heaven's light, hardly look like people at all, but rather like monsters. They are involved in what is evil and false instead of what is good and true, and so they are involved in things contrary to wisdom and discernment. As a result, their life is not even called "life," but "spiritual death."

81. Since heaven does reflect a person overall and in detail because of the Lord's Divine Human, angels refer to themselves as being "in the Lord." Some of them say they are "in His body," meaning in the good of His love. This accords with what the Lord Himself taught in the words,

Stay in Me, and I in you: as the branch cannot bear fruit on its own, without staying in the vine, so neither can you, without staying in Me; . . . for without Me you can do nothing; . . . stay in my love; . . . if you follow my commands, you will stay in my love. (John 15:4-10)

82. Since this is how the Divine is perceived in the heavens, every individual who accepts any inflow from heaven has grafted into him a tendency to think of God in human guise. People of ancient times did this; people do it today, outside the church as well as within it. The unsophisticated visualize Him as a venerable figure surrounded by radiance.

But everyone who has set this inflow from heaven aside through self-intelligence and an evil life, has stifled this ingrafted tendency. People who have destroyed it through self-intelligence prefer an invisible God; people who have stifled it through an evil life prefer no God at all. Neither class knows that an ingrafted tendency like this exists, since it is not within them. Yet this is the actual heavenly Divine, it is what first and foremost flows into man from heaven. This is because man is born for heaven, and no one enters heaven without some concept of the Divine.

83. This is why someone who is not engaged in the concept proper to heaven—the concept of the Divine which is heaven's source—cannot be brought up even to the first threshold of heaven. The moment he comes near, he feels an opposition, a forceful resistance. This is because his more inward elements, which are supposed to accept heaven, are closed, not being in the form of heaven. In fact, the closer he gets to heaven, the more tightly these more inward elements are closed.

This is what happens to people in the church who deny the Lord, and to people who, like the Socinians, deny His Divine. As for what happens to people who are born outside the church, in ignorance of the Lord because they lack the Word, this will come out in later pages.

84. The question of the ancients' having an anthropomorphic concept of the Divine is settled by the appearances of the Divine to Abraham, Lot, Joshua, Gideon, Manoah and his wife, and others, who did see God as a person, but did worship Him as God of the universe, calling Him "God of heaven and earth," and "Jehovah." It was the Lord who appeared to Abraham; this He teaches in *John* (8:56). We can see that this was the case in the other instances, judging from the Lord's words,

That no one has seen the Father or His face, or heard His voice. (John 1:18, 5:37)

85. But it is very hard for people to grasp the fact that God is a Person if they form their conclusions on the basis of the outer person's sensory data. The only way the sense-oriented person can think about the Divine is through models from the world or worldly objects. So the only way he can think of a Divine or a spiritual person is the same way he thinks of a physical or natural one. As a result, he arrives at the conclusion that if God were Man, He would be as big as the universe, that if He ruled heaven and earth, He would use many assistants the way kings on earth do.

Tell such people that there is not the kind of spatial extension in heaven that there is on earth, and they simply cannot understand it. For, anyone who does his thinking on the basis of nature and from nature's light alone, invariably bases his thought on the kind of expanse that is presented to his eyes. But people go utterly astray when they think this way about heaven. Distance there is not like distance on earth. Here it is a limited distance and therefore measurable; there it is an unlimited distance and therefore immeasurable.

But the topic of distance or extension in heaven will come up later, when we deal with space and time in the spiritual world.

Further, everyone knows how far eyesight reaches—even to the sun and the stars, remote as they are. Anyone who thinks more deeply also knows that inner sight—the sight of thought—has a far wider outreach, and he therefore knows that the more inward the sight, the wider the field. Then what about Divine sight, the inmost and highest of all?

Since thoughts do have this kind of outreach, all the elements of heaven are communicated to each individual there. So are all the elements of the Divine which constitutes and fills heaven, as indicated in the previous chapter.

86. It baffles the inhabitants of heaven that people think they are smart if they think about the Lord by turning their minds to something invisible, something that cannot be confined in any form—also that they call people unintelligent and simple if they think otherwise. But it is just the other way around. The angels say, "Let these people who think they are smart really examine themselves. Do they not see nature in God's place? Some, the nature that is right in front of their eyes, some a nature that is not right in front of their eyes? And aren't they so blind that they don't know the nature of God, of an angel, of a spirit, of their own soul which will live after death, of the life of heaven within man, and of a host of other things that go to make up intelligence? But the people they call simple know all these things in their own fashion. They have a concept of their God as being the Divine in human form, a concept of an angel as a heavenly person, a concept of their soul, which will live after death, as being like an angel, and a concept of the life of heaven on man's part as being to live according to Divine laws."

These latter are the people the angels call intelligent and fit for heaven. The former kind they call unintelligent.

12.

THERE IS A CORRESPONDENCE BETWEEN EVERYTHING IN HEAVEN AND EVERYTHING IN MAN

87. The nature of correspondence is unknown nowadays; this for several reasons. The foremost reason is that man has moved himself away from heaven through love of self and love of the world. For a person who loves himself and the world primarily focuses on worldly things only, since these appeal to his outward senses and gratify his inclinations. He does not focus on spiritual things because these appeal to the inner senses and gratify the mind. As a result, people of this kind reject spiritual things, calling them too lofty to think about.

The ancient people behaved differently. As far as they were concerned, a knowledge of correspondences was the finest of all knowledges. They drew discernment and wisdom through it; through it, church people were in touch with heaven. For this knowledge of correspondences is an angelic knowledge.

Using correspondence itself, the most ancient people (who were celestial people) thought like angels and actually talked with angels as a result. For the same reason, the Lord often appeared to them and taught them. Nowadays, though, this knowledge has so vanished that even the nature of correspndence is unknown.

88. Now, without insight into the nature of correspondence, nothing can be known in clear light about the spiritual world, nothing about its inflow into the natural world, or even about what the spiritual is relative to the natural; nothing can be known in clear light about man's spirit, called his soul, and how it acts on the body, nothing about man's state after death. Because of this, the nature and character of correspondence needs to be presented. This will pave the way for further matters.

89. Let us then first state the nature of correspondence. The whole natural world corresponds to the spiritual world—not just the natural world in general, but actually in details. So anything in the natural world that occurs from the spiritual world is called a correspondent. It is vital to understand that the natural world emerges and endures from the spiritual world, just like an effect from the cause that produces it.

The natural world means all the expanse under the sun, receiving warmth and light from it. All the entities that are maintained from this source belong to that world. The spiritual world, in contrast, is heaven. All the things that are in the heavens belong to that world.

90. Since man is both a heaven and an earth in smallest form, on the model of the greatest (see n. 57 above), he has a spiritual world and a natural world within him. His spiritual world comprises his more inward elements, belonging to his mind and having to do with discernment and intention. His natural world comprises his more outward elements, belonging to his body and having to do with its senses and behavior. So anything that occurs in his natural world (his body, its senses, and its actions) *from* his spiritual world (his mind, its discernment, and its intention) is called a correspondent.

91. The nature of correspondence is visible in man in his face. In a face which has not been trained to pretend, all the mind's affections stand out visibly, in a physical form as in their imprint. This is why the face is called the index of the mind, a person's spiritual world contained within his natural world.

In much the same way, the elements of discernment are represented in speech and the elements of intention in bodily attitudes. So these things that happen in the body—face, speech, or attitudes alike—are called correspondences.

92. This may also serve to clarify what the inner person is and what the outer person is. The inner is what is called the spiritual person; the outer, the natural. Further, the two are quite distinct, as are heaven and earth, in such a way that, further still, everything that happens or emerges in the outer or natural person happens and emerges from the inner or spiritual.

93. All this has to do with the correspondence of the inner or spiritual realm of man with his outer or natural realm. Now we must deal with the correspondence of the totality of heaven with the details of man.

94. It has been pointed out that the whole heaven reflects a single person, that it is a person in all appearance, and that it is therefore called the Greatest Man. It has also been pointed out that the angelic communities that constitute heaven are therefore arranged like the members, organs, and viscera in a person. So there are some which are in the head, some in the chest, some in the arms, and some in specific parts of them (cf. nn. 59-72 above).

So communities that are in a particular member there correspond to the like member in man—those in the head, for example, correspond to the head in a person, those in the chest to the person's chest, those in the arms to his arms, and so on. Man has being from this correspondence, for man has being only from heaven.

95. The division of heaven into two kingdoms, one called celestial and one called spiritual, has been pointed out above in the appropriate section. In general, the celestial kingdom corresponds to the heart and to everything dependent on the heart throughout the body. The spiritual kingdom corresponds to the lungs and to everything dependent on them throughout the body. Heart and lungs constitute two kingdoms in man, with the heart's domain extending through the arteries and veins, and the lungs' dominion through the nerve and motor tissues. Both are involved in whatever effort or activity occurs.

There are also two kingdoms in every individual's spiritual world, which is called his spiritual person. One of these belongs to his intention and the other to his discernment. Intention's dominion extends through affections for what is good, and discernment's through affections for what is true. These kingdoms correspond to the kingdoms of the heart and the lungs in the body.

The situation in the heavens is similar. The celestial kingdom is the seat of heaven's intention, where the ''good'' of love reigns. The spiritual kingdom is the seat of heaven's discernment, where what is true reigns. These are what correspond to the functions of the heart and lungs in man.

This correspondence is why ''the heart'' in the Word indicates intention, also the good of love; while ''the breath'' of the lungs indicates discernment and what is true of faith. This is also why affections are attributed to the heart, even though they are not in or from the heart.

96. The correspondence of heaven's two kingdoms with the heart and lungs is the general correspondence of heaven with man. Less general is the correspondence with his particular members, organs, and viscera, whose nature will now be noted.

In the Greatest Man, or heaven, people in the head are those who are involved in everything good more than others are. They are in fact involved in love, peace, innocence, wisdom, discernment, and in joy and happiness as a result.

They flow into the head, and into things dependent on the head, in man; and they correspond to such things.

In the Greatest Man, or heaven, the people who are in the chest are involved in the good of charity and faith. They flow into man's chest, and correspond to it.

In the Greatest Man, or heaven, people in the loins or organs for generation are involved in marriage love. People in the feet are in the outmost good of heaven, which is called natural-spiritual good. People in the arms and hands are involved in the power of what is true from what is good. People in the eyes are involved in discernment; people in the ears, in hearkening and obedience; people in the nostrils, in perception; people in the mouth and tongue, in discussing on the basis of discernment and perception. People in the kidneys are involved in truth as examining, distinguishing, and correcting. People in the liver, pancreas, and spleen are involved in various kinds of cleansing of what is good and true. Other functions are performed elsewhere.

These flow into parallel elements in man, and correspond to them. The inflowing of heaven is into the functions and uses of the members of the body. The uses, being from the spiritual world, take form by means of such materials as occur in the natural world. So they present themselves in their effect, which is the source of correspondence.

97. This is why these same members, organs, and viscera are used in the Word to denote parallel things; for everything in the Word has meaning according to correspondence. "Head" is therefore used to denote discernment and wisdom, "chest," charity; "loins," marriage love; "arms" and "hands" the power of what is true; "feet," what is natural; "eyes," discernment; "nostrils," perception; "ears," obedience; "kidneys," examination of what is true; and so on.

This is also why it is natural for people talking about

intelligence and wisdom to speak of "a good head," to speak of someone involved in charity as "a bosom friend," to refer to someone perceptive as "having a sharp nose," someone discerning as "sharp-sighted," someone powerful as "having a long arm," someone who wills something from his love as "willing from his heart."

These expressions, and many others in people's language, stem from correspondence. They actually stem from the spiritual world, though people do not realize it.

98. The existence of this correspondence between everything heavenly and everything human has been demonstrated to me by an abundance of experience—such an abundance that I am so thoroughly convinced about these matters as to find them quite obvious, beyond any doubt. But listing all this experience is not our task at this point, and the very abundance precludes it. You may find it assembled in *Arcana Coelestia* in the treatment of correspondences, representations, the inflow of the spiritual world into the natural, and interaction between soul and body.

99. In spite of the fact that everything physical about man corresponds to everything heavenly, still a person is not a picture of heaven as far as his outward form is concerned, only as far as his inner form is concerned. It is the more inward elements of a person, after all, that receive heaven; his outer elements receive the world. So an individual is inwardly a heaven in least form, a reflection of the greatest heaven, so far as his more inward elements do receive heaven. To the degree that his more inward elements are unreceptive, he is not a heaven or a reflection of the greatest.

Be that as it may, his more outward elements, which receive the world, may be in a form that follows some pattern of this world—with different degrees of beauty, therefore. Outward or physical beauty, that is, goes back to parents and to formation in the womb. Thereafter it is maintained by means of a general inflow from the world. As a result, the form of an individual's natural person may differ radically from the form of his spiritual person.

A number of times, I have been shown what the form of an individual's spirit was like, and with some people who looked lovely and charming, the spirit looked misshapen, black, and monstrous—something you would call a reflection of hell rather than of heaven. With others who were not beautiful, the spirit looked graceful, radiant, and angelic. After death, a person's spirit looks the way it actually was within his body while it dwelt there in the world.

100. But correspondence includes even more than just man. There is an intercorrespondence of the heavens, the second or middle heaven corresponding to the third or inmost, and the first or outmost heaven corresponding to the second or middle. This first heaven corresponds to physical forms in man, called members, organs, and viscera.

So man's body is where heaven finally leaves off; it is what heaven stands on like a base. But this arcanum will be explained more fully elsewhere.

101. But the following fact must certainly be known: all the correspondence that exists with heaven is with the Lord's Divine Human, since heaven is from Him and He is heaven, as has been pointed out in the preceding chapters. For unless the Divine Human did flow into all the elements of heaven—and, following correspondences, into all the elements of earth—neither angel nor man would exist.

This clarifies again why the Lord became Man, why He covered His Divine with a Human from beginning to end. This happened because the Divine Human which has sustained heaven before the Lord's coming was no longer adequate to keep everything going, since man, the "base" of the heavens, had undermined and destroyed the pattern.

102. Angels are baffled when they hear that there actually are people who ascribe everything to nature and nothing to the Divine, people who believe that their bodies, where so many heavenly marvels are assembled, are just put together out of natural elements—who believe nature to be the source even of man's rationality.

Yet if only they could raise their minds a bit, they would see that things like this are from the Divine, not from nature, that nature was created simply to clothe the spiritual, to act as its correspondent and to give it presence in the lowest realm of the overall design. Angels compare people like this to owls, who see in the dark but not in the light.

13.

HEAVEN HAS A CORRESPONDENCE WITH EVERYTHING ON EARTH

103. The nature of correspondence has been described in the last section, along with the explanation that all the specific components of the animate body are correspondences. Next we need to point out that all things on earth—in general, everything in the world—are correspondences.

104. All things on earth are divided into three classes called kingdoms—the animal kingdom, the vegetable kingdom, and the mineral kingdom. Things in the animal kingdom are correspondences of the first level, because they are alive. Things in the vegetable kingdom are correspondences in the second level, because they simply grow. Things in the mineral kingdom are correspondences of the third level, since they neither live nor grow.

Correspondences in the animal kingdom are the various kinds of living creatures, ones that walk and creep on the earth as well as ones that fly in the air. The different kinds are not listed here because they are well known.

Correspondences in the vegetable kingdom are all the things that grow and bloom in gardens, forests, fields, and meadows. These are not listed either, since they too are well known.

Correspondences in the mineral kingdom are the more and less noble metals, precious and ordinary stones, various kinds of earths, and even liquids. In addition to these, correspondences are things made out of them by human diligence for human use—for example, all kinds of foods, items of clothing, houses, buildings, and many other things.

105. Things above the earth like the sun, the moon, and the stars, and things in the atmospheres like clouds, storms, rain lightning, and thunder, are correspondences too.

Things that stem from the sun, from its presence or its absence, like light and shade, heat and cold, are also correspondences. So are things which depend on these phenomena, like the seasons of the year, called spring, summer, fall, and winter, and the parts of the day, like morning, noon, evening, and night.

106. In short, all the things that occur in nature, from the smallest to the greatest, are correspondences. Their being correspondences stems from the fact that the natural world and everything in it emerges and persists from the spiritual world, with both worlds emerging and persisting from the Divine. It is said that something also persists because everything does persist to the extent that it keeps emerging, persisting being really a continual emerging. This is said also because nothing can persist on its own, only from something prior to itself, and therefore from a First. If it is ever separated from this First, it utterly wastes away and vanishes.

107. A correspondent is anything that emerges and persists in nature as a result of the Divine design. The Divine design is a product of the Divine "good" that issues from the Lord. It has its beginning from Him, issues from Him through the successive heavens into the world, and finishes there in the extremities. Things there that are there in accord with the design are correspondences.

The things which are in accord with the design there are all the things that are good and are thoroughly fitted for use, everything good being good according to its use. The form has to do with what is true, since the true is the form of the good.

This is why everything in the whole world—everything participating in the nature of the world—that is in the Divine design, has to do with the good and the true.

108. It is proposed, then, that everything in the world emerges as a result of the Divine, being clothed in whatever elements in nature enable it to be there, to serve a use, and in this way to correspond. There is clear support for this in the visible details of both the animal and the vegetable kingdom. In each kingdom there are things of such a nature that anyone who thinks deeply can see that they come from heaven. As illustrations, we may cite a few of the myriads that exist, beginning with some from the animal kingdom.

Here, the existence of a kind of innate knowledge in all sorts of animals is widely recognized. Bees know how to gather honey from flowers, how to build little cells out of wax where their honey can be stored, providing food for themselves and their dependents against the coming winter. Their queen lays eggs, while other bees take care of them and tuck them away so that new progeny will be born from them. They live within a kind of governmental structure that they all know innately. They protect useful members and eject useless ones or deny them food. Then there are other marvelous things given them from heaven for the sake of use. Their wax serves the human race worldwide for light, and their honey for flavoring foods.

[2] And what about caterpillars, the most unattractive members of the animal kingdom? They know how to get nourishment from the juice of appropriate leaves, and how after a precise time to form a cocoon around themselves—to put themselves in a womb, so to speak—and to hatch offspring of their own kind in this way. Some of them change into nymphs and chrysalids first, and make new threads. Then, after exhausting labor, they are fitted out with a new body adorned with wings. They fly through the air as though it were their heaven, they consummate their marriages, lay their eggs, and provide a posterity for themselves.

[3] Beside these particular examples, all the winged crea-

tures of the sky in general know the foods that are good for them. They know not only what these foods are, but where they are. They know how to build themselves nests, lay and incubate eggs in them, hatch their chicks, feed them, and send them away from home when they are ready to be on their own. They know the enemies to avoid; they know the friends to seek out—all this from the beginning of infancy. And how can I leave out miracles within the egg itself, where everything necessary for the forming and nourishment of the incipient chick lies ready and properly arranged? And beyond this there are countless other examples.

[4] Is there anyone—anyone who thinks with a trace of cogent wisdom, that is—who would claim that these wonders come from any source but the spiritual world?—the spiritual world, which the natural world serves by clothing its output in a body, or by giving effective presence to things that, causally regarded, are spiritual?

Why is it that both earthbound and flying animals are born into all this knowledge, but not man, who is actually superior to them? The reason is that animals are engaged in the true design of their life. They have not been able to destroy the elements from the spiritual world that are within them because they have no rationality.

Man, whose thinking arises from the spiritual world, is different. With the support of his rationality, he has corrupted the output of the spiritual world within himself, through a disorderly life. So he must be born into complete ignorance, and be led back from there into the design of heaven by Divine means.

109. Many examples might be used to show how things in the vegetable kingdom correspond. For example, there is the growth of seeds into trees, their putting forth leaves, bearing flowers and then fruit in which, in turn, they lay seeds. These events occur in sequence and they come together in such a marvelous order that there is no way to describe it briefly. It would take volumes, and still the deeper secrets, more basic to the function of plants, could not be fully understood.

Inasmuch as these matters too have their origin in the spiritual world or heaven, which is in human form (as pointed out in the pertinent chapter above), even the details of the plant world have a certain relationship to things within man. There are people in the learned world who recognize this.

An abundance of experience has made it clear to me that everything in that kingdom is a correspondence as well. Often, for example, when I was in a garden looking at trees, fruits, flowers, and vegetables, I noticed correspondences in heaven. Then I talked with the people involved and was taught where they came from and what their quality was.

110. But nowadays heaven is the only source of knowing the spiritual things in heaven to which natural things on earth correspond. The knowledge of correspondences is simply demolished. So I should like to use a few examples to show what the correspondence between spiritual and natural things is like.

In general, the land animals correspond to affections. The gentle and useful ones correspond to good affections, the ruthless and unserviceable ones to evil affections. Specifically, cows and calves correspond to affections of the natural mind, sheep and lambs to affections of the spiritual mind. The various kinds of winged creatures, on the other hand, correspond to intellectual elements in the one mind or the other.

So in the Israelitish Church (which was a "representative church"), different animals like cows, calves, rams, sheep, female and male goats, male and female lambs, even pigeons and turtledoves were accepted for holy service and used for sacrifices and burnt offerings. In that use they actually corresponded to spiritual things which were discerned in heaven according to correspondences.

The reason that animals, genus by genus and species by species, are affections, is that they are alive. For nothing possesses life except out of affection and according to affection. This is why every animal has innate knowledge in keeping with the affection of his life.

Even man is much the same as far as his natural person is concerned. So he is in fact likened to animals in everyday idioms. For example, we call a gentle person a sheep or a lamb, a cruel one a bear or a wolf, a shrewd one a fox or a snake, etc.

111. There is a similar correspondence with things in the vegetable kingdom. In general, a garden corresponds to heaven viewed as to its discernment and wisdom. So heaven is called "the garden of God" and "Paradise," and also, by man, "a heavenly Paradise." Trees, species by species, correspond to perceptions and insights of what is good and true, the raw material of discernment and wisdom. So the ancient people, who were involved in the knowledge of correspondences, held their holy worship in groves. This is also why trees are mentioned so many times in the Word and used as analogues to heaven, the church, and man—trees like the vine, the olive, the cedar, and others. The good things people do are compared to fruits.

Foods derived from plants—especially from field-grown grains—correspond to affections for what is good and true, because these nourish spiritual life the way earthly foods nourish natural life.

So bread in general corresponds to an affection for everything good because it supports life more commonly than other foods, and because the word "bread" is used to denote all kinds of food. It is by reason of this correspondence that

the Lord calls Himself the Bread of Life. This is why bread
was put to holy use in the Israelitish Church, placed on a
table in the tabernacle, and called "the bread of Presence."
All Divine worship performed with sacrifice and burnt of-
fering was called bread, as well. This correspondence is
also the reason that the most holy act of worship in the
Christian Church is the Holy Supper, in which the bread
and the wine are given.

These few examples may suffice to establish what correspondence is like.

112. Now we may state briefly how heaven is yoked with
earth by means of correspondences.

The Lord's kingdom is a kingdom of purposes which are
useful functions—or a kingdom of useful functions which
are purposes, which amounts to the same thing. The universe
has therefore been so created and formed by the Divine that
wherever useful functions occur, they may clothe themselves in the kinds of material that enable them to stand up
in action or effectiveness. They do so clothe themselves
beginning in heaven, and then in the world—that is, step
by step and in order right down to the outmost elements of
nature.

We can therefore see that the correspondence between
natural and spiritual, between the world and heaven, is by
useful functions; and these functions make the bond. The
forms that clothe functions are correspondences, and bonds,
to the extent that they are the forms that belong to the
functions.

In the world's nature, with its threefold kingdom, all the
things that occur according to the Design are forms that
belong to functions, or results shaped by functions for the
sake of function. So all the things in it are correspondences.

But as far as man is concerned, the degree to which he
lives according to the Divine design—in love to the Lord,

that is, and charity toward the neighbor—determines the extent to which his actions are functions in form, are correspondences through which he is bonded with heaven. Loving the Lord and the neighbor, generally, is equal to fulfilling useful functions.

It is further worth knowing that it is man by whom the natural world is bonded with the spiritual world—that man is the medium of connection. For there is a natural world within him and a spiritual world as well (see above, n. 57). So man is a medium of connection to the extent that he is spiritual. But to the extent that he is natural and not spiritual, he is not a medium of connection. The Divine inflow into the world does continue even without man as a medium. It continues into the things in man that come from the world, but not into his rationality.

113. Just as everything that follows the Divine design corresponds to heaven, everything that disagrees with the Divine design corresponds to hell. The things that correspond to heaven all have to do with what is good and true; the things that correspond to hell all have to do with what is evil and false.

114. Now we may say a bit about the knowledge of correspondences and the use of that knowledge.

We have already noted that the spiritual world—heaven—is connected to the natural world through correspondences. As a consequence, communication with heaven is given to man through correspondences.

The angels of heaven do not think on the basis of natural phenomena, the way men do. So when a person is involved in the knowledge of correspondences, he can be united with angels as touches the thoughts of his mind. So he can be bonded to them as touches his spiritual or inner person.

To provide a bond between heaven and man, the Word was composed by pure correspondences. The whole Word and its details have correspondence. If man were involved in the knowledge of correspondences, then he would understand the Word in its spiritual meaning. In this way it would be granted him to understand arcana of which he sees no trace in the literal meaning.

The Word does contain a literal meaning and a spiritual meaning. The literal meaning is composed of worldly things, while the spiritual meaning is composed of heavenly things. Since the bond between heaven and earth is by correspondences, this kind of Word has been provided, in which the details do correspond, right down to the smallest letters.

115. I have been taught from heaven that the most ancient people on our earth, who were celestial people, did their thinking by means of actual correspondences. The natural things of this world, the things before their very eyes, served them as means for this kind of thinking. Being like this, they associated with angels and talked with them.

Through them, heaven was bonded to earth. On this account, that era was called the Golden Age, the age when, early writers say, heavenly beings dwelt with men and communed with them as friend with friend.

But after their era, there came people who did not think by means of actual correspondences, but by means of knowledge about correspondences. So there was even then a bond between heaven and man, but not such an intimate one. Their era is the one called the Silver Age.

Then came people who knew some correspondences, but did not do their thinking by means of this knowledge. This was because they were involved in natural "good," and not, like their predecessors, in spiritual "good." Their era is known as the Bronze Age.

After their era, man became increasingly external, and finally carnal. At this point, the knowledge of correspondences was completely destroyed, and along with it the awareness of heaven and of many related matters.

The very naming of these eras after gold, silver, and bronze comes from correspondence. Gold, by correspondence, denotes celestial "good," in which the most ancient people were involved. Silver denotes spiritual "good," in which the ancient people were involved; and bronze denotes natural "good," in which their immediate descendants were involved. Iron, after which the last era was named, denotes what is true without what is good.

14.

THE SUN IN HEAVEN

116. This world's sun is not visible in heaven, nor is anything that comes from it, because all such things are natural. Nature actually begins with that sun, and everything produced by means of it is called natural. But the spiritual realm, where heaven is, is higher than nature and quite distinct from anything natural. These realms communicate with each other only by means of correspondences.

The nature of this distinction can be understood with the aid of the information given above (n. 38) about levels. Material about correspondence in the last two chapters may aid comprehension of the nature of the communication.

117. But in spite of the fact that neither this world's sun nor anything from it is visible in heaven, there is still a sun there. There is light and warmth, there are all the things we have on earth and countless others. However, they are not from the same source, for things in heaven are spiritual and things in the world are natural.

Heaven's sun is the Lord. Heaven's light is Divine truth, its warmth Divine good, issuing from the Lord as if from a sun. This is the source of all the things that emerge or appear in the heavens. But in subsequent chapters there will be information about light and warmth and the things that come into being in heaven from this source. Here we deal only with that sun.

The reason the Lord is seen as a sun in heaven is that He is Divine love, the source from which all spiritual things emerge and—via the world's sun—all natural things. That love is what shines like a sun.

118. The Lord's actual appearing in heaven like a sun is not just something angels have told me about, but something I have been allowed to see several times. So now I should like to describe briefly what I have seen and heard about the Lord as a sun.

The Lord does not appear as a sun *in* heaven, but high above the heavens; not overhead or straight up, but in front of the angels' faces, at a medium elevation. He appears in two places, one before the right eye and one before the left, with a perceptible space between. To the right eye He looks exactly like a sun, with something like the same fire and size as earth's sun has. To the left eye He does not look like a sun but like a moon, with a similar but more glistening luster, of a size similar to our earth's moon. However, it appears to be surrounded by miniature moons, each of them shining and glistening in like manner.

The reason the Lord appears in two places, and so differently, is that His appearance to anyone depends on the way He is accepted. He looks one way to people who accept Him with the good of love, and another way to people who accept Him with the good of faith.

To people who accept Him with the good of love, He looks like a sun, fiery and flaming in keeping with their acceptance. These people are in His celestial kingdom. To people who accept Him with the good of faith, though, He looks like a moon, lustrous and glistening in keeping with the acceptance. These people are in His spiritual kingdom.

This is because the good of love corresponds to fire, so that fire in a spiritual meaning is love. The good of faith corresponds to light, and light in a spiritual meaning is faith.

He appears before the eyes because the more inward elements, those of the mind, see through the eyes. They look from love's good through the right eye, and from faith's good through the left eye. For everything on the right side of an angel—or of a man —corresponds to the good which is the source of the true; while things in the left correspond to the true that comes from the good. Faith's good is basically something true derived from something good.

119. This is why in the Word the Lord in respect to love is compared to the sun, while in respect to faith He is compared to the moon. Also, love for the Lord, from the Lord, is indicated by "the sun," and faith in the Lord, from the Lord, by "the moon." So in the following passages:

> The light of the moon will be like the light of the sun: while the sun's light will be increased sevenfold, like the light of seven days.(Isaiah 30:26)
>
> When I destroy you, I will cover the heavens and darken the stars; I will cover the sun with a cloud, and the moon will not make her light shine forth; I will darken all the lights in the heavens above you, and set darkness over your land.
>
> (Ezekiel 32:7,8)
>
> I will dim the sun at its rising, and the moon will not make her light shine forth.
>
> (Isaiah 13:10)
>
> The sun and the moon will be darkened, and the stars will withhold their radiance; . . . the sun will be turned to darkness, and the moon to blood.
>
> (Joel 2:2, 10,31;4:15)
>
> The sun was blackened like a hairy sack, and the moon made like blood, and the stars fell on the earth.   (Revelation 6:12)
>
> Immediately after the distress of those days, the sun will be darkened and the moon will not give her light, and the stars will fall from heaven.   (Matthew 24:29)

and elsewhere.

In these passages, love is indicated by "the sun" and faith by "the moon," while awareness of what is good and what is true are indicated by "the stars." These are described as darkening, losing their light, and falling from heaven, when they no longer exist.

The Lord's appearing as a sun in heaven is also confirmed by the way He was transfigured in front of Peter, James, and John,

. that His face shone like the sun.

(Matthew 17:2)

This is the way the Lord looked to His disciples when they were withdrawn from the body and in heaven's light. For this reason, the ancient people, who had a representative church, faced toward the sun in the east when they were engaged in Divine worship. They, in turn, are the source of building temples to face the east.

120. The amount and nature of Divine love can be determined by comparison with this world's sun, which burns most intensely. Believe it or not, Divine love is far more fiery. The Lord as the sun therefore does not flow directly into the heavens, but the warmth of His love is tempered bit by bit in transit. The tempering agents look like gleaming bands around the sun. Besides this, the angels are shielded by a cloud, appropriately thin, so as not to be hurt by the inflow.

So the heavens are spaced according to acceptance. The higher heavens, being involved in love's good, are nearest to the Lord as the sun. The lower heavens, being involved in faith's good, are farther from it. People involved in nothing good whatever, though, like those in hell, are actually farthest away; and they are just as far away as they are opposed to what is good.

121. However, when the Lord appears *in* heaven, as often happens, He does not appear clothed with the sun, but in angelic form, distinguished from angels by something Divine shining from His face. He is not actually there in person, for His person is continually clothed with the sun; He is there with an effective presence by means of an appearance. It is quite usual in heaven for things to appear as present at the point where sight is focused or terminated, in spite of the fact that this may be quite remote from the place where they actually are. This presence is called the presence of inner sight, and will be mentioned further below.

The Lord has in fact appeared to me outside the sun, in an angelic form a bit below the sun on high; also close at hand in a similar form, with His face shining; and once in the midst of some angels as a flaming radiance.

122. This world's sun looks to angels like something dark at the other end of things from the sun of heaven. Our moon looks like something gloomy at the other end from heaven's moon, consistently. The reason is that anything fiery in this world corresponds to love of self, with any light from it corresponding to falsity stemming from that love. Love of self is quite contrary to Divine love; and the falsity that stems from it is quite contrary to Divine truth. Anything contrary to Divine love and Divine truth is darkness to angels. As a result, the meaning in the Word of "worshipping earth's sun and moon" and "prostrating oneself to them" is loving oneself and the false things that stem from self-love. On the elimination of these practices, see Deut. 4:9; 17:3-5; Jer. 8:1,2; Ez. 8:15, 16, 18; Rev. 16:8; Matt. 13:6.

123. Since the Lord, because of the Divine love which is in Him and from Him, is visible in heaven as a sun, all the people in heaven turn steadily toward Him. People in the celestial kingdom turn toward Him as a sun; people in the spiritual kingdom turn toward Him as a moon. But the people in the hells turn toward the dark and gloomy entities that come from the contrary source, and so turn their backs to the Lord. This is because all the people in the hells are involved in self-love and love of the world, and are therefore opposed to the Lord.

The people who turn toward the dark place where earth's sun is are toward the rear in the hells, and are called genii. The people who turn toward the gloomy place where the moon is are farther forward in the hells, and are called spirits. So the people who are in the hells are described as being in the gloom, while people in heaven are described as being in the light. "Gloom" refers to the falsity that comes from what is evil, and "light" to the truth that comes from what is good.

This turning occurs because all people in the other life direct their attention to the controlling forces within themselves—that is, to their loves. It is also these more inward elements that make the face of an angel or spirit; and in the spiritual world there are no fixed compass points like those in the natural world—it is the face that determines the direction.

Man too, in spirit, turns himself in a similar fashion. People involved in self-love and love of the world are turning themselves away from the Lord, and people involved in a love of Him and love toward their fellowmen are turning toward Him. But man, being involved in a natural world where compass points are determined by sunrise and sunset, is unaware of this.

Since this matter is hard for people to grasp, it will be clarified later, in dealing with directions, space, and time.

124. Because the Lord is heaven's sun, and all the things that come from Him face Him, the Lord is the common center, the source of every direction and boundary. For the same reason too, all the things beneath are in His presence and under His guidance, whether they are in the heavens or on earth.

125. These observations let us see in clearer light the statements made in previous sections about the Lord, to the effect that

He is the God of heaven (nn. 2-6).

His Divine constitutes heaven (nn. 7-12).The Lord's Divine in heaven is love for Him and charity toward fellowman (nn. 13-19).There is a correspondence with heaven of everything on earth, and through heaven, a correspondence with the Lord (nn. 81-115).

Finally, earth's sun and moon have correspondence (n. 105).

15.

LIGHT AND WARMTH IN HEAVEN

126. People who use only nature as the basis for their thinking cannot possibly grasp the fact that there is light in the heavens, yet the fact is that there is so much light that it exceeds by many times the light of noonday on earth. This I have often witnessed, even at evening and night times. At first I was puzzled when I heard angels saying that earth's light was hardly anything but shadow compared to heaven's light. But having seen, I can assert that this is true. Its brilliance and radiance are of a quality beyond description. What I have seen in the heavens I have seen in this light—therefore more clearly and distinctly than in the world.

127. Heaven's light is not a natural light, like the world's light, but a spiritual one. It actually comes from the Lord as the sun, this sun being Divine love, as stated in the last chapter.

In heaven, that which issues from the Lord as the sun is called the Divine-True. However, it is essentially the Divine-Good made one with the Divine-True. From it angels have light and warmth—light from the Divine-True and warmth from the Divine-Good. This enables us to conclude that heaven's light, coming as it does from this kind of source, is spiritual and not natural, likewise heaven's warmth.

128. The reason the Divine-True is light to angels is that angels are spiritual and not natural. Spiritual beings see because of their sun, natural beings from theirs. Divine truth is the source of angels' discernment, and discernment is their inner sight which flows into their outer sight and produces it. So things that are visible in heaven from the Lord as the sun apppear in that light.

This being the source of light in heaven, then, this light varies according to the acceptance of the Divine-True from the Lord, or, that is, according to the intelligence and wisdom the angels are involved in. It is therefore different in the celestial kingdom than it is in the spiritual kingdom, and different in each particular community. The light in the celestial kingdom looks fiery, since the angels there accept light from the Lord as the sun. The light in the spiritual kingdom, on the other hand, is white, since the angels there accept light from the Lord as the moon (see above, n. 118).

Further, the light is not the same in one community as in another. It varies even within one community, with the people at the center being in more light and those toward the borders in less (see n. 43).

In a word, angels have light to the precise degree that they are accepting of the Divine-True—that is, are involved in intelligence and wisdom from the Lord. This is why heaven's angels are called angels of light.

129. Since the Lord in the heavens is the Divine-True, and the Divine-True there is light, the Lord—and every true thing that comes from Him—is called ''light'' in the Word, as in the following passages:

> Jesus said, ''I am the light of the world; whoever follows Me will not walk in darkness, but will have the light of light.''   (John 8:12)
> As long as I am in the world, I am the world's light.   (John 9:5)
> Jesus . . . said . . . ''The light is with you for a short while only; while you have light, walk, lest darkness overtake you: . . . while you have light, believe in the light so that you may be children of light . . . I have come into the world as light, so that anyone who believes in Me will not stay in darkness.''   (John 12:35, 36, 46)
> Light has come into the world, but men have loved darkness more than light.   (John 3:19)

John says of the Lord:

This is the true light that enlightens every man. (John 1:4, 9)

The people who sit in darkness have seen a great light; and on those who were sitting in the shadow of death, light has risen.

(Matthew 4:16)

I will make you a covenant for the people, a light for the nations. (Isaiah 42:6)

I have set you up as the light of the nations, so that you would be my salvation right to the end of the earth. (Isaiah 49:6)

The nations that have been saved will walk toward His light. (Revelation 21:24)

Send forth Thy light and Thy truth, may they lead me. (Ps. 43:3)

In these and other passages, the Lord is called light by reason of the Divine-True that comes from him. The truth itself is likewise called light. Since light exists in heaven from the Lord as the sun, when He was transfigured in front of Peter, James, and John

His face looked like the sun, and his clothes like light, gleaming and white as snow, as no fuller on earth could whiten them.

(Mark 9:3, Matthew 17:2)

The reason the Lord's clothes looked this way was that they pictured the Divine-True from Him in the heavens. "Clothes" in the Word refer to truths, for which reason it is said in *David,*

Jehovah, Thou surroundest Thyself with light like a garment. (Psalm 104:2)

130. It has been proposed that light in the heavens is spiritual, and that this light is the Divine-True. This can be inferred from the fact that man too has spiritual light, and has enlightenment from it to the extent to which he is engaged in intelligence and wisdom from the Divine-True. Man's spiritual light is the light of his discernment, which properly focuses on truths, arranging them analytically in patterns, constructing theorems, and coming to consecutive conclusions on this basis.

The natural person is unaware of the reality of the light which enables the intellect to see this sort of thing, for he neither sees it with his eyes nor senses it with his thought. But many people do recognize it, nevertheless, and distinguish it from a natural light that involves people who think naturally rather than spiritually. People think naturally who focus only on the world, and give nature credit for everything. But people think spiritually who focus on heaven, and give the Divine credit for everything.

The existence of a true light that enlightens the mind (quite distinct from the light called natural illumination) has been presented to my perception and sight many times. I have gradually been inwardly raised into that light; and as I was raised, my intellect was enlightned to the point that I could perceive what I had not perceived before—ultimately things totally incomprehensible to thought from natural illumination. At times I resented the fact that they were incomprehensible, when they were at the same time so clearly and obviously perceptible in heavenly light.

Since light is a property of discernment, we can talk about discernment rather as we do about the eye, saying, for instance, that it sees and is in the light when it perceives, that it is veiled or shaded when it does not perceive, and many similar expressions.

131. Inasmuch as heaven's light is the Divine-True, it is also Divine wisdom and intelligence. So "being raised into heaven's light" means the same thing as "being raised into intelligence and wisdom," and "being enlightened." As a result, light among angels exists corresponding precisely to the level of their intelligence and wisdom.

Since heaven's light is Divine wisdom, everyone's quality is recognizable in heaven's light; the whole quality of what is within each person shows in his face. Not the least element is concealed. More inward angels love to have everything that belongs to them show because they intend only what is good. This is not the case with people who are below heaven and do not intend what is good. Such people have an intense fear of being seen in heaven's light. And strange as it seems, people in hell look human to each other, but in heaven's light they look monstrous, with frightening faces and bodies—they are the very models of their own evil.

Man, as far as his spirit is concerned, has a similar appearance when angels look at him. If he is good, he looks like a beautiful person in proportion to his goodness; while if he is evil he looks monstrous, misshapen, in proportion to his evil.

So we can see that everything becomes obvious in heaven's light—everything becomes obvious because heaven's light is the Divine-True.

132. Because the Divine-True is light in the heavens, everything true anywhere is radiant, be it within an angel or outside him, within the heavens or outside them. True things outside the heavens, though, are not radiant the same way true things within the heavens are. True things outside the heavens have a cold radiance, like something snow-white without warmth. This is because they do not draw their essential substance from what is good the way true elements within heaven do. That cold light therefore vanishes when heaven's light penetrates it; and if evil underlies it, it turns to gloom. This I have seen several times, this and many other noteworthy phenomena involving shining truths, which I omit at this point.

133. Some description of heaven's warmth is now in order. Heaven's warmth is essentially love. It issues from the Lord as the sun, whose nature is Divine love within the Lord and from the Lord you may find stated in the preceding chapter. So we can see that heaven's warmth is just as spiritual as heaven's light, since it comes from the same source.

There are two things that issue from the Lord as the

sun—the Divine-True and the Divine-Good. The Divine-True presents itself in the heavens as light, and the Divine-Good as warmth. Yet the Divine-True and the Divine-Good are united in such a way that they are not two entities, but one. However, they are separated with angels, since there are some angels who accept the Divine-Good more than the Divine-True, and some who accept the Divine-True more than the Divine-Good. The ones who accept more Divine-Good are in the Lord's celestial kingdom, while the ones who accept more Divine-True are in the Lord's spiritual kingdom. The most perfect angels are the ones who accept both to the same degree.

134. Heaven's warmth, like heaven's light, varies from place to place. It is one thing in the celestial kingdom and another in the spiritual kingdom, and it is also different in each particular community there. It varies not only in degree, but in quality. It is more concentrated and pure in the Lord's celestial kingdom because the angels there accept more Divine-Good. It is less concentrated and pure in the Lord's spiritual kingdom because the angels there accept more Divine-True. In each particular community, too, it varies according to the acceptance.

There is warmth in the hells, too, but it is unclean. Warmth in heaven is what is meant by "holy and heavenly fire" while the warmth of hell is meant by "profane fire" and "hellfire." Each one refers to love—heavenly fire to love for the Lord and love toward the neighbor, and to every affection proper to these loves; while hellfire refers to love of self and love of the world and to every craving proper to these loves. The identity of love and warmth from a spiritual source is shown by the warming that follows upon love. A person is kindled and warmed in proportion to his love's extent and quality, and love's full heat shows itself when it is attacked. This is why, too, it is possible to speak of being kindled, warming up, blazing, boiling, or burning, when speaking of the affections proper to a good love and the cravings proper to an evil love as well.

135. The sensation of warmth at the touch of love coming from the Lord as the sun occurs because the more inward elements of angels are involved in love as a result of the Divine-Good that comes from the Lord. Their more outward elements, which are kindled by this means, are in warmth as a result. This is why love and warmth in heaven correspond to each other, so that a person is in a warmth in keeping with the quality of his love, in line with what has just been said.

The world's warmth does not penetrate heaven at all, since it is too crude, being natural rather than spiritual. This situation is not the same with people on earth, though, since they are in both the spiritual world and the natural world. As far as their spirits are concerned, they grow warm in direct proportion to their love. But as far as their bodies are concerned, they grow warm from both sources—warmth of spirit and the warmth of the world. The former flows into the latter because the two correspond.

The kind of correspondence that exists between the two kinds of warmth can be determined from animals, from the fact that their loves (the primary one being a love of generating offspring of their own kind) burst into action depending on the presence and abundance of warmth from the earth's sun, which warmth occurs only in spring and summer times. People who believe that the earth's inflowing warmth arouses these loves are quite mistaken. An inflow of the natural into the spiritual does not occur, only an inflow of the spiritual into the natural. This latter inflow follows from the Divine design, while the latter contradicts the Divine design.

136. Like men, angels have discernment and intending.

Heaven's light constitutes the life of their discernment, since heaven's light is the Divine-True and the consequent Divine wisdom. Heaven's warmth constitutes the life of their intending, since heaven's warmth is the Divine-Good and the consequent Divine love. The angels' very life comes from warmth, and not from light except as there is warmth in it. Life's dependence on warmth is obvious, since if warmth is taken away, life ceases.

There is a similar situation with faith apart from love, or with the true apart from the good. For the truth that is ascribed to faith is light, and the good ascribed to love is warmth.

These principles emerge even more clearly from observation of the world's warmth and light, to which heaven's warmth and light correspond. It is from the world's warmth, combined with light, that everything on earth comes to life and blooms. They are combined in spring and summer time. But from light without warmth, nothing comes to life and blooms—everything becomes sluggish and dies. They are not combined in winter time. Then warmth is gone, while light continues.

This correspondence is the basis of heaven's being called "a paradise," since there what is true is combined with what is good—or faith with love—like light with warmth in springtime on earth.

All this confirms the truth discussed in the appropriate chapter above (nn. 13-19), that the Lord's Divine in heaven is love for Him and charity toward the neighbor.

137. It says in *John:*

> In the beginning was the Word, and the Word was with God, and God was the Word: . . . all things were made by means of It, and without It nothing was made that was made. In It was life, and the life was the light of men. . . . He was in the world, and the world was made by means of Him, . . . And the Word was made flesh, and dwelt among us, and we saw His glory.   (John 1:1,3, 4, 10, 14)

It is obviously the Lord who is meant by "the Word," since it says that the Word was made flesh. But precisely what "the Word" means is still unknown, so let us explain. The Word is the Divine-Truth that is in the Lord and from the Lord. Therefore He is there referred to as light, whose identity with the Divine-True has been explained earlier in this chapter.

The making and creating of everything by means of the Divine-True is next to be explained. [2] In heaven, all power belongs to the Divine-True—without this, there is absolutely none. All angels are called powers because of the Divine-True, and depending on the degree to which they are acceptances and receiving vessels, they are powers. By means of what is true they prevail over the hells and over all who set themselves against them. A thousand foes cannot withstand one ray of heaven's light, which is the Divine-True. Since angels are angels by reason of their acceptance of the Divine-True, it follows that the whole heaven has no other basis of existence; for heaven is composed of angels.

[3] The idea that the Divine-True has so much power in it is one which people cannot believe if their only concept of what is true is that it has to do with thinking or speaking. These have no intrinsic power, except as other people act on them out of obedience. But the Divine-True has intrinsic power, such power that through it heaven was created and earth was created, with all the things they contain.

Light may be shed on the fact that the Divine-True has so much power by means of a pair of comparisons: by considering the power of what is true and good within man, and by considering the power of light and warmth from the sun in the world.

The power of what is true and good in man: Whatever a person does, he does by virtue of his discernment and his intending. By virtue of his intending, he acts through what is good; by virtue of his discernment, he acts through what is true. For all the things that are in his intending have to do with what is good, and all the things that are in his discernment have to do with what is true. From these, then, the person activates his whole body, with thousands of elements in it acceding freely to their bidding and urging. This demonstrates that the whole body is constructed for submission to what is good and true—constructed therefore on the basis of what is good and true.

[4] *The power of light and warmth from the sun in the world:* All growing things in the world—things like trees, grains, flowers, grasses, fruits, and seeds—emerge solely by reason of the sun's warmth and light. So their inherent productive power is obvious. What power must Divine light not have then, which is the Divine-True, and Divine warmth which is the Divine-Good? For these are the sources of heaven's existence and the world's as well, since the world exists by reason of heaven, as stated above.

This shows us how to understand the statements that all things were made by means of the Word, that without it nothing was made that was made, and that the world was made by means of Him—this means by means of the Divine-True from the Lord.

This is also why in the book of Genesis it speaks of light first, and later about things derived from light (Genesis 1:3,4). This is why, too, everything in the universe—in heaven and in the world alike—has to do with the good and the true, and with their bonding, if it is really to be anything at all.

139.* It needs to be realized that the Divine-Good and the Divine-True which occur in the heavens from the Lord as the sun, are not in the Lord but from the Lord. Within

---

* [There is no n. 138 in the original.]

the Lord there is only Divine Love, which is the Reality from which all things arise. Arising from Reality is what "issuing" means. This can be illumined by comparison with the world's sun. The warmth and light that are in the world are not in the sun but from the sun. Within the sun there is only fire, and from that fire the other things emerge and issue forth.

140. Since the Lord as the sun is Divine Love, and Divine Love is itself the Divine-Good, the Divine that issues from Him (which is His Divine in heaven) is called the Divine-True in order to identify it clearly, even though it is the Divine-Good united with the Divine-True. This Divine-True is what is called the Holy Spirit that issues from Him.

16.

THE FOUR MAJOR REGIONS IN HEAVEN

141. In heaven, as in the world, there are four major regions, east, south, west, and north. Each set is determined by its own sun—in heaven, by heaven's sun, which is the Lord, and in the world by the world's sun. Beyond this, however, major differences arise.

The first difference is that in the world we call "south" the direction where the sun reaches its greatest height above the earth, "north" its opposite position below the horizon, "east" the direction where the sun rises at the equinoxes, and "west" where it sets at those times. In the world, then, all the major regions are determined from the south.

But in heaven, that direction is called "east" where the Lord is seen as the sun. The opposite direction is west, south in heaven is to the right, and north is to the left. This holds true no matter which way people turn their faces or bodies. So in heaven, all the major regions are determined from the east.

The reason for calling it east [*oriens*] where the Lord is seen as the sun, is that the whole source [*origo*] of life is from Him as the sun. Further to the extent that warmth and light—or love and intelligence—from Him are accepted among angels, the Lord is said to have risen [*exoriri*] among them. This is also why the Lord is called "the East" in the Word.

142. A second point of difference is that the east is always in front of angels, the west behind, south to the right, and north to the left. But since this is hard to grasp in a world where people turn to face any direction, it will be explained.

All heaven turns toward the Lord as toward its common center; so all angels turn that way. The tendency of every vertical on the earth toward a common center is recognized. But the vertical line in heaven differs from the vertical line in the world, since in heaven the frontal parts face the common center, while in the world the lowest parts do. The vertical line in the world is what we call "the centripetal" and "gravity." Angel's more inward elements are turned forward, and since the more inward elements manifest themselves in the face, the face is what determines the major regions.

143. But the idea that the east is in front of angels *wherever they turn their faces or bodies*—this is still harder to grasp in the world, since any direction may be in front of a person on earth, depending on which way he turns. So we will explain this, too.

Angels, like people on earth, turn and direct their faces wherever they wish, but for them the east is still always before their eyes. But the turns angels make are not like the turns people on earth make, being in fact from a different source. They look alike, but they are not. The dominant love is the source. From it derive all delineations for angels and for spirits. For as stated above, their more inward elements really are turned toward their common center—in heaven, therefore, toward the Lord as the sun. As a result, since (a) the love is inescapably in front of their more inward elements, and (b) the face arises from these elements, being actually their outward form, the love that dominates is always in front of the face. In the heavens, then, this is the Lord as the sun, since He is the source of their love. And because the Lord is with angels in His love, it is the Lord who causes them to focus on Him whichever way they turn.

There is no way at this point to make these matters clearer; but in subsequent chapters, particularly on the subjects of representations and manifestations, and time and space in heaven, they will be presented to the understanding more clearly.

The phenomenon of angels' constantly having the Lord before their faces is one I have been granted to know and observe from a good deal of experience. While I have been in company with angels, my attention has been drawn to the Lord's presence before my face. Even though it was not seen, it was perceived in the light. Angels too have often asserted the truth of this.

Because the Lord is constantly before angels' faces, people on earth say that those who believe in Him and love Him have God before their eyes and faces, look to Him, and see Him. Such human idioms come from the spiritual world, for many elements of human speech originate there, though man does not know that this is their source.

144. The existence of this kind of "turning" ranks among heaven's wonders. For many people there can be in one place, one turning his face and body one way and another another way, and yet all of them will see the Lord in front of them. Each will have the south to his right, the north to his left, and the west behind him.

It also ranks among heaven's wonders that, even though all the angels' view is toward the east, they still have a view toward the other three regions. This view, though, stems from their more inward sight, which is a property of thought.

It also ranks among heaven's wonders that no one is allowed to stand behind someone else and look at the back of his head. This confuses the inflow of the good and the true that come from the Lord.

145. Angels see the Lord one way, and the Lord sees angels another way. Angels see the Lord with their eyes, while the Lord sees angels in the forehead. The reason for singling out the forehead is that the forehead corresponds to love. The Lord flows into their intending through their love; He makes Himself visible through their discernment, to which the eyes correspond.

146. In the heavens that make up the Lord's celestial kingdom, the major regions are not the same as the ones in the heavens that make up His spiritual kingdom, the reason being that to the angels in His celestial kingdom the Lord is seen as the sun, while to the angels in His spiritual kingdom He is seen as the moon, and the east is where the Lord is seen. The distance between the sun and the moon in heaven is thirty degrees, so the offset of the regions is the same.

The division of heaven into two kingdoms called the celestial kingdom and the spiritual kingdom, is described in its own chapter (nn. 20-28), as is the Lord's appearance in the celestial kingdom as the sun and in the spiritual kingdom as the moon (n. 118). Still, heaven's regions are not confused by this phenomenon, since spiritual angels cannot ascend to celestial angels, nor the latter come down to the former (see above, n. 35).

147. This shows what the Lord's presence is like in the heavens. Namely, it is everywhere; it is with each individual involved in the good and the true that emanate from Him, and therefore it is with angels in whatever belongs to Itself (as stated above, n. 12). Angels' perception of the Lord's presence takes place in their more inward elements. From these elements their eyes see; so they see Him outside themselves, there being no interruption.

This enables us to decide how to understand the Lord's "being in them" and their "being in the Lord," as in the Lord's words,

Dwell in Me, and I in you.   (John 15:4)

Whoever eats My flesh and drinks My blood dwells in Me, and I in him.

(John 6:56)

"The Lord's flesh" means the Divine-Good, and "blood" means the Divine-True.

148. All the people in the heavens dwell in different areas according to the major regions. To the east and west live the people who are involved in the "good" of love—to the east the ones in clear perception, to the west the ones in veiled perception. To the south and north dwell the ones who are involved in wisdom from love's "good"—to the south the ones in wisdom's clear light, to the north the ones in wisdom's veiled light.

The homes of angels in the Lord's spiritual kingdom are arranged similarly to those of angels in the Lord's celestial kingdom, but with a difference like that between the good of love and the light of the true from what is good. Love in the celestial kingdom is love for the Lord, and the light of the true that comes from it is wisdom. But love in the spiritual kingdom is love toward the neighbor, which is called charity, and the light of the true that comes from it is intelligence, also called faith (see above, n. 23). There is also the difference in the regions, since the regions in the two kingdoms are thirty degrees apart, as stated above (n. 146).

149. Angels' dwellings are arranged in similar fashion within each community of heaven. To the east live the people engaged in the greatest degree of love and charity, to the west those in less. To the south live the people in the greatest degree of wisdom and intelligence, to the north those in less.

The reason they live in different areas is that every community reflects heaven, and indeed is a heaven in smaller form (see above, nn. 51-58). The same holds true of gatherings. They tend toward this arrangement because of heaven's form, which enables each individual to know where he belongs.

The Lord takes care that there be people of each type in every community, so that heaven may be similar in form throughout. The arrangement of the whole heaven does differ from that of a community the way a larger whole differs from a particular component. For communities toward the east are better than those to the west, and ones to the south better than ones to the north.

150. This is why the major regions in the heavens indicate the kinds of things prevalent among the people living there. Specifically, "east" means love and its "good" in clear perception; "west" the same in veiled perception; "south" means wisdom and intelligence in clear light, and "north" the same in veiled light.

Since these regions do have this kind of meaning, they have the same meaning in the Word's inner or spiritual sense; for the Word's inner or spiritual sense accords completely with the phenomena of heaven.

151. The opposite holds true for the people who are in the hells. The people who are there do not look toward the Lord as the sun or the moon. They look away from the Lord toward that darkness that occupies the place of the world's sun, or toward that gloom that occupies the place of earth's moon. Those called genii look toward the darkness that occupies the place of the world's sun and those called spirits, toward the gloom that occupies the place of earth's moon. It may be seen above (n. 122) that the world's sun and earth's moon are not visible in the spiritual world, but that a black something, in the opposite direction from heaven's sun, occupies the place of its sun, and a gloomy something, in the opposite direction from heaven's moon, occupies the place of earth's moon.

As a result, they have regions directly opposite to heaven's regions. Their east is where that dark or gloomy something is, their west toward heaven's sun. Their south is on the right and their north on the left—this too regardless of the way they turn their bodies. Nothing else is possible for them, because every axis of their more inward elements (and therefore every boundary) tends and strives in this one direction. At n. 143 it may be seen that the axis of the more inward elements—and the actual boundary therefore of everything in the other life—follows from love. The love that belongs to the people who are in the hells is love of self and love of the world; and these loves are meant by the world's sun and earth's moon (see n. 122). Further, these loves are contrary to love for the Lord and love toward the neighbor. This is why they turn toward darkness, away from the Lord.

The homes of the people who are in the hells are also arranged according to their regions. People involved in evil things that stem from love of self range from their east to their west; people involved in evil's falsities range from their south to their north. But more on these matters later, in discussing the hells.

152. When an evil spirit enters the company of the good, normally the regions there are disordered, so that the good can barely tell where their east is. I have seen this happen a number of times, and have heard about it from spirits who complained of it.

153. Evil spirits are at times observed to be oriented by heaven's regions. At such times, they have intelligence and a perception of what is true, but no affection for what is good. So as soon as they turn back to their own regions, they are without intelligence and perception of what is true. Then they claim that the truths they had heard and perceived were not true, but false. They want falsities to be true as well.

As regards this turning, I have been taught that for evil people, only the understanding can be turned in this fashion,

not the intending. I have also been taught that this is provided by the Lord, to the end that anyone can see and
recognize things that are true, but that no one will accept
them unless he is involved in something good. For the good
is what accepts truths; what is evil never does.

There is a similar situation in regard to man, since he can
be corrected by means of truths, though ultimately he cannot
be corrected beyond the extent to which he is involved in
what is good. This, I have been taught, is why man can
likewise be turned toward the Lord; but if he is involved
in something evil as to his life, he promptly turns away and
strengthens himself in the falsities of his evil against the
truths which he had understood and seen. This happens
when he thinks by himself on the basis of what lies deeper
within himself.

17.

CHANGES OF STATE OF ANGELS IN HEAVEN

154. By "changes in angels' states," we understand their changes in love and faith, hence in wisdom and intelligence, and therefore in their state of life. "States" are predicated of life and of matters pertaining to life. Since an angelic life is a life of love and faith and of their derivative wisdom and intelligence, "state" is predicated of these aspects, and reference is made to states of love and faith and states of intelligence and wisdom.

Let us then proceed to describe how these states change for angels.

155. Angels are not unvaryingly in the same state as to love, nor, consequently, as to wisdom, all their wisdom being from love and proportional to love. Sometimes they are in a state of intense love, sometimes in a state of mild love. This declines by degrees from its maximum to its minimum. When they are at the peak of love, they are in the light and warmth of their life, surrounded by radiance and delight. When they are at the bottom of the scale, they are in shade and cold, or in a shrouded and unpleasant state. They do return from this last state to the first, and so on. These changes follow each other, never exactly the same.

These states come in sequence like the daily changing states of light and shade, warmth and cold, or morning, noon, evening, and night in the world, showing an unfailing variety during the year. They even correspond—morning to the state of angels' love in full radiance, noon to the state of their wisdom in full radiance, evening to the state of their wisdom veiled, and night to a state of no love or wisdom. Note however that night has no correspondence with the states of people in heaven. There is rather a correspondence with the daybreak that precedes the morning; night's correspondence is with people in hell.

This correspondence is why "day" and "year" in the Word mean states of life in general, "warmth" and "light" meaning love and wisdom, "morning" the first and highest level of love, "noon" wisdom in its full light, "evening" wisdom in its shade, "daybreak" the veiled condition just before morning, and "night" the absence of love and wisdom.

156. Along with the states of more inward elements (which pertain to angels' love and wisdom), the states of the different things visible to their sight around them change. For the things around them choose a form that accords with the things within them. What these things are, and what they are like, will be described in later chapters, where we discuss representations and appearances in heaven.

157. Every angel undergoes and traverses changes of state like these, and so in general does every community. But each individual in a community does so differently, since individuals differ in love and wisdom. Some, that is, are at the center, in a more perfect state than the surrounding ones out to the borders (see above, nn. 43 and 128). Listing the differences would take too long, since every single one undergoes changes consonant with the quality of his love and faith.

As a result, one is in a radiant and joyful state when another is in an obscure and disagreeable state, even within the same community at the same time. This happens differently from one community to another as well. It happens differently in communities of the celestial kingdom than in communities of the spiritual kingdom.

Overall, the varieties of their changes of state are like the varieties of kinds of days in different zones on earth. Some are having morning while others are having evening, some warmth while others cold, and vice versa.

158. I have received information from heaven as to why these changes of state occur there. Angels have said that there are many reasons.

The first is that anything pleasant about life and heaven (which they get from the love and wisdom the Lord gives) would deteriorate bit by bit if they experienced it without respite, just as happens to people who experience pleasures and comforts without variety.

A second reason is that angels have self-images [*proprium*] just as people on earth do. It is loving themselves, and everyone in heaven is kept away from his self-image. To the extent that they are kept away from it by the Lord, they experience love and wisdom; but to the extent that they are not kept away, they experience love of self. Since everyone loves his own self-image, and since it influences him, they have changes of state or fluctuations, in series.

A third reason is that this helps perfect them because it is a mean by which they get used to being kept in the experience of love of the Lord, and kept away from love of self. Then too, their perception and awareness of what is good are made more delicate by fluctuations between things pleasant and unpleasant.

Angels have also told me that the Lord does not cause their changes of state, because the Lord as the sun is always flowing in with warmth and light—that is, with love and wisdom. The angels themselves are the reason, because they love their self-images, which is always leading them astray.

This was illustrated by comparison with the word's sun. Per se, it is not the cause of changes in states of warmth and cold or light and shade, of individual years and days, since it remains constant. The reason is intrinsic to the earth.

159. I have been shown how the Lord as the sun looks to angels in the celestial kingdom in their first state, their second, and their third. I saw the Lord as the sun, at first a red-gold color, flashing with an indescribable brilliance. I was told that this is how the Lord as the sun looks to angels in their first state.

After that, I saw a large cloudy ring around the sun, which began to dim the flashing red-gold color that had caused the original brilliance. I was told that this is how the Lord looks to them in their second state.

Then I saw this ring thicken, so that the sun seemed less ruddy. This continued bit by bit until finally it had become virtually white. I was told that this is how the sun looks to people in the third state.

After this, I saw this white object move to the left, toward heaven's moon, and join with its light, with the result that the moon blazed out immoderately. I was told that this was the fourth state for people in the celestial kingdom, and the first in the spiritual kingdom.

I was also told that in both kingdoms, changes of state fluctuate this way—not everywhere at once, but in one community after another, these states, finally, not being precisely periodical, but happening more slowly or more quickly without their noticing.

Again, they said that the sun itself undergoes neither such changes nor such movement. It looks that way as changes of state progress on the angels' level, since the Lord has an appearance to every individual in keeping with the quality of that individual's state. So He looks ruddy to people who are experiencing intense love, less ruddy and ultimately white as the love wanes. They said that the quality of people's own state was depicted by the cloudy ring, which superimposed on the sun those apparent variations of flame and light.

160. When angels are in this last state—that is, when they experience their self-image—they begin to feel depressed. I have talked with them while they were in this state, and I have seen the depression. However, they said that they felt hope for a prompt return to their original state—to heaven, so to speak; since for them, heaven is being kept away from their self-image.

161. There are changes of state in the hells, too; but these will be described below, in the discussion of hell.

18.

TIME IN HEAVEN

162. Regardless of the fact that everything in heaven happens in sequence and progresses the way things do in the world, still angels have no idea or concept of time and space. This lack is so complete that they simply do not know what time and space are. At this point, we will discuss time in heaven; space will be discussed in its own chapter.

163. The reason angels do not know what time is (although everything progresses in sequence for them the ways things do in the world, so completely that there is no difference), is that there are no years and days in heaven, but changes of state. Wherever there are years and days, there are times. Where there are changes of state, there are only states.

164. The reason for the existence of times in the world is the sun's apparent sequential progression from one degree to another, producing the times called "seasons of the year." It also seems to travel around the earth and produce the times called "times of day." Both these phenomena occur with fixed periods.

Heaven's sun is different. It does not produce days and years by sequential progression or orbital motion, but apparently causes changes of state. And this does not happen at fixed intervals, as has been shown in the last chapter. This is why angels are incapable of any concept of time, thinking instead in terms of state. It may be seen above (n. 154) what "state" is.

165. Since angels, unlike people on earth, have no concepts derived from time, they have no concepts about time or about matters involving time. They do not even know what these "matters involving time" are, such as a year, a month, a week, a day, an hour, today, tomorrow, or yesterday. When angels hear about these things from men (for angels are constantly kept in touch with man by the Lord), they perceive instead state and matters involving state. So man's natural concept is transformed into a spiritual concept among angels.

As a result, times in the Word refer to states; and matters involving time, like the ones just listed, refer to their corresponding spiritual matters.

166. A similar principle applies to all the phenomena that occur because of time—for example, to the four seasons of the year, called spring, summer, autumn, and winter. It applies to the four times of day called morning, noon, evening, and night. It applies to the four ages of man called infancy, adolescence, maturity, and old age. It applies to other things that either occur because of time or follow in temporal sequence. Man thinks in terms of time when he thinks about these matters; but an angel thinks in terms of state. Consequently anything temporal in these phenomena on man's level is transformed into a concept of state on the angel's level. Spring and morning are transformed into a concept of a state of love and wisdom as in the first state of angels. Summer and midday are changed into a concept of love and wisdom as in their second condition; autumn and evening, to the third; night and winter, to a concept of the kind of condition prevailing in hell.

This is why times in the Word refer to matters such as these (see above, n. 155). This shows how natural things in a person's thought become spiritual with angels accompanying him.

167. Since angels have no idea of time, they have a

different concept of eternity that people on earth do. Angels
see in eternity an infinite state, not an infinite time.

I was thinking about eternity once, and using a time-
concept I could see what "to eternity" meant, but not what
"from eternity" meant. So I could not see what God had
been doing before creation, from eternity. When this began
to distress me, I was lifted into a sphere of heaven, and
therefore into the perception of eternity which angels have.
Then the light dawned, that we should not think about eternity on the basis of time, but should start from state. Then
we would grasp what "from eternity" means—which is
what actually happened to me.

168. Angels who talk with people on earth never use the
natural concepts proper to man, all derived from time, space,
matter, and the like. They use spiritual ideas, all derived
from states and their various changes within angels and
outside them. The angelic concepts, however, which are
spiritual, change instantly and spontaneously into natural
concepts proper to man, corresponding precisely to the spiritual ones, when they flow into the individual. Neither angels nor men are aware that this is happening, yet all
heaven's inflow into people on earth is of this kind.

Some angels were once let intimately into my thoughts,
all the way into the natural ones that had considerable content derived from time and space. But because they did not
understand anything at that juncture, they quickly drew
back. After they had drawn back, I heard them say that they
had been in darkness.

[2] I have been made aware by experience of the nature
of angels' ignorance of time. There was a particular person
from heaven whose character was such that he could have
access even into natural ideas, the kind proper to man. I
talked with him later person to person, so to speak. At first
he did not understand what it was that I was calling "time,"

so I had to explain to him in detail how the sun seems to travel around our earth, producing years and days, so that the years are divided into four seasons, also into months and weeks, with days divided into twenty-four hours. I explained that these happen over and over at fixed periods, which is the basis of "times." He was amazed to hear this, and told me he had not known about matters like these, but he did know what states were.

[3] In the course of our conversation, I also said that the absence of time in heaven is known in the world; people do talk as though they knew. For they refer to those who die as "leaving the temporal" and as "going beyond time," meaning that they have left the world. I mentioned too that some people are aware that times originate in states, because times are wholly relative to their states of affection. They seem short when people are involved in pleasant and happy affections, long when they are involved in unpleasant or disagreeable ones; in states of hope or expectation they seem of various lengths. As a result, scholars are investigating the nature of time and space, some even knowing that time pertains to the natural person.

169. A natural person may believe that his thinking would cease if concepts of time, space, and matter were removed, since all man's thinking is based on them. It would help him to realize, though, that thoughts are limited and restricted to the extent that they draw upon time, space, and matter. They are not limited, and they expand, to the extent that they do not draw upon these, since the mind is proportionally raised above bodily and worldly matters.

This is where angels get their wisdom; this is why it might well be called unfathomable—because it does not fit into concepts composed solely from things physical and worldly.

19.

REPRESENTATIONS AND APPEARANCES IN HEAVEN

170. Anyone who does his thinking from natural illumination [*lumen*] alone cannot grasp the idea that anything in heaven could be like anything on earth. This is because he has thought and concluded from that illumination that angels are only minds, that minds are sorts of airy vapors, and that they therefore do not have the senses that man does—no eyes, that is; and without eyes there are no objects of sight. However, angels have all the senses man has, and in fact far more sensitive ones; for the light in which they see is far clearer than the light in which man sees.

See above (nn. 73-77) on angels' being people in most perfect form, and enjoying all the senses; on light in heaven being far clearer than light in the world, see nn. 126-132.

171. There is no brief way to describe the nature of the things visible in the heavens to angels. They are largely similar to things on earth, but more perfect in form and more abundant.

The occurrence of such objects in heaven is confirmed by what the prophets saw. Ezekiel, for example, saw the things relating to the new temple and the new earth described in chapters 40-48; Daniel the things from chapter 7 to chapter 12; John the things in *Revelation* from the first chapter to the last. And others saw things described in both the historical and the prophetic parts of the Word.

Things like these became visible to them when heaven was opened to them; and heaven is said to be opened when the more inward sight—the sight of man's spirit—is opened. For what is in the heavens cannot be seen by the eyes of man's body, but by the eyes of his spirit. When the Lord pleases, these are opened, as the person is taken out of the natural illumination in which he is engaged because of his body's senses, and is raised into spiritual light, in which he is engaged because of his spirit. It is in this latter light that I have seen things in the heavens.

172. But the things one sees in the heavens, even though they are largely similar to things on earth, are dissimilar in essence. For the things in heaven arise from heaven's sun, while the things on earth arise from the world's sun. The things that arise from heaven's sun are called spiritual; while the things that arise from the world's sun are called natural.

173. The things that occur in the heavens do not occur in the same way as things on earth do. In the heavens, all things arise from the Lord, according to their correspondence with angels' more inward elements. Angels do have more inward and more outward elements. The contents of their more inward elements relate to love and faith—to intending and discernment therefore, since intending and discernment are their receiving vessels. Their more outward elements, though, correspond to their more inward ones. This correspondence of more inward to move outward things has been presented above (nn. 87-115).

This may be illustrated by what has already been said in the chapter, "Light and Warmth in Heaven." The equivalence of angels' warmth and the quality of their love, of their light and the quality of their wisdom, is set forth in nn. 128-134. A similar principle applies to the other things that present themselves to angel's senses.

174. When I have been allowed to associate with angels, I have seen things there exactly as I have seen things in the world, so vividly that I had no way of knowing that I was not in the world, in some king's hall. I have talked with angels like one person with another.

175. Since all the things that correspond to more inward things actually re-present them, they are called "representations." Since they do vary depending on the states of the deeper things in the angels, they are called "appearances." This is despite the fact that the things visible to angels' eyes in the heavens, the things perceived by their senses, are visible and perceived just as realistically as things on earth are by man— actually with far more clarity, crispness, and vividness.

The appearances that occur in heaven are called "real appearances," because they do really occur. There are also unreal appearances; they are things that do become visible, but do not correspond to more inward things. But more on these later.

176. I should like to cite just one example to illustrate what kinds of things are visible to angels in consequence of correspondences.

To angels involved in intelligence, there appear gardens and parks full of every kind of tree and flower. The trees are set in a very beautiful design, twining into arched entrances opening through, and with walks here and there. Everything is so beautiful that there is no way to describe it.

People stroll there who are engaged in intelligence. They gather flowers, make wreaths, and adorn little children with them. There are kinds of trees and flowers there unknown in the world—in fact, kinds that cannot occur. There are fruits on these trees reflecting the "good" of the love that engages these intelligent angels. They see this kind of thing because a garden and a park (as well as fruit trees and flowers) correspond to intelligence and wisdom.

The presence of such things in heaven is known on earth,

but only to people involved in what is good, people who have not smothered heaven's light within them with natural illumination and its deceptions. For on the subject of heaven, they both think and say that such things exist there as *the ear has never heard, nor the eye seen.*

20.

THE CLOTHES ANGELS ARE SEEN WEARING

177. Since angels are people, living together as people on earth do, they have clothes, houses, and many similar things. But there is this difference, that since angels are in a more perfect state, everything they have is more perfect. As angelic wisdom surpasses human wisdom so much as to be indescribable, so too does everything they perceive, everything presented to them. For everything they perceive, everything presented to them, corresponds to their wisdom (see above, n. 173).

178. Like everything else, the clothes angels wear correspond, and truly exist because they correspond (see above, n. 175). Their clothes correspond to their intelligence. So all the people in heaven are seen dressed in accord with their intelligence; and since one person surpasses another in intelligence (see nn. 43,128) one will have more outstanding clothes than another. The most intelligence have clothes that gleam as if aflame, some radiant as if alight. The less intelligent have shining white clothes without radiance, and those still less intelligent have clothes of various colors. The angels of the inmost heaven, though, are naked.

179. Because angel's clothes correspond to their intelligence, they correspond to what is true; for all intelligence comes from the Divine-True. So it makes no difference whether you say that angels are dressed in keeping with intelligence or in keeping with the Divine-True.

The reason the clothes of some gleam as if aflame and some are radiant as if alight, is that flame corresponds to what is good and light to what is true. The reason the clothes of some are shining and white, without radiance, and some are of various colors, is that the Divine-Good and the Divine-True are less luminous, and are variously accepted, among the less intelligent. "Shining" and "white" correspond to what is true, and colors to variants of it. The reason angels of the inmost heaven are naked is that they are in a state of innocence, and innocence corresponds to nakedness.

180. Since angels wear clothes in heaven, they have appeared wearing clothes when seen in the world, like those seen by the prophets, and those seen at the Lord's tomb, whose

> faces were lightning, and whose garments were gleaming and white.   (Matthew 28:3, Mark 16:5, Luke 24:4, John 20:12f)

and like those seen in heaven by John, whose

> clothes were linen, and white.   (Rev. 4:4, 19:14)

And because intelligence comes from the Divine-True,

> The Lord's clothes, when He was transfigured, were gleaming, and white as light.   (Matthew 17:2, Mark 9:3, Luke 9:29)

The equivalence of light and the Divine-True emanating from the Lord has been presented above (n. 129). This is why "clothes" in the Word refer to things true, and to resulting intelligence. So in *John,*

> The people who have not defiled their clothes will walk with me in white, because they are worthy. Whoever conquers will be clothed in white garments. . . .   (Rev. 3:4, 5)

> Blessed is the man who keeps watch, and cares for his clothing.   (Rev. 16:15)

On the subject of Jerusalem, meaning the church that is involved in what is true, in *Isaiah,*

> Arise, put on strength, O Zion; put on your beautiful garments, O Jerusalem.
>
>   (Is. 52:1)

and in *Ezekiel,*

> Jerusalem, I have girded you with linen, and enfolded you with silk, your clothes are of linen and silk.   (Ez. 16:10, 13)

plus many other places. The person who is not involved in things true is called "not wearing a wedding garment" in *Matthew:*

> When the king entered . . . he saw a man not wearing a wedding garment, and said to him, "Friend, how have you come in without a wedding garment?" Therefore he was expelled into the outer darkness.
>
> (Matthew 22:11-13)

The "wedding house" means heaven and the church, by reason of the Lord's bond with them through His Divine-True. The Lord is therefore called the Bridegroom and Husband in the Word, and heaven and the church, the Bride and Wife.

181. It has been proposed that angels' clothes do not simply seem to be clothes, but truly are clothes. This is confirmed by the fact that they not only see them, but feel them to the touch. Further, they have a number of clothes, they take them off and put them on, they put away the ones they are not using, and take them out again in order to use them. Their wearing different clothes I have witnessed thousands of times.

I have asked where these clothes came from, and they said they were from the Lord, that they were given to them, and that at times they are clothed without their knowing it.

They also said that their clothes changed with their changes of state, that in the first and second states they had gleaming and shining clothes, and in the third and fourth somewhat darkened clothes. This resulted from correspondence, since they undergo changes of state as to intelligence and wisdom (on these matters, see above, nn. 154-161).

182. Inasmuch as everyone's clothes in the spiritual world are in accord with his intelligence (in accord, then, with the truths that produce intelligence), people in hell, lacking truths, are presented clothed, but only in torn, dirty, offensive clothes, each in accord with his folly. They can wear nothing else. The Lord provides that they be clothed, so that they may not be seen naked.

21.

ANGELS' HOMES AND HOUSES

183. Since there are communities in heaven, and angels live like people, angels have homes. These, like their clothes, vary depending on the individual's state of life. There are splendid ones for angels in a more deserving state, and less splendid ones for angels in a lower state.

I have talked with angels about the homes in heaven a number of times. I have told them that nowadays hardly anyone believes that they have homes or houses—some because they do not see them, some because they do not know that angels are people, and some because they think the angelic heaven is the sky above them, visible to their eyes. Since this looks empty, and since they think angels are airy shapes, they draw the conclusion that angels live in the upper atmosphere. Nor do they grasp the fact that there are the same kinds of thing in the spiritual world as there are in the natural world, since they have no knowledge of the spiritual.

[2] Angels have told me that they know this kind of ignorance is prevalent in the world nowadays, and, incredibly, especially in the church. In the church it is more characteristic of the intelligent than of those referred to as "the simple." The angels further affirmed the possibility of knowing from the Word that angels are people, seeing that the ones who have been seen have been seen as people. This was also the way the Lord was seen, who took to Himself everything of His that was Human.

According to angels, then, since they are people they

have houses and homes. They do not fly in the air, as the ignorance of some people would have it (an ignorance which angels refer to as madness), nor are they winds, in spite of the fact that they are called spirits. People can grasp this if only they extend their thinking about angels and spirits beyond their basic preconceptions. This happens when they do not place in question or under direct consideration *whether it is so*. For there is a general idea, common to all people, that angels are in the human form, that they have dwellings called heavenly homes that are more splendid than homes on earth. But this general idea, which results from the inflow of heaven, promptly collapses into nothing when *whether it is so* is made the center of attention and thinking. This happens primarily with learned people who through their self-conscious intelligence have closed off heaven and the path of its light.

[3] The same thing happens with belief in man's living after death. People who talk about this, and do not also think pedantically about the soul or doctrinally about the resumption of the flesh, believe that man will live after death. They believe he will dwell among angels if he has lived well, that he will see magnificent sights and feel joys. But the moment someone focuses on the doctrine of resumption of the flesh, or on some theory about the soul, and his thinking encounters the question of whether a soul like this exists (hence *whether it is so*), then his original idea is put to flight.

184. But it would be better to interrupt with samples from experience. Whenever I have talked face to face with angels I have been with them in their dwellings. Their dwellings are just like the dwellings on earth which we call homes, except that they are more beautiful. They have rooms, suites, and bedrooms, all in abundance. They have courtyards, and are surrounded by gardens, flowerbeds, and lawns.

Where people are closely associated, the houses are adjoining, one beside another, arranged in the form of a city with avenues, streets, and squares just like cities on our earth. I have been allowed to go walking through them, to sightsee, and on occasion to enter homes. This has happened to me when I was fully awake, when my inner sight was opened.

185. I have seen palaces of heaven so noble as to defy description. The higher parts glowed as if they were made of pure gold, the lower as though made of precious gems; each palace was more splendid than the last. Inside, the same—the rooms were decorated with accessories such that words and arts fail to describe them.

Outside, on the south prospect, there were parks where everything likewise glowed, with here and there leaves gleaming like silver and fruit like gold. The flowers in their plots formed virtual rainbows. At the borders more and more palaces were visible, as far as the eye could see.

The designs of heaven's buildings are so perfect that you would say they represent the very essence of the art; and small wonder, since the art of architecture comes from heaven.

The angels told me that these and countless other such things still more perfect are set before their eyes by the Lord. Yet these please their minds even more than their eyes. This is because they see correspondences in the details, and through them see things Divine.

186. Now in regard to correspondences, I have been taught that it is not just the palace or home that corresponds to what angels have more deeply within them from the Lord—it is each and everything within them and outside. I have been taught that the house itself corresponds, broadly, to their "good," the particular things in the houses to different elements that constitute that good, and the outdoor things to true elements that stem from what is good, and to perceptions and insights.

Since they do correspond to the good and true elements in angels from the Lord, they correspond to their love. As a result, they correspond to wisdom and intelligence, since love is a matter of what is good, wisdom of what is good and what is true together, and intelligence of what is true stemming from what is good. This sort of thing, I have been taught, is what angels perceive when they look at their houses, the contents, and the surroundings. This is also why these things delight and move their minds more than their eyes.

187. This has clarified the reason the Lord called Himself the Temple that is in Jerusalem (John 2:19, 21), and why the New Jerusalem appeared made out of pure gold, with gates of pearl and foundations of precious stones (Rev. 21). The reason was that the Temple represented the Lord's Divine-Human. "The New Jersualem" means the church that was to be founded in the future, the "twelve gates" the true things that lead to what is good, and the "foundations" the true elements on which it rests.

188. The angels who make up the Lord's celestial kingdom live for the most part in the higher regions that look like mountains rising from the earth. The angels who make up the Lord's spiritual kingdom live in less lofty regions that look like hills. The angels in the lowest heavens live in regions that look like rocky crags.

These things too occur by reason of correspondences, since more inward things correspond to higher ones and more outward to lower. As a result, "mountains" in the Word mean celestial love; "hills" mean spiritual love; and "rocks," faith.

189. There are angels who do not live in communities, but apart, home by home. These live in the center of heaven, because they are the best of angels.

190. The homes angels live in are not constructed, as are homes in the world, but are given freely to them by the Lord—to each in accordance with his acceptance of what is good and true. They change slightly in keeping with changes of the state of their more inward elements (on these, see above, nn. 154-160).

Angels regard all their possessions as gifts from the Lord, and are given whatever they need.

22.

SPACE IN HEAVEN

191. In spite of the fact that everything in heaven seems to be in a place and in space just like things in the world, angels have no concept or idea of place or space. As this can only look like a paradox, I should like to bring it out into the light; for it has a major bearing.

192. All journeys in the spiritual world occur by means of changes of the state of more inward things, to the point that journeys are simply changes of state. This is how I have been brought into the heavens by the Lord; this is how I have been brought to planets in the universe. My spirit has been brought, while my body stayed in one place. This is how all angels travel. So they do not have any spatial intervals, and without spatial intervals, there are no spaces. Instead, there are states and changes of state.

193. Since this is how journeys occur, nearness are clearly similarities, and distances dissimilarities, in the state of more inward elements. Consequently, people who are in similar states are near each other, and people who are in dissimilar states are far apart. There are no spaces in heaven except outward states that correspond to inner ones.

There is no other source of the various heavens' distinctness, of that of communities in each heaven or of individuals in each community. This also gives rise to the complete separation of the hells from the heavens, since they are in opposite states.

194. This is the reason too that in the spiritual world one person becomes present to another if only the other earnestly desires his presence. For by so doing he sees the other in thought, and puts himself in his state. Conversely, one person is taken from another as far as he turns away from him. Since all turning away stems from opposition of affections and disagreement of thoughts, large groups of people in a single region will be visible for as long as they are in accord. But the moment they disagree, they vanish.

195. When anyone travels from one place to another—be it within his community, within his own grounds, in his gardens, or to others outside his community—he gets there more quickly if he is willing and more slowly if he is unwilling. The route itself becomes longer or shorter in keeping with his willingness, even while it remains the same route. I have often witnessed this, and marvelled at it.

Again, this makes it clear that distances (and therefore spaces themselves) exist solely in keeping with the states of the more inward elements of angels. And this being the case, no concept or idea or space can find its way into their thinking, even though spaces exist for them just as much as they do in the world.

196. This can be understood more clearly by considering man's thoughts, in that spaces do not exist for them. For whatever a person earnestly gives his mental attention to becomes, so to speak, present to him.

Further, we realize on reflection that distances are visually perceived only by means of intervening objects on earth, seen all at once, or from the realization that we know a particular thing to be a given distance away. This results from the existence of a continuum, and in a continuum distances are perceived only through items that are discontinuous.

This is all the more true for angels, since their sight is coordinated with their thought and their thought with their affection; also because things near and far appear and vary in keeping with the condition of the more inward elements of the angels, as mentioned above.

197. As a result, places and distances in the Word (and everything that depends at all upon space) mean things which involve state. This includes distances, near, far, paths, roads, journeys, miles, and furlongs; plains, fields, gardens, cities, and avenues; motion, and various measurements; long, wide, high, and deep; and countless other things. For most of the things man has in his thought from the world derive something from space and time.

I should like to interject here only the meaning of "length," "breadth," and "height" in the Word. [2] In the world, "long" and "wide" are applied to things spatially long and wide—likewise "high." But in heaven, where there is no spatial thinking, "length" means "state in respect to what is good," "width" means "state in respect to what is true," and "height" means their being distinguished as to their level (see n. 38).

The reason these three dimensions have this kind of meaning is that length in heaven is the dimension from east to west, where people are who are involved in the good content of love. Width in heaven is the dimension from south to north, where people are who are involved in what is true arising from what is good (see above, n. 148). Height in heaven applies to either in respect to its level.

This is why "length," "width," and "height" have this kind of meaning in the Word. Note, for example, Ezekiel 40-48, where measurements of length, width, and height are used to describe the new temple and the new earth, with courtyards, suites, doors, gateways, windows, suburbs—all of which refer to a new church and the good and true elements in it. Why else would all these measurements be listed?

[3] The New Jersualem is described in a similar vein in *Revelation* as follows:

> The city lies foursquare, with its length equal to its width. The city
> was measured with a reed, the result being twelve thousand furlongs:
> the length, breadth, and height are equal.   (Rev. 21:16)

Here, since "the New Jersualem" means a new church,
its dimensions mean what belongs to the church. "Length"
means the good content of its love; "width" means the
"true" that stems from that "good"; and "height" means
the good and the true as far as degrees are concerned.
"Twelve thousand furlongs" means everything good and
true taken together. Why else would the height be twelve
thousand furlongs, like the length and the breadth?

One can see in *David* that "width" in the Word means
what is true:

> Jehovah, "You have not imprisoned me in the hand of the enemy, You
> have set my feet in a wide place."   (Psalm 31:9)

> I called upon Jah out of a narrow place; He answered me in
> breadth.   (Psalm 118:5)

Elsewhere, too, as in Isaiah 8:8 and Habakkuk 1:6; and
in other passages besides.

198. All this makes it possible to see that in heaven, even
though there are spaces as there are in the world, nothing
there is evaluated by spatial criteria, only by criteria of state.
Spaces cannot even be measured there the way they are in
the world. They can only be seen as a result of the state,
and in accord with the state of angels' more inward elements.

199. The precise primary reason is that the Lord is present
with each individual in proportion to love and faith, with
everything seeming near or far in proportion to His presence,
this being the way everything in heaven is prescribed. This
is how angels come to have wisdom, because this is how
they come to have outreach of thought, and how there occurs
a communication of all the elements in the heavens.

In short, this is how they think spiritually, not naturally
like men.

23.

HEAVEN'S FORM, WHICH PATTERNS ASSOCIATIONS AND COMMUNICATIONS THERE

200. To some extent, the nature of heaven's form can be deduced from things described in the preceding sections. For example, heaven is alike in greatest and smallest elements (n. 72), so that each community is a heaven in smaller form and each angel a heaven in smallest form (nn. 51-58). As the entire heaven reflects a single person, each community of heaven reflects a person in smaller form, and each angel in smallest form (nn. 59-77). In the middle are the wisest, around them to the circumference the less wise; and this holds true of each community (n. 43). In heaven, angels involved in the good content of love live on the east-west axis, and angels involved in things true because of what is good live on the south-north axis, which holds true for each community (nn. 148-149).

These things are all in keeping with heaven's form, so the general nature of heaven's form can be deduced from them.

201. It helps to know the nature of heaven's form, because it patterns not only all associations but also all communications as well. Further, since it patterns all communication, it patterns all outreach of thoughts and affections, and therefore all the intelligence and wisdom that angels have.

This is why the degree to which a person is in the form of heaven—is a form of heaven—determines how wise he is. It amounts to the same thing whether you say "in the form of heaven" or "in the order of heaven." For the form of anything stems from an order and follows it.

202. Let us begin by saying something about what "being in heaven's form" actually is. Man is created after heaven's model and after the world's model (see above, n. 57). His inner part is created after heaven's model and his outer after the world's. It makes no difference whether you say "according to the form" or "after the model."

However, since man has destroyed heaven's model (hence its form) in himself by evil elements of his intention and consequent false elements of thought, and has introduced the model and form of hell instead, what lies within him is closed off from the moment of birth. This is why man, unlike every kind of animal, is born into complete ignorance. In fact, for the model or form of heaven to be restored to him, he needs to be taught about matters relating to order. For as already said, form follows order.

The Word contains all the laws of Divine order, since the laws of Divine order are the commandments it contains. To the extent that a person knows them and lives by them, what lies within him is set free. Then the order or model of heaven is formed anew in him. We can see from this what "being in the form of heaven" means—namely, living by the contents of the Word.

203. To the extent that anyone is in the form of heaven, he is in heaven; in fact he is a heaven in smallest form (n. 57). Therefore he participates in intelligence and wisdom to the same extent. For as stated above, all the thought of his understanding and all the affection of his intention reach out round about into heaven in keeping with its form, communicating marvelously with the communities there, and they in turn with him.

[2] There are people who believe that thoughts and affections do not really reach out around them, but are within them. This is because they see within themselves, not farther away, the things they are thinking about. They are quite

mistaken, however. For just as eyesight has an outreach to remote objects, and responds to the arrangement of the things it sees in that outreach, so the more inward sight proper to the understanding has an outreach in the spiritual world (although, for reasons given above, n. 196, man has no awareness of this). The only difference is that eyesight is affected naturally, being made of materials from the natural world; while the sight of the understanding is affected spiritually, being made of materials from the spiritual world, which all have to do with what is good and true.

The reason man does not know this is that he is unaware of the existence of a light that enlightens his understanding. Yet apart from the light that enlightens his understanding, man could not think at all (on this light, see above, nn. 126-132).

[3] There was a particular spirit who believed that he thought independently, without any outreach beyond himself or consequent communication with communities beyond him. In order for him to learn that he was wrong, his communication with neighboring communities was suspended. As a result, he was not only deprived of thought, he actually collapsed as though he were dead—though he did wave his arms like a newborn baby. After a while, communication was restored to him; and gradually, as it was restored, he came back to the state of his own thought.

[4] So the other spirits who witnessed this admitted that all thought and affection flow in according to communcation. And since this is true of all thought and affection, it is true of all life; for all of a person's life rests in the ability to think and feel, or (which is the same thing) to understand and to intend.

204. It must be realized, though, that intelligence and wisdom vary from person to person depending on the communication. People whose intelligence and wisdom are fashioned from things genuinely true and good are in touch with communities according to heaven's form. People whose intelligence and wisdom are fashioned not from things genuinely true and good but still from things in harmony with them have an intermittent communication, only more or less coherent, since it is not a communication with communities in the sequence proper to heaven's form. But people who do not participate in intelligence and wisdom, owing to their participation in falsities stemming from what is evil, are in communication with communities in hell. The extent of the outreach is proportional to the fixity of their participation.

It should also be realized that this communication with communities is not a communication with them that reaches the conscious perception of their inhabitants. It is rather a communication with their quality, the quality in which they participate and which emanates from them.

205. All the people in heaven are connected according to spiritual relationships, which have to do with the good and the true in their proper pattern. This is true of the entire heaven, of each community, and of each household. As a result, angels involved in like good and truth recognize each other the way relatives and kinfolk do on earth, just as though they had known each other from infancy.

There is a similar connection of the good and true elements that make up wisdom and intelligence within each individual angel. These recognize each other in similar fashion; and as they recognize each other, they join together.

Consequently, people whose good and true elements are assembled according to heaven's pattern see successive things in sequence, and see how they fit together over a wide range beyond themselves. This does not hold true for people whose good and true elements are not assembled according to heaven's form.

206. This is what form is like within each heaven, patterning the communication and outreach of thoughts and affections for angels, and patterning therefore their intelligence and wisdom. But the communication of one heaven with another is different—that is the communication of the third or inmost heaven with the intermediate one, and the communication of these two with the first or outermost one. Communications between heavens, for that matter, should be called inflow rather than communication. It will be discussed forthwith.

The existence of three heavens, distinct from each other, has been presented above in the appropriate chapter (nn. 29-40).

207. From the relative positions of the heavens, it is possible to conclude that there is not a communication from one to another, but rather an inflow. The third or inmost heaven is high above, the second or intermediate is lower, and the first or outermost is still lower. All the communities of each heaven have this same arrangement, as for example the ones in elevated areas that look like mountains (n. 188). At their summits live angels of the inmost heaven, lower down those of the second, and lower still those of the outermost. This holds true universally, for areas of high elevation and areas not. A community of a higher heaven is not in touch with a community of a lower heaven except by way of correspondences (see above, n. 100); and communication by way of correspondences is what is called inflow.

208. One heaven is connected with another, or a community of one heaven with a community of another, by the Lord alone through direct and indirect inflow. The direct inflow is from Him Himself; the indirect is through the higher heavens in sequence to the lower ones.

Because the connection of the heavens through inflow is from the Lord alone, every possible precaution is taken lest any angels of a higher heaven look down into a lower heaven and talk with anyone there. The moment this happens, the angel loses his intelligence and wisdom.

As to the reason for this, each angel has three levels of life, like the three levels of heaven. People who are in the inmost heaven have their third or inmost level opened, their second and first levels closed. People who are in the intermediate heaven have their second level opened, their first and third levels closed. And people who are in the outermost heaven have their first level opened, their second and third level closed.

So the moment an angel of the third heaven looks down into a community of the second heaven and talks with someone there, his third level is closed. Once it is closed, he has lost his wisdom. For his wisdom is located on the third level; he has none on the second or first.

This is the intent of the Lord's words in *Matthew:*

> The person who is on the roof, let him not come down to get anything that is in his house; and the person who is in the field, let him not turn back to get his clothes. (Matthew 24:17f.)

and in *Luke:*

> In that day let the person on the roof, whose vessels are in the house, not go down to bring them up; and the person who is in the field, let him not turn backward: remember Lot's wife. (Luke 17:31f.)

209. There is no such thing as an inflow from the lower heavens into the higher ones, this being in violation of order. Rather, the inflow is from the higher heavens into the lower ones.

The wisdom of angels of a higher heaven surpasses the wisdom of angels of a lower one by a ratio on the order of thousands to one. This is why angels of a lower heaven cannot talk with angels of a higher one. In fact, they do not see them when they look at them. Their heaven looks like something cloudy overhead. On the other hand, angels of a higher heaven can see ones who are in a lower one, but engaging in conversations with them is not allowed—only with loss of their wisdom, as already stated.

210. The thoughts, affections, and consequent words of angels of the inmost heaven are never grasped in the intermediate one, since they are so transcendent. But when it pleases the Lord, something from that heaven appears flame-like in the lower heavens. Corresponding phenomena in the intermediate heaven appear in the outermost heaven as something bright, sometimes as a shining multicolored cloud. From the cloud itself, its rise, descent, and form, angels are aware for a while of what is being said there.

211. This may serve to show what heaven's form is like, that in the inmost heaven it is most perfect of all, in the intermediate heaven perfect but on a lower level, and in the outermost heaven on a lower level still; also that the form of one heaven continually derives from another through an inflow from the Lord.

But there is no understanding what communication through inflow is like without knowing what degrees of height are like, and knowing that there is a difference between these degrees and degrees of length and width. On the nature of these two kinds of degrees, (see n. 38).

212. As for the details of heaven's form and the way it moves and flows, this is incomprehensible even to angels. Some of this can be conceptualized by means of the form of all the parts of the human body, surveyed and analyzed by someone both precise and wise. For in the appropriate sections above, we have shown that the whole heaven reflects a single person (nn. 59-72) and that all the parts in a person correspond to the heavens (nn. 87-102).

Just how incomprehensible this form is, how impossible to sort out, one may roughly gather simply from the nerve fibers that connect each and every part. Their nature, the way they move and flow in the brain, never is visible, for the countless elements involved are so interwoven that, taken together, they look like a pliant, continuous mass. But in fact each thing and everything that belongs to intention and understanding flows along the fibers by most distinct paths into actions. One can see how these fibers gather again in the body by noting the various plexuses—the cardiac, the mesenteric, and others—and also the nodes called ganglia, where many fibers enter from all directions, intermix, and leave differently connected for their functions. This happens again and again. In addition, similar features are to be found in every inner part, member, organ, and muscle.

Anyone who surveys matters such as these and their wonders with a knowing eye will be quite stunned. Yet what the eye sees is only a little; what it does not see is even more marvelous because it is of a more inward nature.

The correspondence of this form with heaven's form can be clearly seen in the way all the elements of intention and understanding work within that form and in keeping with it. In fact, whatever a person intends slips down through that form into act, and whatever he thinks moves through the fibers from beginning to end, resulting in sensation. And since this is the form of thought and intention, it is the form of intelligence and wisdom.

This is the form that corresponds to heaven's form. This enables us to know that this is the form through which all the affection and thought of angels reach out, and to know that they participate in intelligence and wisdom to the extent that they are in this form.

On the derivation of this form from the Lord's Divine-Human, see above (nn. 78-86).

This material has been appended to make known the fact that heaven's form is of such nature that even in its general principles it can never be exhaustively probed, such that it is incomprehensible even to angels, as already stated.

24.

GOVERNMENTS IN HEAVEN

213. In view of the fact that heaven is divided into communities, the larger ones consisting of several hundred thousand angels (n. 50), with the members of each community being involved in like "good" but not in like wisdom (n. 43), there are necessarily governments there. For order must be kept, and matters of order cared for.

But governments in the heavens are of different kinds. They are not the same in the communities that constitute the Lord's celestial kingdom as they are in the communities that constitute the Lord's spiritual kingdom. They vary according to the forms of service appropriate to each community.

Still, there is no government in heaven that is not a government of mutual love; the government of mutual love is heavenly government.

214. Government in the Lord's celestial kingdom is called "justice," because everyone there is involved in the good content of love to the Lord from the Lord. Any action arising from this love is called "just."

Government there belongs to the Lord alone. He Himself guides them, and in life-related matters teaches them. The true things called judgments are written in their hearts. Everyone knows and perceives and sees them. So "legal points" never come to court, only life-related questions of justice. The less wise consult the wiser about these matters, and the wise consult the Lord and bring back the replies.

Their heaven, or the center of their joy, is living justly from the Lord.

215. Government in the Lord's spiritual kingdom is called "judgment," because they are involved in spiritual "good," which is that of charity toward the neighbor. This "good" is essentially true, and what is true is a property of judgment just as what is good is a property of justice.

These angels are guided by the Lord too, but indirectly (n. 208). As a result they have officials, fewer or more depending on the need of the community involved. They also have laws, which they abide by in their life together.

The officials administer everything according to the laws. They understand them because they are wise; and in cases of doubt, they are enlightened by the Lord.

216. Since government on the basis of what is good (the kind that exists in the Lord's celestial kingdom) is called "justice," and government on the basis of what is true (the kind that exists in the Lord's spiritual kingdom) is called "judgment," justice and judgment are mentioned in the Word in connection with heaven and the church. "Justice" means celestial "good" and "judgment" spiritual "good" which, as already stated, is essentially true. Note the following passages:

> There will be no end to peace on the throne of David and on His kingdom until it is established, and until it is founded on judgment and justice from now even till eternity.   (Isaiah 9:7)

"David" here means the Lord, and "His kingdom" means heaven, as we can see from the following passage:

> I will raise up for David a just Branch, and he will reign as king, and act discerningly, and do judgment and justice in the land.
>
> (Jeremiah 23:5)
>
> Let Jehovah be exalted, because He dwells on high: He has filled Zion with judgment and justice.   (Isaiah 33:5)

"Zion" too means heaven and the church.

> I Jehovah make . . . judgment and justice on earth, because I find pleasure in them.   (Jeremiah 9:24)
>
> I will betroth you to Myself for eternity, and I will betroth you to Myself in justice and judgment.   (Hosea 2:19)

Jehovah, Thy justice is in the heavens like mountains of God, and Thy
judgment like the great deep.   (Psalm 36:5-6)
They ask Me for judgments of justice, they long for the approach of
God.   (Isaiah 58:2)

and elsewhere.

217. There are various forms of government in the Lord's
spiritual kingdom, different from one community to another.
The differences depend on the kinds of service the communities undertake.

Their kinds of service are patterned after those involved
in all the members of man, to which they correspond. The
variety of these is well known. One kind of service is appropriate for the heart, another for the lungs, another for
the liver, another for the pancreas and spleen, and others
for each sensory organ.

Just as these have different functions in the body, communities have different functions in the Grand Man, which
is heaven, since it is communities that correspond to these
bodily organs. On the correspondence of everything in
heaven to everything in man, see the appropriate chapter
(above, nn. 87-102).

But all the forms of government there agree in one respect,
in focusing on the public good as their objective, and within
this good, the good of each individual. This happens because
everyone in all heaven is under the care of the Lord, who
loves everyone and provides out of Divine Love that the
common good be the source from which individuals receive
their own good. Each one receives what is good as he loves
the whole. For to the extent that one loves the whole, he
loves everyone and each one. And because this love is the
Lord's, he is beloved by the Lord to that extent, and is given
what is good.

218. This may serve to show what the officials are
like—they are in fact the ones who more than others are
involved in love and in wisdom, the ones therefore who,

out of love, intend what is good for everyone and who out of wisdom know how to provide that it happens.

People like this do not domineer and give orders; they minister and serve. For doing good to others out of a love for what is good, is serving; and providing that it happens is ministering. They do not make more of themselves than of others, but less, for they give first priority to the good of the community and the neighbor, and lower priority to their own good. What has first priority is greater; what has lower priority is less.

They do nevertheless have honor and glory. They live in the center of the community, higher up than others, and in splendid mansions. They do accept this honor and glory—not for themselves, however, but for obedience' sake. Everyone there knows, in fact, that this honor and glory are given them by the Lord, and that they are to be heeded on this account.

This is the meaning of the Lord's words to the disciples:
Whoever wants to become great among you shall be your servant, and whoever wants to be first among you, let him be your slave. Just as the Son of man did not come to be served, but to serve.

(Matthew 20:26-28)

Whoever is greatest among you shall be as the least; and whoever is leader, as one who serves.   (Luke 22:26)

219. A similar government, on the smallest scale, exists in each household. Here there is a head of the household and there are servants. The head loves the servants and the servants the head, so out of love they work for each other. The head teaches how to live and says what to do; the servants obey and fulfill their functions. Performing useful tasks is the delight of everyone's life. Clearly then, the Lord's kingdom is a kingdom of useful activities.

220. There are governments in the hells as well; for unless there were governments, the people there could not be kept fettered. But the governments involved are the opposites of governments in heaven. They all come under the heading of love of self.

Everyone there wants to rule over others and to be on top. Given people who are not on their side, they hate them, wreak vengeance on them, and are violently hostile toward them; for this is what love of self is like.

As a result, the worst do the ruling, and are obeyed out of fear. But more on this later, in speaking explicitly of the hells.

25.

DIVINE WORSHIP IN HEAVEN

221. Divine worship in heaven is outwardly rather like Divine worship on earth, but inwardly it is different. They do have teachings, sermons, and church buildings. The teachings are consistent in essentials, but in the higher heavens they are characterized by a deeper wisdom than in the lower heavens. The sermons are in keeping with the teachings. And just as they have homes and mansions (nn. 183-190), they have church buildings where the preaching takes place.

The reason why these things occur in heaven as well as on earth is that angels are constantly being perfected in wisdom and love. They have understanding and intention just as men do. Their understanding is of a kind that can continually be perfected, and so is their intention. Understanding is perfected by means of true elements that pertain to intelligence; and intention through good elements that pertain to love.

222. In actual fact, Divine worship in the heavens does not consist in going to church and paying attention to the sermon, but in a life characterized by love, charity, and faith according to the teachings. Church sermons function simply as a means for instruction in matters pertinent to life.

I have talked with angels about this, mentioning the belief in the world that Divine worship is just going to church, paying attention to the sermon, taking communion three or four times a year, following church law in other ritual matters, as well as making time for prayers and behaving committedly. The angels responded that these were outward matters that should indeed be observed, but that they were useless without something inward as their source, this inward something being a life in keeping with the laws taught by doctrine.

223. To learn what the meetings in churches are like, I have been allowed on occasion to enter and hear the sermons. The clergyman stands in a pulpit toward the east. Directly in front of him sit the angels who are especially involved in the light of wisdom, with those in lesser light on their right and left. They are stretched out in a circular arrangement so that all of them are within the clergyman's range of vision. To each side, where his sight does not reach, no ones sits.

Newcomers sit near the door, which is toward the east of the church, left of the pulpit. No one is allowed to stand behind the pulpit—if there is anyone there, the clergyman becomes confused. The same thing happens if someone in the group disagrees, which necessitates his turning his face away.

The sermons are characterized by such wisdom that none on earth can be cited in comparison: they are in the heavens, in a more inward light.

In the spiritual kingdom the church buildings seem to be made of stone, in the celestial kingdom, of wood. This is because stone corresponds to what is true, which people in the spiritual kingdom are involved in, while wood corresponds to what is good, which is what people in the celestial kingdom are involved in. In this latter kingdom the buildings are not called churches, but houses of God. In the celestial kingdom the buildings have no grandeur, but in the spiritual kingdom they do have more or less grandeur.

224. I talked with a particular clergyman about the holiness that envelops people who are listening to sermons in the churches. He told me that something holy, earnest, and reverent comes to each one, in keeping with his more inward elements that have to do with love and faith. This results from the presence of something intensely holy within love and faith because the Lord's Divine is there. He knew of nothing outwardly holy apart from these; and when he did think about outward holiness apart from these, said that there might perhaps be something that counterfeited holiness in outward appearance, either cleverly assumed or simply hypocritical. Some false fire of love of self and the world might arouse and maintain this kind of holiness.

225. All clergymen belong to the Lord's spiritual kingdom, none to the celestial kingdom. The reason they belong to the Lord's spiritual kingdom is that there, people are engaged with things true arising from what is good, and all proclamation stems from things that are true. The reason none come from the Lord's celestial kingdom is that people there are engaged in the good content of love, seeing and perceiving true things from that locus, but not talking about them. But in spite of the fact that angels of the celestial kingdom do see and perceive true things, they still have sermons, because thereby they are given light in the true elements they know and are perfected in many they did not know. The moment they hear them, they grasp, they love; and they make them part of their life by living by them. They say that living by things true is loving the Lord.

226. All clergymen are appointed by the Lord, and as a result have the gift of proclaiming. No one else is allowed to teach in the churches. They are called proclaimers, not priests. This is because heaven's priesthood is the celestial kingdom. Priesthood means, in fact, the good content of love for the Lord, in which the people who belong to that kingdom are involved. Heaven's kingship, on the other hand, is a spiritual kingdom, since kingship means things true stemming from what is good, in which the people who belong to that kingdom are involved (see above, n. 24).

227. The teachings which the sermon follow focus without exception on life as their goal—none on faith apart from life. The teaching of the inmost heaven is more filled with wisdom than is the teaching of the intermediate heaven, which in turn is more filled with wisdom than is the teaching of the outmost heaven. The teachings are in fact adapted to the grasp of the angels of each heaven.

The essential element of all the teachings is the acknowledgement of the Lord's Divine Human.

26.

THE POWER OF HEAVEN'S ANGELS

228. People who have no knowledge of the spiritual world and its inflow into the natural world cannot grasp the fact that angels have power. They think angels can have no power because they are so pure and rarefied as to be invisible. But people who look more deeply into the causes of things feel differently. They realize that all the strength man has comes from his understanding and intention, since without these he could not move the smallest part of his body.

Understanding and intention are his spiritual person. This activates the body and its members by his every signal. For what this spiritual person thinks, the mouth and tongue say; what he wills, the body performs, actually granting strength at his pleasure.

Man's intention and understanding are governed by the Lord through angels and spirits. And since this is true of his intention and understanding, it is true of everything bodily, since this stems from them. Believe it or not, man cannot take a single step without heaven's inflow.

A great deal of experience has demonstrated the truth of this to me. Angels have been allowed to activate my steps, my motions, my tongue, and my speech as they wished, by flowing into my intention and thought. I have been convinced that I could do nothing independently.

Afterwards, the angels said that each and every person is governed in this fashion; and that this can be known from the church's doctrine and from the Word. For man prays that God send His angels to lead him, guide his steps, teach him, inspire him what to think and say, etc. Still, when someone thinks on his own, apart from doctrine, he says and believes otherwise.

These matters have been related in order to make known the kind of power angels have with man.

229. The power angels have in the spiritual world is so great that if I were to cite at this point everything I have seen, it would be beyond belief. If there is something left there that needs to be removed because it is in opposition to the Divine design, they raze and destroy it by sheer force of will, with a look. I have seen mountains, under the control of evil people, razed and destroyed, sometimes shaken from boundary to boundary as if by an earthquake, the central peaks parting into a chasm, the evil ones on them engulfed. Also, I have seen hundreds of thousands of evil spirits routed by them and hurled into hell. A multitude is powerless against them, as are ploys, stratagems, and factions. They see them all and wreck them in a second (but more on this subject may be found in the account of *The Last Judgment and Babylon Destroyed*). This is the kind of strength angels have in the spiritual world.

We can see from the Word that angels have similar power in the natural world when they are allowed to use it. See, for example, their giving whole armies over to slaughter, their introducing a plague from which seventy thousand people died—we read of this angel,

> The angel stretched out his hand against Jerusalem to destroy it; but Jehovah, repenting of His evil, said to the angel who was destroying people, "It is enough; withdraw your hand." And David saw the angel who struck the people. (II Samuel 24:15-17)

There are other instances as well. Angels are called "powers" because they have such power, and in *David* we read,

> "Bless Jehovah, ye angels most powerful in strength" (Psalm 103:20).

230. It does need to be realized, however, that angels

have no power on their own, that all their strength is rather from the Lord. They are "powers" to the extent that they admit this. Any one of them who believes he has strength on his own promptly becomes so feeble that he cannot withstand a single evil spirit. This is why angels attribute absolutely no credit whatever to themselves, refusing any praise or honor for what they do and crediting it to the Lord.

231. The Divine-True that comes from the Lord is what possesses all the power in the heavens; for the Lord, in heaven, is the Divine-True made one with the Divine-Good (see nn. 126-140). To the extent that angels welcome this, they are "powers."

Each one is his own truth and his own good, since each one is of the same quality as his discernment and intention. Discernment has to do with what is true, being wholly composed of what is true. Intention has to do with what is good, being wholly composed of what is good. For anything a person discerns he calls true, and anything he intends he calls good. This is why every person is his own truth and his own good.

To the degree, then, that an angel is true from the Divine and good from the Divine, he is a "power," because to this degree the Lord is with him. Since no angel is engaged in just the same, identical "good" and "true" as another (for in heaven as in the world there is unending variety (see n. 20), no angel is possessed of the same power as another.

The ones who make up the arms in the Grand Man or heaven are possessed of the greatest power, because they are involved in things true more than others are, and the good from all of heaven flows into their true elements. So too the strength of the whole person is channeled into the arms, and the whole body puts its energies to work through them. This is why "arms" and "hands" are used in the Word to mean "power."

So sometimes a naked arm appears in heaven, powerful enough to shatter anything in its way, even a vast boulder in the earth. Once it actually moved toward me, and I realized that it could crush my bones to powder.

232. The fact that the Divine-True that comes from the Lord possesses all power, and the fact that angels have power insofar as they welcome the Divine-True from the Lord, have been cited above (n. 137). Angels, however welcome the Divine-True to the extent that they welcome the Divine-Good. All power actually belongs to true things that stem from what is good, none to true things apart from what is good. Likewise, all power belongs to what is good by means of things true, none to what is good apart from things true. Power arises from the bonding of these two.

It is the same with faith and love. For it makes no difference whether you say "the true" or "faith"—everything of faith is true. And it makes no difference whether you say "the good" or "love"—everything of love is good.

The amount of power angels have through things true that stem from what is good, can be seen in the fact that an evil spirit simply looked at by an angel collapses and ceases to look human until the angel turns his eyes elsewhere. The reason this happens at the gaze of angels' eyes is that angels' sight stems from heaven's light, and heaven's light is the Divine-True (see above, nn. 126-132). Eyes, in fact, correspond to things true stemming from what is good.

233. Granted that all power belongs to true things that stem from what is good, no power whatever belongs to false things that stem from what is evil. All the people in hell are involved in false things that stem from what is evil. So they have no power whatever against what is true and what is good. But we shall speak later about the kind of power they do have among themselves, and of the kind of power evil spirits have before they are cast into hell.

27.

ANGELS' LANGUAGE

234. Angels talk with each other just the way people in the world do, and they talk of various things—household matters, political matters, issues of moral life and issues of spiritual life, for example. There is no noticeable difference, except that they talk with each other more intelligently than men do, since they talk more profoundly, from thought.

I have often been allowed to associate with them, to talk with them as friend with friend—occasionally as stranger with stranger. At such times, being in a state like theirs, I had no way of knowing that I was not talking with people on earth.

235. Angelic speech, like human speech, is divided into units. Too, it is just as much spoken aloud and heard aloud, for angels have mouths, tongues, and ears. They have an atmosphere in which their speech sounds are pronounced; but it is a spiritual atmosphere, fit for angels who are spiritual. Angels breathe in their atmosphere and use breath to pronounce words just the way men do in theirs.

236. There is a single language for everyone in all heaven. They all understand each other, no matter what community they come from, near or far. The language is not learned there—it is native to everyone. It actually flows from their affection and thought. The sound of speech corresponds to their affections, and the distinctions of sound—the speech units—to thought-concepts stemming from affection. Because the language does correspond to these elements, it too is spiritual, being affection sounding and thought speaking.

[2] Anyone who gives the matter explicit attention can come to the realization that every thought comes from an affection, which in turn belongs to love, and that the concepts of thought are the various forms in which the general affection is parcelled out. For no thought or concept whatever exists apart from an affection—this is the source of their soul and life.

This is why angels know simply from conversation what another person is like—from the sound, they know what his affection is like, and from the distinctions of sound or speech units they know what his mind is like. The wiser angels can tell from a single sentence what the dominant affection is like, since they focus particularly on this.

[3] It is recognized that an individual has various affections—one when he feels happy, another when he feels sad, or gentle and compassionate, or candid and honest, or loving and charitable, or zealous and touchy, or deceitful and cunning, or eager for honor and fame, and so on. But a dominant affection or love lies within each of these. For this reason, the wiser angels, perceiving this, know from conversation the whole state of another person.

[4] I have been shown the truth of this by an abundance of experience. I have heard angels lay bare someone's life simply by listening to him. They have also told me that they know all about another's life from a few concepts of this thought, since from these they know his dominant love, which contains everything in an order. This and nothing else, they say, is a person's book of life.

237. Angelic language has nothing in common with human language except a few words that derive their sounds from particular affections. Even then, the likeness is not with the actual words, but with their sound, to which we will return later.

The lack of common ground between angelic language

and human languages is evidenced by angels' inability to pronounce a single word of a human language. They have tried, and have been unable. They can actually pronounce nothing unless it agrees completely with their affection. Anything that does not agree opposes their very life; for life belongs to affection, and their speech flows from it.

I have been told that people's first language on our earth was in accord because it came to them from heaven; also that the Hebrew language agrees in some respects.

238. Since angels' speech does correspond to their affection, which belongs to love, and since heaven's love is love for the Lord and love toward the neighbor (see above, nn. 13-19), we can see how choice and pleasant their conversation is. It actually touches not just the ears, but the more inward reaches of the minds of those who hear it.

There was one particular hardhearted spirit with whom an angel spoke. Eventually he was so touched by the conversation that he burst into tears, saying that he couldn't help it, love was talking, and he had never cried before.

239. Angels' speech is full of wisdom, too, because it comes from their more inward thought. Their more inward thought is wisdom, as their more inward affection is love. Their love and wisdom come together in speech.

As a result, their speech is so full of wisdom that they with a single word can express things that men could not compass in a thousand words. Then, too, their thought-concepts embrace things such as men cannot grasp, let alone verbalize. Consequently, the sounds and sights of heaven are called inexpressible, and such as ear simply has not yet heard, nor eye seen.

[2] I have been granted knowledge of this on the basis of experience. On occasion, I have been assigned to the state in which angels were, and in that state have talked with them. At such times I understood everything. But when

I was sent back into my earlier state—hence to the natural thinking proper to man—and wanted to recall what I had heard, I could not. For there were thousands of things that had no equivalent in concepts of natural thought, that were therefore inexpressible except simply through shiftings of a heavenly light—not at all by human words.

[3] The concepts of angels' thinking, which are the sources of their words, are changes in heaven's light as well; and the affections which give rise to their tones of voice are changes in heaven's warmth. This is because heaven's light is the Divine-True, or wisdom, and heaven's warmth is the Divine-Good, or love (see above, nn. 126-140). Angels derive affection from Divine love and thinking from Divine wisdom.

240. Since angels' speech emanates directly from their affection (for as stated at n. 236 above, thought concepts are different forms in which general affections are parcelled out), angels can say more in a minute than man can say in half an hour. They can also set down in a few words the contents of many written pages. This too has been demonstrated to me by an abundance of experience.

So angels' thought-concepts and the words of their language make a one, like an effective cause and its result. For in the words, there is set forth as a result what was present in the thought-concepts as a cause. This is why each word encompasses so much. When the details of angel's thought (and hence the details of their speech) are made visible, they look like a delicate wave or an ambient atmosphere, containing countless elements appropriately arranged, elements from their wisdom which enter another's thought and move him. Anyone's thought-concepts, angel's or man's, can be made visible in heaven's light whenever it pleases the Lord.

241. Angels who come from the Lord's celestial kingdom talk the way angels do who come from the Lord's spiritual

kingdom, except that celestial angels talk from a more inward thought than spiritual angels. Further, since celestial
angels are involved in the good proper to love to the Lord,
they talk from wisdom; while spiritual angels, being involved in the good proper to charity toward the neighbor
(which is essentially true, see n. 215), talk from intelligence.
For the derivative of what is good is wisdom, and the derivative of what is true is intelligence.

So the speech of celestial angels is rather like a gentle
stream, soft and unbroken, while the speech of spiritual
angels is rather energetic and distinct. Further, the speech
of celestial angels uses the sounds *u* and *o* a good deal,
while the speech of spiritual angels uses the sounds *e* and
i. The vowels serve for tone, and within the tone is the
affection. For as mentioned above (n. 236), the tone of
angels' speech corresponds to affection, and the distinct
sound-units—the words—correspond to thought-concepts
that stem from affections.

Because vowels do not belong directly to language, but
rather involve using resonance to raise the pitch of its sound-
units for specific affections dependent on a general state,
vowels are not represented in Hebrew, and are also pronounced in different ways.

Angels recognize from this what a person is like as far
as affection and love are concerned. The speech of celestial
angels lacks the hard consonants, and rarely puts two consonants together without slipping in a syllable beginning
with a vowel.

This is why the little word "and" slips in so often in the
Word, as may be clear to people who read the Word in
Hebrew. For in Hebrew, this little word is soft, and in both
its forms is a vowel sound. It is possible to tell somewhat
from the sounds in the Hebrew Word whether a word belongs to a celestial class or to a spiritual class—that is,

whether it deals with what is good or with what is true. Words that deal with what is good use the sounds *u* and *o* a good deal, and *a* to some extent. Words that deal with what is true use rather *e* and *i*.

Since affections do find expression primarily in tones, in human speech words using *u* and *o* sounds are preferred when dealing with major issues such as heaven and God. Musical sounds rise in this direction, too, when such matters are involved. This is why the art of music is so adept at expressing different varieties of emotion.

242. There is a kind of harmony in angelic speech that defies description. The source of this harmony is this: the affections and thoughts that give rise to speech pour out and spread in accord with heaven's form, and heaven's form provides the pattern for all friendship and all communication. On the form of heaven as the pattern for angels' friendships and for the flow of their affections and thoughts, see above (nn. 200-212).

243. A language like that of the spiritual world is instinctive in every individual, but it is in the realm of his more inward understanding. However, since this realm does not, in man's case, find its way into words that parallel affections the way it does with angels, man is unaware that the language is there. Still, this is why man is at home with this language of angels and spirits when he enters the other life, and knows how to speak it without being taught. But more on this below.

244. As stated above, there is one language for everyone in heaven. But it does vary in that the speech of the wise is more profound, more rich with shadings of affections and thought-concepts. The speech of the less wise is more outward, without the same richness. The speech of simple folk is still more outward, and is consequently made up of words from which meaning is gathered, the way it happens when people on earth talk to each other.

There is also a language that uses the face, trailing off into something audible that is altered by concepts. There is also a language in which representations of heaven are combined with concepts and one formed from concepts presented to sight. There is also a language using bodily motions corresponding to affections, and picturing things similar to those conveyed by words. There is a language by means of shared elements of affection and shared elements of thought, there is a thundering language, and there are others.

245. The speech of evil and hellish spirits is, predictably, natural, since it does come from their affections. But it comes from evil affections and therefore from dirty concepts, which angels wholly spurn. So the languages of hell are opposed to the languages of heaven, which means that evil people cannot stand angelic speech nor angels hellish speech. To angels, hellish speech is like a foul smell that hurts the nostrils.

The language of hypocrites (the ones who can pretend to be angels of light) is like the language of angels as far as the words are concerned. But as to affections and resultant thought-concepts, it is wholly opposite. So when the inward quality of their speech is perceived, the speech itself sounds like a grinding of teeth, and strikes horror.

28.

ANGELS' SPEECH WITH MAN

246. Angels who talk with man do not talk in their own language but in the person's language. They also talk in other languages a person knows, but not in languages unfamiliar to him. The reason for this is that when angels are talking with someone, they turn toward him and bond themselves to him. The bond of angel to man brings the two into a similar kind of thinking. And since a person's thought is connected to his memory, where speech comes from, the two are in command of the same language.

Further, when an angel or spirit comes to a person and is bonded to him by turning toward him, he gains entrance to his whole memory—so much so that as far as he is aware, he on his own knows everything the person knows, including languages.

[2] I have talked with angels about this, and have said that they might claim to be talking with me in my own dialect because it seemed that way to them, but that in fact they were not the ones who were doing the talking, but I, this being supported by the fact that angels cannot utter a single word of human language (n. 237). Besides, human language is natural, while angels are spiritual, and spiritual beings cannot produce anything by natural means.

Their response was that they know their bond with the person they are talking to is a bond with his spiritual thinking. But since this does flow into his natural thinking, which in turn is connected to his memory, it seems to the angels as though the person's language is their own, that all his

knowledge is theirs. This happens, they say, because it is
the Lord's good pleasure that there should be with men this
bond, this virtual incursion of heaven. The condition of man
today, however, is different, so that this kind of bonding
no longer occurs with angels, only with spirits who are not
in heaven.

[3] I have talked with spirits about this same subject too.
They, in contrast, wanted to believe not that the person was
speaking but that they were speaking within the person, not
that the person knew what he was doing, but that they
knew—hence that everything the person knew came from
them. I wanted to prove to them at length that this was not
true, but it was pointless.

Later on, in dealing with the World of Spirits, we will
note who are meant by "spirits" and who are meant by
"angels."

247. The intimacy of the bond between angels and spirits
and man (so intimate that they have no awareness that a
person's attributes are not their own) results also from the
fact that there is such a bond between the spiritual and
natural worlds that they are virtually one. However, since
man has alienated himself from heaven, it has been arranged
by the Lord that there be angels and spirits with each individual, and that the individual be led by the Lord by means
of them. This is why the bond is so intimate.

It would have been different if man had not alienated
himself. In that case, he could have been led by the Lord
through a general inflow from heaven, without having spirits
and angels yoked to him. But more in detail on this later,
in dealing with the bond between heaven and man.

248. The speech of angels or spirits with man sounds just
as "audible" as the speech of one person with another.
However, it is not audible to people nearby, only to the
individual himself. This is because the speech of an angel

or spirit flows into the person's thought first, and comes by an inner path to his physical ear; it thus activates it from within. But the speech of one person with another travels through the air first, comes by an outer path to his physical ear, and activates it from the outside. We can see then that the speech of an angel or spirit with a person is heard within him; and since it does also activate the physical ear, it is also audible.

In evidence of this descent from within of an angel's or spirits speech, I have observed that it also travels to the tongue and makes it quiver slightly, though not with the kind of motion that occurs when the person himself is using his tongue to enunciate speech sounds.

249. Talking with spirits, however, rarely happens nowadays, because it is dangerous. For in this case spirits know what they otherwise do not know, that they are with someone. Evil spirits, you see, are by nature ones who harbor a murderous hatred toward man, with no greater desire than to destroy him soul and body—which actually happens to people who overindulge in fantasies to the point that they cut themselves off from the pleasures appropriate to the natural person.

Actually, people who lead a lonely life may at times hear spirits talking with them, without risk. But the spirits who are with them are moved away by the Lord from time to time so that they may not know they are with the person. For most spirits are not aware that there is any world but the one they are in, or therefore that there are people somewhere else. Consequently, a person is not allowed to carry on a conversation with them, for if he could speak, they would know.

People who think a great deal about religious matters and become wrapped up in them to the point that they virtually see them within themselves, also begin to hear spirits talking with them. For when someone deliberately becomes absorbed in religious matters, no matter what kind, without interrupting them with various considerations that serve worldly uses, these religious matters travel inward, settle there, and take over the person's whole spirit. They even enter the spiritual world and affect spirits who are there. But people like this are ones who see visions and who get carried away. No matter what spirit they hear, they believe he is the Holy Spirit, when in fact there are spirits who take delight in carrying people away.

Spirits like this see false things as true, and having seen them, convince themselves and in turn convince any people they have access to. Since these spirits began to convince them of evil matters to which obedience was owed, they have gradually been removed.

Spirits who delight in carrying away can be distinguished from other spirits by their belief that they are the Holy Spirit, and that what they say is Divine. These spirits do not hurt the person because he holds them in honor with Divine worship.

I have talked with them a number of times, and at such times the disgusting things they impart to their worshippers have been laid bare. They live together toward the left, in a barren area.

250. No one is allowed to talk with angels except people who are involved in true things derived from what is good—especially people involved in a recognition of the Lord and of the Divine within His Human, since this is the truth the heavens are engaged in. For as shown above, the Lord is the God of heaven (nn. 2-6); the Lord's Divine constitutes heaven (nn. 7-12); and the Lord's Divine in heaven is love for Him and charity from Him toward the neighbor (nn. 13-19). All heaven, taken in a single grasp, reflects a single person, as does each community of heaven, and each angel is in a perfect human form—all this from the Lord's Divine-Human (nn. 59-86).

We can see, then, that conversation with angels of heaven happens only for people whose inward reaches have, by things Divinely true, been opened all the way to the Lord. For the Lord flows into these things in an individual, and when the Lord flows in, so does heaven.

The reason things Divinely true open the more inward reaches is that man is so created that as far as his inner person is concerned he is a reflection of heaven; while as far as the outer is concerned, he is a reflection of the world (n. 57). The inner person cannot be opened except by the Divine-True emanating from the Lord, since this is the light of heaven and the life of heaven (nn. 126-140).

251. The inflow of the Lord Himself into man is into his forehead, and from there into the whole face, since the forehead corresponds to love, and the face corresponds to all the more inward elements of the person. The inflow of spiritual angels into man is into his head all the way across the pate and the temples, the whole area under which the cerebrum lies, since this part of the head corresponds to intelligence. But the inflow of celestial angels is into the part of the head under which the cerebellum lies, called the occiput, from the ears around to the nape of the neck, for this area corresponds to wisdom.

All the speech of angels with man comes by these paths into his thought. I have grasped by this means just who the angels were who were talking with me.

252. People who talk with heaven's angels see what is in heaven as well, since they are seeing from the light of heaven in which their more inward reaches are. The angels too see through them what is on earth. For in such people heaven is bonded to earth and earth bonded to heaven, since as already noted (n. 246), when angels turn toward a person,

they join themselves to him so completely that they have
no knowledge that the person's attributes are not their own.
This applies not only to elements of his language, but also
to elements of sight and hearing. The person, in turn, has
no knowledge that the things that flow in through angels are
not his own.

The most ancient people on this earth were involved in
this kind of bond with heaven's angels, so that their era was
called the Golden Age. Since they did recognize the Divine
in Human form (that is, the Lord), they talked with heaven's
angels as their friends, and heaven's angels in turn talked
with them as their friends. In them, heaven and earth made
a one.

But after that era, man steadily moved away from heaven
by loving himself more than the Lord and the world more
than heaven. As a result, he began to feel the delights of
love of self and the world as distinct from the delights of
heaven, eventually to the point that he did not recognize
any other delight. Then his more inward reaches which had
lain open to heaven, were closed, and his more outward
reaches were opened to the world. Whenever this happens,
a person is in the light as far as everything in the world is
concerned, and in darkness as far as everything in heaven
is concerned.

253. Since that era, only seldom has anyone talked with
heaven's angels, though some have talked with spirits who
were not in heaven. The inner and outer realms of man are
so constituted that they are either turned toward the Lord
as their common center (n. 124), or they are turned toward
the person himself, which means away from the Lord.
Things which are turned toward the Lord are also turned
toward heaven; things which are turned toward the person
himself are also turned toward the world. Things turned in
this latter direction are hard to raise up. Still the Lord does

raise them as much as possible by turning the love, and this is done by means of true things from the Word.

254. I have been told how the Lord spoke with the prophets through whom the Word came. He did not speak with them the way He did with the ancient people, by flowing into their more inward reaches, but rather by means of spirits whom He sent to them. These the Lord filled with His look, and in this fashion He inspired the words which they were dictating to the prophets. Consequently it was not an inflow, but dictation.

Further, since the words came directly from the Lord, the details were filled with what is Divine, and contain an inner meaning of such nature that angels of heaven grasp the words in a celestial and spiritual meaning, while men grasp them in a natural meaning. In this way, the Lord has used the Word to bond heaven and earth together.

I have also been shown what it is like for spirits to be filled with what is Divine by the Lord by means of a look. A spirit filled by the Lord with what is Divine has no awareness that he is not the Lord, or that it is not the Divine which is speaking. This lasts until he has finished speaking. Afterwards he realizes that he is a spirit, and that he has not spoken on his own, but rather from the Lord.

Since this was the state of the spirits who spoke with the prophets, the prophets say that Jehovah spoke. Even the spirits themselves called themselves ''Jehovah,'' as can be illustrated not only by prophetic passages, but even by historical passages of the Word.

255. To make it known what the bonding of angels and spirits to man is like, I may relate some noteworthy items which offer light and conviction on this topic. When angels or spirits turn toward someone, it seems to them absolutely as though the person's language were theirs and they had no other. This is because they are involved in the individual's language rather than in their own, which they cannot call to mind. But the moment they turn away from the person, they are involved in their own angelic and spiritual language, and know nothing of the person's language.

Something like this has happened to me when I associated with angels and was in a state like theirs. Then I too spoke with them in their own language. I knew nothing of my own, which I could not call to mind. The moment I was not associated with them, I was involved in my own language.

It is worth noting that when angels or spirits turn toward a person, they can talk with him no matter how far away he is. They have talked with me from a distance just as audibly as though they were at hand. But when they turn away from someone and talk with each other, nothing at all is audible to the person, even though this may take place right next to his ear. Evidently then, all bonding in the spiritual world depends on turning a particular way.

It is also worth noting that many spirits can talk with a person at once, and he with them. Actually, they send a particular spirit from themselves to the person they want to talk with. This emissary spirit turns toward the person, and the many turn toward this spirit of theirs. In this way they focus their thoughts, which the spirit then presents. To the spirit, it seems as though he were speaking on his own, to the others that they are doing the same. So a bonding is effected between many and one by this turning in particular directions.

But much more will be said later on about these emissary spirits, called "subordinates," and about communication through them.

256. No spirit or angel may talk with a person from his own memory, only from the person's memory. Angels and spirits do have a memory just as men do. If a spirit were from his own memory to talk with someone, then it would seem to that person as though the things he was thinking were his own, yet they would still belong to the spirit. It is like recollecting something he has never heard or seen. I have been granted knowledge of the truth of this by experience.

This phenomenon gave rise to the belief among some early people that after several thousand years they would return to their former life and all its events, also that they had already made such a return. They based this on the fact that occasionally a sort of recollection would occur to them of things they have never seen or heard. This happened because spirits had from their own memories flowed into their thought concepts.

257. There are also spirits called natural and corporeal spirits. When they come to someone, they do not join with his thoughts the way other spirits do. They rather enter his body and take over all his senses. They speak with his mouth; they act with his limbs. To them, it seems wholly as though everything of the person's belonged to them. These are the spirits that ''possess'' people. But they have been cast into hell by the Lord, and thus completely taken away; so that possessions of this kind do not occur nowadays.

29.

WRITTEN MATERIALS IN HEAVEN

258. Inasmuch as angels do have a spoken language, and their language involves words, they also have written materials; their mind convey meaning through written materials as they do through speech. Several times, I have been sent pages inscribed with writing—some just like hand written pages, some like pages published in print in the world. I could even read them in similar fashion, but I was not allowed to get more than one or two meanings from them. This is because it is not in keeping with the Divine design for anyone to be taught by means of books from heaven, only by means of the Word. For only by this means is there a communication and a bonding of heaven with the world, and thus of the Lord with man.

It is clear in *Ezekiel* that pages written in heaven were visible to the prophets:

> When I looked, behold a hand sent me by the spirit, and in it a scroll of a book which he unrolled before me. It was written on the front and on the back.

> (Ezekiel 2:9-101)

also in *John:*

> I saw in the right hand of Him who sat upon the throne a book written within and on the back, sealed with seven seals.

> (Revelation 5:1)

259. The existence of books in heaven is provided by the Lord for the sake of the Word, for in its essence the Word is the Divine-True, the source of all heavenly wisdom for men and angels alike. It was in fact dictated by the Lord; and what is dictated by the Lord travels through the heavens in order and comes to rest with man. Consequently it is adapted both to the wisdom angels are involved in and to the intelligence people are involved in.

This is why angels too have the Word and read it as men on earth do. Their doctrinal tenets are derived from it, and their sermons come from it (*cf*. n. 221).

It is the very same Word. To be precise, its natural meaning, which is the literal meaning to us, does not exist in heaven. A spiritual meaning exists instead, which is the inner meaning. The nature of this meaning may be seen in the booklet, *The White Horse Mentioned in Revelation*.

260. Once a small page was sent me from heaven, with only a few words written on it in Hebrew letters. I was told that each letter enfolded secrets of wisdom, and that these were within the bends and curves of the letters and therefore in the sounds as well. I could see from this the meaning of these words of the Lord:

> I tell you in truth, until heaven and earth perish, one jot or one title will not pass from the law.   (Matthew 5:18)

It is recognized within the church that the Word is Divine to its every tip [*apex*]. But it is not known as yet just where this Divine element lies hidden "in every tip," and so this should be prevented.

In the inmost heaven, writings are made up of various curved and rounded forms. The curves and roundings are in keeping with heaven's form. By their means angels present arcana of their wisdom, and many things beyond the power of words to express. Further—remarkably—angels know this way of writing without study or teacher; it is conferred on them like the spoken language itself (*cf*. n. 236). So this writing is heavenly writing. It is conferred on them because all the outreach of angels' thoughts and affections, and therefore all the sharing of their intelligence and wisdom, proceed according to heaven's form (n. 201). As a result, their writing flows into this form.

I have been told that the earliest people on this earth, before letters were invented, had this kind of writing, also that is was carried over into the letters of the Hebrew language, which in early times were all curved, with none separate and straight the way they are today. This is why there are things Divine in the Word, and arcana of heaven even in its jots, tips, and tittles.

261. This writing, made by figures drawn from the heavenly form, is used in the inmost heaven, where people are above all others involved in wisdom. Through these figures they present the affections from which thoughts flow, following in sequence according to the substance of the matter in question. This is why these writings enfold secrets that cannot be plumbed by thinking. I have been allowed to see these writing, too.

In the lower heavens, however, writings of this kind do not exist. In these heavens, writing is like writing in the world, with similar letters. Still, they are not comprehensible to men because they are in an angelic language, and angelic language is of such nature that it has nothing in common with human languages (n. 237). With the vowels they express feelings; with the consonants thought concepts derived from feelings, and with words so composed they express the meaning of the matter (see above, nn. 236, 241).

Further, this writing can enfold in a few words more than man can describe in many pages. I have seen these writings, too. In the lower heavens, they have a Word written in this manner; and in the inmost heaven they have one written in celestial form.

262. It is interesting to note that written materials in the heavens flow naturally from angels' thoughts themselves—such as effortless process that it is as though the thought simply projected itself. The hand does not hesitate in choosing a particular word, since the words (those written as well as those spoken) correspond to their thought concepts, and all correspondence is natural and spontaneous.

There do occur in heaven writings without the aid of hands, but these do not last.

263. I have also seen things written from heaven composed soley out of numbers in an order and sequence, quite as is done with things written with letters and words. I have been informed that these written materials come from the inmost heaven; also that their heavenly writing (treated above, nn. 260-261) is presented in numbers to angels of a lower heaven when thought descends from it; and also that this numerical writing likewise involves hidden things, some of which cannot be grasped by thought nor expressed in words.

Numbers do in fact correspond and indicate according to correspondence just like words. There is the difference, though, that numbers involve generalities while words involve details. And since a single generality involves countless details, numerical writing enfolds more hidden things than alphabetic writing.

This has enabled me to see that numbers in the Word mean things just as much as the words do. The meanings of the simple numbers such as 2, 3, 4, 5, 6, 7, 8, 9, 10, and 12, and of the composite numbers 20, 30, 50, 70, 100, 144, 1000, 10,000, 12,000 and others, can be found in the appropriate passages of *Arcana Coelestia*.

In this kind of writing in heaven, a number is always prefixed on which the following depend in sequence, as if on their subject. For this number is, so to speak, the title of the matter treated, by which the following numbers are limited to the specific topic.

264. As for people who know nothing about heaven, who are unwilling to hold any concept of it except as something pure and airy where angels float around like intelligent minds without hearing or sight, they are unable to think of angels as having language and writing. In fact, they locate the actual occurence of everything in the material realm. Yet the things that exist in heaven occur with just as much reality as things in the world, and the angels who are there have everything useful for life and useful for wisdom.

30.

THE WISDOM OF HEAVEN'S ANGELS

265. It is hard to grasp the nature of angels' wisdom, since it so surpasses human wisdom that no comparison is possible, and anything so surpassing appears to be nothing at all. There are some overlooked means of describing it which, before they are recognized, are like shadows in the mind, and often conceal the essential quality of the subject. Still, they are of such nature that they can be known, and once known, grasped, if only the mind finds pleasure in them. For pleasure brings light with it, since it stems from love; and if people love the kind of thing that has to do with Divine and heavenly wisdom, a light from heaven shines on them, and enlightenment occurs.

266. The nature of angels' wisdom can be deduced from the fact that angels are in heaven's light, and heaven's light is essentially the Divine-True or Divine Wisdom. This light illuminates at once the sight of their inward realm that belongs to the mind, and the sight of their outward realm that belongs to the eyes (on the identity of heaven's light with the Divine-True or Divine Wisdom, see above, nn. 126-133).

Angels are also in heavenly warmth, which essentially is the Divine-Good or Divine Love, the source of their affection and longing for being wise (on the identity of heaven's warmth with the Divine-Good or Divine Love, see above, nn. 133-140).

As for the fact that angels are engaged in wisdom—even to the extent that they could be called ''wisdoms''—this can be inferred from the fact that all their thoughts and affections flow according to the heavenly form, which is the form of Divine Wisdom, it may also be inferred from the fact that their more inward reaches, which receive wisdom, are arranged on that heavenly form (on the fact that angels' affections and thoughts, and consequently their intelligence and wisdom, flow according to heaven's form, see above, nn. 201-212).

[2] There is evidence for angels' having surpassing wisdom also in the fact that their speech is wisdom's speech, flowing directly and freely from thought, and this in turn flowing from affection in such fashion that their speech is "thought from affection" in an outward form. This is why nothing diverts them from the Divine inflow, nothing of that "outward" that for man intrudes in his speech from unrelated thoughts (on angels' speech being a speech of their thought and affection, see nn. 234-245).

Still another factor contributes to this wisdom of angels, namely the agreement with their wisdom of everything they see with their eyes and perceive by sense. For these are correspondences, and consequently are objective entities in forms that portray elements appropriate to wisdom (on the proposition that all things visible in heaven are correspondences to the more inward elements of angels, and that they are portrayals of their wisdom, see above, nn. 170-182).

[3] Especially, angels' thoughts are not limited and constrained by ideas derived from space and time the way human thoughts are. For spaces and times belong to nature; and things that belong to nature lead the mind away from spiritual matters and deprive intellectual sight of its outreach (on the proposition that angels' concepts do not contain time and space and are therefore less limited than human concepts, see above, nn. 162-169 and 191-199).

Angels' thoughts are not drawn down into earthly or

material matters nor interrupted by anxieties over the necessities of life. So they are not drawn away from the pleasures of wisdom by such matters the way the thoughts of people in the world are. All things come to them from the Lord free; they are clothed, fed, and housed free (nn. 181-190). And beyond this, they are granted pleasures and comforts in the measure that they accept wisdom from the Lord.

All this has been related to show where angels get such wisdom.

267. The reason angels can accept such wisdom is that their more inward reaches are open; and wisdom, like all perfection, increases toward more inward things. Consequently, it increases in the measure that these are opened.

There are three levels of life in every angel, which correspond to the three heavens (see nn. 29-40). Angels in whom the first level is opened are in the first or outmost heaven. Angels in whom the second level is opened are in the second or intermediate heaven. But angels in whom the third level is opened are in the third or inmost heaven. The wisdom of angels in the heavens is matched to these levels. Consequently, the wisdom of angels of the inmost heaven vastly surpasses the wisdom of angels of the intermediate heaven; and their wisdom in turn vastly surpasses that of angels of the outmost heaven (see above, nn. 209, 210; and on the nature of the levels, see n. 38).

The reason for these distinctions is that the elements present on a higher level are details, while those of a lower level are generalities, the generalities being inclusive of the details. The ratio between the details and the generalities is on the order of thousands or ten thousands to one. Consequently the ratio of the wisdom of angels of a higher heaven to the wisdom of angels of a lower heaven is the same.

But even the wisdom of these latter angels surpasses man's wisdom, for man is involved in the physical and the body's sense impressions; and man's physical sense impressions are on the lowest level of all.

This shows what kind of wisdom is proper to people who do their thinking on the basis of sense impressions, that is, people called "sense-oriented people." In fact, they are not involved in wisdom at all, only in information.

It is different though with people whose thoughts are raised above sense impressions; and still more different with people whose more inward reaches are opened all the way into heaven's light.

268. The extent of angels' wisdom can be determined from the fact that in the heavens there is a sharing of everything. The understanding and wisdom of one person are conveyed to another; heaven is a joint participation in everything good. This is because heavenly love is of such nature that it wants what it has to belong to another. So no one in heaven sees any good thing of his as good within himself, unless it is also in someone else—which is a source of heaven's happiness, too. Angels derive this attitude from the Lord, whose Divine Love is of the same quality.

I have been allowed to know at first hand that there is this kind of sharing in the heavens. Once some simple folk were taken up into heaven, and while they were there, they entered into angelic wisdom as well. During that time, they understood things they could not grasp before, and said things they could not have uttered in their former state.

269. Words cannot describe what angels' wisdom is like—it can only be illustrated by a few generalities. Angels can express in a word what man cannot express in a thousand words. What is more, one angelic word contains countless elements that cannot be expressed by the words of a human language. In fact, the smallest things angels say contain hidden elements of wisdom in flawless connection that human information never approaches.

Then too, what angels cannot complete with the words of their language they supply with tone, which contains an affection for the subjects in their proper order. For as stated above (nn. 236, 241), they do express affections by tones, while by words they express thought concepts arising from affections. This is why things heard in heaven are called "inexpressible."

By the same token, angels can expound in a few words the details set down in a volume of a written work, and can introduce into each word elements that raise it toward a more inward wisdom. For their language is of such nature that it is in accord with their affections, and each word is in accord with their concepts. The words are changed in countless ways depending on the series of matters involved in the whole thought-complex.

[2] More inward angels can know a person's whole life from the tone, from a few spoken words. From the tone, patterned by means of the concepts involved in the words, they perceive his dominant love, which has recorded in it, so to speak, all the details of his life.

This may serve to show what angels' wisdom is like.

The ratio between their wisdom and human wisdom is on the order of ten thousand to one. It is rather like the motor impulses of the whole body, which are beyond counting, in comparison to the resulting action which to human senses looks like a simple unit. Or it is like thousands of entities seen through a perfect microscope, compared to the one indistinct entity seen by the naked eye.

[3] I should like to illustrate this with an example. An angel, out of his wisdom, described regeneration, citing arcana on the subject in proper sequence to the hundreds. Each of these he filled with concepts involving deeper arcana, all this from beginning to end. He actually explained how the spiritual person is conceived anew, is carried in the

womb, so to speak, is born, grows up, and is perfected step
by step. He said he could amplify the number of arcana to
several thousand, those he had mentioned being only about
the regeneration of the outer person, and there being countless more about the regeneration of the inner.

I could see from this, and from other similar things I have
heard from angels, what great wisdom they have, and how
great relatively is the ignorance of man, who hardly knows
what regeneration is and does not know a single phase of
the process while he is involved in it.

270. Let us now speak about the wisdom of angels of the
third or inmost heaven, and how far it surpasses the wisdom
of angels of the first or outmost heaven.

The wisdom of angels of the third or inmost heaven is
beyond understanding, even for people who are in the outmost heaven. This is because the more inward reaches of
angels of the third heaven are opened to the third level,
while the more inward reaches of angels of the first heaven
are opened only to the first level. Further, all wisdom increases toward the inner, and is perfected in proportion to
its openness (see nn. 208, 267).

[2] Since the more inward reaches of angels of the third
or inmost heaven are opened to the third level, Divine true
things are virtually inscribed on them. For the more inward
elements of the third level—more than those of the second
and first levels—are in heaven's form. Heaven's form stems
from the Divine-True, and is therefore in accord with Divine
Wisdom. This is why these angels seem to have things
Divine and true virtually inscribed on them, or virtually
inherent and innate. Consequently, the moment they hear
things genuinely true and Divine, they acknowledge and
grasp them; and thereafter they virtually see them in themselves.

This being the nature of angels of the third heaven, they

never apply logic to things Divine and true. Still less do they debate about anything true as to whether it is so or not, nor do they know what "believing" or "having faith" are. What they say is, "What is faith? I perceive, I see that this is so."

They cite comparable situations by way of illustration. It would be just as though someone out with a friend were to see a house and all the various things in and around it, and were to tell his friend that he ought to believe that these things existed, and were what they seemed to be. Or it would be as though someone saw a garden with trees and fruit, and told his friend that he ought to have faith that it was a garden, that those were trees and fruit, when he could actually see them plainly with his own eyes. This is why these angels never use the term "faith," nor have any concept of it. Consequently, they do not apply logic to things true and Divine, much less debate about anything true as to whether it is so or not.

[3] But angels of the first or outmost heaven do not have things true and Divine inscribed on their more inward natures in this way, since nothing but the first level of life is opened to them. They do therefore apply logic to these matters, and people who do this scarcely see past the obvious form of the matter they are reasoning about. Nor do they go farther into a subject than to bolster it by various means. Having done this, they say that these are matters of faith, and that people ought to believe.

[4] I have talked about this with angels who told me that the difference between the wisdom of angels of the third heaven and that of angels of the first heaven is like the difference between clear and cloudy. They proceeded to compare the wisdom of angels of the third heaven to a splendid palace full of everything functional, surrounded on all sides by parks, which in turn were encircled by splendid

things of many sorts. They told me that these angels, being involved in true elements of wisdom, were able to go into the palace and see everything, to walk in the parks at will, and to enjoy it all.

It is quite different for people who apply logic to matters of truth, and even more different for people who debate about them. Since they do not see matters of truth in the light of what is true, deriving them instead from other people or from the literal meaning of the Word, which they do not understand in depth, they say that people should believe these things or have faith, and then are not willing to have a deeper view of things intrude. Angels say that such folk are not able to reach the first threshold of the palace, let alone go inside or walk in the parks, since they stop at the first step.

It is different with people who are involved in matters of actual truth. Nothing holds them back from moving and walking without restriction. For true things, seen, lead where they will, even into broad meadows, because each single element of truth is subject to infinite extension, and is bound up with an abundance of others.

[5] These angels went on to say that the wisdom of angels of the inmost heaven consists primarily of seeing Divine and heavenly matters in individual objects, and marvels in a sequence of several. For everything visible to their eyes has a correspondence; so that when they see a palace and gardens, their focus does not become fixed on the kind of thing that lies before their eyes. Instead, they see the inner realities from which these things stem, to which they therefore correspond. This occurs with constant variation, depending on the appearance of the objects, so that they see countless elements in a pattern and connection, which so delights their minds that they seem to be taken out of themselves (on the proposition that everything visible in the heav-

ens corresponds to things Divine from the Lord within angels, see above, nn. 170-176).

271. The reason angels of the third heaven are like this is that they are involved in love for the Lord, and this love opens the more inward reaches of the mind to the third level, and is what receives everything proper to wisdom.

We also need to realize that angels of the inmost heaven are constantly being perfected in wisdom, in a different way from that characteristic of angels of the outmost heaven. Angels of the inmost heaven do not store Divine true things away in their memories, or make some kind of information out of them. Rather, the moment they hear them, they grasp them and put them to work in life. This is why Divine true things stay with them as though inscribed; for anything that is actually applied to life is "inside" in this way.

The situation is different with angels of the outmost heaven. They do store Divine true things away in their memories at first, and conceal them in information. From there, they retrieve and use them to perfect their understanding, willing them and applying them to life without any inward perception of their truth. Consequently, everything is relatively cloudy to them.

It is worth noting that angels of the third heaven are perfected in wisdom by what they hear, not by what they see. Whatever they hear from exhortation does not go into their memories, but directly into their perception and intention, and becomes part of their life. But whatever these angels see with their eyes does go into their memories, and they apply logic to it and talk about it. This may serve to show that the path of hearing is their path of wisdom.

This too has its source in correspondence, for the ear corresponds to obedience, and obedience has to do with living. But the eye corresponds to intelligence, and intelligence has to do with doctrine.

The state of these angels is described very often in the Word, as in *Jeremiah:*

> I will put my law in their mind, and write it on their heart; . . . No longer will anyone teach his friend, or anyone his brother, saying "Know Jehovah," for all that exist will know me, from the least of them to the greatest of them.   (Jeremiah 31:33-34)

And in *Matthew:*

> Let your speech be "Yes, yes, No, no," anything beyond this comes from what is evil.   (Matthew 5:37)

The reason "anything beyond this comes from what is evil" is that it does not come from the Lord. For the true things that are within the angels of the third heaven do come from the Lord because they are involved in a love for the Lord. Love for the Lord, in that heaven, is willing and doing what is Divine and true, for the Divine-True is the Lord in heaven.

272. Another factor beside the ones just cited bears on the ability of angels to accept this kind of wisdom—a major factor in heaven, namely their lack of love of self. For to the extent that anyone is free of this love, he is able to become wise in Divine matters. It is this love that closes the more inward realms and turns them toward itself. As a result, all people in whom this love is dominant are in darkness as far as matters of heaven are concerned, no matter how much light they have in matters of the world.

But because angels on their part are free of this love, they are involved in wisdom's light. In fact, the heavenly loves they are involved in (love for the Lord and love toward the neighbor) open the more inward reaches because these loves come from the Lord and the Lord Himself is within them (on the proposition that these loves make up heaven overall and form the heaven within each particular individual, see above, nn. 13-19).

Because heavenly loves do open the more inward reaches to the Lord, all angels turn their faces toward the Lord (n. 142). In the spiritual world it is in fact love that turns each individual's more inward elements toward itself; and wherever love turns the more inward elements, it turns the face. For there the face acts as one with what lies within, and is actually the outer form of the more inward things.

Since a love does turn the more inward elements and the face toward itself, it bonds itself to them as well, for love is a spiritual bond. Consequently, it also conveys its own possessions to them. As a result of this turning, with the consequent bonding and sharing, angels have wisdom (on the proposition that all bonding in the spiritual world occurs according to "turning," see n. 255 above).

273. Angels are constantly becoming more perfect in wisdom. However, they cannot to eternity become perfect to any extent that could cause a ratio to exist between their wisdom and the Lord's Divine Wisdom. For the Lord's Divine Wisdom is infinite, while that of angels is finite, and no ratio exists between the infinite and the finite.

274. Since wisdom perfects angels and makes up their life, and since heaven with its good things flows in for each individual in proportion to his wisdom, everyone there longs for wisdom and hungers for it, very much the way a hungry man longs for food. Information, discernment, and wisdom are spiritual nourishment, the way food is natural nourishment; they do correspond to each other.

275. The angels in one heaven—even the angels in one community of heaven—are not in like wisdom, but in unlike. Those in the center are in the greatest wisdom, those round about to the borders in less. The decline in wisdom proportional to the distance from the center is like the decline of a light pointed into darkness (see above, nn. 43, 128). For angels, the light too is at a level of intensity parallel to that of their wisdom, because heaven's light is Divine Wisdom, and everyone is in light in proportion to his acceptance of that wisdom (on heaven's light and the variable acceptance of it, see above, nn. 126-132).

31.

ANGELS' STATE OF INNOCENCE IN HEAVEN

276. Few people in this world know the nature and quality of innocence; no one who is involved in what is evil knows at all. There is something visible to the eyes, something about the face, speech, and motions particularly of children, but people do not know what this is, and are still more ignorant of the fact that this is where heaven conceals itself within man.

To make this known, I should like to proceed step by step, speaking first about the innocence of childhood, then about the innocence of wisdom, and finally about heaven's state in respect to innocence.

277. The innocence of childhood (or of children) is not real innocence, since it resides only in their outward form, not in their inner one. It is, however, possible to learn from it what innocence is like. It actually glows from their faces, some of their motions, and their beginnings of speech. It qualifies their lack of internal thought; for they do not yet know what is good or what is evil, what is true or what is false, and thought stems from these knowledges.

[2] As a result, they have no self-generated discretion, no intention or resolution, and therefore no purpose of anything evil. They have no selfhood amassed out a love of self and the world. They do not credit themselves with anything, ascribing to their parents everything they have received. They are contented and happy with little trifles given them as presents. They have no worry about food and clothing, or about what is going to happen. They do not

focus their attention on the world and covet a great many things from it. They love their parents, their nurse, and their little friends, with whom they innocently play. They allow themselves to be led; they listen and obey.

[3] Because they are in this state, they accept everything by means of life. They have, as a result, without knowing the source, suitable habits; they have speech; they have the first elements of memory and thought, which their state of innocence helps them accept and absorb.

But as stated above, this innocence is outward because it belongs to the body only, not to the mind. Actually, their mind has not yet taken shape. For the mind is understanding and intention, consequently thought and affection.

[4] I have been told from heaven that children are especially under the Lord's guardianship, with an inflow from the inmost heaven, where the state is one of innocence; also that this inflow passes through their more inward reaches, exerting no influence in transit except by means of innocence. Also, this is why innocence comes out in the face and in certain motions; further, this is what profoundly moves parents, causing the love that is called *storge* [a Greek word for parental affection].

278. The innocence of wisdom is genuine innocence because it is inward. For it belongs to the mind itself, that is therefore, to intention itself and consequently to understanding. When there is innocence within these functions, there is wisdom as well, for wisdom is proper to them.

This is why it is said in heaven that innocence lives in wisdom, and that an angel's wisdom is in proportion to his innocence. Angels support the truth of this with the fact that people who are in a state of innocence do not credit anything good to themselves, but rather attribute and ascribe everything they have received to the Lord. Further, there is the fact that they want to be led by Him, not by themselves.

They love everything that is good, they take pleasure in everything that is true; since they both know and perceive that loving what is good (that is, willing and doing it) is loving the Lord, and loving what is true is loving the neighbor. They live content with what they have, whether it be little or much, knowing that they receive as much as is good for them. They have few things if a little is good for them, and many things if an abundance is good for them. They do not know what is good for them—only the Lord knows; in His sight all the things He provides are eternal.

[2] So they are not worried about what is going to happen. They refer to worry about what is going to happen as "anxiety about tomorrow's affairs," which, according to them, is suffering about the loss or lack of things that are not needed for life's useful employments. Socially, they never act from a purpose of what is evil, but from what is good, right, and honest. They call acting for a purpose of what is evil, "cunning," something they flee like a snake's venom, because it is utterly opposed to innocence.

Because there is nothing they love more than being led by the Lord, and because they give Him credit for everything they receive, they are kept away from their selfhood; and to the extent that they are kept away from their selfhood, the Lord flows in. This is why the things they hear from Him—whether by means of the Word or by its exposition—they do not store away in memory, but promptly obey, that is, intend and do. Intention is their very memory.

These angels usually seem artless in outward form, but they are wise and skillful within. They are the ones meant by the Lord,

Be wise as serpents, and artless as doves.

(Matthew 10:16)

This is the nature of the innocence called "the innocence of wisdom."

[3] Now innocence credits itself with nothing good, but

ascribes everything good to the Lord; it loves to be led by the Lord in this way, which results in an acceptance of everything good and true, the source of wisdom. For this reason, man has been so created as to be in innocence (albeit outward innocence) during childhood; and when he grows old he is in inward innocence—that is, so created as to come through the outward into the inward, and again into the outward because of the inward. Consequently, as a person ages he deteriorates physically and becomes like a child all over again, but like a wise child—that is, an angel. For in the highest sense, a "wise child" is an angel.

This is why "child" in the Word means someone innocent, and "old man" means a wise person with innocence in him.

279. Something like this happens with everyone who is being regenerated. Regeneration is rebirth, as far as the spiritual person is concerned. First, the individual is guided into the innocence of infancy, meaning that he knows nothing true and is capable of nothing good on his own, only from the Lord, and that he wants and longs for these things simply because the one is true and the other is good. These are granted by the Lord as the person advances in age. First he is guided into knowledge about them, then from "knowledge about" into understanding, and finally from understanding into wisdom, with innocence ever in attendance—innocence meaning, as already stated, that he knows nothing true and is capable of nothing good on his own, only the Lord. Apart from this faith and a perception of it, no one can receive any element of heaven. The innocence of wisdom resides principally within it.

280. Since innocence is being led by the Lord rather than by self, all the people in heaven are involved in innocence. For all the people who are there love being led by the Lord. They know, in fact, that leading oneself is being led by selfhood; and selfhood is loving oneself; and anyone who loves himself does not let himself be led by anyone else.

This is why an angel is in heaven to the extent that he is involved in innocence. That is, he is to this extent involved in the Divine-Good and the Divine-True; for involvement in these is being in heaven.

The heavens are therefore distinguished according to innocence. People who are in the outmost of first heaven are in innocence of the first or outmost level. People who are in the intermediate or second heaven are in innocence of the second or intermediate level. People who are in the inmost or third heaven, then, are in innocence of the third or inmost level. Consequently, they are the very innocencies of heaven, since they more than others love being led by the Lord like children by their father. So too, they accept into their intention the Divine-True that they hear either directly from the Lord or indirectly through the Word and explanations of it, and so apply it to their lives. This is why they have so much more wisdom than angels of the lower heavens (see nn. 270-271).

Because they are like this, these angels are nearest to the Lord, the source of their innocence. They are also kept apart from their selfhood to the point where they virtually live in the Lord. They look artless in outward form, even like children in the sight of angels of the lower heavens—very small. They look like people who are not very wise, even though they are the wisest of heaven's angels. They realize, in fact, that on their own they have no wisdom, and that being wise is recognizing this fact. Then too, what they do know is practically nothing in comparison to what they do not know. Knowing, recognizing, and grasping this is, in their words, the first step toward wisdom.

These angels are naked, because nakedness corresponds to innocence.

281. I have talked with angels about innocence a good deal, and have received the following information. Innocence is the inner Reality [*Esse*] of everything good; therefore a good thing is good to the extent that it contains innocence. As a result, wisdom is wisdom to the extent that it derives from innocence, and so are love, charity, and faith. This is why no one can enter heaven unless he has innocence, which is what the Lord meant by saying,

> Let the children come to me; do not forbid them, for of such is the kingdom of the heavens. I tell you truly, anyone who does not receive the kingdom of the heavens like a child, will not enter it.
>
> (Matthew 19:14; 18:3; Mark 10:14-15; Luke 18:16-17)

Here as elsewhere in the Word, ''children'' means people who are innocent. The condition of innocence is described by the Lord (Matthew 6:24-25), but in pure correspondences. The reason why any good thing is good to the extent that it contains innocence, is that everything good is from the Lord, and innocence is willingness to be led by the Lord.

I have also been informed that what is true cannot be bonded to what is good, or vice versa, except by means of innocence. This is another reason why an angel is not an angel of heaven unless there is innocence within him. For heaven is not within anyone unless what is true is bonded to what is good within him. This bonding of the true and the good is called ''the heavenly marriage,'' and the heavenly marriage is heaven.

I have also been informed that genuine marriage love derives its manifest form from innocence, since it comes from the bonding of the good and the true that the two minds, husband's and wife's, are involved in. As this bonding descends, it makes itself known in the form of marriage love; for the married partners, like their minds, love each other. This is the source of childlike, innocent play in marriage love.

282. Since innocence is the actual inner reality of what is good in heaven's angels, we can see that the Divine-Good emanating from the Lord is innocence itself. For that is the Good that flows into angels, influences their inmost elements, and arranges and fits them for the acceptance of every good thing of heaven. A similar thing happens in infants, whose more inward reaches are not only formed by the passage of innocence from the Lord, but constantly fitted and arranged to accept the good of heavenly love. For the good quality of innocence works from the center, being the inner reality of everything good, as mentioned above.

We may conclude from this that all innocence is from the Lord. This is why the Lord is called "the Lamb" in the Word, since a lamb means innocence.

Because innocence is the central element of everything good in heaven, it so influences minds that people who feel it (which happens when an angel of the inmost heaven draws near) seem to themselves not to be under their own authority, to be moved by such delight, virtually transported, that all the world's delight is nothing in comparison. I say this from direct experience.

283. All people who are involved in the goodness of innocence are influenced by innocence, with the influence being proportional to the involvement in that "good." But people who are not involved in the goodness of innocence are not influenced by it. So all the people who are in hell are utterly opposed to innocence. They do not know what innocence is. On the contrary, their nature is such that the more innocent a person is, the greater is their ardor to inflict harm on him. This is why they cannot stand the sight of children. The moment they see them, they are on fire with a vicious passion to hurt.

This may serve to show that man's selfhood, and consequently his love of self, are opposed to innocence. For all the people who are in hell are involved in their selfhood and therefore in love of self.

32.

THE STATE OF PEACE IN HEAVEN

284. Anyone who has not been involved in heaven's peace cannot grasp the nature of the peace angels experience. As long as a person is involved in his body, he cannot accept heaven's peace and therefore cannot perceive it, since man's perception is on the natural level. In order to perceive it, he needs to be of such nature that he can be lifted and led out of the body as to his thought and made present in the spirit, thereby being with angels.

Since I have perceived heaven's peace in this manner, I am able to describe it. I cannot put into words what it is like intrinsically, since human words are inadequate. I can only describe in words what it is like in comparison to that "peace of mind" that belongs to people who are content in God.

285. There are two inmost elements of heaven, innocence and peace. They are called inmost because they come directly from the Lord. Innocence is the source of everything good in heaven; and peace is the source of all the delight of what is good—every good thing has its own delight. Both of them—what is good as well as what is pleasant—belong to love. For what is loved is called "good," and is also felt as pleasant. It then follows that these two inmost elements, innocence and peace, come from the Lord's Divine Love, and affect angels from their very center.

On innocence as the inmost element of what is good, see the chapter immediately preceding, where the subject was the state of innocence of heaven's angels. The present chapter treats of peace as the inmost element of what is pleasant arising from the "good" of innocence.

286. We may first state the source of peace. There is a Divine peace in the Lord, arising from the union within Him of the Divine Itself and the Divine-Human. The Divine side of peace in heaven is from the Lord, arising from His bond with heaven's angels, and specifically from the bonding of what is good and what is true in each individual angel. These are the sources of peace.

We can conclude from this that peace in the heavens is something Divine, most deeply touching everything good there will happiness—essentially a Divine joy of the Lord's Divine Love because of His bond with heaven and with each individual there. This joy, perceived by the Lord in angels and by angels because of the Lord, is peace. From it, by secondary development, angels receive everything blessed, pleasant, and happy—that is, what people call "heavenly joy."

287. These being the sources of peace, the Lord is called "the Prince of peace," and states that peace comes from Him and is in Him. Then too, angels are called "angels of peace," and heaven "the heaven of peace," as in the following passages:

A boy is born to us; a Son is given us, on whose shoulder sovereignty shall rest. And His name shall be called Wonderful, Counselor, God, Hero, Father of eternity, Prince of peace. There shall be no end of the increase of sovereignty and peace.

(Isaiah 9:6-7)

Jesus said, "I leave peace with you; I give you my peace. Not as the world gives do I give to you." (John 14:27)

I have said these things so that you would have peace in me.(John 16:33)

May Jehovah lift His face to you, and give you peace. (Nu. 6:26)

The angels of peace weep bitterly; the paths are destroyed.(Isaiah 33:7-8)

The work of justice shall be peace, . . . and my people shall live in the home of peace. (Isaiah 32:17-18)

[2] We may verify the fact that "peace" in the Word means Divine and heavenly peace from other passages where it is mentioned, such as the following:

Isaiah 52:7, 54:10, 59:8; Jeremiah 16:5, 25:37, 29:11; Haggai 2:9; Zechariah 8:12; Psalm 37:37; *et al.*

Since peace means the Lord and heaven (also heavenly joy and the delight of what is good), the greeting of ancient times was, "Peace be with you," and consequently still is today. The Lord encouraged this, saying to the disciples whom He sent out,

When you enter a house, say first, "Peace be to this house." If a son of peace be there, your peace will rest upon it.   (Luke 10:5-6)

Then too, the Lord Himself said, "Peace be with you" (John 20:19, 21, 26) when he appeared to the apostles.

[3] A state of peace is also to be understood in the Word by this—

that Jehovah said, "I have smelled the scent of quietness" (as in Exodus 29:18, 25, 41; Leviticus 1:9, 13, 17; 2:9; 6:15, 21; 23:12, 13, 18; Numbers 15:3, 7, 13; 28:6, 8, 13; 29:2, 6, 8, 13, 36).

In the heavenly sense, a perception of peace is meant by "the scent of quietness."

Because peace does mean all this—the union in the Lord of His Divine Itself with the Divine-Human, the Lord's bond with heaven, the church, and all the people in heaven and the church who accept Him—the Sabbath was established as a reminder to them, was given its name from "quietness" or "peace," and was the holiest symbol of the Church. So too the Lord called Himself "the Lord of the Sabbath" (Matthew 12:8, Mark 2:27-28; Luke 6:5).

288. Heaven's peace, being something Divine which most deeply touches with blessedness the good itself which is in angels, does not reach their conscious perception except as follows:

through a pleasure of heart when they are engaged in the good proper to their lives, through a sense of fitness when they hear something true that is in harmony with their good, and

through an exhilaration of mind when they perceive their bonding.

From this source, though, it flows into all the deeds and thoughts of their lives, presenting itself to all outward appearance as joy.

[2] But as to nature and amount, peace varies in the heavens in proportion to the innocence of the people who are there, since innocence and peace walk hand in hand. For as stated above, innocence is the source of everything good in heaven, and peace the source of everything pleasant belonging to that "good."

This enables us to establish the possibility of saying here about a state of peace the same things said in the last chapter about the state of innocence in heaven, innocence and peace being connected like what is good and what is pleasant about it. For what is good is detected by its own proper pleasantness, and what is pleasant is recognized by its goodness.

This being the case, we can see that angels of the inmost or third heaven are involved in the third or inmost level of innocence. Also angels of the lower heavens are involved in lower levels of peace because they are in lesser levels of innocence (see above, n. 280).

[3] The inseparability of innocence and peace (like that of what is good and what is pleasant about it) is observable in children, who, being in innocence, are also in peace. And since they are in peace, everything within them is playful.

But the peace within infants is an outward peace; inward peace, like inward innocence comes only with wisdom. Since it does come only with wisdom, it comes only as what is good and what is true are joined together, for this is the source of wisdom.

Heavenly or angelic peace comes to people on earth who

are involved in wisdom because of the joining together of what is good and what is true, and who consequently see themselves as content in God. But these qualities, as long as people are living in the world, lie hidden away in their more inward recesses, being uncovered when they leave their bodies and enter heaven, for then the more inward recesses are opened.

289. Since this is the way Divine peace arises—from the Lord's bond with heaven, and in the individual case of each angel, from the bonding of what is good and what is true—angels are in a state of peace when they are in a state of love; for then what is good is joined to what is true within them (on the regular fluctuation of angels' states, see above, nn. 154-160).

Something like this happens with a person who is being regenerated. When the bonding of the good and the true takes place within him (which happens especially after temptations), he enters a condition of joy stemming from heavenly peace.

That peace is like the morn or dawn in springtime, when, once the night is done, all things of earth begin to live anew from the rising of the sun; the scent of leaves is wafted here and there, awakened by the dew that falls from heaven; the gentle warmth of spring makes fertile the soil and grants as well a joy to human minds. This is because morning and dawn in springtime correspond to the state of peace of angels in heaven (see n. 155).

290. I have also talked with angels about peace. I have told them that in the world, peace is defined as a time when wars and hostilities between nations cease, or enmity and strife between individuals, together with a belief that inner peace is "peace of mind" because problems have been taken away —especially a calm and pleasure at the success of business ventures.

Angels have told me, however, that "quietness of mind," calm and pleasure at the removal of problems and the success of business ventures, may look like peace, but that they are not peace except in people who are involved in some heavenly "good" because peace does not occur except within that "good." Peace actually flows from the Lord into the inmost part of such people, descends and flows down into their lower levels, and presents a peace of the inner mind [*mentis*], a calm of the outer mind [*animi*], and a joy in consequence.

But for people who are involved in something evil, peace does not occur. Something like quietness, calm, and pleasure does appear when they get what they want, but this is outward only, not at all "inner." In fact, enmity, hatred, revenge, and many evil desires are raging within, with the outer mind being borne into these desires the moment such people see someone who is not on their side, and breaking out openly unless there is also fear present.

Angels have also told me that this is why such people's pleasure dwells in madness, while the pleasure of people involved in what is good dwells in wisdom. The difference is like that between hell and heaven.

33.

HEAVEN'S BOND WITH THE HUMAN RACE

291. It is known within the church that everything good is from God and nothing from man, and that it is not right therefore for anyone to count anything good to be his own. It is also known that what is evil is from the devil. This is why people who are speaking from the church's doctrine describe people who behave well (and people who talk reverently and preach) as being led by the Lord, in contrast to people who behave badly and talk irreverently.

There could be no substance to all this unless there were a bond between man and heaven, and a bond with hell, and unless these were bonds with his intention and his understanding. For it is out of these that the body acts and the mouth speaks.

Let us describe what this connection is like.

292. Good spirits and evil spirits are in company with each individual. Through the good spirits a person has a bond with heaven; through the evil spirits he has a bond with hell. These spirits are in a World of Spirits which is halfway between heaven and hell, and will be treated explicitly below.

When these spirits come to someone, they enter his whole memory and consequently his whole thought process. Evil spirits enter those elements of memory and thought that are evil, good spirits those elements of memory and thought that are good.

The spirits have no awareness whatever of being with the person. While they are there, rather, they believe that all the things that belong to the person's memory and thought are their own. Nor do they see the person, since the things that exist in our subsolar world do not fall within their range of vision.

The Lord takes the greatest possible care lest spirits know that they are with someone. If in fact they should become aware of this, they would talk with him, and then the evil spirits would destroy him. For evil spirits, being bonded with hell, have no greater desire than to destroy someone—not only as to his soul (that is, his faith and love), but even as to his body.

It is different when they do not talk with the person. Then they are not aware that what they are thinking, what they are saying among themselves, comes from him. For they do talk among themselves from the person as a source, yet in the belief that the matters are their own. Each one values and loves what belongs to him. So the spirits are bound to love and value the person, even though they are not aware of it.

By many years of constant experience, this nature of the bonding of spirits with man has become so well known to me that nothing is more familiar.

293. The reason spirits who are in contact with hell are in touch with man as well, is that man is born into involvement with all kinds of evil things, with his earliest life made up of nothing else. So unless there were spirits of his own quality in touch with him, he would not be able to live, let alone to be led away from his evils and reformed. So he is kept in his own life by evil spirits, and kept back from it by good spirits. Because of these two, then, he is in a balance; and because he is in a balance, he is in his free state. He can be led away from evils and guided toward the good; he can also have the good grafted into him, which cannot happen unless he is in a free state. Also, the free

state cannot occur for him unless spirits from hell are working from one side and spirits from heaven from the other,
with the person in the middle.

It has also been pointed out that man, insofar as he exists
from what he inherits and therefore in his own right, would
have no life unless he were allowed to be involved in something evil, nor if he were not in a free state. It has also been
pointed out that he cannot be compelled toward the good,
and that that which is compelled does not stick; similarly,
that anything good which a person accepts in a free state
is grafted into his intention and becomes virtually a part of
him. This is why man has communication with hell and
communication with heaven.

294. We may now describe the nature of heaven's communication with good spirits and hell's communication with
evil spirits, and the consequent nature of the bond of heaven
and hell with man.

All spirits (who are in the World of Spirits) are in touch
with either heaven or hell—the evil ones with hell and the
good ones with heaven.

Heaven is divided into communities, and so is hell. Each
spirit is related to a particular community. He also continues
in existence as the result of an inflow from that source; so
he acts in unison with it. This is why man is joined to heaven
and hell as he is joined to spirits, each individual with the
community he is involved in as far as his own affection—or
his own love—is concerned. For all heaven's communities
are distinguished according to affections for the good and
the true, and all hell's communities are distinguished according to affections for the evil and the false (on heaven's
communities, see above, nn. 41-45, then nn. 148-151).

295. The spirits connected to a person are of the same
quality as the person himself in affection or love. But the
good spirits are put in connection with him by the Lord,
while the evil ones are invited by the person himself.

However, the spirits with a person are changed in keeping with changes of his affections. So he has some spirits in early childhood, others in later childhood, others in young adulthood and maturity, and still others in old age. There are present in early childhood spirits who are in innocence, who therefore are in communication with the heaven of innocence, which is the inmost or third heaven. In later childhood, spirits are present who are involved in an affection for learning, who are therefore in communication with the outmost or first heaven. In young adulthood and maturity, spirits are present who are involved in an affection for what is true and what is good, hence in intelligence, who are therefore in communication with the second or intermediate heaven. But in old age, spirits are present who are involved in wisdom and innocence, who are therefore in communication with the inmost or third heaven.

This connection, however, occurs from the Lord with people who can be reformed and regenerated. It is different with people who cannot be reformed and regenerated. Good spirits are connected with them also, so that they can be restrained from evil by them as far as possible, but their direct contact is with evil spirits who are in communication with hell. As a result, they have the same kinds of spirits as they themselves are as people. If they are in love with themselves, or with money, or with revenge, or with adultery, similar spirits are with them. These spirits virtually take up residence in their evil affections. To the extent that the person cannot be restrained from an evil act by the good spirits, they set him afire. And to the extent that an affection dominates him, they cling and do not depart.

So an evil person is bonded with hell, and a good person is bonded with heaven.

296. This government of man by the Lord through spirits occurs because man is not in heaven's design. In fact, he is born into involvement in evil things which belong to hell—exactly opposite, therefore, to the Divine design. So he has to be brought back into the design, and he cannot be brought back except indirectly, through spirits.

It would be different if man were born into involvement in the good which is in accord with heaven's design. Then he would not be governed by the Lord through spirits, but by the design itself, therefore by a general inflow.

Man is governed by this general inflow in respect to the things that come from his thought and intention into act—in respect therefore to his speech and behavior. For both of these flow in a natural pattern, so that the spirits attached to the person have no share in his speech and behavior.

Animals as well are governed by the general inflow from the spiritual world because they are involved in the pattern of their life, unable to overthrow or destroy it because they have no rational faculty. On the distinction between people and animals, (see above n. 39).

297. Still on the subject of heaven's bond with the human race, it is worth knowing that the Lord Himself flows into every individual in accordance with heaven's pattern—into his inmost recesses as well as into things outermost—and arranges them to receive heaven. He rules man's outmost elements from his inmost ones and his inmost ones from his outmost ones at the same time, keeping together in the way everything, in general and in detail.

This inflow of the Lord is called the direct inflow. The other inflow, then, which occurs by means of spirits, is called the indirect inflow. The latter is maintained by means of the former.

The direct inflow, which belongs to the Lord Himself, is from His own Divine-Human, and is into the individual's intention and through his intention into his understanding. So it is into the person's "good," and through the good into what he has that is true. Or (which is the same thing) it is into love, and through love into his faith—not the other way around, and surely not into faith without love or into something true apart from something good, or into an understanding that does not arise from intention.

This Divine inflow is constant, and among good people is received into what is good, but not among evil people. Among these latter it is either rejected, stifled, or corrupted. This is the cause of their evil life, which spiritually understood is a death.

298. The spirits who are with an individual—both those bonded with heaven and those bonded with hell—never flow into the individual out of their own memory and consequent thought. For if they did flow in out of their own thought, the individual would be wholly unaware that the things that belonged to them were not his own (see above, n. 256). Rather, an affection of a love for what is good and true flows through them into the person from heaven, and an affection for what is evil and false from hell. To the extent, then, that the individual's own affection is in harmony with what is flowing in, this is accepted by him in his thought, because man's more inward thought is completely in accord with his affection or love. To the extent that it is not in harmony, however, it is not accepted.

Thus we can see that, since thought is not inserted into a person by spirits, but only an affection for something good or an affection for something evil, man has a choice because he has an area of freedom. Thus in thought he can accept the good and reject the evil, for he knows from the Word what is good and what is evil. Whatever he accepts in thought because of affection becomes part of him; whatever he does not accept in thought because of affection does not become part of him.

This allows us to conclude what the inflow in man of the

good from heaven is like, and what the inflow of evil from hell is like.

299. I have also been allowed to learn the source of man's anxiety, distress of mind, and the more inward sadness known as depression.

There are spirits who are not yet closely bonded with hell because they are still in their first state (these will be described later, when we discuss the World of Spirits). These love disorganized and vicious things that are like elements of food in the process of becoming fecal matter in the intestines. They are present therefore whenever such things occupy a person, because these matters are pleasant to them; and because of their own affection, they say evil things to each other.

The affection of their speech flows from this into the individual. If this affection is opposed to that of the individual, he is affected by sadness and depressive anxiety; if however it agrees, he is affected by delight and exhilaration.

These spirits appear next to the belly—some on its left side, some on its right, some lower, some higher, nearer and farther away —differently, that is, depending on the affections they are involved in.

From an abundance of evidence, I have been granted knowledge and corroboration that this is the source of anxiety of mind. I have seen them; I have heard them; I have felt the anxieties that welled up from them. I have talked with them. They have been driven off and the anxiety has ceased; they have returned and the anxiety has returned. I have precisely observed its increase and decrease in proportion to their approach and departure.

So it has become clear to me why some people, who do not know what conscience is because they have no conscience, blame its distress on their intestines.

300. Heaven's bond with man is not like the bond of

person with person, but is rather a bond of more inward elements that belong to his mind, thus one that pertains to his spiritual or inner person. There is also a bond with his natural or outer person through correspondences, which bond will be discussed in the next chapter, where the topic will be "Heaven's Bond with Man through the Word."

301. The proposition that heaven's bond with the human race and the human race's bond with heaven are so arranged that one is maintained by the other will also be presented in the next chapter.

302. I have talked with angels about heaven's bond with the human race, noting that while a churchman might say that everything good is from the Lord and that angels are with man, few of them believe that angels are intimately connected to man, and fewer still that they are within his thought and affection.

The angels have replied that they knew this faith and profession existed in the world, especially within the church—which surprised them, since within the church is the Word, which teaches people about heaven and its bond with man. Yet such a bond exists that a person cannot have the least thought without spirits present; and his spiritual life depends on this bond.

They have stated that the reason for the ignorance of this fact was man's belief that he lives on his own, apart from any connection with the First Reality [*Esse*] of life, and his lack of awareness that his connection exists through the heavens. Yet if this connection were disengaged, a person would instantly drop dead.

If people only believed the way things really are—that everything good is from the Lord and everything evil from hell—then they would not make anything good in themselves a matter of merit, nor would anything evil be charged to them. For in that case, they would focus on the Lord in everything good that they thought and did, and everything evil that flowed in they would throw back into the hell it came from.

But since people do not believe in any inflow from heaven or from hell, and since then in their judgment everything they think and wish is within them and therefore from them, they make the evil their own, and defile with a sense of merit the good that flows in.

34.

HEAVEN'S BOND WITH MAN THROUGH THE WORD

303. People who think from a more inward rationality are able to see that there is a connection of all things through intermediate things with a First, and that anything which is not connected disintegrates. They do know, when they think, that nothing can exist on its own—everything needs something prior to itself, so everything derives from a First. They know that the connection with the prior is like the connection of an effect with its efficient cause. When the efficient cause is taken away from its effect, then the effect breaks up and collapses.

Learned people, having held this opinion, have both seen and stated that existence is a perpetual coming into being, that all things therefore are constantly coming into being or existing from a First because they [originally] came into being from it.

But there is no way to describe briefly the nature of the connection of each particular entity with its prior and therefore with the First which is the source of everything, since this is varied and diverse. We can say broadly only that there is a connection of the natural world with the spiritual world; and that this is the source of the correspondence of all the things that exist in the natural world with all the things that exist in the spiritual world (on this correspondence, see nn. 103-115); then that there is a connection, and consequently a correspondence, of all the elements of man with all the elements of heaven (on this, see also nn. 87-102 above).

304. Man has been so created that he has a connection and bond with the Lord, but only an association with angels. The reason he has only an association with angels, not a bond, is that from creation man is like an angel as far as the more inward reaches of his mind are concerned—he has intention like an angel's and understanding like an angel's. This is why a person becomes an angel after death and has wisdom like angels' wisdom then, if he has lived according to the Divine design. So when we mention man's bond with heaven, we understand this to mean his bond with the Lord and his association with angels. For heaven is not heaven because of anything that belongs to angels, but because of the Lord's Divine (on the proposition that the Lord's Divine constitutes heaven, see above, nn. 7-12).

[2] But over and above this, man has something that angels do not—a presence not only in the spiritual world as to his more inward elements, but a presence in the natural world at the same time as to his more outward elements. His more outward elements, which are in the natural world, are all the elements of his natural or outer memory, and the things from that source that belong to his thoughts and imagination. In general, these are insights and data with their enjoyments and pleasures, to the extent that they have a worldly flavor, and also many pleasures that belong to the body's sensory capacities. Beyond these, there are the senses themselves, and speech, and behavior. All of these are the outmosts in which the Lord's Divine inflow comes to rest; for this inflow does not stay in anything intermediate, but persists through to its outmosts.

This enables us to conclude that the outmost form of the Divine design is in man; and since this is the outmost, it is the basis and foundation.

[3] To proceed, then, we note that the Lord's Divine inflow does not stop in anything intermediate, but as stated

persists to its outmosts. We note that the "intermediate" through which it passes is the angelic heaven, while its outmost is in man. We note that nothing exists which is not connected. From these reasons, it follows that heaven's connection with the human race is of such nature that one exists by reason of the other—the situation of the human race without heaven would be like that of a chain whose shackle was gone, and the situation of heaven without a human race like that of a house without a foundation.

305. But since man has broken this connection with heaven (which he has done by turning his more inward elements away from heaven, toward the world and himself, through a love of himself and the world, so withdrawing himself that he no longer serves as a basis and foundation for heaven), the Lord has arranged an intermediate to be in place of heaven's basis and foundation, and to join heaven and man together. This "intermediate" is the Word.

How the Word serves as such an intermediate is presented at some length in *Arcana Coelestia*. All this material may be found collected in the booklet, *The White Horse Mentioned in the Apocalypse* and also in the *Appendix to the Heavenly Doctrine*.

306. I have been taught from heaven that the earliest people had a direct revelation, since their more inward elements were turned toward heaven. Further, this was the source of the Lord's bond with the human race at that time. Later, however, this kind of direct revelation no longer occurred, but rather an indirect revelation by means of correspondences. In fact, every element of their Divine worship was made up of these, so that the churches of that era were called "representative churches." In those days they knew what a correspondence was and what a representation was; they knew that all things on earth corresponded to spiritual things in heaven and in the church—or depicted [*reprae-*

sentarent] them, which is the same thing. So the natural entities which were the outward forms of their worship served them as means for thinking spiritually—that is, thinking with angels.

After the knowledge with correspondences and representations was forgotten, the Word was composed, in which all the words and their meanings are correspondences, so that they have within them the spiritual or inner meaning in which angels are involved. As a result, when a person reads the Word and grasps it according to the meaning of the letter, angels are grasping it as to its inner or spiritual meaning. Actually, all the thinking of angels is spiritual, while all the thinking of man is natural. These kinds of thinking do indeed look different, but they are nevertheless one because they correspond.

This is why, after man moved away from heaven and broke the tie, the Lord arranged a way of bonding heaven with man through the Word.

307. I should like to illustrate how heaven is connected with man through the Word by means of some passages from the Word.

In the Apocalypse, the New Jerusalem is described in the following words:

> I saw a new heaven and a new earth, and the former heaven and the former earth had passed away . . . . and I saw the holy city Jerusalem . . . descending from God out of heaven. . . . The city was four-square, its length equal to its width; and the angel measured the city with a reed, to twelve thousand furlongs; and the angel measured the city with a reed, to twelve thousand furlongs; the length, width, and height . . . were equal. And he measured its wall, a hundred and forty-four cubits; the measure of the man, which is that of the angel: . . . The wall's construction was of jasper; but the city itself was of pure gold, and like pure glass; and the wall's foundations . . . were adorned with every precious stone. . . . The twelve gates were twelve pearls; . . . and the streets of the city were pure gold like clear glass.   (Rev. 21:1, 2, 16-19, 21)

The person on earth who reads this understands it only in its literal meaning—namely that the visible heaven is going to perish, and earth with it, and that a new heaven is going to come into being. Then the holy city Jerusalem will descend on a new earth, and in all its specifications will be as described.

But the angels who are with this person understand it quite differently. To be specific, they understand spiritually the details which the person understands naturally.

[2] By "a new heaven and a new earth," they understand a new church. By "the city Jerusalem descending from God out of heaven" they understand its heavenly teaching, revealed by the Lord. By the "length," "width," and "height" which are equal, and by the twelve thousand furlongs, they understand all the good and true elements of that teaching in a single grasp. By its "wall," they understand the true things that keep it safe. By "the wall's dimension, a hundred and forty-four cubits" which is "the measure of the man, which is that of the angel," they understand all these protective true elements in a single grasp, and what their quality is. By "its twelve gates" which were of pearls, they understand true elements that introduce—"pearls" do mean such true elements. By "the wall's foundations" made of precious stones, they understand the insights on which the teaching is based. By the "gold like pure glass," the substance of the city and its street, they understand the good that belongs to love, which makes the teaching and its true elements radiant.

Angels do comprehend all these things in this fashion—not, that is, the way man does. Man's natural ideas do in this manner make a transition to spiritual ideas among angels, without their knowing anything of the Word's literal meaning, as for example about the new heaven, the new earth, the new city Jerusalem, its wall, the wall's foundations, or the dimensions.

Still, angels' thoughts constantly make one with man's thoughts because they correspond. They make a one almost like a speaker's words and their import in a listener who does not focus on the words but simply on understanding.

[3] This shows how heaven is bonded with man by means of the Word. Let us take another example from the Word:

> In that day there will be a highway from Egypt to Assyria, and Assyria will come into Egypt, and Egypt into Assyria, and the Egyptians will serve Assyria. In that day Israel will be a third one to Egypt and Assyria, a blessing in the middle of the land, which Jehovah of Hosts will bless, saying, ''Blessed be my people the Egyptian, and the work of my hands the Assyrian, and my inheritance Israel.''(Isaiah 19:23-25)

From the Word's literal meaning and its inner meaning, we can decide how man thinks and how angels think when this is read. Man, from the literal meaning, thinks that the Egyptians and the Assyrians are going to be turned to God and accept Him, and that they are going to be united to the Israelite nation. But angels, in keeping with the inner meaning, think about the individual who belongs to the spiritual church that is described in that meaning, whose spiritual element is Israel, whose natural is the Egyptian, and whose rational (which is the intermediate element) is Assyria.

The second and first senses still are a unity because they correspond. So when angels think spiritually and man naturally in this way, they are bonded together almost like soul and body. The Word's inner meaning is then its soul, and the literal meaning is its body.

This is what the Word is like throughout. This shows that it is a means of bonding heaven with man, and that its literal meaning functions as a base and foundation.

308. By means of the Word, there is also a bonding of heaven with people who are outside the church, where the

Word does not occur. For the Lord's church is universal, and exists in all people who recognize something Divine and live in charity. They are then taught by angels after death, and accept Divine truths. This is discussed below in the appropriate chapter on the heathen.

In the Lord's sight, the universal church in the various lands is like one person, just as heaven is (see above, nn. 59-72). But the church where the Word is found, and where the Lord is known by means of it, is like the heart and like the lungs within that person. It is recognized that all the internal organs and members of the whole body draw their life from the heart and lungs by various paths. It is this way too with that part of the human race that lives outside the church where the Word is found, and that makes up the members of that person.

Heaven's bond through the Word with people who are far away can also be compared to light which spreads in all directions from a center. There is a Divine light within the Word. The Lord is present there, with heaven, and as a result of this presence even faraway people are in light. It would be different if no Word existed. These matters can be further explained by the points made above about heaven's form which determines associations and communications there.

This arcanum, however, is intelligible to people who are in a spiritual light, not to people who are in a natural light only. For people who are in a spiritual light see clearly countless things which people only in a natural light do not see, or see only as a fuzzy unit.

309. If this kind of Word had not been granted on this planet, this planet's people would have been cut off from heaven; and being cut off from heaven, they would no longer have been rational. People's rationality does in fact arise from the inflow of heaven's light.

The human being of this planet, you see, is of such nature that he cannot take in a direct revelation and be taught by it about Divine truths, as is possible for people who live on other planets (who have been discussed in a separate treatise). Our human being is in fact more involved in worldly matters than they, and therefore more involved in outward concerns; while it is inward elements that are receptive to revelation. If the outward elements did receive what is true, it would not be understood.

This nature of our planet's inhabitants is clearly visible in people within the church, who, even though they are informed from the Word about heaven and hell and life after death, still deny it at heart. We find among these also people who grasp especially at a reputation for erudition, who on this account might be believed to be wiser than others.

310. Sometimes when I have talked with angels about the Word, I have mentioned that it is looked down on by some people because of its plain style, that absolutely nothing is known about its inner meaning, and that consequently people do not believe that so much wisdom does lie hidden within it.

Angels have responded that the Word's style, plain though it may seem in the literal meaning, is actually of such nature that nothing whatever is of comparable excellence, since Divine wisdom lies not just within every meaning, but within every word. They have stated that this wisdom shines out in heaven. They have been eager to declare that it was heaven's light because it was the Divine-True, for the Divine-True in heaven does shine (see above, n. 132). They have also stated that without such a Word, none of heaven's light would exist among people of our planet, and that there would therefore be no bonding of heaven with them. For in the measure that heaven's light is present with someone this bonding exists; and in the same measure he has a revelation of the Divine-True by means of the Word. Man's ignorance of this bond (through the Word's spiritual meaning corresponding to its natural meaning) stems from the fact that people on this planet do not know anything about angels' spiritual thought and speech, or its difference from man's thought and speech. Unless they know this, they are wholly incapable of knowing what an inner meaning is, or therefore of knowing that this kind of bond can be established by means of it.

They have also told me that if a person knew that this kind of meaning existed, and did his thinking from some knowledge of it when he read the Word, he would come into a more inward wisdom and would then be still more closely bonded to heaven. For by this means, he would move into concepts like those of angels.

35.

HEAVEN AND HELL ARE FROM THE HUMAN RACE

311. It is quite unknown in the Christian world that heaven and hell are from the human race. In fact, it is believed that angels were created at the beginning, resulting in a heaven; and that the Devil or Satan was an angel of light, but was cast out with his faction because he became rebellious, resulting in a hell.

The existence of this kind of belief in Christendom utterly amazes angels, particularly because people do not know anything at all about heaven even though it is a leading matter of the church's doctrine. Because such ignorance is prevalent, the angels have wholeheartedly rejoiced that it has pleased the Lord to unveil to people at this time an abundance of information about heaven and about hell, so dispelling, as far as possible, the shadows which are increasing daily because the church has arrived at its end.

[2] They therefore want me to declare on their behalf that in all of heaven there is not a single angel who was created at the beginning, nor is there in hell any devil who was created an angel of light and cast down. Rather, all the individuals in both heaven and hell are from the human race. In heaven are the ones who lived in heavenly love and faith in the world; in hell are the ones who lived in hellish love and faith. Further, hell taken as a whole is what is called the Devil and Satan. The hell which is in back, where the people called evil genii live, is called the Devil; and the hell which is in front, where the people called evil spirits

233

live, is called Satan. [3] The nature of each of these hells will be described in subsequent pages.

They said that the source of Christendom's acceptance of this kind of faith about people in heaven and hell was in a few passages in the Word understood only in their literal meaning, not enlightened by any real doctrine from the Word. The literal meaning of the Word, however, unless real doctrine illuminates it, leads minds off in different directions, resulting in various kinds of ignorance, in heresies, and in errors.

312. Another reason the churchman has this belief is that he believes no person enters heaven or hell before the time of the Last Judgment. He has conceived this to mean that everything visible will then be destroyed and that new things will emerge, that the soul will return to its body, the person living as a person again because of this coming together. This belief includes the other one about angels—their being created at the beginning—because there is no way to believe that heaven and hell are from the human race when it is believed that no one arrives there before the end of the world.

[2] In order that people might be convinced that this is not so, I have been allowed to have fellowship with angels and also to talk with people in hell—this for several years now, sometimes constantly from morning to evening—and in this way to become knowledgeable about heaven and about hell. This has been allowed so that the churchman might no longer remain in his mistaken faith about resurrection at the time of judgment, about the interim condition of souls, and then about angels and the devil. This faith, being a faith in something false, is full of shadows; and for people who consider these matters from their own intelligence, it induces doubt and ultimately denial. For in their hearts they say, ''How can such a vast sky, with so many

constellations, with the sun and the moon, be destroyed and dispersed? How can the stars then fall from heaven onto the earth, when they are larger than the earth? How can bodies eaten by worms, destroyed by decay, scattered in all directions, be gathered back together to their souls? Where has the soul been all this time, and what has it been like without the power of sensation it possessed in the body?'' [3] They raise many other similar questions which, being unintelligible, do not fit in with faith, and which for many people destroy faith in the life of the soul after death, in heaven and hell, and likewise in other matters of the church's faith.

This destruction can be observed in people who say, "Who has come to us from heaven and told us that it is real? Who has told us what hell is, or whether it exists? What is this business about man being tormented by fire to eternity? What is the day of judgment? Has it not been expected for centuries, all in vain?''—along with many questions that involve a denial of everything.

[4] To prevent people who think like this (as is common with many who sound educated and learned because of worldly things, which they enjoy) from further confusing and misleading people of simple faith and heart, from casting hellish shadows on matters of God, heaven, eternal life, and other corollary matters, the more inward reaches of my spirit have been opened by the Lord, and I have in this way been allowed to talk with all the people I was acquainted with during their physical life, after they had died. I have talked with some of them for days, with some for months, with some for a year. I have talked with other people as well—so many that a hundred thousand would be an understatement. Many of these were in the heavens, and many in the hells.

I have even talked with some people a couple of days after their death, telling them that now their funeral services and arrangements were being organized for their burial. They responded that it was good to cast off the thing that had served them for a body and for bodily functions in the world. They wanted me to state that they were not dead, that they were alive, just as human as ever, that they had only journeyed from one world to another; also that they were unaware of any loss, since they were in a body and its sensations just as before, involved in understanding and intention just as before, having similar thoughts and affections, similar sensations, and similar desires, to those they had had in the world.

[5] Many people just recently deceased, once they saw that they were still alive, still people just as before, even in a similar state (for after death, everyone's first state of life is like the one he had in the world, changing gradually for him toward heaven or toward hell)—many such people were moved by a fresh joy in being alive, and said they had never believed it. At the same time, they were amazed that they had been in such ignorance, such blindness about the condition of their own life after death. They were even more amazed that church folk were in the same kind of ignorance and blindness, when of all people in all lands of the earth, they could be in light in these matters.

Thereafter, they saw for the first time the reason for this blindness and ignorance —namely that outward things, the worldly and the physical, so completely occupied and filled people's minds that they could not be raised into heaven's light, nor could church matters beyond the outer forms of doctrine be contemplated. For from worldly and physical concerns, when they are loved as much as they are these days, only shadows flow in when people go deeper.

313. Many of the learned from Christendom are stunned to see themselves after death—in a body, clothed, and housed the way they were in the world. When they recall what they had thought about life after death, spirits, heaven, and hell, they are struck with shame and admit that they had thought nonsense, and that people of simple faith had thought far more wisely than they.

An investigation was made of some learned people who had reinforced themselves in ideas like these and who gave nature credit for everything. It was discovered that their more inward reaches were quite closed and their more outward reaches opened, so that they were not looking toward heaven but toward the world and therefore toward hell. For to the extent that a person's more inward reaches are opened, he looks toward heaven; but to the extent that his more inward reaches are closed and his more outward ones opened, he looks toward hell. For man's more inward reaches are designed to accept everything that belongs to heaven, and his more outward to accept everything that belongs to the world; and people who accept the world and not heaven with it, accept hell.

314. The conclusion that heaven is from the human race can be drawn from the fact that angels' minds and human minds are alike. Both enjoy the faculty of understanding, perceiving, and intending; both are designed to accept heaven. For the human mind is just as discerning as the angelic mind. The reason it is not so discerning in the world is that it is within an earthly body, within which a spiritual mind thinks in natural fashion. But it is quite different when it is released from its tie with the body. Then it no longer thinks in a natural way, but in a spiritual way; and when it does, it thinks about matters unintelligible and inexpressible to the natural person—so it discerns like an angel. This allows the conclusion that the inside of man, which is called his spirit, is essentially an angel (see above, n. 57), which, once it is released from its earthly body, is just as much in the human form, and is an angel (on the angel's perfect human form, see above, n. 73-77). But when the inside of a person is not opened upwards, only downwards, then after the ultimate release from the body it is in a human form, but in a dreadful and diabolical one. For it cannot look up toward heaven, only down toward hell.

315. A person who has been taught about the Divine design can also understand that man is created to become an angel because the outmost form of the design is within him (n. 304), in which something can be constructed that belongs to heavenly and angelic wisdom, and which can be restored and increased.

The Divine design never comes to a halt halfway, and constructs something there without an outmost form, since it is not in its fullness and perfection. It proceeds rather to an outmost form, and once it is in its outmost form, it does construct something, and by the means there gathered, it restores itself and produces something further, which occurs by means of "procreations." So this is the locus of the seedbed of heaven.

316. The reason the Lord rose again not only in spirit, but in body as well, is that He glorified His whole human when He was in the world—that is, He made it Divine. Actually, the soul which He had from the Father was Divine in its own right, and the body was made a representation of that soul (that is, of the Father), and therefore also Divine. As a result, He alone of all people rose again in both respects. This He made clear to the disciples, who believed they were seeing a spirit when they saw Him, by saying,

See my hands and My feet, that I am Myself; touch Me and see, for a spirit does not have flesh and bones, as you see that I have.(Luke 24:36-38)

showing thereby that He was a person not only in spirit, but even in body.

317. To let it be known that man does live after death, and comes into heaven or hell depending on his life in the world, I have been shown many things about the human state after death. These will be treated below, under the topic of the World of Spirits.

36.

THE HEATHEN OR PEOPLE OUTSIDE THE CHURCH IN HEAVEN

318. It is a general opinion that people who are born outside the church, who are called heathen or gentiles, cannot be saved because they do not possess the Word and therefore have no knowledge of the Lord; and without the Lord there is no salvation. Yet we need only one fact to show that they are saved—the fact that the Lord's mercy is universal, that is toward individuals, and that they are born just as human as people within the church, who are relatively few; also that it is not their fault that they have no knowledge of the Lord.

Anyone who thinks with some enlightened rationality can see that no one is born for hell. The Lord is actually Love itself, and His love is a desire to save everyone. So He provides that everyone may have a religion, and through it may have a recognition of something Divine and a more inward life. For living by something religious is living more inwardly. Then the person focuses on the Divine; and to the extent that he does focus on this he does not focus on the world, but moves away from the world. He therefore moves away from a worldly life, which is a more outward life.

319. People can know that the Gentiles are saved just as Christians are if they know what constitutes heaven in man. For heaven is in man, and people who have heaven in themselves come into heaven. Heaven in man is recognizing the Divine and being led by the Divine. The first and foremost element of every religion is recognition of what is

240

Divine: a religion that does not recognize something Divine is not a religion. The laws of every religion focus on worship—that is, on how the Divine is to be revered so that the worship may be accepted by Him. And when this occupies a person's mind—that is, to the extent that he wants this or loves this—he is led by the Lord.

It is known that Gentiles lead just as moral a life as Christians—some of them better than Christians. A moral life is lived either for the sake of something Divine or for the sake of people in the world. A moral life that is lived for the sake of what is Divine is a spiritual life. The two look alike in outward form; but in inward form they are quite different. For the person who lives a moral life for the sake of what is Divine is led by what is Divine, while the person who lives a moral life for the sake of people in the world is being led by himself.

[2] Let an example shed light on this. The person who does not wrong his neighbor because it is against religion, therefore against what is Divine, refrains from wrongdoing from a spiritual source. But the person who does not wrong his neighbor simply out of fear of the law, or of loss of reputation or prestige or profit—therefore for the sake of himself and the world—refrains from wrongdoing from a natural source, and is being led by himself. The life of the latter is natural, while the life of the former is spiritual. The person whose moral life is spiritual has heaven within him, but the person whose moral life is not spiritual does not have heaven within him. The reason is that heaven flows in from a higher level and opens a person's more inward reaches, flowing through the more inward into the more outward. But the world flows in from a lower level and opens the more outward but not the more inward. For inflow does not occur from the natural world into the spiritual, but from the spiritual into the natural. This is why, if heaven

is not accepted at the same time as the world the more inward reaches are closed.

This enables us to see just which people do accept heaven in themselves and which people do not. [3] But the heaven in one person is not the same as the heaven in someone else. It varies in each individual depending on his affection for the good and for what is true that derives from it. People who are engaged in an affection for what is good because of what is Divine, love the Divine-True, for the good and the true love each other and want to be joined together. Gentiles, consequently, although they are not involved in things genuinely true in the world, do ultimately accept them in the other life because of their love.

320. There was a particular spirit from the Gentiles who in the world had lived in charity according to his religious persuasion. When he heard some Christians discussing matters of belief (spirits discuss much more thoroughly and keenly than men, especially the topic of things good and true), being surprised that they argued so much, he said that he did not want to hear these discussions because they were being carried on on the basis of appearances and fallacies. "If I am good," he informed them, "I can know which things are true from what is good itself; and what I do not know I can acquire."

321. I have been taught in many ways about Gentiles who have led a moral life, living in obedience and good order and mutual charity according to their religious persuasion and who have thereby acquired some element of conscience. I have learned that they have been accepted in the other life and are taught there with painstaking care by angels about the good and true elements of faith. I have been told that when they are taught, they behave temperately, understandingly, and wisely, readily both accepting truths and absorbing them. For they have not fashioned principles of falsity for themselves in opposition to the true elements of faith, principles which would have to be broken down (to say nothing about libels against the Lord) as have many Christians who do not favor any idea of Him except as an ordinary man. It is different with Gentiles, who, on hearing that God became Man and thereby made Himself known in the world, promply recognize and worship the Lord. They say that God made Himself expressly known because He is the God of heaven and earth and because the human race belongs to Him.

It is a matter of Divine Truth that there is no salvation apart from the Lord, but this has to be understood as meaning that there is no salvation except from the Lord.

There are many planets in the universe, all full of inhabitants. Hardly any of them know that the Lord donned a human nature on our planet. Still, because they do worship the Divine in human form, they are received and led by the Lord; on this topic, one may refer to the booklet, *Earths in the Universe*.

322. There are both wise and simple people among the Gentiles, just as there are among Christians. To help me learn what they are like, I have been allowed to talk with them, sometimes for hours or days. But nowadays there are not the wise ones there were in olden times, especially in the Ancient Church, which was distributed over much of the Asian continent, and from which religion spread to many heathen. To let me know what they were like, I have been allowed to hold friendly conversation with some of them.

A particular person was with me who had once been one of the wiser ones and had consequently been well known in the learned world. I talked with him on various topics, and was given to believe that it was Cicero. Since I knew that he was wise, my conversation with him was about wisdom, understanding, order, the Word, and lastly the Lord.

[2] On wisdom, he said that no other wisdom exists than that which belongs to life, and that wisdom could not be predicated of anything else. On understanding, he said that wisdom was its source. On order, he said that it comes from the highest God, and that living by that order is being wise and understanding. In connection with the Word, when I read him a passage from the prophets he was overjoyed, mainly because the individual names and words pointed to more inward matters. He was quite astonished that educated people nowadays do not find pleasure in this kind of pursuit.

I saw clearly that the more inward reaches of his mind were opened. He said that he could not stay there, because he perceived something holier than he could bear, and was being deeply moved as a result.

[3] Eventually, my conversation with him was about the Lord, His birth as a Man, yet begotten by God, His putting off the maternal human and putting on the Divine Human, and His being the one who rules the universe. His response was that he knew many things about the Lord, and in his own way could grasp that it could not have happened in any other way if the human race were to be saved.

Meanwhile, some evil Christians were spouting various libels. But he paid no attention to them, saying that this came as no surprise, since in their physical lives they had not absorbed the kind of thing they should have, and that until this kind of libel is broken down, they are unable to let in ideas that affirm, the way people can who lack knowledge.

323. I have also been allowed to talk with other people who had died in olden times and who had been among the wiser ones then. I first saw them in front of me at a distance, and they were able there to grasp the more inward elements of my thought very completely. From a single thought-concept they could know a whole series, and fill it with delightful elements of wisdom with charming representations. This led to my perceiving that they were among the wiser ones; and I was told that they were from olden times.

Thereupon they came nearer, and when I read them a passage from the Word, they were thoroughly delighted. I perceived their actual delight and pleasure, which arose mainly from the fact that each and every thing they heard from the Word was representative and indicative of things celestial and spiritual.

They stated that in their own times, when they lived in the world, their manner of thinking and speaking—of writing as well—was of the same kind, and that this was their pursuit of wisdom.

324. As far as the Gentiles who are living noawdays are concerned, however, they are not wise, but many are simple-hearted. Eventually, though, the ones who have lived in mutual charity do accept wisdom in the other life. I may cite an example or two of these.

While I was reading the seventeenth and eighteenth chapters of Judges (about Micha, whose idol and teraphim and Levite the Danites stole), there was a spirit from the heathen who during his physical life had been an idol-worshipper. When he listened attentively to what happened to Micah, the pain he suffered because of his idol which the Danites stole, the pain came upon him, and affected him so severely that he scarcely knew what he was thinking on account of it. This pain was perceived, as was an innocence in the details of his affections at the same time.

Some Christian spirits were nearby, noticed him, and were amazed that this idol-worshipper was moved by such an affection of mercy and innocence.

Thereafter, good spirits talked with him, saying that the idol was not to be worshipped, and that he could understand this because he was a human being. Rather, he should think beyond the idol, about God the Creator and Guide of all heaven and all the earth, and that this God was the Lord.

While they were saying this, I was allowed to perceive the more inward condition of his worship, which was conveyed to me as far holier than that of the Christians.

We may conclude from this that Gentiles enter heaven more readily than Christians noawadays, in keeping with the Lord's words in Luke:

> Then they will come from the East and from the West, and from the North and the South, and will take their places in the kingdom of God: and lo, there are last ones who will be first, and there are first ones who will be last.   (Luke 13:29f)

For in the condition in which that Gentile was, he could absorb all the elements of faith and accept them with an inner affection. There was a mercy in him that was a quality of love, and within his ignorance there was innocence. When these are present, all the elements of faith are accepted freely, and even with joy. Thereafter he was received among the angels.

325. I heard a single chorus at a distance one morning; from representations of the chorus I was granted a recognition that they were Chinese. They were bringing a kind of woolly goat, then a cake made of millet, and an ivory spoon, and a kind of conceptualization of a floating city.

They wanted to come closer to me, and when they were at hand, they said they wanted to be alone with me so that they could bring what they were thinking out into the open. But they were told that they were not alone, and that there were others who felt insulted at their wish to be alone, since they were guests.

Once they perceived this resentment, they sank into thought as to whether they had been false to the neighbor and whether anyone had claimed for himself what belongs to others. Since all thoughts in the other life are communicated, I was allowed to perceive this agitation of their minds. It had to do with the realization that they had accidentally wounded others. Then there was an element of shame as a result, and elements at the same time of other honest affections; from which one could recognize that they were gifted with charity.

Shortly thereafter I talked with them, eventually about the Lord. When I called Him the Christ, there was a particular perceptible distaste among them. But the reason was disclosed, namely that they had brought this distaste with them from the world because they knew that Christians lived worse lives than they did, lives without charity. But when I called Him "the Lord," they were deeply moved.

They were then taught by angels that Christian doctrine above all others in the whole world enjoins love and charity, but that there are few people who live by it.

There are Gentiles who have realized from conversation and report while they lived in the world, that Christians lived evil lives—in adultery, for example, in hatred, in strife, in drunkenness—in a kind of behavior that horrified them, because this kind of behavior is opposed to their religious principles. In the other life, these people are relatively hesitant about accepting true elements of faith. But they are taught by angels that Christian doctrine, even the faith itself, teaches something quite different. Christians, though, live by their doctrinal precepts less than Gentiles do. When they grasp this, they accept true elements of faith and worship the Lord, albeit gradually.

326. It is customary for Gentiles who have worshipped some god in an image or statue, or some idol, to be introduced when they enter the other life to people who stand in lieu of their gods or idols, so that they may shed their illusions. After they have been with them for a few days, they are brought away.

People who have worshipped men are introduced sometimes to the people themselves, sometimes to others who stand in their stead. Many of the Jews, then, are introduced to Abraham, Jacob, Moses, or David. But when they see that these have the same human nature as others and that they can be of no assistance to them, they are ashamed, and are taken to their places in keeping with their lives.

Among the Gentiles in heaven, the most beloved are the Africans. They accept the good and true elements of heaven more readily than others. They want first of all to be known as obedient, but not as faithful. They say that Christians, since they possess a doctrine of faith, can be called faithful; but not they themselves unless they accept it—or, in their own words, are able to accept it.

327. I have talked with some people who were in the Ancient Church (by the Ancient Church, we mean the one after the Flood, spread over many realms, namely through Assyria, Mesopotamia, Syria, Ethiopia, Libya, Egypt, Philistia as far as Tyre and Sidon, and through the land of Canaan on both sides of the Jordan), people who at that time had known about the Lord, had known that He was going to come, had absorbed the good elements of faith, but eventually had deviated and become idolaters.

They were toward the front on the left, in a place full of shadows, and in wretched condition. Their speech was rather fluty, in monotone, and almost devoid of rational thought. They said they had been there for many centuries, and that they were released occasionally so that they could serve others in different functions, which were menial.

This led to thought about many Christians who are not outwardly idolaters, but are inwardly, being worshippers of themselves and the world and denying the Lord at heart—what lot awaits them in the other life.

328. It may be seen above (n. 308) that the Lord's church is distributed over the whole world—it is universal—that it includes all people who live in the good of charity in accord with their own religious persuasion; that the church where the Word is known and the Lord is known through it, is to those outside that church like the heart and lungs in a person, from which all the members of the body live—differently in keeping with their forms, locations, and connections.

37.

CHILDREN IN HEAVEN

329. Some people hold the belief that only children born within the church enter heaven, not children born outside the church. The reason they give is that children within the church have been baptized, and by means of baptism have been introduced into the faith of the church.

These people, however, do not know that no one gains heaven or faith by means of baptism. Baptism simply serves as a sign and reminder that the person needs to be reborn, and that the person born within the church can be reborn because the Word is there, in which are Divine truths for regeneration. The Lord also is known there and He is the source of regeneration.

May they know, then, that every child, wherever he was born—within the church or outside it, of godly or of godless parents —every child is accepted by the Lord when he dies and is brought up in heaven. According to the Divine design, he is taught and filled with affections for what is good. By means of these, he is filled with insights into what is true. Then, as he is made complete in understanding and wisdom, he is introduced into heaven and becomes an angel.

Everyone who thinks rationally is capable of understanding that no one is born for hell, but everyone for heaven; and that the individual himself is at fault for entering hell, with children being incapable of guilt as yet.

330. Children who die are just as much children in the other life. They possess the same childlike mind, the same innocence within their ignorance, the same gentleness in all respects. They are only in beginnings in order to become angels. For children are not angels, but do become angels.

Actually, everyone who departs this world finds himself in a similar life state—the child in a child's state, the adolescent in an adolescent's state, the young adult, the adult, the aged, in the state of a young adult, an adult, or an elderly person—although later each individual's state does change. The state of children has an advantage over that of others in this respect, that children are in innocence, and evil is not yet rooted in them by their real life. Their innocence is of such nature that all the elements of heaven can be grafted into it, for innocence is a container for the true that belongs to faith and the good that belongs to love.

331. The state of children in the other life is much better than that of children in this world, since they are not clothed with an earthly body, but with one like an angel's. An earthly body is intrinsically heavy. It does not accept basic sensations and basic impulses from the more inward or spiritual world, but from the more outward or natural world. So children in this world learn to walk, to control their movements, and to talk. Even their senses, such as sight and hearing, are opened only by practice.

It is different with children in the other life. Because they are spirits, they act immediately in accord with what is within them, walking without practice. They even talk—at first, to be sure, from general affections that are not resolved into thought-concepts. But before long, they are introduced into these as well, which can happen because their more outward aspects are at one with their more inward ones.

On the flow of angels' speech from affections differentiated by means of thought-concepts, with the result that their speech is wholly shaped by thoughts from affections, (see above nn. 234-245).

332. As soon as children are revived (which happens

immediately after their decease), they are borne into heaven and entrusted to angels of the feminine gender who during their physical life had loved children tenderly and had also loved God. Because they had in the world loved all children with a virtually maternal tenderness, they accept these as their own. And the children, from their inborn nature, love them as though they were their own mothers. Each woman has as many children as she wants from her spiritual parental affection.

This heaven appears in front of the area of the forehead, right on the line or ray along which angels look toward the Lord. It has this location because all children are under the direct care of the Lord. Also the heaven of innocence, which is the third heaven, flows in among them.

333. Children vary in their native qualities. Some have the nature of spiritual angels, some the nature of celestial angels. Children of celestial nature appear toward the right in heaven; children of spiritual nature appear toward the left.

In the Grand Man who is heaven, all children are in the region of the eyes. Those of a spiritual nature are in the region of the left eye, and those of a celestial nature are in the region of the right eye. This is because the Lord appears in front of the left eye to angels in the spiritual kingdom, and in front of the right eye to angels in the celestial kingdom (see above, n. 118).

Since children are in the region of the eyes in the Grand Man or heaven, we can see that they are under the Lord's direct observation and care.

334. Let us describe briefly how children are raised in heaven. From their guardian, they learn to talk. Their first speech is simply an affectional sound that gradually becomes clearer as thought-concepts become involved. For thought-concepts stemming from affections are the basis of all angelic speech (material on this subject may be found in the appropriate chapter, nn. 234-245).

First of all, there are subtly instilled into their affections (which all spring from innocence) the kinds of thing that are presented to their sight, quite delightful things. Because they are from a spiritual source, elements of heaven flow in simultaneously within them, and the infants' more inward levels are opened by this means. So day by day they become more perfect.

Once this first stage is completed, they are transferred to another heaven where they are educated by teachers; and so the process continues.

335. Children are taught mainly by means of representations suited to their native gifts—representations so beautiful, and so filled from within with wisdom at the same time, that no one could ever believe it. In this way, step by step, an understanding is instilled into them which draws its soul from what is good.

At this point I may describe a pair of representations I have been privileged to see, which may be taken as typical of other representations.

At the outset, they were portraying the Lord rising from His tomb, and at the same time the union of His Human with His Divine. This happened in such a wise way that it surpassed all human wisdom, yet at the same time it was in the innocent style of infants.

They represented a concept of a tomb, but not a concept of the Lord with it except so indirectly that one could scarcely tell that it was the Lord, as though He were a great way off. This is because there is something funereal about the tomb which they were dispelling by this means.

After this, they carefully let into the tomb something airy that looked thin and water-like, by which they indicated (albeit with a suitable indirectness) the spiritual life inherent in baptism.

After this, I saw their depiction of the Lord's descent to those who were bound and His ascent with them to heaven, all done with matchless care and reverence. The childlike aspect was that they let down little cords, not at all obvious, very delicate and slight, with which they supported the Lord in His ascent. Ever present was a holy fear lest any element in the portrayal border on anything that did not contain something spiritual and heavenly.

There are other portrayals in which they are engaged, by which they are guided to recognitions of what is true and affections for what is good, for example plays adapted to the minds of children.

336. I was also shown how delicate their understanding is. While I was praying the Lord's Prayer, and they were flowing into my thought-concepts from their own understanding, I sensed that their inflow was so delicate and mild that it was composed almost entirely of affection. At the same time, though, one could notice that their understanding had been opened by the Lord, for what came from them seemed to be flowing through them.

The Lord flows into children's concepts above all from their inmost realms, for nothing has closed these, as is the case with adults —no principles of falsity against understanding what is true, no life of evil against accepting what is good and thus becoming wise.

This leads to the conclusion that children do not enter the angelic state immediately after death, but are led into it step by step by means of insights into what is good and true, all in keeping with the whole heavenly design. For the slightest elements of the inner nature of every one of them are known to the Lord. So they are led in accord with each and every shift in their own tendency, toward acceptance of things true derived from what is good, and of things good derived from what is true.

337. I have also been shown how everything is instilled into them by means of pleasant and charming things suited to their gifts. I have been allowed to see children most beautifully clothed with garlands of flowers glowing in the loveliest heavenly hues around their breasts and their slender arms.

Once I was allowed to see some children and their nurses, with some virgins in a garden park—not a wooded park, but one with banks of laurel with most elegant gateways and paths giving access to its inner areas. The children themselves were garlanded with the same flowers, and as they entered, the shrubbery over the entrance became more joyfully radiant.

We can thus ascertain the quality of their delights, and can also ascertain that they are led into the good elements of innocence and charity by means of charming and pleasant things, with these good elements constantly instilled into the pleasant and charming means by the Lord.

338. I have been shown, by a means of communication common in the other life, what children's concepts are like when they see any particular object. It was as though each and every thing was alive, so that life is inherent in the individual concepts of their thought. I could also see that children on earth have virtually the same concepts when they are involved in their play, not yet having the kind of considered opinion adults do about what is inanimate.

339. It was stated above that angels are either of a celestial or of a spiritual bent. The ones of a celestial bent are clearly distinguished from the ones of a spiritual bent. The former think and speak a little more gently, so that almost nothing is noticeable except a fluent something stemming from a love of what is good, for the Lord, and toward the neighbor. The latter do not function so gently; instead, something rather like fluttering wings is noticeable in certain situations among them. This is evident from their indignation, among other things.

340. Many people manage to suppose that children remain children in heaven and are like children compared to angels. People who do not know what an angel is have managed to confirm themselves in this opinion by the likenesses in churches here and there where angels are portrayed as children; but the actual situation is quite different.

Understanding and wisdom constitute an angel. Just as long as children do not possess these attributes, they are with angels but are not themselves angels. But once they become understanding and wise, they become angels. Further—which surprised me—they do not then look like children, but like adults. For at that point they are no longer of a childlike nature, but of a more mature, angelic nature. This is inherent in understanding and wisdom.

The reason that children look more mature as they become more perfect in understanding and wisdom is that understanding and wisdom are spiritual nourishment itself. So the very things that nourish their minds are nourishing their bodies as well. This stems from correspondence, for the form of their bodies is nothing but the outward form of their more inward elements.

It is worth knowing that children in heaven do not mature beyond the beginning of young adulthood, and remain at that point to eternity. To let me be quite sure that this is the case, I have been allowed to talk with some people who were reared as children in heaven and grew up there. I have talked with some when they were children, and then with the same people when they were young adults. I have heard from them about the course of their lives from the one age to the other.

341. On the basis of statements made above (nn. 276-283) about the innocence of angels in heaven, we may establish that innocence is what accepts all the elements of heaven, and that the innocence of children is therefore the matrix of all affections for what is good and true. The statements we refer to are the following: that innocence is wanting to be led by the Lord and not by oneself, that a person is involved in innocence to the extent that he is moved out of his own selfhood, and that the measure of his freedom from his selfhood is the measure of his involvement in the Lord's "Selfhood." The Lord's "Selfhood" is what is known as the Lord's righteousness and worth.

The innocence of children, however, is not real innocence because thus far it lacks wisdom. Real innocence is wisdom; for to the extent that a person is wise he loves to be led by the Lord—which is the same as saying that a person is wise to the extent that he is led by the Lord.

[2] So infants are led from the outward innocence in which they are first involved (which is known as the innocence of infancy) into inward innocence, which is the innocence of wisdom. This latter innocence is the goal of all their instruction and advancement. So when they attain the innocence of wisdom, the innocence of childhood which had served them as a matrix in the interim is bonded to them.

[3] The nature of children's innocence was depicted to me as something wood-like, almost devoid of life, which is brought to life as they are perfected through the agency of insights into what is true and affections for what is good. Afterwards, the nature of real innocence was depicted by a very beautiful child, very much alive, and naked. Actually, the innocents who are in the inmost heaven and therefore nearest the Lord, look quite like children in the sight of other angels. And some are naked, since innocence is portrayed by a nakedness which does not occasion shame. This is what we read about the first man and his wife in the

Garden (*Genesis* 2:25); this is also why, when their state of innocence came to an end, they were ashamed of their nakedness and hid (*Genesis* 3:7, 10, 11).

In summary, the wiser angels are, the more innocent they are; and the more innocent they are, the more they look like children to themselves. This is why "infancy" in the Word indicates innocence (see above, n. 278).

342. I have talked with angels about children—whether they were free of evils because they did not have any realized evil like adults. But I was told that they are just as much involved in what is evil, that they too are actually nothing but evil. But like all angels, they are withheld from what is evil and held in what is good by the Lord, so completely that it seems to them that they in their own right are involved in what is good. For this reason, after they become mature in heaven, to prevent them from involvement in the false notion that the good they have is from themselves and not from the Lord, they are occasionally allowed to slip back into their inherited evil elements, and are left in them until they know and realize and believe that this is in fact the case.

One particular person who had died as an infant and grown up in heaven held this kind of opinion. [2] He was the son of a certain king. So he was allowed to slip back into his inborn life of evil things; and I saw then from his life-sphere that he had a passion for dominating others and took acts of adultery lightly. For him, these were evils acquired by heredity from his parents. But once he recognized that this was his own quality, he was again accepted among the angels he had been with before.

[3] In the other life, a person never suffers punishment because of inherited evil, because it does not belong to him. That is, he is not at fault for being what he is in this respect. Rather, he suffers punishment because of the realized evil

that does belong to him—that is, the amount of inherited evil that he has made his own by his life activities.

This remission of grown-up children into the state of their hereditary evil is not to make them suffer punishment, but to let them know that in their own right they are nothing but evil, and that they are delivered from the hell within them into heaven because of the Lord's mercy. So they know that they are not in heaven because of their own worth, but because of the Lord. This prevents them from showing off in front of others because of the good within them, for this is in opposition to the good of mutual love, just as it is in opposition to the true content of faith.

343. Several times, when numbers of children were with me in groups at the same time (these were still wholly in a childlike state), they sounded like something soft and disorganized, as though they were not yet coordinated as they would be when more mature. Surprisingly, some spirits who were with me could not refrain from urging them to speak (this kind of desire was innate in the spirits). But every time, I noticed that the children balked and did not want to talk. The refusal and resistance—accompanied by a kind of resentment—are things I have often perceived. When they were given the ability to talk, they kept saying only that it wasn't so.

I was taught that this is what children's temptation is like, to accustom and introduce them not only to resisting what is false and evil, but also to not thinking, speaking, or acting solely at the prompting of someone else. This has the ultimate goal of their not letting themselves be led by anyone but the Lord alone.

344. From the matters just cited we can draw conclusions as to the nature of the upbringing of children in heaven. Specifically, it is a matter of their introduction, by means of understanding what is true and wisdom in what is good, into angelic life, which is love to the Lord and mutual love, both containing innocence.

How different this is from the upbringing of children on earth in many cases can be deduced from the following example.

I was in the street of a large city and saw some small boys involved in a fight. People crowded around, looking on with great pleasure, and I was told that the parents themselves urged their children into these fights.

The good spirits and angels who were seeing these events through my eyes were so repelled that I could feel their horror —particularly at the fact that parents were egging their children into such situations. They said that parents in this way snuff out at this early age all mutual love that infants have from the Lord, and lead them into attitudes of hatred and vengefulness. As a result, by their deliberate behavior they shut their children out of heaven, where there is nothing but mutual love. Let any parents who wish their children well, then, beware of this kind of behavior.

345. Let us now state the nature of the difference between people who die as adults and people who die as children.

People who die as adults have a plane acquired from the earthly, material world, and take it with them. This plane is their memory and its natural, physical affection. This remains settled and then quiesces, but all the while it is serving as an outmost plane for their thought after death, since their thought flows into it.

As a result, the nature of this plane and the way the rational corresponds with its contents determine the nature of the person himself after death.

In contrast, children who died in childhood and were brought up in heaven do not have this kind of plane. Instead, they have a "natural-spiritual" plane. This is because they draw nothing from the physical world and the earthly body.

Consequently, they are incapable of involvement in such crude affections and their resultant thoughts; in fact they draw everything from heaven.

Particularly, children do not know that they were born in the world, so they believe they were born in heaven. This means that they do not know what a birth other than a spiritual one is—a spiritual birth being one that occurs by means of insights into things good and true, and by the intelligence and wisdom that make a person a person. Since these things come from the Lord, they believe that they belong to the Lord Himself, and love this fact.

Still, the state of people who have matured on earth can become just as perfect as that of children who grow up in heaven, if they set aside bodily and wordly loves (which are loves of self and the world) and accept spiritual loves in their place.

38.

WISE AND SIMPLE PEOPLE IN HEAVEN

346. People believe that the wise will have more glory and distinction in heaven than the simple, because it is stated in *Daniel*,

> The intelligent will shine as with the radiance of the firmament, and people who turn many to righteousness like the stars, to eternity. (Daniel 12:3)

But few people know just who are meant by "the intelligent" and by "people who turn many to righteousness." By and large, it is believed that this means the people who are known as scholarly and learned, especially ones who have done teaching in the church and have been better than others at teaching and preaching, and of these, primarily the ones who have converted large numbers of people to the faith.

In this world, all people of this kind are believed to be intelligent; yet they are not "the intelligent in heaven" described in Daniel unless their intelligence is a heavenly intelligence. The nature of this intelligence is to be described in the sections which follow.

347. Heavenly intelligence is an inner intelligence arising from a love of what is true, not for the sake of any glory in the world, not for the sake of glory in heaven, but for the sake of what is true itself, which occasions a most inward emotion and delight.

People who are moved and delighted by the truth itself are moved and delighted by heaven's light—and if they are moved by heaven's light, then they are moved by the Divine-True and in fact by the Lord Himself. For heaven's light is the Divine-True, and the Divine-True is the Lord in heaven (see above, nn. 126-140).

The only area where this light can enter is the more inward reaches of the mind, since the more inward reaches of the mind are made to receive this light. It enters in such a way that it does in fact move and delight. For anything that flows in from heaven and is received, has within itself something pleasurable and delightful. This is the source of a genuine affection for what is true, which is an affection for what is true for the sake of what is true.

People who are engaged in this affection (or, what is the same thing, people who are engaged in this love) are engaged in heavenly intelligence, and do shine in heaven like the radiance of the firmament. The reason for their radiance is that the Divine-True, wherever it occurs in heaven, is bright (see above, n. 132). Further, the firmament of heaven refers by correspondence to that aspect of intellect, in angels or men alike, that is in heaven's light.

[2] In contrast, people who are engaged in a love for what is true for the sake of glory in the world or for glory in heaven, cannot shine in heaven. This is because they are not delighted and moved by heaven's light itself, but by the world's light. This latter light, without the former, is simply darkness. Actually, a glory of self is dominant because it is the "end for which." And when that glory is the goal, then the person in question focuses primarily on himself and regards the truths that promote his glory only as means to an end, as slaves. For the person who loves Divine truths for the sake of his own glory focuses on himself, not the Lord, within the Divine truths. Consequently he deflects his sight (which is a matter of understanding and faith) from heaven to the world, and from the Lord to himself. This is why he is in the world's light and not in heaven's light.

[3] In outward appearance, to other people, people of this

sort look just as intelligent and learned as people who are in heaven's light. This is because they talk in similar fashion—sometimes outwardly even more wisely because they are spurred by self-love and skilled at imitating heavenly affections. But all the while, in the inner form in which they appear before angels, they are completely different.

We may to some extent determine from this just who are meant by "the intelligent" who will shine in heaven like the radiance of the firmament. Now we may state just who are meant by "people who turn many to righteousness," who will shine like stars.

348. By "people who turn many to righteousness" are meant those who are wise. In heaven, people are called wise who are involved in what is good. The people there who are involved in what is good are the ones who commit Divine truths to life immediately. For when something Divine and true becomes a matter of life, it becomes good. It actually becomes a matter of intention and love, and anything that is a matter of intention and love is called good. Such people are therefore called wise, because wisdom is a matter of life.

In contrast, those people are called intelligent who do not commit Divine truths to life immediately, but who commit them first to memory, from which they are later retrieved and applied to life.

The nature and extent of the difference between the former and the latter may be seen in the chapter dealing with the two kingdoms of heaven, the celestial and the spiritual (nn. 20-28), and in the chapter dealing with the three heavens (nn. 29-40).

People who are in the Lord's celestial kingdom, just like those who are in the third or central heaven, are called "righteous" because they credit no element of righteousness to themselves, but all to the Lord. The Lord's righteousness in heaven is the good that is from the Lord. So such people are meant by "those who turn many to righteousness." These are also the ones the Lord mentioned,

> The righteous shall shine like the sun in my Father's kingdom. (Matthew 13:43)

Their shining like the sun stems from their being engaged in love from the Lord to the Lord; and this love is meant by "the sun" (see above, nn. 116-125). The light these people have is actually flame-like, and their thought-concepts draw on this flame-like element because they accept the good content of love directly from the Lord as the Sun in heaven.

349. Everyone who has gotten himself intelligence and wisdom in the world is accepted in heaven and becomes an angel, each individual in keeping with his kind and amount of intelligence and wisdom. In fact, anything a person acquires in the world does endure, and he takes it with him after death. Further, it is increased and filled—but within, not beyond, the limits of the level of his affection and desire for what is true and good. People who have little such affection and desire accept little, but still just as much as they can accept within the limits of that level. But people who have an abundance of affection and desire accept in abundance. The actual level of affection is like a measure of capacity that is filled full, with more for the person whose measure is large, and less for the one whose measure is small. The reason for this is that love (to which affection and desire belong) accepts whatever is suitable to it; so the amount of love determines how much it can accept.

This is the meaning of the Lord's words,

> To everyone that has, it shall be given, so that he shall have a greater abundance. (Matthew 13:12; 25:29)

> Into the bosom shall be given good measure, pressed down, shaken, and overflowing. (Luke 6:38)

350. Everyone is admitted to heaven who has loved what is true and good for the sake of what is true and good. The people who have loved a great deal, then, are the ones who are called wise; the people who have loved a little are the ones who are called simple. The wise in heaven are in a bright light, the simple in less light, each in proportion to the level of his love for what is good and true.

Loving what is true and good for the sake of what is true and good, is intending and doing what is true and good. For the people who intend and do are the ones who love, not the people who do not intend and do. These are also the people who love the Lord and who are loved by Him, because the good and the true come from the Lord. And since they do come from the Lord, within them (the good and the true) is the Lord. Accordingly, He is with people who accept what is good and true in their lives by intending and acting.

Further, if a person is looked at as he is in himself, he is nothing but what he has that is good and true, and his quality is that of his intention and understanding. So we can see that insofar as a person's intention is formed from what is good and his understanding formed from what is true, he is loved by the Lord.

"Being loved by the Lord" means loving the Lord as well, since love is mutual. The Lord enables His beloved to love.

351. It is believed in the world that people who know a great many things—whether from the doctrine of the church and the Word or from the sciences—see true things more deeply and precisely than others, and are therefore more intelligent and wise. People like this hold the same belief about themselves. But let us next describe what true, counterfeit, and false intelligence and wisdom are.

[2] True intelligence and wisdom are seeing what is true

and good, thereby seeing what is false and evil, and distinguishing these clearly, doing this by a more inward insight and perception.

There are more inward and more outward elements to every individual. The more inward elements are the ones that belong to the inner or spiritual person; the more outward elements are the ones that belong to the outer or natural person. The way the more inward elements are formed and work together with the more outward ones determines the way the person sees and perceives.

A person's more inward elements can be formed only in heaven, while the more outward ones are formed in the world.

When the inner elements are formed in heaven, then the things which are there flow into the outer elements that come from the world, and shape them to correspond—that is, to act in concert with them. When this is done, then the person sees and perceives from what is more internal.

The only way more inward elements can be formed is for the individual to focus on the Divine and on heaven; for as mentioned, the more inward elements are formed in heaven. The person focuses on the Divine when he believes the Divine and believes that this is the source of everything true and good, therefore of all intelligence and wisdom. He also believes the Divine when he wants to be led by the Lord. There is no other way for a person's more inward reaches to be opened.

[3] A person who is involved in that faith and in a life conformable to faith is involved in the ability and capacity to become intelligent and wise. But if he is to become intelligent and wise, he needs to keep learning many things—not just things of heaven, but things of earth as well. He needs to learn things of heaven from the Word and the church, and things of the world from the sciences. To

the extent that he keeps learning and applies this to his life, he does become intelligent and wise. For to this extent, his more inward sight (which is a property of his discernment) and his more inward affection (which is a property of his intention) are perfected.

Simple people of this sort are ones whose more inward reaches are opened, but are not developed by the agency of spiritual, moral, civil, and natural truths. They perceive things true when they hear them, but they do not see them in themselves. Wise people of this sort are ones whose more inward reaches are not only opened, but are developed as well. They both see truths within themselves, and perceive them.

We can see from this what true intelligence and wisdom are.

352. Counterfeit intelligence and wisdom are not seeing and perceiving what is true and good (and thereby what is false and evil) from anything more inward, but believing that things are true and good or false and evil because other people say so, and thereafter corroborating it.

Because people like this do not see what is true from itself, but from someone else, they are just as capable of adopting and believing something false as something true, and of corroborating it so that it seems true. For anything that is corroborated takes on the look of truth, and there is nothing that cannot be corroborated.

Their more inward levels are opened downward only, while their more outward levels are opened insofar as they have engaged in corroboration. As a result, the light they see by is not heaven's light but the world's light, which is called natural lighting [*lumen*]. In this lighting, false things can shine as though they were true. If they are corroborated they can even gleam; but not in heaven's light.

The less intelligent and wise people of this sort are the

ones who have corroborated themselves a great deal; the more intelligent and wise are the ones who have corroborated themselves less.

[2] We can see from this what counterfeit intelligence and wisdom are. But people do not belong to this class who in childhood have assented to things they have heard from their teachers, if in their adolescence (when they think from their own understanding) they do not cling to these opinions but long for truth and seek it because of their longing, being deeply moved when they find it. Because they are moved by what is true for its own sake, they see what is true before they corroborate it.

[3] Let us take an example. There was a discussion among some spirits about the reason animals are born into all the information consonant with their natures, while man is not. The reason was given, that animals are within the proper design of their life, while man is not. So man needs to be led into his proper design by means of insights and information. If, however, man were born into the proper design of his life—which is loving God above all, and the neighbor as himself—then he would be born into intelligence and wisdom, and consequently into faith in everything true, to the extent that his insights concurred.

The good spirits immediately saw this and perceived that it was true, simply from the light of truth. But some spirits who had established themselves in faith alone, thereby pushing love and charity aside, could not understand it. This was because the light of the false which they had corroborated in themselves veiled the light of the true.

353. False intelligence and wisdom are every kind that is devoid of a recognition of what is Divine. In fact, all people who do not recognize what is Divine, but rather recognize nature instead of what is Divine, do their thinking on a physical sense basis and are wholly sense-oriented, no matter how scholarly or learned people believe they are. Their scholarship rises no higher than the kind of material that is visible to their physical sight in the world, which they keep in their memories. And their insight into these matter is almost physical, even though this is the same information that serves really intelligent people for the building up of understanding. By ''information'' we mean the various kinds of experimental findings—those of physics, astronomy, chemistry, mechanics, geometry, anatomy, psychology, philosophy, the history of nations and the realm of literature, criticism, and language study.

[2] There are experts who deny the Divine and do not raise their thoughts any higher than the sensory data that belong to the outward person. Their attitude toward things from the Word is no different from their attitude toward other items of information; they do not make them subjects of thought, or of any insight from an enlightened rational level of mind. This is because their more inward reaches are closed, together with the adjacent more outward levels. This closure stems from their turning away from heaven and deflecting the things which they might see there—which things are the more inward elements of the human mind, as already mentioned. This is why they cannot see what is true and good—because for them these matters are in darkness, while what is false and what is evil are in light.

[3] Still, sense-oriented people are able to calculate, some with greater skill and precision than other people. But they do this from sensory illusions corroborated by their own kinds of data; and because they can calculate, they believe they are wiser than other people.

The fire that kindles their calculation with affection is the fire of self-love and love of this world. These are the people who are involved in false intelligence and wisdom, the ones the Lord meant in *Matthew:*

Seeing, they do not see, and hearing, they do not hear, nor do they understand.   (Matthew 13:13-15)

and elsewhere,

Things are hidden from the intelligent and wise, and revealed to infants.   (Matthew 11:25-26)

354. I have been allowed to talk with many scholars after their departure from this world, with some who had been most prominent, renowned in the learned world for their writing, and with some not so renowned but still possessed of abstruse wisdom.

The ones who denied the Divine at heart, no matter how much lip service they gave it, had become so senseless that they could scarcely grasp a civic truth, let alone a spiritual one. You could tell and even see that the more inward reaches of their minds were so closed off that they seemed black (phenomena like this are presented visually in the spiritual world), and of such nature that they could not stand any heavenly light or receive any inflow from heaven.

This blackness that appeared around their more inward reaches was greater and more widespread in people who had justified themselves in denying the Divine by means of the data of their scholarship.

In the other life, people of this kind accept everything false because it pleases them, soaking it up the way a sponge soaks up water. They reject everything true the way a bony shell sheds whatever falls on it. It has even been claimed that the more inward reaches of people who have justified themselves in denying the Divine and affirming nature, have become bony. Their heads look tough, as though they were made of ivory; and this extends right to the nose, a sign that no element of perceptiveness is left.

People like this sink into abysses that look like swamps. There they are harassed by the hallucinations that their false beliefs become.

Their hellish fire is a passion for glory and renown, which makes one attack another and persecute with hellish zeal people who do not worship them as demigods. They do this to each other by turns.

All worldly learning becomes like this if it does not accept into itself light from heaven by recognition of the Divine.

355. We may determine that these people are like this in the spiritual world when they arrive there after death, simply from this: all the things that are in the natural memory and are directly bonded to the physical senses (such as those fields of learning listed just above), become inactive. All they do is serve their resultant rational processes in conscious thought and speech there. The person does actually carry with him his whole natural memory, but its contents are not within his consciousness and do not occur in his thinking the way they did while he was living in the world. He cannot retrieve anything from it and bring it out into the spiritual light. For these elements are not subject to spiritual light; but the rational processes and capacities for discrimination that a person has gained from data while he lived in the body, these are compatible with the light of the spiritual world. So to the extent that a person's spirit has become rational through insights and data in this world, it is rational after separation from the body. For then the person is a spirit, and the spirit is what thinks in the body.

356. There are, however, people who through insights and data have gained intelligence and wisdom. These are the people who have applied everything to the business of life, and at the same time have recognized the Divine, loved the Word, and lived a spiritual moral life (see above, n. 319). Data have been of use to them as means to becoming wise and also to supporting matters pertinent to faith. I have perceived and even seen the more inward elements of their minds as transparent because of a light—clear-colored, flame-like or azure, like the light of diamonds, rubies, or sapphires that are crystal-clear. This is in keeping with the kinds of support for the Divine and for Divine truths available in their data. True intelligence and wisdom look like this when they come into view in the spiritual world. They derive this appearance from heaven's light, which is the Divine-True emanating from the Lord, the source of all intelligence and wisdom (see above, nn. 126-133).

[2] The planes appropriate to this light—in which variations stand out like colors—are the more inward reaches of the mind. And verifications of Divine truths by things characteristic of nature—hence of data—bring about these variations. Actually, a person's more inward mind examines the contents of his natural memory; and elements that are supportive, it cleanses with the fire of heavenly love, so to speak, detaches, and refines into spiritual concepts. As long as a person is living in the body, he is unaware that this is going on; for at that point he is thinking both spiritually and naturally but is not conscious of what he is thinking spiritually—only of what he is thinking naturally. In contrast, when he arrives in the spiritual world, he is not conscious of what he thought naturally in the world, but of what he thought spiritually. This is how his state changes.

[3] We can see from this that a person becomes spiritual by means of insights and data, and that these are means of becoming wise, but only for people who recognize the Divine in faith and life.

These people are accepted in heaven ahead of others, and live there among the people who are at the center (n. 43) because they are in light more than others. These are the intelligent and wise in heaven, who gleam like the radiance of the firmament and shine like stars. There are simple folk there, too, who have recognized the Divine, loved the Word, and led a spiritual moral life, but who have not developed the more inward reaches of their minds by insights and data in the same way. The human mind is like soil, whose quality depends on its cultivation.

39.

RICH AND POOR PEOPLE IN HEAVEN

357. People have different ideas about who is accepted into heaven. Some are of the opinion that the poor are accepted but not the rich, some that rich and poor alike are accepted, some that the rich cannot be accepted unless they renounce their means and become like the poor. Each one supports his own opinion from the Word. But people who draw a line between the rich and the poor in connection with heaven do not understand the Word.

In its own bosom, the Word is spiritual, although it is natural in the letter. So people who take the Word only in its literal meaning, not in any spiritual meaning, miss the point in many respects, especially about the rich and the poor—for example, about its being as hard for the rich to enter heaven as for a camel to go through the eye of a needle, or about its being easy for the poor because they are poor. For it is said,

Blessed are the poor . . ., for theirs is the kingdom of heaven.(Luke 6:20)

But people who have any awareness of the Word's spiritual meaning think differently. They know that heaven exists for all people who live a life of faith and love, whether they are rich or poor. In the following paragraphs we will state who are meant in the Word by "the rich," and who by "the poor."

I am granted to know with certainty, from much conversation and living with angels, that the rich enter heaven as easily as the poor; also that a person is not shut out of heaven because he has many possessions nor accepted into heaven because he is in poverty. There are rich people there as well as poor ones, and many rich ones are in greater glory and happiness than poor ones.

358. By way of preface, we may note that a person may acquire wealth, may build up such fortune as he can, as long as he does not use craftiness and evil devices. He can eat and drink well, as long as he does not center his life in this. He can be splendidly housed in keeping with his status; he can associate with others like anyone else, he can go to entertainments regularly, talk about worldly matters. There is no need for him to walk around somberly, with a sad, mournful face and a bowed head—he can be cheerful and happy. There is no need for him to give his possessions to the poor, except as affection prompts him. In a word, he can live in outward form just like a man of the world. This creates no problems about his entering heaven provided he thinks about God deeper within himself as he should, and lives honestly and justly with his fellowman.

Actually, a person's quality is that of his affection and thought, or of his love and faith. All the things he does outwardly derive their life from this source. For doing is intending, and speaking is thinking, since he acts from intention and speaks from thought.

For this reason, statements in the Word to the effect that the person is judged according to his deeds and rewarded according to his works, are understood to mean according to his thought and intention, from which his deeds spring or which are within his deeds. For deeds are of no account apart from these elements—they are of the same quality as the affection and thought.

We can see from this that the outer part of man accomplishes nothing; it is rather his inner part, from which the outer derives.

By way of illustration, let us take a person who behaves with honesty and does not cheat others solely because he is afraid of the laws, of losing his reputation and therefore his prestige and profit, and who would cheat others as much as he could if this fear did not hold him in check. His thought and intention are cheating, no matter how honest his deeds appear to be in outward form. Because he is inwardly dishonest and cheating, he has hell within himself. But the person who behaves honestly and does not cheat others because this is against God and against the neighbor, would not want to cheat someone else if he could. His thought and intention are a conscience; he has heaven within himself. The deeds of these two look alike outwardly, but in their inner form they are totally different.

359. Because one person can live like the other in outward form, can become wealthy, dine very well, live and dress in style in keeping with his position, enjoy pleasant and happy occasions, engage in worldly pursuits for the sake of his duties and affairs and for the sake of his mental and physical life, provided he acknowledges the Divine inwardly and intends well toward his neighbor—because of all this, we can see that it is not so difficult as many people believe to proceed along the way to heaven. The only difficulty is being able to resist the love of self and the world and to prevent it from dominating, for this is the source of all evils.

Its not being as hard as people believe is meant by these words of the Lord,

> Learn from me that I am meek and lowly of heart, and you will find rest for your souls; for my yoke is easy, and my burden light. (Matthew 11:29-30)

The reason the Lord's yoke is easy and His burden light is that man, to the extent that he does resist the evils that well up from love of self and the world, is led by the Lord and not by himself. Then the Lord resists these elements within the person, and moves them away.

360. I have talked with some people after death who had, while living in the world, renounced the world and devoted themselves to a life virtually in isolation, making opportunity for devout meditations by withdrawing their thoughts from worldly matters in the belief that this was how to proceed along the way to heaven. But in the other life, they are of mournful character; they avoid others who are not like themselves. They are resentful when they do not receive happiness beyond the lot of others, believing that they have earned it. Nor do they care about other people; they avoid the duties of charity, which are the means to a bond with heaven.

They long for heaven more than others do, but when they are raised to where angels are, they introduce anxieties that disturb the happiness of the angels. So they are removed from that society; and once they are cut off from it, they betake themselves to deserted places where they lead the same kind of life they had led in the world.

[2] People can be formed for heaven only in the world. Here reside the outmost results in which everyone's affection must find its closure. Unless the affection puts itself forth or flows out into action (which happens only in a public community), it is stifled, ultimately to the extent that the person no longer focuses on his neighbor, but only on himself.

We can see from this that a life of charity toward the neighbor—which is doing what is just and right in every word and in every task—leads to heaven, but not a life of piety apart from this. As a corollary, we can also see that training in charity and the consequent growth of its life can exist to the extent that a person is engaged in normal activities. It cannot exist to the extent that he withdraws from these.

[3] Let me speak now of these matters on the basis of experience. Many of those who put their energies into business and trade in the world, and who also became wealthy by this means, are in heaven. However, there are fewer of those who have been highly esteemed and have become rich because of their positions. This is because these latter have been led to love themselves and the world by profits and prestige accruing to them from their managing first matters of justice and propriety, and then monies and honors. In this way they have been led to withdraw their thoughts and affections from heaven, and to turn them toward themselves. For to the extent that a person loves himself and the world and focuses on himself and the world in everything, he alienates himself from the Divine, and withdraws from heaven.

361. The lot of rich people in heaven is such that they live in affluence more than others. Some of them live in mansions, where everything inside gleams as though it were made of gold and silver. They are abundantly supplied with everything that is useful for life; but they do not set their hearts on these things, but on the actual uses. They see these clearly, in the light so to speak; while they see the gold and silver dimly, as though they were relatively in the shade. The reason is that in the world they loved useful activities, and loved gold and silver only as means and servants. So the uses themselves shine in heaven—the good aspect of use like gold, and the true aspect like silver. These people have as much wealth, pleasure, and happiness as they had useful activities in the world.

The following are good uses: providing the necessities of life for oneself and one's dependents; wanting a great deal for the sake of the nation and the sake of the neighbor, whom a wealthy person can benefit in far more ways than a poor one can, and wanting a great deal also because the mind can in this way be withdrawn from an idle life, which is a destructive life because in it a person thinks evilly from the evil that is natural to him. These uses are good to the extent that they have something Divine within them—that is, to the extent that the person concerned focuses on the Lord and heaven, placing his "good" in them and making his wealth only an auxiliary good.

362. There is a very different lot for the rich who have not believed in the Divine and who have rejected from their minds those things that have to do with heaven and the church. These people are in hell, where there is squalor, misery, and poverty. Riches that are loved as an end are turned into things like these—not only the riches, but even the very uses, which were tasteful living, indulgence in pleasures, a full and free giving of their minds to disgraceful practices, or surpassing others whom they despised.

Since these riches and these uses have nothing spiritual within them, only something earthly, they become squalid. Actually, the spiritual element within riches and their uses is like a soul within a body, and like heaven's light in moist soil. So they decay like a body without a soul, and like moist soil without the sky's light. These are people whom riches have led astray and diverted from heaven.

363. For every individual, his ruling affection or love endures after death. It is not uprooted to eternity. Since a person's spirit is exactly like his love and (which is an arcanum) the body of every spirit and angel is an outer form of that love that corresponds exactly to the inner form of his soul and mind—because of all this, a spirit's qualities are recognizable in his face, his deeds, and his speech. A person himself would also be recognizable as to his spirit while he was living in the world, if he had not learned to simulate characteristics other than his own with his face, his behavior, and his speech.

This enables us to conclude that a person remains to eternity like his ruling affection or love. I have been allowed to talk with some people who lived seventeen centuries ago, whose lives are known from their contemporary literature; and I have discovered that the same love they had then, still activated them.

We can also conclude from this that the love of wealth and of uses stemming from wealth endures for everyone to eternity, and is exactly the same as was acquired in the world. There is however this difference, that for people whom riches have served for good uses, the riches are changed into pleasures according to the uses, while for people whom riches have served for evil uses, the riches are changed into squalor—squalor in which they still find delight just as they did in riches on earth for evil uses.

The reason they find delight in squalor is that the sordid pleasures and the disgraceful deeds which were the derivative uses correspond to squalor—as does avarice as well, being a love of wealth apart from use. Spiritual squalor is nothing but this.

364. Poor people do not enter heaven because of their poverty, but because of their life. Each individual's life follows him, whether he is rich or poor. There is no special mercy for one more than for the other. The person who has lived well is accepted; the person who has lived evilly is rejected.

In particular, poverty leads a person astray and draws him away from heaven just as wealth does. There are many of the poor who are not content with their lot, who solicit many things, and who believe that riches are blessings. So when they do not get them, they get angry and think ill of Divine providence; they envy other people their goods. In particular, they too cheat others just as much when they have the chance, and live just as much in squalid pleasures.

It is different, though, with poor people who are content with their lot, reliable and conscientious in their work, and who prefer work to idleness, who behave honestly and with good faith, and lead a Christian life as well.

At various times I have talked with people who were from the country or the common people, who had believed in God while they lived in the world, and had behaved justly and rightly in their jobs. Because they were involved in an affection for knowing what is true, they kept asking what charity was and what faith was, since in the world they had heard a great deal about faith and in the other life a great deal about charity. So they were told that charity is everything that has to do with life, and faith everything that has to do with doctrine. They were told that accordingly charity is intending and doing what is just and right in every task, while faith is thinking justly and rightly; also that faith and charity go together like doctrine and a life in accord with it, or like thought and intention; and that faith becomes charity when a person intends and does what he justly and rightly thinks; and that when this happens, faith and charity are not two things, but one.

They understood this well and were overjoyed, saying that in the world they had not understood believing to be anything other than living.

365. We can conclude from this that the rich enter heaven just like the poor, one as easily as the other. The belief that the poor enter easily and the rich with difficulty is caused by a misunderstanding of the Word where the rich and the poor are mentioned. "The rich" there means in the spiritual sense people amply supplied with deeper knowledges of what is good and true—that is, people within the church where the Word is. And "the poor" means people who lack these knowledges but still long for them—that is, people outside the church, where the Word is not found.

"The rich man" who was clothed with purple and linen and was cast into hell, means the Jewish people. Because they had the Word, and were therefore amply supplied with deeper knowledges of what is good and true, they are called rich. Knowledges of what is good are indicated by "the garments of purple," and knowledges of what is true by "the garments of linen." "The poor man" who lay at his doorway, wanting to fill himself with the crumbs that fell from the rich man's table, and who was carried off into heaven by angels, means the people who did not have deeper knowledges of what is good and true, but still longed for them. (Luke 16:19-31)

"The rich" who were invited to the great dinner and made excuses also means the Jewish people; "the poor" who were brought in to replace them means people outside the church. (Luke 24:16-24)

We must also explain what "the rich man" means of whom the Lord says,

It is easier for a camel to go through the eyes of a needle than for a rich man to enter the kingdom of God.   (Matthew 19:24)

Here "the rich man" means rich people in each sense, natural and spiritual alike. In the natural meaning, the rich are people amply supplied with wealth, who set their hearts on wealth. In the spiritual sense, they are people amply supplied with deeper knowledges and with information (these being spiritual riches), who intend to bring themselves into the realms of heaven and the church by their own understanding with the use of these resources. Since this is opposed to the Divine design, it is stated that it is easier for a camel to go through the eye of a needle. Actually, in the latter sense a camel refers broadly to matters of knowledge and information, while the needle's eye refers to spiritual truth. These meanings of "camel" and "needle's eye" are unknown today, because until now all the information that teaches what is meant in the spiritual sense by what is said in the Word in the literal sense, has been inaccessible. As a matter of fact, there is a spiritual meaning in the details of the Word and a natural meaning as well. For the Word was composed through pure correspondences of natural entities with spiritual ones so that there would be a bond between heaven and earth (or between angels and men) after a direct bond ceased. So we can see just whom "the rich" means there.

We can support the proposition that "the rich" in the Word means in the spiritual sense people involved in deeper knowledges of what is true and what is good, with "riches" meaning these knowledges themselves, which are spiritual riches, from various other passages. *Cf.* Isaiah 10:12-14; 30:6-7; 45:3; Jeremiah 17:3; 48:7; 50:36-37; 51:13; Daniel 5:2-4; Ezekiel 26:7, 12; 27:1-end; Zachariah 9:3-4; Psalm 45:12; Hosea 12:8; Revelation 3:17-18; Luke 14:33; *et al.*

Some passages on the meaning of "the poor" in the spiritual sense, as people who do not have deeper knowledges of what is good and true but who still long for them, are the following: Matthew 11:5; Luke 6:20-21; 14:21; Isaiah 14:30; 29:19; 41:17-18; Zephaniah 3:12-13.

All these passages are explained as to their spiritual meaning in *Arcana Coelestia* n. 10227.

40.

MARRIAGES IN HEAVEN

366. Whereas heaven is made up from the human race, and therefore there are angels of both sexes there, and whereas it stems from creation that woman is for man and man is for woman, each belonging to the other, and whereas that love is born into each, it follows that there are marriages in the heavens just as there are on earth. But marriages in the heavens are very different from marriages on earth. In what follows, then, we shall explain what marriages in the heavens are like, how they differ from and resemble marriages on earth.

367. Marriage in heaven is the bonding of two individuals into one mind. We shall first explain what this bonding is like.

The mind is made up of two parts, one of which is called discernment, the other intention. When these two parts work together, they are called a single mind.

In heaven, the husband takes that part called discernment, and the wife that part called intention. When this bond (which is a matter of more inward elements) comes down into the lower levels that involve their bodies, it is perceived and felt as love. This love is true marriage love.

We can see from this that true marriage love originates from the bonding of two individuals into one mind. In heaven, this is called "dwelling together," and a couple is not called two, but one. This is why two married partners in heaven are not referred to as two angels, but as one.

368. The existence of this kind of bonding of husband

and wife in the most inward elements of their minds, comes from their creation itself. The man is actually born to be discerning—that is, to think from discernment; while the woman is born to be affectional—that is, to think from intention. This can be seen in the bent or inborn nature of each, and from their form as well. In the matter of inborn nature, a man thinks on the basis of reason, a woman on the basis of affection. In the matter of form, a man has a harder, less attractive face, a heavier voice, and a harder body; while a woman has a smoother, more attractive face, a gentler voice, and a softer body.

The same kind of difference exists between discernment and intention, or between thought and affection. The same kind also exists between what is true and what is good, the same between faith and love. For what is true, and faith, are matters of discernment, while what is good, and love, are matters of intention.

This is why "young man" and "man" in the Word mean, in the spiritual sense, a discernment of what is true, while "virgin" and "woman" mean an affection for what is good. This is also why the church is called "a woman" and "a virgin," because of an affection for what is good and true; and why all people who are involved in an affection for what is good are called "virgins" (Revelation 14:4).

369. Everyone—man and woman alike—enjoys faculties of discernment and intention. But in a man discernment is dominant, while intention is dominant in a woman; and the person is in keeping with whatever is dominant. There is, however, no dominance in marriages in heaven. The wife's intention actually belongs to her husband, and the husband's discernment to the wife, because each wants to intend and think like the other—that is, with sharing, and reciprocally. This is the source of their bonding into one.

This bonding is a real bonding. The wife's intention actually enters the husband's discernment, and the husband's discernment enters the wife's intention, especially when they look at each other face to face. For as it has often been said above, there is a sharing of thoughts and affections in the heavens, all the more for a husband and wife because they love each other.

From this we can determine the nature of the bonding of minds that makes a marriage and that begets marriage love in the heavens—namely, that one wants what is his to belong to the other, and that this is mutual.

370. I have been told by angels that so far as two married partners are involved in this bond, they are involved in true marriage love and at the same time in intelligence, wisdom, and happiness; this because the Divine-True and the Divine-Good, the sources of all intelligence, wisdom, and happiness, flow primarily into true marriage love. In the same way, I have been told, true marriage love is the very plane into which the Divine flows because it is as well as marriage of what is true and what is good. For just as it is a bonding of discernment and intention, it is a bonding of the true and the good, since discernment is the recipient of the Divine-True and is also formed out of things true, while intention is the recipient of the Divine-Good, and is also formed out of things good. In fact, what a person intends is good as far as he is concerned, and what a person discerns is true as far as he is concerned. This is why it makes no difference whether you say, "the bonding of discernment and intention" or "the bonding of what is true and what is good."

The bonding of what is true and what is good constitutes an angel, and also constitutes his intelligence, wisdom, and happiness. The nature of an angel is in fact determined by the way what is good within him is bonded to what is true, and what is true to what is good. Or—which is the same thing—an angel's nature is determined by the way love is bonded to faith within him, and faith bonded to love.

371. The reason that the Divine emanating from the Lord flows primarily into true marriage love, is that true marriage love descends from the bonding of what is good and what is true. For as stated above, it makes no difference whether you say, "the bonding of discernment and intention" or "the bonding of the good and the true." The bonding of what is good and what is true finds its origin in the Lord's Divine love toward all the people who are in the heavens or anywhere on earth. Out of Divine love comes the Divine-Good, and the Divine-Good is received by angels and men in Divine truths. The only vessel for the good is the true. So no one can accept anything from the Lord out of heaven if he is not involved in things true. To the extent that the true elements within a person are bonded to what is good, then, the person is bonded to the Lord and to heaven.

This now is the actual origin of true marriage love. Therefore that love is the actual plane of the Divine inflow.

This is why the bonding of what is good and what is true is called in heaven "the heavenly marriage," why heaven in the Word is compared to a marriage and is even called a marriage. This is also why the Lord is called "a bridegroom" and "a husband," while heaven and also the church are called "a bride" and "a wife."

372. When the good and the true are bonded to each other within an angel or a man, they are not two but one. For then the good belongs to the true, and the true to the good. This bonding is like the situation that obtains when a person thinks what he intends and intends what he thinks. Then thought and intention make one—one mind, that is—with the thought actually forming, or presenting in form, what the intention intends, and the intention making it pleasant. This too is why a married pair in heaven is not called two angels, but one angel.

Again, this is the meaning of the Lord's words,

Have you not read that He who made them, made them male and female from the beginning, and said, "for this reason a man will leave father and mother and cleave to his wife, and they two will become one flesh; therefore they are no longer two, but one flesh." Therefore what God has joined together, let not man separate: . . . Not everyone will grasp this saying, except those to whom it is granted.(Matthew 19:4-6, 11; Mark 10:6-9; Genesis 2:24)

This is a description of the heavenly marriage in which angels live, and of the marriage of what is good and what is true as well. "Man not separating what God has joined together" means that what is good should not be separated from what is true.

373. Now it is possible to see from this where true marriage love comes from— namely, that its first formation occurs in the minds of people who are in a married state. From there, it descends and branches out into the body, where it is perceived and felt as love. Actually, anything that is perceived and felt in the body has its origin in the body's spiritual level, because it originates from discernment and intention. Discernment and intention make up the spiritual person.

Anything that descends from the spiritual person into the body comes out there in a different guise, yet still with a resemblance to its source, still concordant, like soul and body or like cause and effect—as we can determine from the points proffered and explained in the two chapters on correspondences.

374. I heard an angel describing true marriage love and its heavenly pleasure as follows. The Lord's Divine in the heavens, which is the Divine-Good and the Divine-True, is so united in two people that they are not two but virtually one. The angel said that two married partners in heaven are that love because each one is his own good and his own truth, in mind and body alike, the body being an image of the mind because it is formed on its model.

From this, he drew the conclusion that the Divine is imaged in two people who are involved in true marriage love. And because the Divine is so imaged, so is heaven, since the whole heaven is the Divine-Good and the Divine-True emanating from the Lord. Further, this is why all the elements of heaven are inscribed on that love—so many blessings and delights as to be beyond counting. He expressed the amount with a word that involved ten thousand times ten thousand.

He was amazed that the churchman does not know anything about this, even though the church is the Lord's heaven on earth and heaven is the marriage of what is good and what is true. He said that he was baffled when he considered the fact that acts of adultery—within the church more than outside it—were committed and even justified; yet their intrinsic delight, in the spiritual meaning and therefore in the spiritual world, is simply the delight of a love of what is false bonded to what is evil, which is a hellish delight because it is directly contrary to heaven's delight, the delight of a love of what is true bonded to what is good.

375. Everyone knows that two married partners who love each other are united quite deeply, and that the essential element of marriage is the union of personalities [*animorum*] or minds. Further, we can know from this that the intrinsic quality of the personalities or minds determines the quality of the union, and also the quality of the love between the two. A mind is formed solely from things true and things good. For all the things that exist in the universe go back to what is good and what is true, and also to their bonding together. So the union of minds is of exactly the same quality as are the true and good things out of which they are formed. As a result, the most perfect union is one of minds formed from things genuinely true and good.

It is worth knowing that there is no greater reciprocal love than that between what is true and what is good. This is why true marriage love descends from that love. What is false and what is evil love each other, too, but this love later changes into hell.

376. We can determine, from what has now been presented about the origin of true marriage love, just who are involved in true marriage love and who are not. The ones who are involved in true marriage love are the ones engaged in the Divine-Good as a result of Divine truths. We can also determine that true marriage love is genuine to the extent that the true elements bonded to the good are more genuine.

And since all the good that is bonded to truths comes from the Lord, it follows that no one can be involved in true marriage love unless he recognizes the Lord and His Divine. For without this recognition, the Lord cannot flow in and be joined to the true elements that are within the person.

377. We can see from this that people are not involved in true marriage love if they are involved in things false, especially if they are involved in things false which are grounded in something evil.

In people who are engaged in evil and thereby in things false, the more inward reaches of the mind are closed off. As a result, no origin of true marriage love can exist within them. Rather, in the outer or natural person below, separated from the inner, there occurs a bonding of what is false and what is evil, which bonding is called the hellish marriage.

I have been allowed to see what marriage is like between people who are involved in things false grounded in evil, which is called hellish marriage. They talk with each other, they join together because of lust. But inside, they are aflame with a murderous hatred for each other, such a hatred that it is beyond description.

378. True marriage love does not occur between two

people of different religions because what is true for one is not in harmony with what is good for the other; and two different and discordant elements cannot make one mind out of two. So the origin of their love derives nothing from what is spiritual; if they live together and agree, it is for natural reasons only.

For this reason, marriages in the heavens are formed with people within a community, involved in similar good and truth, not with people outside a community. It may be seen above (nn. 41ff.) that all the people there who are within a community are engaged in similar good and truth, and are different from the people who are outside.

This was depicted in the Israelite nation as well, by the fact that marriages were contracted within the tribe, even within the family, and not outside.

379. True marriage love cannot occur between one husband and several wives. This destroys its spiritual source, which is for one mind to be formed out of two. In the same way, it destroys the inner bonding of what is true and what is good, which is the source of the essence of that love.

Marriage with more than one is like a discernment divided among several intentions, or like a person not committed to one church but to several—in this way his faith is actually pulled apart so as to become nothing.

Angels say that the taking of several wives is absolutely opposed to the Divine design. They know this for many reasons, including the fact that the moment they think about marriage with several people, they are estranged from inner blessedness and heavenly happiness. Then they become like drunkards because what is good is disjoined from its truth within them. And since the more inward reaches of their minds come into this state as a result of the mere thought with some intent, they clearly perceive that marriage with more than one does close their inner person, and causes a love of licentiousness to take over for true marriage love; and a love of licentiousness leads away from heaven.

[2] They go on to say that man can hardly understand this because there are so few who are involved in actual marriage love. And people who are not involved in it know absolutely nothing about the deep delight within that love—knowing only about the delight of licentiousness that turns into something unpleasant after a brief liaison. The delight of true marriage love, though, not only lasts into old age in the world, but becomes a delight of heaven after death, being then filled with a more inward delight that keeps becoming more perfect to eternity.

Angels have also said that the blessings of true marriage love can be listed into the many thousands with not even one of them familiar to man, or within the mental grasp of anyone who is not involved in the marriage of the good and the true, from the Lord.

380. A love of having one rule over the other destroys completely both true marriage love and its heavenly delight. For as stated above, true marriage love and its delight rest in having the intention of one belong to the other, mutually and reciprocally. Love of ruling in marriage destroys this, because the one who rules wants only his intention to be in the other, and wants no element of the other's to be in himself in return. As a result, it is not mutual; there is no sharing of the love of the one and its delight with the other, or vice versa. Yet this sharing and its resultant bonding are the inner delightfulness itself that is called blessedness in marriage. A love of ruling stifles the blessedness completely, and stifles with it all celestial and spiritual love, to the point that its very existence is unknown. If they mention it at all, people like this consider it so worthless that they either laugh or bridle at the mere mention of any blessedness from it.

[2] When one intends or loves what the other does, each has a freedom, since all freedom belongs to love. But neither has freedom where there is ruling. The one is a slave; so is the ruler, since he is led like a slave by his craving to rule. But if a person does not know what the freedom of a heavenly love is, he will not understand this at all.

Still, it is possible to know from the statements above about the origin and essence of true marriage love that as ruling enters the picture, minds are not bonded but separated. Ruling enslaves; and an enslaved mind has either no intention or an opposing one. If there is no intention, there is no love either. If there is an opposing intention, then there is hatred in the place of love.

[3] The more inward elements of people who live in this kind of marriage clash with each other and fight like two adversaries, no matter how restrained and composed more outward affairs may be, for the sake of peace and quiet. The clash and battle of their more inward elements is uncovered after death. They usually get together; then they quarrel with each other like enemies and tear into each other. They are then actually behaving in accord with the state of their more inward elements.

I have been allowed to see their fights and vicious attacks several times, and some of them were full of vengefulness and cruelty. For everyone's more inward elements are let loose in the other life, no longer repressed by outward considerations, because of reasons involving the world. Each individual then is actually just what he is inwardly.

381. There does occur in some people a kind of copy of true marriage love, even though it is not true marriage love unless they are involved in a love of what is good and what is true. It is a love that looks like true marriage love for a number of reasons—to be taken care of at home, for security, to be at peace, to have leisure time, to be taken care of in ill health and old age, for the sake of children who are loved. For some people it is impelled by fear, either on account of the spouse or on account of reputation or of misfortunes. For some people it is lust that prompts it.

Also, marriage love varies between married partners. It can be greater or less in one, and little or none in the other. And because it varies, one can have a heaven and the other a hell.

382a. Genuine marriage love exists in the inmost heaven, because the angels there are involved in the marriage of the good and the true, and in innocence as well. Angels of the lower heavens are also in true marriage love, but only to the extent that they are involved in innocence, since true marriage love, seen in its own right, is a condition of innocence. As a result, the pleasures between partners who are in true marriage love are heavenly. To their minds they are almost like the games of innocence, like games among little children. For nothing fails to give pleasure to their minds; in fact, heaven flows with its joys into the details of their lives.

As a result, true marriage love is portrayed in heaven by very beautiful things. I have seen it portrayed by a virgin of indescribable beauty, clothed in a white cloud. It has been said that true marriage love is the source of all the beauty of angels in heaven. The affections and thoughts that arise from it are depicted by diamond-like auras glittering as though with fiery gems and rubies, with a charm that moves the inner reaches of the mind.

In short heaven depicts itself in true marriage love, because heaven, for angels is the bonding of the good and the true, and this bonding produces true marriage love.

382b. Marriages in the heavens are different from marriages on earth, in that marriages on earth have the added purpose of generating offspring, while this is not the case in the heavens. Instead of this generating, there is in the heavens a generating of what is good and what is true.

The reason the latter generating replaces the former is that their marriage is a marriage of what is good and what is true (as stated above), and in that marriage the good and the true, and their bonding, are loved more than anything else. As a result, these are the increase from marriages in the heavens.

This is why "births" and "generations" in the Word indicate spiritual births and generations, of what is good and what is true; why "mother" and "father" indicate what is true bonded to the good that gives birth; why "sons and daughters" indicate the true and good elements that are born; why "sons-in-law and daughters-in-law" indicate their bondings, and so on.

We can see from this that marriages in the heavens are not like marriages on earth. There are spiritual weddings in the heavens, not called "weddings" but "bondings of minds, arising from the marriage of the good and the true." But on earth there are weddings because they are not matters of the spirit alone, but of the flesh as well. Further, since there are no "weddings" in the heavens, married partners are not referred to as "husband" and "wife"; rather a person's spouse, because of the angelic concept of bonding two minds into one, is referred to by a word that means "each other's."

We can learn from this how to understand the Lord's words about weddings. (Luke 20:35-36)

383. I have also been allowed to see how married partners are brought together in the heavens. Throughout heaven, like people come together and unlike people distance themselves. So each community of heaven is made up of like people. Like are borne toward like not on their own, but by the Lord (see above, nn. 41, 43, 44f.). Partner is borne toward partner in the same way, if their minds can be joined into one. So at first sight they love each other very deeply, see themselves as married partners, and begin a marriage. Consequently, the Lord alone is the source of all marriages in heaven. They do also hold marriage banquets with many people attending; the festivities vary from community to community.

384. Because marriages on earth are the seedbeds of the human race and also of heaven's angels (for as presented in the appropriate chapter, heaven is from the human race), and because marriages have a spiritual origin, the marriage of the good and the true, with the Lord's Divine flowing primarily into that love—because of all this, earthly marriages are very holy to heaven's angels. Correspondingly, adulterous relationships, being opposed to marriage love, look sacrilegious to them. For just as angels see in marriages the marriage of the good and the true, which is heaven, so they see in adulterous relationships the marriage of the evil and the false, which is hell. As a result, whenever they hear a mention of adultery they turn away. This is also why heaven is closed to a person when he commits adultery for pleasure's sake. And once heaven is closed, the person no longer recognizes the Divine or any element of the church's faith.

I have been allowed to perceive, from an atmosphere breathed out from hell, that all the people in hell are opposed to true marriage love. The atmosphere was like a constant effort to break up and destroy marriages. I could see from this that the dominant delight in hell is a delight in adultery, also that a delight in adultery is as well a delight in destroying the bond between the good and the true, the bond that constitutes heaven.

It follows from this that a delight in adultery is a hellish delight, wholly opposed to delight in marriage, which is a heavenly delight.

385. There were some spirits who, as a result of their practice during physical life, used to trouble me with particular ingenuity. They did this by means of a very delicate, almost wave-like inflow, such as is proper to upright spirits; but I perceived that there was cunning and other such properties within them, to beguile and deceive. Eventually I talked with one of them, who, I was told, had been an army officer when he had lived in the world. Since I perceived that there was something lewd in his thought-concepts, I talked with him about marriage in a spiritual language with representations that fully expressed the ideas, many at a time. He said that during his bodily life he had been completely casual about acts of adultery.

But I was given to answer him that acts of adultery are unspeakable, despite the fact that to people like him, because of the pleasure they grasp for and their resultant rationalizing, such acts do not seem so, but even seem legitimate. Further, he could know that this was true from the fact that marriages are the seedbeds of the human race and consequently the seedbeds of the heavenly kingdom, which means that they should never be defiled, but should be held sacred. He sought also to have known this because true marriage love (as he ought to realize, being in the other life and in a perceptive state) comes down from the Lord through heaven, and because mutual love, the mainstay of heaven, is derived from that love as from a parent. Further still, he could know it from the fact that the moment adulterers even draw near to heavenly communities, they smell their own foul odor and rush headlong toward hell. Or at the very least, he could have known that violation of marriage was against Divine laws and against the civil laws of all nations—and against the true light of reason because it was against both the Divine design and the human design, among other reasons. But he replied that he had not given thought to such matters during his physical life. He wanted to discuss whether this was all true, but he was told that truth does not allow of arguments because arguments are defensive of pleasures and therefore of things evil and false. He should first think about the things he had been told because they were true. Or he might think from the principle very widely recognized in the world, that no one should do to someone else what he does not want someone else to do to him. So if anyone had taken that kind of advantage of *his* wife, whom (as happens at the beginning of every marriage) he loved, then when he was in an angry mood over it, if he talked about it in that mood, wouldn't he too have found acts of adultery despicable? And then, being strong-minded, wouldn't he have resolved himself more than other people against these acts, even to the point of condemning them to hell?

386. I have been shown how the delights of marriage love progress toward heaven, and the delight of adultery toward hell.

The progress of marriage love's delights was a progress into delights and joys constantly increasing, so as to be countless and indescribable; and the more inward they became, the more countless and indescribable they became, until they finally reached the very blessings and joys of the inmost heaven, the heaven of innocence. This took place with the fullest freedom. For all freedom stems from love; so the fullest freedom stems from true marriage love, which is heavenly love itself.

In contrast, the progress of adultery was toward hell, step by step toward the deepest hell, where nothing exists that is not cruel and fearful.

This kind of lot awaits adulterers after their life in the world. ''Adulterers'' means people who find pleasure in acts of adultery and not in marriage relationships.

41.

ANGELS' OCCUPATIONS IN HEAVEN

387. It is not possible to list or describe the occupations in heaven in detail, only to say something about them in general. For they are beyond counting, and differ also depending on the functions of the particular communities. Each community does in fact perform a specific function; for just as communities are distinguished on the basis of good elements (see above, n. 41), so they are distinguished on the basis of uses, since the good elements in all of them are good elements in action, which are uses. Everyone there actively serves a use, for the Lord's kingdom is a kingdom of uses.

388. In the heavens as on earth there are many kinds of service, because there are ecclesiastical, civil, and domestic concerns. The existence of ecclesiastical concerns is demonstrated by the statements and descriptions above (nn. 221-227) about Divine worship. The existence of civil concerns is demonstrated by the statements and descriptions about governments in heaven (nn. 213-220); while that of domestic concerns is demonstrated by the material on angels' homes and houses (nn. 183-190) and on marriages in heaven (nn. 366-386). We can see from these sources that the occupations and responsibilities within each heavenly community are manifold.

389. All the elements in the heavens are set up in accord with the Divine design, which is maintained through responsibilities discharged by angels. Matters of the common good or use are cared for by wiser angels, while more limited matters are cared for by the less wise, and so on. They are ranked exactly as uses are in the Divine design.

So too, each occupation has a worth attached in keeping with the worth of the use.

Yet the angel does not claim this worth for himself; he rather attributes it all to the use. And since the use is the good which he performs, and everything good is from the Lord, he attributes it all to the Lord.

As a result, if anyone is thinking about honor for himself and secondarily for the use (not for the use and secondarily for himself), he cannot carry out any responsibility in heaven; for he is looking backwards, away from the Lord, at himself first and at the use second.

When we say "use," it means the Lord as well, because as just stated, use is good, and what is good is from the Lord.

390. We can determine from this how things are ranked in the heavens—namely, that the extent to which anyone loves, values, and respects a use determines the extent to which he loves, values, and respects the personage [*persona*] to whom that use is attached. It holds also that the personage is loved, valued, and respected to the extent that he attributes the use to the Lord and not to himself. For to this extent he is wise; and to this extent he fills the uses that he does, from what is good.

Spiritual love, value, and respect are nothing but love, value, and respect for the use in the personage—respect for the personage on the basis of use, not respect for the use on the basis of the personage.

If anyone looks at people on a spiritual, true basis, he looks at them in this way only. For he sees one person as like another, whether he is of great or slight importance, differing only in wisdom. And wisdom is loving use—that is, the welfare of the fellow citizen, the community, the nation, and the church.

Love for the Lord too rests in this, because the Lord is

the source of everything good that is good as a result of use.
So too does love toward the neighbor, because the neighbor
is the loveworthy good within the fellow citizen, the community, the nation, and the church—the good which should
be done for them.

391. All the communities in the heavens are distinguished
according to their uses because they are distinguished according to things that are good (as stated above, nn. 41ff.),
good things being good in action or good elements of charity, which are uses.

There are communities whose occupations involve taking
care of infants. There are other communities whose occupations involve teaching and training them as they grow up.
There are others who similarly teach and train boys and girls
who are well disposed because of their training in the world
and who therefore enter heaven. There are others who in-
struct good, simple folk from Christendom and lead them
into the path to heaven. There are some which do the same
for various non-Christian peoples. There are some who protect newly arrived spirits, fresh from the world, from the
attacks of evil spirits. There are some that help people who
are in the lower earth, and some too who help people who
are in the hells, restraining them so that they do not torture
each other beyond set bounds. Then there are communities
that help people who are being revived from the dead.

Broadly speaking, angels of a particular community are
sent to people on earth, to watch over them, to lead them
away from evil affections and consequent evil thoughts and
to instill, to the extent that the people accept them freely,
good affections, thereby governing people's deeds or words
by removing evil intentions as far as this is possible.

When angels are with people on earth, they live in their
affections, so to speak—near at hand to the extent that a
person is involved in something good on the basis of things

that are true, farther away to the extent that his life is remote from such things.

All these activities of angels, however, are activities of the Lord through the angels, because the angels do not perform them on their own, but from the Lord. This is why "angels" in the Word—in its inner meaning—do not mean angels, but rather something belonging to the Lord. This is also why angels in the Word are called "gods."

392. These occupations of angels are their common activities, but each individual has his own particular contribution. For every common use is made up of countless elements that are called intermediate, auxiliary, or subsidiary uses. All these particular elements, are ranged and structured according to the Divine design and taken together, constitute and complete a common use, which is a common good.

393. Eccelesiastical concerns in heaven occupy people who in the world loved the Word and eagerly sought truths from it—not with an eye to prestige or profit, but the use both of their own lives and of the lives of others. In proportion to their love and eagerness for use, they are in enlightenment and in the light of wisdom in heaven. They come into this condition because of the Word in the heavens, since it is not natural, the way it is in the world, but spiritual (see above, n. 259).

These people fill the function of preachers, and in keeping with the Divine design, the ones who surpass others in wisdom from enlightenment are in the higher places there.

[2] Civic concerns occupy people who in the world loved their country and its common good more than their own, and who acted justly and rightly out of a love for the just and the right. To the extent that they sought just laws eagerly, from love, and became discerning as a result, they have the capability of supervising areas of service in heaven.

They do this in whatever place or on whatever level their discernment occupies, their discernment being on the same level as their love of use for the sake of the common good.

[3] Beyond this, there are so many areas of service and supervision in heaven, so many tasks as well, that they cannot be listed for their abundance. There are few in the world by comparison.

No matter how many people there are, they are all caught up in joy for their task and work, out of a love of use—no one depends on self-love or a love of profit. Nor does anyone have a love of profit for the sake of his livelihood, since all the necessities of life are given to them free. They are housed free, clothed free, and fed free.

We can see from this that people who loved themselves and the world more than use have no lot in heaven. In fact, everyone's love or affection stays with him after his life in the world; it is not uprooted to eternity (see above, n. 363).

394. In heaven, correspondence determines the task each individual is engaged in; and the correspondence is not with the task, but with the use of each task (see above, n. 112), with everything having a correspondence (n. 106). When someone in heaven is engaged in an occupation or task that corresponds to his use, he is in a state of life exactly like the one he was in in the world, because the spiritual and the natural act as one through correspondences. But there is still a difference, in that he is involved in a more inward pleasure because he is involved in a spiritual life which is a more inward life, more receptive of heavenly blessedness.

42.

HEAVENLY JOY AND HAPPINESS

395. Hardly anyone nowadays knows what heaven and heavenly joy are. People who have thought about the one or the other have come up with such a broad and crude concept that it is hardly a concept at all. From spirits who come from the world into the other life, I have had a most marvelous opportunity to find out what kind of idea they had about heaven and heavenly joy; for left to themselves as they were in the world, they think in much the same way.

The reason they do not know what heavenly joy is, is that the people who thought about it formed their opinions on the basis of outward joys proper to the natural person, without knowing what the inner or spiritual person was or therefore what was pleasant or blessed in him. So even if they had been told by people involved in a spiritual or inner delight what heavenly joy was and what it was like, it would have been incomprehensible. In fact, it would have dropped down into an unfamiliar concept, not therefore into their perception; and so it would have been among the matters that the natural person cast aside.

Yet everyone could know that when a person leaves behind his outer or natural person, he enters an inner or spiritual one. He could know from this that heavenly delight is an inner and spiritual delight, not an outer and natural one, and also that being inner and spiritual, it is more pure and choice, moving the more inward reaches of the person that belong to his soul or spirit.

Simply from this, everyone can see that he will have the same kind of delight that his spirit had, and that the delight of the body, called ''delight of the flesh,'' is not heavenly by comparison. Whatever is in a person's spirit when he leaves the body stays with him after death, for then the person lives as a spirit.

396. All delights flow out of love; for whatever a person loves, he feels as delightful. There is no delight from any other source. It follows from this that the nature of the love determines the nature of the delight.

All delights of the body, or the flesh, flow out of love of self and love of the world. All cravings and their pleasures are from the same sources as well. But all delights of the soul or spirit flow out of love for the Lord and love toward the neighbor. All affections for what is good and true flow from the same source as well, as do all deeper forms of happiness.

These latter loves, together with their delights, flow in from the Lord out of heaven along an inner path which is from above, and move the more inward reaches. The former loves, together with their pleasures, in contrast, flow in from the flesh and from the world along an outer path which is from below, and move the more outward reaches.

So the more inward reaches, those of the soul or spirit, are opened and focused away from the world, toward heaven, to the extent that these two loves of heaven are accepted and actually moving. But the outer reaches, of the body or the flesh, are opened and focused away from heaven, toward the world, to the extent that these two loves of the world are accepted and actually moving.

As loves flow in and are accepted, their delights flow in at the same time—heaven's delights in the more inward reaches, the world's delights in the more outward; for as stated, all delight belongs to love.

397. Heaven is intrinsically of such nature that it is full of delights, even to the point that, seen in its own right, it is nothing but blessed and delightful. This is because the Divine-Good, emanating from the Lord's Divine Love, constitutes heaven in general and in detail for every individual there, Divine Love being a will that everyone be saved and that everyone be most profoundly and fully happy. This is why it is all the same whether you say, "heaven" or "heavenly joy."

398. Heaven's delights are indescribable and innumerable. But not one of those countless delights can be known or believed by a person who is involved in the pleasure only of the body or the flesh, because his more inward reaches, as stated above, are focused away from heaven and toward the world, that is, backwards. For if anyone is totally involved in the pleasure of the body or the flesh (or in love of self and of the world, which is the same thing), he feels no touch of delight except in prestige, profit, or bodily and sensory pleasure. These so quench and stifle the more inward delights that belong to heaven that their very existence is disbelieved. So this kind of person would be quite bewildered if he were told that delights do occur once those of prestige and profit are gone, and that the subsequent delights of heaven in their stead are countless, and of a quality that defies comparison with delights of the body and the flesh, which are primarily in prestige and profit. We can see in this the reason for ignorance of the nature of heavenly joy.

399. The extent of heaven's joy can be determined simply from the fact that everyone there enjoys sharing his own delight and blessedness with someone else. And since everyone in heaven is like that, you can see how vast heaven's delight is. For as presented above (n. 268), there is a sharing by all with each individual, and by each individual with all.

This kind of sharing flows from heaven's two loves which, as stated, are love for the Lord and love toward the neighbor. These loves are inherently inclined to impart their delights. Love for the Lord is like this because the Lord's love is a love of imparting everything it has to everyone because it wills everyone's happiness. A like love exists in individuals who love Him, because the Lord is in them. As a result, there is a mutual sharing of delights among angels. It will be seen below that love toward the neighbor is also like this, which enables us to establish the fact that these loves are inherently inclined to impart their delights.

It is different with the loves of self and the world. Love of self diverts and takes away all delight from others, and turns it toward itself, since it wills well only to itself. Love of the world wants the neighbor's possessions to be its own. As a result, these loves are inherently inclined to destroy delights for other people. If they are inclined to share anything, it is for their own sake, not another's. So in relation to others, they are not inclined to share but to destroy, except to the extent that others' delights touch or enter themselves.

I have quite often been allowed to see by living experience that this is the nature of the loves of self and the world when they rule. Whenever spirits have come near who had been involved in these loves while they lived as people in the world, my delight has receded and died away. I have also been told that if people of this kind even move in the direction of a particular heavenly community, the delight of the members of that community is lessened in precise proportion to their nearness. And remarkably enough, the evil ones are involved in their delight at such a time.

This has enabled me to see what the state of such a person's spirit is like within his body, for it is similar to that which obtains after separation from the body. That is, he craves or covets the delights or goods of someone else, and finds delight to the extent that he gets them.

We can see from this that the loves of self and the world are destructive of heaven's joys, and hence diametrically opposed to heavenly loves, which are inclined to share.

400. It should however be realized that the delight that occupies people who are involved in loves of self and the world when they move toward a particular heavenly community is a delight of their covetousness, and therefore diametrically opposed to heaven's delight. They become involved in the delight of their covetousness as a result of stealing and carrying off the heavenly delight of people who are involved in it.

It is different when no theft or carrying off occurs. Then they cannot approach; because as far as they do, they become caught in torment and pain. This is why they seldom dare come very near.

This too is something I have been allowed to learn by many instances, of which I should like to cite a particular one. [2] Spirits who come from the world into the other life want nothing more than entrance to heaven. Almost all of them request it, believing that heaven is nothing but admission and acceptance. So, since they desire this, they are taken to a particular community of the outmost heaven.

For people who are involved in the love of self and the world, as soon as they reach heaven's first threshold, they begin to hurt and feel so deeply tormented by pain that they feel hell rather than heaven within themselves. So they dive down headlong from the place, finding no rest until they are in hells with their own kind of people.

[3] It has often happened that people like this have been eager to know what heavenly joy was; and when they heard that it was in the inward reaches of angels, they wanted to have it conveyed to themselves. So this was arranged; for

what a spirit wants when he is not yet in heaven or hell, is granted him if it is useful.

Once the communication was established, they began to be so tormented that they could not control their bodies for the pain. They seemed to force their heads all the way down to their feet, to collapse on the ground, and to writhe in circles like snakes because of the deep torment.

Heavenly pleasure produced this effect in people who were involved in pleasures derived from love of self and the world. The reason is that these loves are diametrically opposed, and when one opposite acts on another, this kind of pain occurs. And since heavenly pleasure flows in along an inner path, and flows into an opposing pleasure, the more inward elements that are involved in that pleasure are twisted backwards—in opposition to themselves, that is. This is the source of the torment.

[4] Their opposition, as stated above, stems from the will of love to the Lord and love toward the neighbor to share everything they have with others. This is actually their pleasure; while love of self and love of the world want to carry off what belongs to others and divert it to themselves. So far as they can accomplish this, they are involved in pleasure.

We can also learn from this why hell is separated from heaven. For all the people who are in hell were while they lived in the world involved in pleasures of the body and the flesh only, stemming from a love of self and the world. All the people who are in the heavens, though, were while they lived in the world involved in pleasures of the soul and spirit stemming from a love for the Lord and a love toward the neighbor. Since these loves are opposed to each other, the hells and the heavens are completely separate. This holds true even to the point that a spirit who is in hell does not dare reach even a single finger outside, or lift the top of his head. For no matter how slightly he reaches or lifts, he is racked and tormented. This too I have seen quite often.

401. If a person is involved in a love of self and the world, then as long as he lives in the body he feels delight from these loves and in the particular enjoyments that derive from them. But if a person is involved in love for God and in love toward the neighbor, then as long as he lives in the body he does not openly feel pleasure from them and from the good affections that derive from them. He feels only a blessedness that is almost imperceptible because it is hidden away in his more inward reaches, covered over by more outward elements that belong to his body, and dulled by the world's concerns. But these states change completely after death. Then the pleasures of self and the world are turned into things painful and fearful because they are turned into what is called hell fire. Or at times they are turned into things foul and squalid corresponding to their unclean enjoyments—things which, remarkably enough, they find pleasant.

But the hidden pleasure, the almost imperceptible blessedness that existed within people in the world who were involved in love for God and in love toward the neighbor—this is then turned into the pleasure of heaven, perceptible and palpable in all possible ways. In fact, this blessedness that had lain concealed in their more inward parts while they lived in the world is then uncovered and released into open sensation, because then they are in the spirit and that pleasure was proper to their spirit.

402. All of heaven's delights are closely connected with uses, and are contained within them, because uses are the good things of love and charity in which angels are involved. So a person's delights are of the same quality as his uses, and on the same level as his affection for use.

The equation between heaven's delights and the delights

of use can be demonstrated by a comparison with the body's five senses in man. Each sense is granted a delight in keeping with its use—sight has its own delight, as do hearing, smell, taste, and touch. Sight has its pleasures from beauty and forms, hearing from harmonies, smell from scents, taste from flavors.

People who reflect on the matter know the uses which these particular senses perform—especially people familiar with correspondences. The reason sight has the kind of delight it has lies in the use it performs for the discernment, which is inner sight. The reason hearing has the kind of pleasure it does, lies in the use it performs for both the discernment and the intention by means of attentiveness. The reason smell has the delight it does lies in the use it performs for the brain, and also for the lungs. The reason taste has the delight it does lies in the use it performs for the digestive system, and thereby for the whole body by nourishing it. True marriage delight, which is a purer and more exquisite delight of touch, is the most valuable of all because of its use, which is begetting the human race, and thereby heaven's angels.

These delights are contained within these sensory capacities because of an inflow of heaven, where all delight belongs to use, and is in proportion to it.

403. On the basis of a supposition gained in the world, some spirits believed that heavenly happiness would consist of a leisurely life in which they would be waited on by others. But they were informed that under no circumstances would any happiness consist in their being idle and getting pleasure out of it. This would mean each individual's wanting other people's happiness for himself; and when each individual wanted this, no one would have any. This kind of life would not be active, but idle, a life in which they would become sluggish. They could however realize that there is no happiness in life apart from activity, and that leisure belong to that life only for invigoration, so that they may get back promptly to the active part of their life.

After that, it was demonstrated in many ways that angelic life consists in performing good acts of charity which are uses, and that angels find all their happiness in use, from use, and in keeping with use. In order to discomfort people like this—people who held the notion that heavenly joy consisted of living idly, taking leisurely whiffs of eternal joy—they were allowed to feel what this kind of life was like. They felt that it was very gloomy, and that as all their joy vanished, they would soon become disgusted with it and sick of it.

404. Some spirits, believing themselves better informed than the rest, kept saying that in the world they had held a belief in heavenly joy as consisting of praising and honoring God—that this was "an active life." They were told, however, that praising and honoring God is not the right kind of active life, that God has no need of praises and honor. He rather wants people to perform useful deeds, that is, the good things that are called good works of charity. But these folk were incapable of putting any notion of heavenly joy into good works of charity—only a notion of slavery. Yet angels bore witness that this is in fact the freest state because it arises from inward affection, and is bonded to an indescribable pleasure.

405. Almost all the people who enter the other life think that hell is the same for everyone and that heaven is the same for everyone. Yet in each case there are infinite varieties and differences—nowhere is hell exactly the same, nowhere is heaven exactly the same for one person as for another. In the same way, no person, spirit, or angel exists anywhere who is exactly like another, even in his facial features. When I merely thought that there might be two exactly alike or equal, the angels shuddered, saying that every "one" is formed by the harmonious agreement of many, whose quality as a "one" depends on the quality of the agreement. So each community of heaven makes a one, and all the communities of heaven make a one—this from the only Lord, by the means of love.

In similar fashion, uses exist in the heavens with all variety and diversity. The use of one person is in no case exactly like the use of another; so too the pleasure of one is in no case exactly like the pleasure of another. Beyond this, the pleasures of each particular use are countless, and these countless elements are likewise diverse. Still, they are closely connected in a pattern so designed that they depend on each other in the same way as do the uses of each member, organ, and inner part of the body. It is even more like the use of each tissue and fiber within each member, organ, and inner part, with all of them, every single one, so joined together that each sees its good within the other and therefore in all, and all see their good in each. On the basis of this all-encompassing and detailed view, they act as one.

406. From time to time, I have talked with spirits who have just arrived from the world, about the state of eternal life—in particular, the significance of knowing who the Lord of the kingdom is, what the government is like, and what the structure of the government is. In the same way, for people in the world who move to another nation, the first thing is to find out who the ruler is and what he is like, what the government is like, and many matters concerning that nation. How much more pertinent is this in that kingdom where they are to live to eternity!

So they should know that the Lord is the one who rules heaven—and the universe as well, for whoever rules the one rules the other. This means that the kingdom where they now are is the Lord's, and the laws of this kingdom are eternal truths, all based in the law that they love the Lord above all and the neighbor as themselves. But there is more to it than that; if they want to be like angels, they should love the neighbor more than themselves.

On hearing this, they could make no reply because they had heard something like this in their bodily life and had not believed it. They were amazed at the existence of this kind of love in heaven, and at the possibility of anyone's loving his neighbor more than himself. However, they were told that all good things increase tremendously in the other life, and that life in the body is of such nature that people cannot progress beyond loving the neighbor as themselves, because they are involved in bodily concerns. But once these are set aside, love becomes more pure—eventually angelic, which means loving the neighbor more than oneself. For in the heavens, doing good for someone else is pleasant; doing good for oneself is not pleasant unless it is done so that the good may belong to someone else—that is, for someone else's sake. This, they were told, is loving the neighbor more than self.

As to the possibility of this love, they were told that it could be demonstrated by the marriage love of people who preferred death rather than harm to their spouse, by parents' love toward their children, in that a mother would rather suffer hunger herself than see her little one hungry, by real friendship, too, in that people will risk dangers for their friends—even by polite and pretended friendship, too, which tries to imitate the real thing, in that people offer the better things to those for whom they profess good will—doing this verbally, at least, though not with the heart. Finally, the possibility of this love can be demonstrated by the nature of love, which is such that its joy is being of service to others, not for its own sake, but for service's sake.

Still, these matters were incomprehensible to people who loved themselves more than others, who in bodily life were eager for profit—especially to misers.

407. One individual who during his bodily life had been more influential than others, retained even in the other life a will to rule. He was informed that he was in a different kingdom, an eternal one, and that his rule on earth had died. Now no one was valued except for what was good and true, and for the Lord's mercy that he was involved in as a result of his life on earth. He was then informed that it was the same in this kingdom as on earth, where people were valued for their wealth and their good standing with the boss. Here, wealth was made up of what is good and true, and good standing with the "boss" was the mercy a person had become engaged in because of his life in the world with the Lord. If he wanted to rule on any other basis, he was a revolutionary, because he was in someone else's kingdom. He was profoundly uncomfortable when he heard this.

408. I have talked with spirits who thought that heaven and heavenly joy consisted of being great. They were told, however, that in heaven the greatest person is the one who is least. For "least" is used to describe a person who has no power and wisdom, and wants no power and wisdom, from himself, but only from the Lord. This kind of least person has the greatest happiness; and it follows from his having the greatest happiness that he is the greatest, since it is from the Lord that he can do everything and is wiser than others.

And what is being greatest except as it involves being happiest? Actually, it is happiness that influential people seek with their influence, and rich people with their wealth.

These spirits were also informed that heaven did not consist of wanting to be least with the ultimate purpose of being greatest, for then there was a longing and desire to be greatest. Rather, heaven was the heartfelt desire for something better for others than for self, helping others for the sake of their happiness, with no underlying purpose of being rewarded—simply out of love.

409. Actual heavenly joy, as it exists in its full reality, is beyond description. For it exists in the inmost recesses of the angels' life, then in the details of their thought and affection, and then in the details of their speech and the details of their behavior.

It is as though the more inward elements were opened wide and spread out to receive what is pleasant and blessed, which was distributed along particular fibers and therefore throughout the whole. As a result, its perception and feeling are of such quality as to be beyond description, because whatever begins in the inmost recesses, flows into the more particular, derived elements, and progresses toward more outward things with constant increase.

As for the good spirits who are not yet involved in that delight because they have not yet been promoted to heaven, when they perceive the delight from an angel because of the sphere of his love, they are filled with such delight that they fall into a kind of sweet swoon. This has sometimes been done with spirits who wanted to know what heavenly joy was.

410. Some particular spirits wanted to know what heavenly joy was, so they were allowed to feel it until they could not bear it any more. Yet this was still not angelic joy; it was barely a kind of least angelic quality which they were allowed to feel through communication. It was so slight that it was almost cold, yet they called it most heavenly because it was the deepest joy within them. This demonstrated not only the existence of levels of heaven's joy, but also the fact that the deepest joy of one person barely reaches the outmost or the intermediate joy of another. It demonstrates also that a person is involved in his own proper heavenly joy when he accepts the deepest joy within himself, and that he cannot endure anything deeper—something painful results.

411. Some particular spirits, not evil ones, slipped into a stillness rather like falling asleep, and in this condition they were brought over into heaven, in respect to the more inward elements of their minds. For before the more inward elements of their minds have been opened, spirits can be brought into heaven and taught about the happiness of the people who are there.

I saw them remain in this stillness for half an hour, and then saw them when they had slipped back into the more outward concerns they were in before, retaining a memory of what they had seen.

They said that they had been among angels of heaven, and had seen stunning things there, all gleaming as though they were made of gold, silver, and precious stones, in wonderful forms that shifted marvelously. They said that the angels were not enraptured with these outward things, but with what they depicted, which were inexpressible Divine things, of infinite wisdom. These were their joy. They had also seen countless things, of which not even a ten thousandth part could be described in human words, things that would not fit into concepts that have any matter-centered content.

412. Almost all the people who enter the other life are in ignorance as to what heavenly blessedness and happiness are, since they do not know the nature and quality of inner joy. They grasp at perception only through physical and worldly joys and pleasures. What they are unaware of, they think is nothing; yet it is physical and worldly pleasures that are relatively nothing.

For this reason, upright people who do not know what

heavenly joy is are brought first of all into heavenly gardens, beyond the most imaginative conceptions, so that they may learn and realize this. At this point, they conclude that they have arrived in a heavenly paradise; but they are informed that this is not really heavenly happiness. So they are allowed to experience more inward states of joy, which they can perceive, moving toward what is most inward for them. Then they arrive at a state of peace to the very core, stating that nothing of this is expressible in any way, or conceivable. Then they arrive at a state of innocence that touches their very inmost capacity for feeling.

This is how they are granted acquaintance with the real nature of spiritual and celestial good.

413. But to enable me to know the nature and quality of heaven and heavenly joy, the Lord has long and often granted me perception of the delightful qualities of heavenly joys. So I can know this because it comes from live experience; but I can never describe it. Still, in order to offer at least some notion of these matters, let me say a little.

Heavenly joy is an affection made up of countless delights and joys which all together present a kind of general entity. Within this general entity, or this general affection, are harmonies of countless affections that do not come through sharply to perception, but only dimly, because this involves a most general kind of perception. Still, I have been able to perceive that there are countless elements involved, arranged in a way that can in no way be described. The quality of these countless elements flows from heaven's design.

An arrangement like this exists within the detailed, smallest bits of affection, which are presented and perceived (in keeping with the ability of the person who has them) only as a most general unity. In short, infinite elements in a most perfectly arranged form are involved in every general entity, with nothing that is not alive and moving. And all the individual elements come from things most inward, because heavenly joys come forth from things most inward.

I have perceived also that joy and delight seem to come from the heart, spreading very gently through all the deepest fibers and from there into gathered fibers, with such a profound feeling of pleasure that the fibers are virtually nothing but joy and delight, with every derived perceptive and sensitive element alive with happiness. Next to these joys, the joys of physical pleasures are like coarse and acrid dust relative to a pure and very soft aura.

I have noticed that when I wanted to convey all my pleasure to someone else, there was a constant inflow of deeper and fuller pleasure in its place, and that the amount of inflow was in proportion to the extent to which I wanted this. I have perceived that this stems from the Lord.

414. People who are in heaven progress steadily toward the springtime of life, and the more thousands of years they live, the more pleasant and happy the springtime. This goes on forever, with the increase keeping pace with the growth and level of their love, charity and faith.

As the years go by, women who have died aged, debilitated by age, who have lived in faith in the Lord, charity toward the neighbor, and happy true marriage love with their husbands, come more and more into the flower of youth and young womanhood—into a beauty that outstrips every concept of beauty that sight can possibly perceive. It is goodness and charity that provide this form and present this image of themselves, making the pleasant and beautiful content of charity so radiate from the smallest details of the face that these women are actual forms of charity. Some people have seen them, and have been stunned.

Charity has this kind of form, vividly evident in heaven, because charity itself is what is depicting itself and being depicted. This holds true to the point that the whole angel, especially his face, is virtually charity appearing and perceived openly. When this form is seen, there is an indescribable beauty that moves the deepest life of the mind with charity.

In a word, growing old in heaven is growing young.

People who have lived in love for the Lord and in charity toward the neighbor become such forms, or such beauties, in the other life. All angels are such forms, with a variety beyond counting. They constitute heaven.

43.

THE VASTNESS OF HEAVEN

415. The vastness of the Lord's heaven can be determined from many things mentioned and explained in the preceding pages. It follows especially from the fact that heaven is from the human race (see above, nn. 311-317)—not only from that portion born within the church, but from the portion outside (nn. 318-328). So it is made up out of all the people, from the very beginning of this planet, who have lived involved in what is good.

Anyone who knows anything about the sections and regions and kingdoms of this planet can figure out what a tremendous number of people there is on this whole sphere of nations. If he gets into some higher mathematics, he will discover that several thousand people die on a given day, some myriads of millions in the space of a year. This has been going on from earliest times, with several thousand years intervening. All these people entered the other world, called the spiritual world, after death; and they still constantly do.

It is impossible to say how many of these became or are becoming angels. I have been told that the majority of people in ancient times did because people then thought more inwardly and more spiritually, and were consequently involved in heavenly affection. But not so many did in later periods, because as time passed men became more outward, began to think more on the natural level, and consequently were involved in earthly affection.

We can determine to begin with, then, that heaven is large simply on the basis of the inhabitants of this planet.

416. The vastness of the Lord's heaven can be established simply from the fact that all children, whether born within or outside the church, are adopted by the Lord and become angels. The number of these amounts to a quarter or a fifth of the whole human race on the planet.

You may see above (nn. 329-345) that every child, wherever born, within or outside the church, of godly or ungodly parents, is accepted by the Lord when he dies. He is raised in heaven, taught and permeated with affections for what is good in keeping with the Divine design, given insights of what is true by means of these affections, and thereafter, as he is perfected in intelligence and wisdom, is led into heaven and becomes an angel. So you can see how vast the number of heaven's angels has become simply from these, from first creation to the present day.

417. We can determine how vast the Lord's heaven is from the fact that all planets visible to the eye in our solar system are earths. Beyond this, there are countless more in the universe, all full of inhabitants. They have been discussed in a special work on planets, from which I should like to cite the following words:

> It is well known in the other life that there are many planets with people on them, and spirits and angels from them. For anyone there who wants to talk with spirits from other planets out of a love for what is true and for a consequent use, is allowed to do so, and thereby to become convinced of the plurality of worlds and informed that the human race is not from one planet alone, but from countless ones.
>
> I have talked about this several times with spirits from our planet, and said that a person of intellectual capacity can learn, from many things he knows, that there are many planets with people on them. He can conclude on rational grounds that such masses as the planets represent, some larger than this planet, are not empty lumps created just to travel and promenade around the sun, shedding their feeble light for this one planet, but that their function should be more worthy than that.
>
> If a person believes—as he should—that the Divine created the universe for no other purpose than the establishment of the human race,

and consequently heaven (for the human race is heaven's seedbed), then he cannot help believing that there are people wherever there is a planet.

We can know clearly that those planets which are visible to our eyes because they are within the bounds of this solar system are earths, since they are bodies of earthly matter; for they reflect sunlight and do not look like stars when they are examined through a telescope, *i.e.*, reddish-yellow from flame, but like earths, with dimly differentiated areas. Further, like our globe, they are borne and proceed around the sun along the path of the zodiac, causing both years and the seasons of the year, which are spring, summer, fall, and winter. In similar vein, they rotate on their axes the way our globe does, making days and the times of day—morning, midday, evening, and night. Further still, some of them have moons (called satellites) circling their spheres in fixed periods, the way our moon circles ours. And the planet Saturn, being a very long way from the sun, has a great luminous belt that does give that planet light, albeit reflected.

If anyone knows this, and thinks rationally, can he say that these are empty bodies?

Beyond this, I have talked with spirits about the possibility of people believing that there are more earths than one in the universe on the grounds that the star-covered sky is so vast. There is such an unfathomable number of stars there, each one a sun in its own place or within its own system, like our sun, only different in size. If anyone ponders this properly, he will decide that this whole vast thing cannot possibly exist except as a means to an end, the goal of creation, which end is a heavenly kingdom where the Divine can live with angels and men.

The visible universe, the heavens studded with such a tremendous number of stars, which all are suns, is simply a means for the establishment of earths, with people on them, as a basis for a heavenly kingdom.

As a result, a rational person has to think that such a vast means to such a noble end was not constructed for the sake of the human race on a single planet. What would that be for the Divine, which is infinite, for which thousands or tens of thousands of planets, all full of inhabitants, are not enough—are scarcely anything?

There are spirits whose special passion is getting knowledges because these alone delight them. So these spirits are allowed to travel around, even to go from this solar system to others, and gather knowledges.

They have said that there are planets with people on them not only in this solar system, but beyond it, in the star-covered heaven, a tremendous number (these spirits are from the planet Mercury).

On preliminary calculation, if there were a million planets in the universe, with a total of 300,000,000 (three hundred million) people on each planet, and two hundred generations within six thousand years, with each person or spirit given a space of three cubic cubits, then the total of these people or spirits gathered together would not fill the volume of this globe—would barely exceed the volume of one planetary satellite, which would constitute a space in the universe of almost unnoticeable minuteness, since the satellites are barely visible to the naked eye.

What does this amount to for the Creator of the universe? For Him, it would not be enough if the whole universe were filled, for He is infinite.

I have talked about this with angels, who said that they had a similar notion of the scarcity of the human race relative to the infinity of the Creator, although they were not thinking in spatial terms but in terms of states. To their notion, they said, the greatest number of myriads of planets they could possibly think of would still be nothing at all to the Lord.

In the booklet just mentioned, the reader may find information on planets in the universe, their inhabitants, and the spirits and angels who come from them. Those contents have been revealed and shown to me to let it be known that the Lord's heaven is vast, and wholly from the human race, also that our Lord is universally recognized as God of heaven and earth.

418. The vastness of the Lord's heaven can also be determined from the fact that heaven, taken as a whole, reflects a single person and corresponds as well to everything in detail that a person comprises. This correspondence cannot possibly be filled up, since it is a correspondence not only with individual members, organs, and tissues of the body in general, but in detail and specifically with all the individual component tissues and organs within them, even to individual ducts and fibers. A correspondence exists not only with these, but even with the organic substances that receive heaven's inflow on a more inward level, the person's

source of the more inward dynamics underlying his personality [*animus*]. For anything that emerges on a deeper level
within a person, does so in forms made of substance; anything that does not emerge in substances serving as "subjects," is nothing.

All these elements have a correspondence with heaven,
as may be concluded from the section on the correspondence
of all elements of heaven with all elements of man (nn. 87-
102).

The reason this correspondence cannot possibly be filled
up is that the more angelic groupings there are which correspond to a given member, the more perfect heaven becomes. In the heavens, all perfection increases in proportion
to abundance.

The reason for this increase of perfection in the heavens
in proportion to abundance is the existence there of a single
goal for all, with a common focus of all on that goal. This
goal is the common good. When this is supreme, then good
results to individuals from the common good, and what is
good for everyone results from the good of individuals. This
happens because the Lord turns everyone in heaven toward
Himself (see above, n. 123), thereby making them one in
Himself.

This formation of perfection by the agreement and accord
of many elements (especially from a source like this and in
such firm connection) is discernible to anyone on the basis
of moderately enlightened reason.

419. I have been allowed to see the spread of both the
inhabited heaven and uninhabited heaven; and I saw that the
spread of the uninhabited heaven was so great that it could
not be filled to eternity, even though there existed many
myriads of planets, with each planet having as great a number of people as ours (on this subject, see again the booklet,
Earths in the Universe, n. 168).

420. Some people think that heaven is not vast, but small, basing this on certain passages from the Word understood according to their literal meaning. For example, they have based this opinion on passages which state that only the poor are accepted in heaven, or only the elect, or only people within the church and not people outside it, or only people for whom the Lord intercedes, or that heaven is closed when it is full, and that the time for this is predetermined.

But these people do not realize that heaven is in no way closed—there is no predetermined time, no specified number—"the elect" means people who are involved in a life characterized by what is good and true, "the poor," people who are not involved in insights of what is good and true and still long for them (because of this longing, they are also called "the hungry").

People who have adopted this opinion of heaven's smallness from the Word as misunderstood, know heaven only as being in a single place where all people are gathered. Yet heaven is made up of countless communities (see above, nn. 41-50). Further, they know heaven only as something granted to the individual by direct mercy, with admission and acceptance therefore out of good will alone.

They do not understand that, out of mercy, the Lord leads every individual who accepts Him, or that the individual who accepts Him is the person who lives by the laws of the Divine design, the rules of love and faith. This being led by the Lord, from infancy to the end of earthly life and on into eternity, is what mercy means.

If only they knew that every single person is born for heaven—accepted if he accepts heaven into himself in the world, and shut out if he does not.

PART II

THE WORLD OF SPIRITS

AND MAN'S STATE AFTER DEATH

44.

WHAT THE WORLD OF SPIRITS IS

421. The world of spirits is neither heaven nor hell; rather it is a place, or state, midway between the two. It is where a person first arrives after death, being, after some time has passed, either raised into heaven or cast into hell from it, depending on his life in the world.

422. The world of spirits is both a place midway between heaven and hell and a person's "midway" state after death. I have been able to see that it is a midway place from the fact that the hells are beneath it and the heavens above; and to see that it is a midway state from the fact that as long as a person is there, he is not yet in either heaven or hell.

Heaven's state in a person is the bonding of what is good and what is true within him; and hell's state, the bonding of what is evil and what is false within him. When what is good is bonded to what is true in a person who is a spirit, he enters heaven, because, as we have said, that bonding is heaven within him. But when what is evil is bonded to what is false within him he enters hell, because that bonding is hell within him.

This bonding occurs in the world of spirits, because then a person is in a midway state. It does not matter whether you say the bonding of discernment and intention, or the bonding of what is true and what is good.

423. We need first to talk about the bonding of discernment and intention and its resemblance to the bonding of what is good and what is true, since this bonding takes place in the world of spirits.

Man has both discernment and intention. His discernment receives things true, and is formed out of them. His intention receives things good, and is formed out of them. As a result, a person calls "true" whatever he discerns and consequently thinks; and he calls "good" whatever he intends and consequently thinks.

Man has an ability to think from his discernment, and thereby to grasping what is true and also what is good; yet he does not think this from intention unless he intends and does it. When he intends it, and does it intentionally, then it exists in his discernment and his intention alike—it therefore exists in the person. For discernment alone does not constitute a person, nor does intention alone; rather it is discernment and intention together. So whatever exists in both these abilities exists in the person and has become part of him, but anything that exists only in the discernment is with the person but not within him. It is only an element of his memory, a matter of information within his memory which he can think about when he is not "in himself" but "outside himself," with other people. So too, he can talk about it and reason about it, and put on affections and manners in keeping with it.

424. Man's ability to think from his discernment without thinking from his intention at the same time is furnished him so that he can be formed anew. For a person is formed anew by means of things true, which belong to his discernment as we have said. Actually, man is born into involvement in all kinds of evil, as far as his intention is concerned. This means that on his own he does not intend what is good to anyone but himself. And anyone who intends what is good only to himself is pleased by the evils that befall others, especially when they are to his own advantage. In fact, he wants to funnel everyone else's good things to himself, whether these be matters of prestige or of profit; and he is inwardly happy to the extent that he can accomplish this.

For the correction and re-forming of this kind of intention, man has been given the capacity to discern things that are true, and thereby to tame the affections for what is evil that gush from his intention. This is the source of man's ability to think true things from his discernment, and to speak and do them. All the same, he cannot think them from his intention until his quality is such that he intends and does them on his own—that is, from his heart. When this is a person's quality, then the things he thinks from his discernment are part of his faith, and the things he thinks from his intention are part of his love. Consequently, faith and love are then bonded together for him, like discernment and intention.

425. A person has heaven within himself, then, to the extent that true elements belonging to his discernment are bonded to good elements belonging to his intention—that is, to the extent that he intends true things and therefore does them—because the bonding of what is good and what is true is heaven, as stated above. Conversely, a person has hell within himself to the extent that false elements belonging to his discernment are bonded to evil elements belonging to his intention, because the bonding of what is false and what is evil is hell. But to the extent that true elements belonging to his discernment are not bonded to good elements belonging to his intention, the person is in a midway state.

Practically everyone nowadays is in the condition of knowing true things and pondering them on the basis of both knowledge and discernment—performing many of them, or few, or none, or acting counter to them out of a love for what is evil and a consequent faith in what is false. To provide either heaven or hell for him, then, he is brought into the world of spirits right after his death. There a bonding takes place—a bonding of the good and the true for people who are going to be raised into heaven, and a bonding of the evil and the false for people who are going to be cast into hell.

For no one, in heaven or in hell, is allowed to have a divided mind, to discern one thing and to intend something else. Rather, what a person intends, he will discern, and what he discerns, he will intend. So in heaven, the person who intends what is good discerns what is true; while in hell, the person who intends what is evil discerns what is false. Consequently, in the world of spirits false elements are taken away from good people, and they are given the true ones that are appropriate for and fit in with their goodness. By the same token, true elements are there taken away from evil people, and they are given the false ones that are appropriate for and fit in with their evil.

This enables us to see what the world of spirits is.

426. There is a vast number of people in the world of spirits, because this is where they first gather; it is where everyone is examined and made ready.

There is no set limit to their stay there. Some barely enter it before they are either borne into heaven or cast into hell. Others stay there only a few weeks, some several years, though not more than thirty. The differences in length of stay arise from the extent to which the more inward elements of the person correspond—or do not correspond—with his more outward elements.

In the following pages we shall tell how a person in that world is led from one state to another and is made ready.

427. After death, immediately on their arrival in the world of spirits people are precisely classified by the Lord. Evil people are promptly attached to the hellish community where, as to their ruling love, they were during their life in the world; and good people are promptly attached to the heavenly community where, as to their love and charity and faith, they were during their life in the world. In spite of this classification, however, they do assemble in that world. All people who were friends or acquaintances during bodily life, particularly wives and husbands, and brothers and sisters, talk with each other whenever they want to.

I have seen a father talking with his six children and recognizing them, and many other talking with their relatives and friends. But since they were of different dispositions because of their lives in the world, it was not long before they were separated. In fact, people who enter heaven or hell from the world of spirits do not see or know each other any more unless they are of like disposition as a result of a like love.

The reason they see each other in the world of spirits but not in heaven or hell, is that people in the world of spirits are led into states like those they had in the world, one after another. Later though, everyone is resolved into a steady state like that of his ruling love. In this state, people recognize each other only on the basis of likeness of love, because likeness forms bonds, and unlikeness severs (as shown above, nn. 41-50).

428. Just as the world of spirits is a midway state between heaven and hell within a person, it is also a midway place. The hells are beneath it, and the heavens are above it.

All the hells are blocked off on the world of spirits' side. They are accessible only through holes and crevices like those in rocks, and through broader gaps which are guarded so that no one can get out unless he is given permission. This happens when there is some urgent need, as will be described later. Heaven too is enclosed on all sides; the only access to an angelic community is by a narrow way, and its beginning is similarly guarded. It is these "exits" and "entrances" that are called the "gates" and "doors" of hell and heaven in the Word.

429. The world of spirits looks like a valley among mountains and cliffs, with dips and rises here and there. The doors and gates to heavenly communities are not visible, except to people who have become ready for heaven; other people do not find them. For a given community, there is a single entrance out of the world of spirits, which leads to a single way that divides into several as it climbs.

The gates and doors to the hells are not visible except to people who are about to enter; for these people they are opened. Once they are opened, one can see dark, sooty-looking caves, leading down on a slant into the depth, where again there are many gates. Out of these caves drift disgusting vapors and stenches, which good spirits flee because they find them repulsive, while evil spirits hungrily track them down because they find them delightful. For just as each one found pleasure in his own evil in the world, so after death he finds pleasure in the stench to which his evil corresponds. In this respect, they can be compared to predatory birds and beasts like ravens, wolves, or pigs, who fly or run to corpse-like or dung-like objects when they catch the scent.

I heard a person screaming violently, as if from inward torture, when a breath of heaven reached him. Yet he was calm and happy while a breath of hell was reaching him.

430. There are two gates within every individual, as well. One of them gives access to hell, and is open to the evil and false elements that come from there. The other gates gives access toward heaven, and is open to the good and true elements that come from there.

The gate of hell is open in people who are involved in something evil and consequently in what is false. Only through crevices overhead does some light from heaven flow in, which enables such people to think, to use logic, and to talk. Conversely, the gate of heaven is open in people who are involved in something good and consequently in what is true.

There are actually two paths that lead to a person's rational mind—a higher or inner path, through which the good and the true come in from the Lord, and a lower or outer path through which the evil and the false climb in from hell. The rational mind is the central area where these two paths are headed. As a result, a person is rational in proportion to the amount of heaven's light that is let in. To the extent that this light is not let in, he is not rational, even though he may seem so to himself.

We mention these matters to show what the correspondence of man with heaven and hell is like. As long as his rational mind is in process of formation, it corresponds to the world of spirits, the things above it to heaven, and the things below it to hell. In people who are being made ready for heaven, the things above the rational mind are opened and the things below it are closed toward the inflow of what is evil and false. But in people who are being readied for hell, the things below it are opened and the things above closed toward the inflow of what is good and true. As a result, these latter can only look downward—toward hell, that is, while the former can only look upward—toward heaven, that is.

Looking upward is looking toward the Lord, since He is the common center on which all the heavens focus. Looking downward, however, is looking away from the Lord toward an opposing center on which all hell focuses (see above, nn. 123, 124).

431. In the pages above, the term "spirits" has been used to mean people who are in the world of spirits; while the term "angels" has been used to mean people who are in heaven.

45.

EVERYONE IS A SPIRIT, AS FAR AS HIS MORE INWARD REACHES ARE CONCERNED

432. If a person gives the matter due consideration, he can recognize that the body does not think, since it is material. Rather, the soul thinks, since it is spiritual.

Man's soul, whose immortality has been the topic of many writers, is his spirit. It is in fact immortal in all respects. It is what thinks in the body, too, since it is spiritual; and the spiritual receives the spiritual and lives spiritually, which is thinking and intending.

So all rational life that is discernible in the body belongs to the soul; none of it belongs to the body. The body, as mentioned above, is in fact material; and the material stuff which is the hallmark of the body is an addendum, almost a kind of accessory, to the spirit, so that a person's spirit can carry on a life and do useful things in a natural world whose constitutents are all material and intrinsically devoid of life.

Since the material does not live, only the spiritual, we can determine that the part of man that lives is his spirit, with the body only serving it, just the way something used as a means serves a living, impelling force. People do say of a tool that it acts, impels, or impinges; but it is a fallacy to believe that this is a property of the tool and not of the person who acts, impels, or impinges through it.

433. Since everything that is alive in the body belongs strictly to the spirit (also everything that acts and senses as a result of life), none of it belonging to the body, it follows that the spirit is the actual person. This is much the same as saying that, seen in his own right, a person is a spirit, and is in comparable form as well. For the part of man that lives and senses is his spirit, and everything in man, from his head to the soles of his feet, lives and senses. This is why, when a person's body is separated from his spirit, which is called dying, he is still a person, still alive.

I have heard from heaven that some people who have died are thinking even while they are lying on mortuary tables, before their awakening, still within their own cold bodies. As far as they know, they are still alive, except that they are unable to move the smallest bit of matter that belongs to their bodies.

434. Man cannot think and intend unless there is a subject, a definable entity, which is a substance from which things proceed and in which things occur. There is no reality to anything which is thought to occur apart from a substantial subject.

We can determine this from the fact that a person cannot see without an organ which is the subject of his sight, or hear without an organ which is the subject of his hearing. There is no reality or existence to sight or hearing apart from these organs.

The same holds true for thought—which is inner sight—and attentiveness—which is inner hearing. Unless these occurred in and from substances which are organic forms which are subjects, they could not happen at all.

We can tell from these considerations that a person's spirit is just as much "in a form" as his body is, that it is in a human form, and that it enjoys abilities of sense and senses just as much when separated from the body as when it was within it. We can tell that every bit of the eye's life, every bit of the ear's life—in a word, every bit of sense life which a person has—is a property not of his body, but of his spirit within these phenomena even to their most minute details.

This is why spirits, just like men, see, hear, and feel—after release from the body not in a natural world, to be sure, but in a spiritual one. The spirit's capacity for natural sensation during its existence in a body came from the material element added to it; but even then, it sensed spiritually in thinking and intending.

435. These matters have been mentioned in order to convince reasonable people that man, seen in his own right, is a spirit, that the bodily aspect, added for the sake of accomplishing things in the natural, material world, is not the person, but simply a tool for his spirit.

Supporting examples from experience vouch for the truth of this, since many people do not grasp rational constructs. In fact, people who have convinced themselves of the opposite proposition use devices of logic based on deceptive sense-impressions to turn these rational constructs into uncertainties.

People who have convinced themselves of the opposite proposition tend to think that the lower animals live and perceive the way man does, and therefore have a spiritual component like man's. But in fact this dies along with the body. However, the spiritual component of animals is not like man's. For man, unlike animals, has an inmost area into which something Divine flows. The Divine lifts man toward Itself and thereby bonds him to Itself, which is why man, unlike animals, is able to think about God and about the Divine elements proper to heaven and the church, to love God because of these elements and in involvement with them, and so to be bonded to Him. Whatever can be bonded to God cannot be destroyed; but anything that cannot be bonded to God is destroyed.

This "inmost" which belongs to man rather than to animals has been described above (n. 39). It is worth repeating that description at this point. For it is important for the dismissal of deceptive views derived from the opposite proposition, views held by many people who lack the capacity to draw rational conclusions on these matters because they lack information and their understanding is not open. The relevant section reads as follows:

> I should like to cite a particular arcanum about the angels of the three heavens. This is something that has not occurred to man before, because he has not understood levels (*cf.* n. 38).
>
> Every single angel and every single person has an inmost and highest level, or something inmost and highest, where the Lord's Divine flows in first or most directly. From this center the Lord assigns places to other relatively inward elements that, according to the sequential levels, lie below in the person. We may call this inmost or highest element the Lord's entryway to angel and man. His very home within them.
>
> It is by this "something inmost or highest" that man is man and is differentiated from non-rational animals, since they do not possess it. As a result, man, unlike animals, can be raised by the Lord toward Himself as concerns his more inward reaches, or what belongs to his inner and outer mind. Man can believe in Him, be moved by love for Him, and so can see Him. As a result also, man can accept intelligence and wisdom, and can talk from rational processes. This also is the source of man's living to eternity.
>
> But it does not come openly to the attention of any angel just what the Lord arranges and takes care of at this center, since this is above his thought and beyond his wisdom.

436. Man's being a spirit as concerns his more inward elements is something I have been granted to know by means of a great deal of evidence. If I were to cite all of it, it would fill volumes, as they say.

I have talked with spirits as a spirit, and I have talked with them as a man in a physical body. When I have talked with them as a spirit, their whole impression was that I was an actual spirit, in a human form, too, just like themselves. This is how my more inward elements looked to them, since when I talked as a spirit, my physical body was not visible.

437. Man's being a spirit as concerns his more inward

elements is demonstrated by the fact that after the spirit has been separated from the body (which happens when a person dies), he is still alive, a person, the way he was before.

To assure me of this, I have been allowed to walk with practically everyone I have ever known during his physical life—with some for hours, with some for weeks or months, with some for years—all for the overriding purpose that I might be assured of this fact, and might bear witness to it.

438. I am allowed to add the following. Every single person, even while he is living in the body, is in a community with spirits as far as his own spirit is concerned, even though he is unaware of the fact. A good person is by means of these spirits in an angelic community; an evil person is in a hellish community; and each person enters that same community after his death. People who join the spirits after death are often told this and shown this.

It is not that a person is visible in that community as a spirit while he is living in the world, since at that point he is thinking on the natural level. But people who are thinking in a manner withdrawn from the body, being then in the spirit, are sometimes visible in their own communities. When they are visible, they are readily identified by the spirits who are there, because they walk along sunk in contemplation, silent. They do not look at anyone else, but act as though they did not see them. The moment any spirit speaks to them they disappear.

439. To illustrate the fact that man is a spirit as far as his more inward elements are concerned, I should like out of my experience to tell what it is like when a person is led out of the body, and when he is led by the spirit to another place.

440. As to the first matter—being led out of the body—it is like this. A person is guided into a particular state which is halfway between being asleep and being awake. In this condition, he is wholly convinced that he is awake. All his senses are as alert as when he is fully awake physically—sight, hearing, and, remarkably, touch, which is then more acutely sensitive than it ever is in physical wakefulness. In this state, spirits and angels have been seen to the life. They have been heard as well, and, remarkably, touched. Then virtually nothing of the body intervenes. This is the condition described as "being led out of the body" and "not knowing whether one is inside or outside the body."

I have been led into this condition only three or four times, simply to let me know what it is like, and at the same time to know that angels enjoy all the senses. So does man, as far as his spirit is concerned, when he has been led out of the body.

441. As regards the second matter—being led by the spirit to another place—I have been shown by live experience what this is like and how it happens, but only two or three times. I should like to cite just one such experience.

While I was taking a walk along city avenues and through the fields, engaged in a conversation with spirits, it was exactly as though I were awake and seeing as usual. I kept on walking without straying. All the while, I was involved in a vision, seeing groves of trees, rivers, mansions, houses, people, and many other things.

But after I had been walking for some hours, I found myself suddenly involved in physical sight, and noticed that I was in another place. Bewildered by this, I realized that I had been in the kind of state people describe as "being led by the spirit to another place." For while the condition lasts, the person pays no attention to his route, even though this might be many miles, nor to the time, though it might be several hours or days, and there is no sense of fatigue. In this state, a person is led by routes which he himself does not know to a chosen place, without straying.

442. These two states of man, however (states which occur when he is involved in his more inward concerns, or in other words, when he is in the spirit), are unusual. They have been shown me only to let me know what they were like, because they are recognized within the church. But talking with spirits, being with them as though I were one of them—this has been granted me while I was completely awake physically, for many years now.

443. Man's being a spirit as far as his more inward elements are concerned can be more fully supported by matters related and set forth above (nn. 311-317) where we deal with the fact that heaven and hell are from the human race.

444. Man's being a spirit as far as his more inward elements are concerned, means as far as those things are concerned that belong to his thought and intention. For these are the more inward elements that make a person a person—their quality, in fact, determines the kind of person he is.

46.

MAN'S AWAKENING FROM THE DEAD AND ENTRANCE INTO ETERNAL LIFE

445. When the body can no longer fulfill its functions in the natural world corresponding to the thoughts and affections of its spirit (which the person receives from the spiritual world), then we say that the person dies. This happens when the lung's respiratory motion and the heart's systolic motion cease.

The person, however, does not die. He is simply separated from the physical component which was serviceable to him in the world. The actual person is still alive.

We say that the actual person lives because the person is not a person because of his body, but because of his spirit. For the spirit does the thinking in a person, and thought together with affection constitutes the person.

We can see from this that when someone dies, he simply crosses from one world into another. This is why "death" in the Word, in its inner meaning, refers to resurrection and to continuity of life.

446. The most inward communication of the spirit is with the breathing and with the motion of the heart—the spirit's thought with the breathing and the affection proper to love with the heart. So when these two motions cease in the body, there is immediately a separation. These two motions (the lungs' respiratory one and the heart's systolic one) are the actual bonds whose breaking leaves the spirit to itself. The body, lacking then the life of its spirit, grows cold and begins to decay.

The reason man's spirit communicates most inwardly with the breathing and with the heart is that all the vital motions are dependent on these two, not just in general, but in every area.

447. After the separation, the person's spirit stays in his body for a while, but not beyond the complete stillness of the heart. This varies with the ailment that causes the person's death, for in some cases, the heart's motion continues for quite a while, and in others, not long.

The moment this motion stops, the person is awakened, but this is accomplished by the Lord alone. "Awakening" means leading a person's spirit out of his body and leading it into the spiritual world, which is usually called "resurrection."

The reason a person's spirit is not separated from his body before the heart's motion has stopped, is that the heart corresponds to affection from love, which is the person's actual life because everyone gets his vital heat from love. Consequently, the correspondence exists as long as the bond lasts, resulting in the presence of the spirit's life within the body.

448. As to the way this awakening happens, I have not simply been told—I have been shown by live experience so that I could have a thorough knowledge of how it happens.

449. I was brought into a condition of unconsciousness as far as my physical senses were concerned—practically, that is, into the condition of people who are dying. However, my more inward life, including thought, remained unimpaired so that I perceived and remembered the things that happened, things that do happen to people who are awakened from the dead.

I noticed that physical breathing was almost taken away; the more inward breathing of the spirit kept on, joined to a slight and still breathing of the body.

Next, a communication was set up between my heartbeat and the celestial kingdom (since that kingdom corresponds to the heart in man). I even saw angels from there, some at a distance; and two of them were sitting by my head. This resulted in the removal of all my personal affections, although thought and perception continued. [2] I was in this condition for several hours.

Then the spirits who were around me left, declaring that I was dead. There was a perceptible aromatic odor, like that of an embalmed body. For when celestial angels are present, then anything that has to do with a corpse is perceived as something aromatic, which prevents spirits from coming near when they perceive it. This is how evil spirits are kept away from a person's spirit when he is just being led into eternal life.

The angels who sat by my head were silent, only their thoughts communicating with mine. When these thoughts are accepted, the angels know that the person's spirit is in a state to be led out of his body. The communication of their thoughts was accomplished by their looking at my face, this being in fact how communication of thoughts takes places in heaven.

[3] Since I still had thought and perception in order to know and remember how awakening happens, I did perceive that the angels first tried to discover what my thinking was, whether it was like the thinking of people who die, which is normally about eternal life. I also perceived that they wanted to keep my mind in that thinking.

Later on, I was told that a person's spirit is kept in its last thought when the body dies, until it returns to the thoughts that stemmed from the affection of its general or ruling love in the world.

Especially, I was allowed to perceive and feel that there was a pulling, a kind of drawing of the more inward elements of my mind—hence of my spirit—out of my body. I was told that this is done by the Lord, and is the source of resurrection.

450. When celestial angels are with someone who has been awakened, they do not leave him; for they love each and every one. But when the spirit is the kind who cannot be in fellowship with celestial angels any longer, then he wants to get away from them.

When this happens, angels from the Lord's spiritual kingdom come, through whom the spirit is granted the benefit of light. For up to this point he had not seen anything; he had only thought.

I was shown how this happens, too. Those angels seemed in a way to roll back a covering of the left eye toward the bridge of the nose, so that the eye was opened and enabled to see. A spirit's whole perception is that this is what happens, but it only seems that way.

Once this covering seems to have been rolled back, something bright but hazy is visible, rather like what a person sees through half open eyelids when he first wakes up. At this point, the bright hazy something seemed to me to be of a heavenly color; but then I was told that this varies.

After this, I felt something being softly rolled off my face, which brought about spiritual thought. This rolling off from the face is an appearance as well, serving to depict that the person has come from natural thought into spiritual thought. The angels take the greatest possible care to prevent the emergence of any concept from the awakened person unless it savors of love.

Then they tell him that he is a spirit.

After the benefit of life has been given, the spiritual angels offer the new spirit every service he could ever wish in that condition, and teach him about the things that exist in the other life, but only as he can comprehend them.

If he is not the kind who is willing to be taught, the person who has been awakened craves release from the fellowship of these angels. Still it is not the angels who leave him; it is he who estranges himself from them. The angels actually love each individual, and want above all to be of service to him, to teach him, and to lead him into heaven. They find their highest delight in this.

When a spirit has thus estranged himself, he is taken away by good spirits, who offer him all kinds of help as long as he is in fellowship with them. But if his life in the world was of a kind to make fellowship with good spirits impossible, then he craves release from them as well. This happens as long and as often as necessary, until he joins the kind of spirits who wholly fit in with his life in the world, among whom he finds his kind of life. Then, remarkably, he leads the same kind of life he led in the world.

451. This introductory phase of a person's life after death, however, lasts only a few days. In the following pages we shall describe how he is guided from one state to another, and finally into heaven or hell. This again is something I have been given to know through a good deal of experience.

452. I have talked with some people on the third day after their departure, at which time the events described above (nn. 449-450) were completed. I have even talked with three people I had known in the world, telling them that their funeral rites were now being arranged for the burial of their bodies. I said, "for their burial." When they heard this, they were struck with a kind of stupefaction, saying that they were alive; people were burying only the thing that had served them in the world.

Later, they were quite amazed that while they lived in the flesh they had not believed in this kind of life after death, especially that almost everyone in the church shared this disbelief.

People who have not believed, in the world, in any life of the soul after the life of the body, are acutely embarrassed when they realize that they are alive. But people who have convinced themselves of this opinion make friends with others of like mind and are separated from people who were in faith. For the most part, they are attached to some hellish community, because people of this sort have denied the Divine and despised the true elements of the church. In fact, to the extent that anyone convinces himself in opposition to the eternal life of his soul, he also convinces himself in opposition to the things that belong to heaven and the church.

47.

AFTER DEATH, PEOPLE EXIST IN A PERFECT HUMAN FORM

453. From matters set forth in a number of chapters above, we can support the conclusion that the form of a person's spirit is the human form—or that the spirit is a person even in form. We refer particularly to the chapters where it is explained that every single angel is in a complete human form (nn. 73-77), that every single person is a spirit as far as his more inward reaches are concerned (nn. 432-444), and that the angels in heaven come from the human race (nn. 311-317).

[2] This can be discerned still more clearly from the fact that a person is a person because of his spirit, not because of his body, the bodily form being appended to the spirit in keeping with the spirit's form, not vice versa. For the spirit is clothed with a body which accords with the spirit's form. This is why a person's spirit acts into the details—even the smallest details—of the body, to the point that any part which the spirit does not activate (that is, in which the spirit is not active) is not alive.

Anyone can know this simply from the fact that thought and intention activate the whole body and all its parts, with such complete control that nothing goes its own separate way. Anything that does go its own separate way is not part of the body, but is rejected as having no living element in it. Thought and intention belong to man's spirit, not to his body.

[3] The reason why the spirit is not visible in a human

350

form to man (either after its separation from the body or within another person) is that the physical organ of sight, the eye, inasmuch as it does its seeing in the world, is made of matter. A material entity sees only what is material, while a spiritual entity sees what is spiritual. As a result, when the material eye is shrouded, or loses its ability to work with the spiritual eye, then spirits are visible in their own form, which is a human one. This applies not only to spirits who are in the spiritual world, but even to the spirit which is in someone else while still in the body.

454. The reason why the spirit's form is the human form, is that as far as his spirit is concerned, man has been created in heaven's form; for all the elements of heaven and its design are brought together in the elements of man's mind. This is the cause of his ability to receive intelligence and wisdom.

It makes no difference whether you say "his ability to receive intelligence and wisdom" or "his ability to receive heaven," as we can support from the matters set forth about heaven's light and warmth (nn. 126-140), heaven's form (nn. 200-212), angels's wisdom (nn. 265-275), and in the chapter on heaven reflecting a person in its form, overall and in its parts (nn. 59-77)—this because of the Lord's Divine-Human, which is the source of heaven and of heaven's form (nn. 78-86).

455. A rational person can understand the matters just presented because he can see from a confluence of causes and from true things in their own proper pattern; but a person who is not rational will not understand them.

There are many reasons for this failure to understand. The chief one is unwillingness, since these matters oppose the false concepts which a person has constituted as his "truths." A person who does not want to understand for this reason closes off heaven's route to his rational capacity—a way which can still be opened if only his intention does not resist (see above, n. 424).

A great deal of experience has been used to show me that a person can understand what is true and can be rational, if only he is willing. Evil spirits who had become irrational by denying in the world the Divine and the true elements of the church, and by resolving themselves in opposition to them, have quite often been turned by Divine power toward spirits who were in the light of what is true. At that point, they grasped everything like angels, stating that these things were true and that they did grasp them all. But the moment they slipped back into their selves and turned toward the love that belonged to their own intention, they grasped nothing, and said things quite the reverse.

[2] I have even heard some hellish spirits say that they both know and observe that their behavior is evil and their thinking false, but that they cannot resist the delight and hence the intention of their love. This, they said, so bears their thoughts along that they see the evil as good and the false as true.

This enabled me to see that people involved in things false because of what is evil were able to understand, able likewise to be rational, but did not want to, their unwillingness being because they loved false things more than true as being in harmony with the evil things they were involved in.

Loving and intending are the same. For a person loves what he intends and intends what he loves.

[3] Since people are in a state which enables them to understand what is true if only they want to, I have been given leave to support with rational considerations spiritual true things pertaining to the church and to heaven. The purpose is then by rational considerations to break up the false things that have closed off the rational ability for many

people, thereby perhaps opening the eye somewhat. For everyone who is involved in things true is given leave to support spiritual true things by means of rational considerations.

Who would ever understand the Word from its literal meaning, if he did not see true elements in it from an enlightened rational ability? What other source is there for so many heresies from the same Word?

456. Daily experience for many years has witnessed to me that the individual's spirit is a person after its separation from the body, and is in a similar form. A thousand times I have seen them, heard them, and talked with them—even about the fact that people in the world do not believe that spirits are what they are, and that people who do so believe are thought of by scholars as simpletons.

The spirits were heartsick at the persistence of this ignorance on earth, especially within the church, saying that this belief had spread primarily from scholars who thought about the soul on the basis of what is sensory and physical. So they gained no concept of the soul, except as being only thought; and when thought is examined apart from any subject in which it occurs and from which it stems, it is like some volatile kind of pure ether, which, on the death of the body, cannot help dissipating. However, since the church, because of the Word, believes in the soul's immortality, they had to credit it with something living like that which thought has, though they did not credit it with any capacity for sensation until it was once again bound to a body.

This view is the basis of the doctrine of resurrection and the faith which holds that this reuniting with a body will happen when the last judgment arrives. As a result of this, when anyone thinks about the soul from this doctrine and theory combined, he fails completely to grasp that the soul is spirit, and that it is spirit in human form.

So it happens that hardly anyone nowadays knows what the spiritual is, let alone that people who are spiritual (as all angels and spirits are) have any human form.

[3] This is why practically all the people who arrive from this world are as bewildered as can be at being alive, at being just as much ''people'' as before, at seeing, hearing, and speaking, at their bodies' ability to touch as before—at there being no difference at all (see above, n. 74). But once this bewilderment is over, then they are bewildered at the fact that the church does not know anything about this condition of people after death, and consequently does not know anything about heaven and hell. All this is in the face of the fact that absolutely all the people who have lived in the world are in the other life, and are living as people.

Further, since they wondered why this (being an essential element of the church's faith) had not been made clear to man by visions, they were informed from heaven that this could have been accomplished—nothing is easier when it pleases the Lord—but that people who had convinced themselves of false beliefs in opposition would still not have believed even if they themselves had seen. Further, they were informed that it is dangerous to support any belief by visions for people who are involved in false beliefs. For at first they would believe, but then they would deny, thus profaning that true belief itself, since profanation is believing and then denying. People who profane true things are driven down into the deepest and harshest of all the hells.

[4] This is the danger meant by the Lord's words:

He has blinded their eyes and hardened their hearts, lest they see with their eyes and understand with the heart, and turn themselves around, and I heal them. (John 12:40)

The fact that people who are involved in false things would not believe even then is meant by these words:

Abraham said to Dives in hell, ''They have Moses and the prophets; let them hear them.'' But he said, ''No, father Abraham; but if one of the dead came to them, they would change their minds." Abraham said to him, however, "If they do not hear Moses and the prophets, they would not believe even if someone rose from the dead."(Luke 16:29-31)

457. When a person's spirit first enters the world of spirits, which (see above) happens shortly after his awakening, it has a face and a sound of voice similar to what the person had in the world. The reason is that at this point he is in a state proper to his more outward elements, the more inward ones being not yet uncovered. This state is the first one people have after their decease.

Later on, the face changes and becomes quite different. It becomes like his dominant affection or love, the kind that engaged the more inward elements of his mind in the world, and that engaged his spirit within his body. For the face of a person's spirit differs markedly from his physical face. His physical face comes from his parents, while his spirit's face stems from his affection, being its image. The spirit comes into this after the life in the body when the more outward elements are removed and the more inward ones unveiled. This state is the person's second [Lat. "third", but *cf.* n. 499 below] one.

I have seen some people just arrived from the world, and recognized them by face and voice; but when I saw them later, I did not recognize them. The ones who were involved in good affections had beautiful faces, while the ones who were involved in evil affections had misshapen faces. Seen in its own right, a person's spirit is nothing but his affection: its outer form is his face.

Another reason faces change is that people in the other life are not allowed to feign affections which do not really belong to them. That is, they are not allowed to put on a face contrary to the love they are engaged in. Absolutely everyone there is resolved into a state in which he speaks the way he thinks, and displays in his expression and gestures what his intentions are.

This, then, is why everyone's face becomes a form and likeness of his affections. And this is why all the people who recognized each other in the world recognize each other in the world of spirits, but not in heaven or hell, as stated above (n. 427).

458. Hypocrites' faces change later than other people's faces because they by practice have formed the habit of arranging their more inward elements into a copy of good affections. As a result, they do not look unattractive for quite a while. However, since this imitative level is stripped off step by step, and the more inward elements of their minds are arranged in the form of their affections, later on they become more misshapen than other people.

Hypocrites are people who have talked like angels, but have given more inward acknowledgment to nature alone, not to the Divine therefore, and who have consequently denied the things proper to the church and heaven.

459. It is worth knowing that the more inwardly a person has loved Divine truths and has lived by them, the more beautiful is his human form after death. For everyone's more inward elements are both opened and formed according to his love and life. Consequently, the more inward the affection, the more it shares in heaven's form, and therefore the more comely is its face.

This is why angels who are in the inmost heaven are the most beautiful—because they are forms of celestial love. People who have loved Divine truths more outwardly and hence have lived them more outwardly are less beautiful. For only relatively outward things shine from their faces; a more inward, celestial love does not shine through these relatively outward things. Neither, then, does heaven's form in its own intrinsic quality. Something rather obscure can be seen in their faces, something not enlivened by the shining through of a more inward life.

In a word, all perfection increases toward more inward levels and decreases toward more outward levels. As perfection rises and falls, so does beauty.

I have seen angelic faces of the third heaven, whose quality was such that no artist, with all his skill, could impart enough of that kind of light to his colors to capture a thousandth part of the light and life you can see in their faces. But the faces of angels of the lowest heaven can be captured to some extent.

460. In conclusion, I should like to offer a particular "arcanum" never before known to anyone—namely that everything good and true that comes from the Lord and constitutes heaven is in a human form. This applies not only overall and most broadly, but in every part and in least detail. This form influences everyone who accepts what is good and true from the Lord, and causes everyone in heaven to be in a human form in keeping with his acceptance.

This is why heaven is alike overall and in detail, why the human form applies to the whole, to each community, and to each angel, as presented in the four chapters that run from n. 59 through n. 86. We need to add to this that the human form applies to the details of thought that stem from heavenly love in angels.

But this arcanum does not fit comfortably into the understanding of any man, though it does fit clearly with angel's understanding, since they are in heaven's light.

48.

AFTER DEATH, A PERSON IS ENGAGED IN EVERY SENSE, MEMORY, THOUGHT, AND AFFECTION HE WAS ENGAGED IN IN THE WORLD: HE LEAVES NOTHING BEHIND EXCEPT HIS EARTHLY BODY

461. Manifold experience has witnessed to me that when a person crosses over from the natural into the spiritual world, which happens when he dies, he carries with him everything that is his, or everything belonging to his person, except his earthly body. For when a person enters the spiritual world, or the life after death, he is in a body the way he was in this world. There seems to be no difference, since he does not feel or see any difference. But his body is spiritual, and so is separated and purified from earthly elements. Further, when something spiritual touches and sees something spiritual, it is just the same as when something natural touches and sees something natural.

As a result, when a person has become a spirit, he cannot tell that he is not in the body he had in the world, and consequently does not know that he has died.

[2] Further, the spirit person enjoys every outward and inward sense he enjoyed in the world. As before, he sees; as before, he hears and speaks, he smells and tastes; as before he feels the pressure when he is touched. He still yearns, wishes, craves, thinks, ponders, is moved, loves, and intends as before. A person who enjoyed scholarly work reads and writes as before. In a word, when a person crosses from one life to the other, or from one world to the other,

358

it is as though he had gone from one place to another and had taken with himself all the things he possessed in his own right as a person. This holds true to the point that one cannot say that a person has lost anything of his own after death, which is a death of the earthly body alone.

He even carries his natural memory with him. For he keeps all the things he has heard, seen, read, learned, or thought in the world from earliest infancy right to the last moment of his life. However, since the natural items that dwell in his memory cannot be reproduced in a spiritual world, they quiesce the way they do with a person who is not thinking about them. Still, they can be duplicated when it pleases the Lord.

We shall have more to say shortly, however, about this memory and its state after death.

A sense-oriented person is quite incapable of believing that a person's condition after death is like this, since he does not grasp it. For a sense-oriented person can only think in terms of nature, even about spiritual matters. So if he does not sense something—that is, see it with his physical eyes and touch it with his hands—he says that it does not exist, as we read of Thomas (John 20:25, 27, 29). On the nature of the sense-oriented person, see above (n. 267).

462a. However, the difference between a person's life in the spiritual world and his life in the natural world is substantial, both in regard to his outer senses and their affections. People who are in heaven have far more delicate senses (that is, they see and hear far more precisely) and they think more wisely than when they were in the world. For they see by heaven's light, which surpasses earth's light by many degrees (see above, n. 126); they hear, too, through a spiritual atmosphere, which also surpasses the earthly one by many degrees (n. 235).

The difference for these outer senses is like the difference between something clear and something veiled by a cloud in the world, or between noonday light and evening shadows. Heaven's light, being the Divine-True, actually gives angels' sight the ability to notice and distinguish the tiniest things. [2] Further, their outer sight corresponds to an inner sight or discernment. For the one sight, for angels, flows into the other so that they act as one, which is why they have such keenness. In like fashion too, their hearing corresponds to their perception, which is a matter of both discernment and intention. So they notice in a speaker's tone and words the tiniest details of his affection and thought —matters of affection in the tone, and matters of thought in the words (see above, nn. 234-245).

For angels, though, the other senses are not so delicate as the senses of sight and hearing, because sight and hearing rather than the others are the servants of their intelligence and wisdom.

If the other senses operated at a like level of delicacy, they would detract from the light and pleasure of their wisdom and bring in a delight in pleasures of various cravings of the body. These veil and cripple the discernment to the extent that they assume leading roles, as happens with people in the world who are sluggish and dull in matters of spiritual truth to the extent that they gratify their taste and give in to the panderings of the sense of physical touch.

[3] From the matters set forth in the chapter on the wisdom of heaven's angels (nn. 265-275), we can conclude that the more inward senses of heaven's angels, belonging to their thought and affection, are more delicate and more perfect than those they had in the world.

As touches the difference between the state of people in hell and their state in the world, this too is substantial. Great as is the perfection and excellence of outer and inner senses for angels who are in heaven, just as great is the imperfection for people who are in hell. But we will deal with their condition later.

462b. As to the retention by people from the world of their whole memory, this has been shown me by many things. I have seen and heard quite a few things worth relating, and should like to tell some of them in a sequence.

There were people who denied crimes and disgraceful things they had committed in the world. So lest people believe them innocent, all things were uncovered and reviewed out of their memory, in sequence, from their earliest age to the end. Foremost were matters of adultery and whoredom.

[2] There were some people who had taken others in by evil devices and who had stolen. Their wiles and thefts were recounted one after another—many of them things hardly anyone in the world had known other than the thieves themselves. They admitted them, too (since they were made clear as daylight), together with every thought, intent, pleasure, and fear which had then combined to agitate their spirits.

[3] There were people who took bribes and made a profit out of judicial decisions. These people were examined from their memory in similar fashion, and from this source everything they had done from the beginning to the end of their tenure of office was reviewed. There were details about how much and what kind, about the time, about the state of their mind and intent, all cast together in their remembrance, now brought out into sight, running past several hundred.

This has been done with other people, and, remarkably, their very diaries where they wrote things like this have been opened and read right in front of them, page by page.

[4] There were people who had lured virgins into dishonor and had violated chastity, who were called to a similar judgment, with details extracted and narrated from their memory. The actual faces of the virgins and other women

were produced just as though they were there, with the locales, the voices, the moods. This was just as immediate as when something is presented to the sight. Sometimes these demonstrations lasted for some hours.

[5] There was one person who thought nothing of disparaging others. I heard his disparaging remarks repeated in their sequence, his defamations as well, in the actual words—whom they were about, whom they were addressed to. All these elements were set forth and presented together in wholly life-like fashion; yet the details had been studiously covered up by him while he had lived in the world.

[6] There was a particular person who had robbed a relative of his inheritance by some crafty device. He too was refuted and judged in a similar way. Strange as it seems, the letters and papers which had passed between them were read in my hearing, and they said that not a word was missing. [7] This same person, shortly before his death, had secretly killed a neighbor by poison. This was laid bare in the following way. A trench seemed to be dug at his feet, and after it was dug out, a man emerged as though from a tomb and shouted at him, "What have you done to me?" Then everything was unveiled—how the poisoner had talked with him as a friend and had offered him a drink, then what he had planned beforehand and what happened afterwards. Once these matters were uncovered, he was sentenced to hell.

[8] In short, each evil spirit is shown clearly all his evil deeds, his crimes, thefts, deceits, and devices. These are brought out of his own memory and proven; there is no room left for denial, since all the attendant circumstances are visible at once.

I have even heard the things which a person thought during a month seen and reviewed by angels out of his memory, a day at a time without error—things recalled as though the person were engaged in them at the time they happened.

[9] We can conclude from these instances that a person carries with him his whole memory, and that nothing is so well hidden in the world that it is not brought out into the open after death, in public, in keeping with the Lord's words,

> Nothing is concealed that will not be uncovered, and nothing hidden that will not be recognized. So what you have said in the darkness will be heard in the light, and what you have said in the ear . . . will be proclaimed on the housetops.

> (Luke 12:2-3)

463. When a person's deeds are being laid bare to him after death, the angels who are given responsibility for examining him look carefully at his face. The examination then spreads through his whole body, beginning with the fingers of one hand, then the other, and continuing in this fashion through the whole.

Because I was puzzled as to the reason for this, it was unveiled, as follows. Just as the details of thought and intention are written on the brain because their origins are there, so they are written on the entire body as well, because all elements of thought and intention move out from their origins into the entire body, where they are bounded as being in their final forms. This is why the things that are written in a person's memory, that have come from intention and consequent thought, are not written on the brain alone, but on the whole person, where they occur in a pattern that follows the pattern of the parts of the body.

This enabled me to see that a person's overall quality is the same as the quality of his intention and consequent thought, even to the point that an evil person is his own "evil" and a good person is his own "good."

We can also draw a conclusion from these considerations about the meaning of a person's "book of life" mentioned in the Word. It is indeed the fact that everything—both deeds and thoughts—is written on the whole person, seeming to be read in a book when called from the memory, and to be seen in visual likeness when the spirit is examined in heaven's light.

I should like to append a noteworthy occurrence that involves man's memory as it endures after death, an occurrence which convinced me that it is not just the broad outlines that have entered the memory which persist, but the most minute details as well: they are never erased.

I saw some books with writing in them, like books in the world, and I was informed that these had come out of the memory of the people who had written them, without a word missing that had been in the book any one of them had written in the world. In the same way, the most minute details of everything can be drawn from someone's memory, even things he himself has forgotten in the world.

The following reason was then unveiled. Man has an outer and an inner memory, the outer one belonging to his natural person, and the inner one belonging to his spiritual person. The details which a person has thought, intended, said, done—even what he has heard and seen—are written on his inner or spiritual memory. There is no way to destroy the things that are there because they are written at once on the spirit itself and on the members of its body, as stated above. So the spirit is formed in keeping with the thoughts and acts of its intention.

I know these things seem very strange, and on this account are almost impossible to believe; still they are true.

Let no one then believe that there is anything a person has thought within himself or done in secret that remains hidden after death. Let him rather believe that each and everything will then be visible as in broad daylight.

464. Even though a person retains possession of his outer or natural memory after death, still the simply natural elements it contains are not brought out again in the other life. Instead, it is the spiritual elements connected to the natural ones by their correspondences.

Yet when these are presented to view, they seem to be in just the same form they had in the natural world. For all the things that are visible in the heavens look like things in this world, even though they are not essentially natural but spiritual, as presented in the chapter on representations and appearances in heaven (nn. 170-176).

[2] The outer or natural memory, however, as concerns such of its contents as derive from what is material, from time and space, and from other things proper to nature, does not serve the spirit in the same function it performed for it in the world. For when a person in this world has thought on the basis of the outer sensory level and not at the same time on the basis of the inner or "intellectual" sensory level, he has thought naturally and not spiritually. In the other life, though, when he is a spirit in the spiritual world, he does not think naturally, but spiritually. Thinking spiritually is thinking "with discernment" or "rationally."

This is why the outer or natural memory becomes dormant as far as material elements are concerned, and only those elements come into play which the person has drawn out through the material elements and made rational while he was in the world.

The reason for the dormancy of the outer memory in regard to its material elements is that these cannot again be brought out. Spirits and angels, in fact, talk from the affections and consequent thoughts that belong to their minds. So things which do not square with these cannot be articulated, as we can conclude from the statements about the speech of angels in heaven and their speech with man (nn. 234-257).

[3] This is why a person is rational after death to the extent that he has become rational by means of language and data in this world, not to the extent that he was skillful with languages and data.

I have talked with many people who were believed to be learned in the world because of their acquaintance with ancient languages like Hebrew, Greek, and Latin, but who had not developed their rational ability by means of what was written in these languages. Some of them seemed as simplistic as people who had no acquaintance with these languages; some seemed stupid, although an arrogance stayed with them as though they were wiser than other people.

[4] I have talked with some people who believed in the world that a person's wisdom depended on how much his memory had in it. These people also stuffed their memories with a mass of material, and talked almost on the basis of this alone. As a result, they did not talk on their own, but echoed others, and did not perfect any rational ability by means of their matters of memory.

Some of them were stupid, some foolish—grasping absolutely nothing true, not knowing whether it was true or not, latching on to all kinds of false things which self-styled scholars market as true. In fact, on their own they cannot see whether anything is true or not, which means they cannot see anything rationally when they listen to other people.

[5] I have also talked with people who had done a great deal of writing in the world—in many different disciplines—and who as a result had a reputation for scholarship over much of the globe. Some of them could actually think logically about matters of truth, about whether things were true or not. Some did understand that they were true while they were talking with people involved in the light of truth, but still did not want to understand. So these people habit-

ually denied the matters of truth when they were involved in their own falsities and therefore in themselves. Some were no wiser than the illiterate masses. Each one, that is, had developed his own rational ability in his own way, by means, so to speak, of the studies he had composed and copied.

But as for people who have been opposed to the true elements of the church, who have done their thinking on the basis of matters of data, and who have convinced themselves of false propositions by this means, they have not developed their rational ability. They have developed only an ability to use logic, an ability people in the world believe to be rationality. It is, however, an ability distinct from rationality. It is a faculty of "proving" whatever one likes, of seeing false rather then true things on the basis of preconceptions and fallacies.

There is no way people like this can be "driven home" to any recognition of things true, since true things cannot be seen from false ones, though false things can be seen from true ones.

A person's rational ability is like a garden with things growing in it, or like fallow ground. [6] His memory is the soil, his true data and his insights are the seeds. Heaven's light and warmth make them come up; without these no sprouting takes place. This latter is what happens if heaven's light (which is the Divine-True) and heaven's warmth (which is Divine love) are not let in. They are the only sources of rational ability.

It grieves angels very deeply that learned people for the most part give nature credit for everything and consequently close off the more inward reaches of their minds, so that they cannot see any element of what is true from the light of what is true, which is heaven's light. As a result, in the other life they lose their faculty of logical thought, to prevent them from using devices of logic to spread false understandings among simple good folk and leading them astray. They are banished to desert areas.

465. One particular spirit was feeling resentful because he did not remember a lot of things he had known in his physical life, feeling sorry for the pleasure he was missing, in which he had previously found the greatest possible delight. He was however told that he had lost nothing whatever, that he knew everything in detail. Further, in the world where he now was, bringing things like these out to his consciousness was not allowed. It was enough that he now had the ability to think and talk much better and more perfectly, without submerging his rational ability the way he had before in thick confusions, in material, physical things, which were useless in the kingdom he had now entered. Now, he was told, he had everything conducive to the function of eternal life; there was no other way he could become blessed and happy. So it was ignorance to believe that in this kingdom intelligence died at the departure and dormancy of the material things in the memory. The situation is like this instead: to the extent that a mind can be led away from the sensory matters in the outer person or the body, it is raised to spiritual and celestial matters.

466. The nature of the memories is sometimes presented to view in the other life, in forms visible only there. Many things are presented to view there which otherwise, for men, issue only as concepts. The more outward memory there takes on a form like a callus; the more inward a form like the medullary substance we find in the human brain, which enables us to know what they are like.

People whose whole preoccupation in their physical life was with the memory, and who therefore have not developed their rational ability, have what looks like a hard callousness, with something like stringy tendons within it. People who have filled their memories with falsities have something that looks hairy and shaggy, because of the disorganized mass of stuff. People who have been preoccupied with memory because of a love of self and the world have something that looks stuck together and calcified. People who have wanted to plumb Divine secrets by means of outward data, especially those of philosophy, unwilling to believe anything unless convinced by these means, have a memory that looks gloomy, and has a quality of absorbing light rays and turning them into shadows. As for decitful and hypocritical people, their memory looks like something hard and bony, like ivory, which reflects light rays.

But as for people who have been involved in what is good from love and in true things of faith, this kind of callus is not visible in them, since their more inward memory sends light rays through into their more outward memory, which rays find their end-points in the objects of concepts of that outer memory—in, so to speak, their foundation or their soil. There they find wholly agreeable vessels. For the outer memory is the last member of a sequence, in which spiritual and celestial elements softly find their end-points and come to rest, when there are good and true elements in it.

467. People who are involved in love to the Lord and in caring about the neighbor have while they are living in the world an angelic intelligence with and within them, but it is hidden away in the most inward reaches of their inner memory. There is no way for this intelligence and wisdom to become manifest to them before they shed what is physical. Then the natural memory is put to sleep, and the people are awakened to a more inward memory, then step by step to a real angelic memory.

468. We may now state briefly how a rational ability is developed.

A true rational ability is made up of true, not false elements; anything made up of false elements is not rational. There are three kinds of true elements—civic, moral, and spiritual.

Civic true elements have to do with matters of legal decision and governmental forms in kingdoms—in general with what is just and fair in this area. Moral true elements have to do with matters of an individual's personal life in relation to groups and associations, generally as concerns what is honest and upright, and particularly as concerns virtues of every kind. Spiritual true elements, though, have to do with matters of heaven and the church, in general to the good that belongs to love and the true that belongs to faith.

[2] There are three levels of life in every individual (see above, n. 267). His rational capacity is opened on the first level by means of civic true elements, on the second level by moral true elements, and on the third by spiritual true elements.

But it does need to be known that a rational ability is not thus formed and opened by virtue of the person's knowing these elements, but by virtue of his living by them. "Living by them" means loving them out of a spiritual affection; and "loving them out of a spiritual affection" is loving what is just and fair because it is just and fair, loving what is honest and upright because it is honest and upright, loving what is good and true because it is good and true. On the other hand, living by them and loving them out of a physical affection is loving them for self's sake, for the sake of reputation, prestige, and profit. So an individual is non-rational to the extent that he loves these true elements out of a physical affection. He does not really love them; he loves that self which these true elements serve the way slaves serve their master. And when true things become a corps of slaves, they do not gain entrance to the person or open any level of his life, not even the first. They simply come to rest in his memory, as data in material form, and bind themselves to his love of self, which is a physical love.

[3] We can establish on this basis how a person becomes rational—namely, on the third level by a spiritual love of the good and the true that belong to heaven and the church, on the second level by a love of what is honest and upright, and on the first level by a love of what is just and fair. Further, these latter two loves become spiritual because of a spiritual love of what is good and true, because this flows into them, binds itself to them, and so to speak forms its own countenance within them.

469. Spirits and angels have just as much memory as man. The things they have heard, seen, though, intended, and done stay with them; and their rational ability is constantly being developed by means of their memory, to eternity. This is why spirits and angels are perfected in intelligence and wisdom by means of their insights of what is true and good, just as men are.

A substantial amount of evidence has enabled me to know that spirits and angels have memory. I have in fact seen that everything they thought and did, openly or secretly, was called out of their memories while they were with other spirits. Then too, I have seen that people who were involved in some particular true matter out of a simple, good motive, were initiated into insights and thereby into intelligence, and then were led away into heaven.

But it needs to be known that they are not initiated into insights, and thereby intelligence, beyond the level of their affection for the good and the true they engaged in in the world—not beyond that level. Every spirit and angel keeps the amount and quality of affection he had in the world. This is later perfected by being filled, which continues to eternity. For there is nothing that cannot keep being filled to eternity; in fact, every particular tnings can be diversified in an infinite number of ways and hence enriched bv different elements, and thereoy muitiplied and made fruitful. There is no end of any good thing, because it comes from the Infinite.

On the constant perfecting of spirits and angels in intelligence and wisdom by means of insights of what is good and true, see the chapters on the wisdom of heaven's angels (nn. 265-275), on Gentiles and people from outside the church in heaven (nn. 318-328), and on little children in heaven (nn. 329-345). On the restriction of this to the level of affection for the good and the true which they engaged in in the world, see n. 349.

49.

A PERSON'S QUALITY AFTER DEATH IS THE SAME AS THE QUALITY OF HIS LIFE IN THE WORLD WAS

470. Every Christian knows from the Word that the life of each individual stays with him after death. For it is stated in many places that the person will be judged and rewarded according to his deeds and works. Further, anyone who does his thinking on the basis of what is good and really true cannot help seeing that a person who lives well goes to heaven and a person who lives evilly goes to hell.

However, the person who is involved in what is evil is unwilling to believe that his state after death depends on his life in the world. He thinks rather (especially when he gets sick) that heaven is granted to an individual out of pure mercy, no matter how he has lived, and that it depends on a faith which he separates from life.

471. There are many places in the Word where it is stated that man will be judged and rewarded according to his deeds and works. I should like to cite a few at this point.

> The Son of man is going to come in the glory of His father with His angels, and then He will recompense everyone according to his works. (Matthew 16:27)
>
> Blessed are the dead, who die in the Lord . . . indeed, says the Spirit, so that they may rest from their labors; . . . their works follow them. (Revelation 14:13)
>
> I will give to each individual according to his works. (Revelation 2:23)
>
> I saw the dead, small and great, standing in front of God; and the books were opened; and the dead were judged by the things which were written in the books, according to their works; . . . the sea yielded

up those who were dead within it, and death and hell yielded up those within them; and all were judged according to their works.
(Revelation 20:12-13)

Lo, I come, . . . and My reward is with Me, that I may give to everyone according to his works.
(Revelation 22:12)

Everyone . . . who hears My words and does them, I will compare to a prudent man, . . . but everyone who hears My words . . . and does not do them, is compared to a stupid man.

(Matthew 7:24, 26)

Not all the people who say to me, "Lord, Lord" will enter the kingdom of the heavens, but rather the person who does the will of My Father who is in the heavens. Many will say to Me in that day, "Lord, Lord, have we not prophesied through Your name, and through Your name cast out demons, and in Your name done many good deeds?" But I will declare to them, "I do not know you: depart from Me, you evildoers."
(Matthew 7:21-23)

Then you will begin to say, "We ate and drank with you; you taught in our streets." But He will say, "I tell you, I do not know you evildoers."
(Luke 13:25-27)

I will reward them according to their work, and according to the deed of their hands.
(Jeremiah 25:14)

[Jehovah] whose eyes are open over all the ways of man, to give to each according to his ways, and according to the fruit of his works.
(Jeremiah 32:19)

I will come to oversee . . . his ways, and I will give him the reward of his works.
(Hosea 4:9)

Jehovah . . . deals with us in keeping with our ways and in keeping with our works.
(Zechariah 1:6)

When the Lord foretells the Last Judgment, He examines nothing but works; and He states in Matthew 25:32-46 that people who have done good works will enter eternal life and people who have done evil works will enter condemnation. The same view is presented in many other passages about man's salvation and condemnation.

We can see that works and deeds are a person's outward life, and that the quality of his inward life takes visible form through them.

472. "Deeds and works," however, does not mean deeds and works simply as they present themselves in outward form; it means also the way they are inside. We all do in fact realize that every deed and work comes out of a person's intention and thought. Unless it did come from this source, it would be movement only, of the kind produced by machines and models. So seen in its own right, a deed or work is only a result which takes its soul and life from intention and thought. Accordingly, it is intention and thought in outward form.

It follows from this that the quality of the intention and thought which produce a deed or work determine the quality of the deed or work. If the thought and intention are good, then deeds and works are good; while if the thought and intention are evil, then the deeds and works are evil, even though the two kinds may look alike in outward form.

A thousand people may behave alike—that is, face us with similar deeds, so similar that we can scarcely tell them apart by their outward form. But each particular one is different, seen in its own right, because it comes from a different intention.

[2] Let us take behaving honestly and fairly with our fellow-citizen as an example. One person can behave honestly and fairly with him in order to seem honest and fair, for his own sake and for the sake of prestige. Another may do the same for the sake of this world and for profit, a third for reward and credit, a fourth to maintain a friendship, a fifth out of fear of the law, of loss of reputation and position, a sixth to attract someone to his own clique, which may well be evil, a seventh to deceive, and others for still different purposes. Yet in spite of the fact that all these people's deeds seem good (for behaving honestly and fairly with the fellow citizen is a good thing), they are still evil because they are not done because of what is honest and fair, because the person loves what is honest and fair, but because of self and the world, which are loved. The honest and the fair

work for this love the way slaves work for their master, who devalues and dismisses them when they do not work for him.

[3] People who act out of a love for what is honest and fair, behave honestly and fairly with their fellow-citizens in ways that look the same in outward form. Some of them act on the basis of what is true in their faith, or from obedience because this is enjoined in the Word; some act on the basis of what is good in their faith, or conscience, because it is a matter of religion; some act on the basis of what is good in charity toward the neighbor, because what is good for him must be taken into account; some act on the basis of what is good in love to the Lord, because the good needs to be done for its own sake, the honest and just therefore for their own sakes, loving what is honest and just because they come from the Lord and because the Divine element that comes from the Lord is within them, making them Divine when viewed in their actual essence.

The deeds and works of these people are inwardly good, and so they are outwardly good as well. For as already stated, the whole quality of deeds and works depends on the quality of the thought and intention they come from. Without these latter they are not deeds and works, only inanimate movements. We can conclude from these considerations what "works" and "deeds" mean in the Word.

473. Deeds and works, being matters of intention and thought, are matters of love and faith as well. Accordingly, their quality depends on the quality of love and faith, for it makes no difference whether you say "the love" or "the intention" of a person, no difference whether you say "the faith" or "the settled thought" of a person. If a person loves something, he also intends it; if he believes something, he also thinks it. If a person loves what he believes, then he intends it, and does it to the extent that he can.

Everyone is capable of knowing that love and faith are within man's intention and thought, not outside them, because intention is what catches fire with love, and thought is what lights up in matters of faith. As a result, the only people who are enlightened are the ones who are capable of thinking wisely; and it is in proportion to this enlightenment that they think what is true and intend what is true—or believe what is true and love what is true, which is the same thing.

474. It is however worth knowing that intention makes the person. Thought makes the person only to the extent that it comes out of intention, with deeds or works coming out of this pair. Another way of saying the same thing is to say that love makes the person, with faith making him only to the extent that it comes out of love, and with deeds and works coming out of this pair. It follows, then, that intention or love is the actual person. For things which come forth belong to the source from which they come; "coming forth" is being brought forth and presented in a form suitable for perception and visibility.

We may conclude from these considerations what a faith separated from love is. It is no faith at all, only information which has no spiritual life in it. In a like vein, we may conclude what a deed or work is without love. It is not a deed or work of life, but a deed or work of death. It contains something that looks like life as a result of evil love and false faith. This "something that looks like life" is what we call "spiritual death."

475. Beyond this, it is worth knowing that the whole person is present in his deeds or works, and that his intention and thought (or his love and faith), which are his more inward elements, are not fulfilled until they occur in deeds or works which are his more outward elements. These more outward elements are the "last things" in which the more inward things find their boundaries. Without boundaries, they are undefined entities which have not yet become present, and which therefore are not yet in the person.

Thinking and intending without doing when doing is possible, are like something on fire which is sealed into a container and extinguished. Or, it is like a seed sown in the sand which does not sprout, but rather dies, together with its power to reproduce. But thinking and intending and consequently doing are like something on fire that gives warmth and light in all directions. This is also like seed sown in the earth which sprouts into a tree or flower and is truly present.

Everyone is capable of knowing that intending and not doing when doing is possible, is not really intending, that loving and not doing what is good when doing is possible is not really loving. This is merely thinking that one intends and loves; that is, it is thought all by itself, which fades away and dissipates.

Love, intention, is the very soul of a deed or work. This soul forms its body in the honest and fair things which the person does. This alone is where a person's spiritual body, or the body of his spirit, comes from. That is, it is formed entirely out of the things the person does out of love or intention (see above, n. 463). In short, all the elements of a person and of his spirit are within his deeds or works.

476. This now enables us to conclude what is meant by the life which a person keeps after death. It is his love and consequent faith, not only potential, but in act as well. So it is his deeds and works because these hold within them all the elements of the person's love and faith.

477. There is a "ruling love" which a person keeps after death, and which never changes to eternity. Everyone has a considerable number of loves, but they all go back to his ruling love and make one with it—or, taken all together, compose it.

All the elements of intention that are in harmony with the ruling love are called "loves," because they are loved. Some of these loves are more inward, some more outward; there are some directly bound and some indirectly bound; some are nearer, some are farther away; there are various kinds of subordination.

Taken all together, they make up a kind of kingdom. Thus they are in fact organized within a person, even though he is completely unaware of their organization. To some extent, however, this is made known to people in the other life, for they have an outreach of thought and affection there that depends on this organization. This is an outreach into heavenly communities if the ruling love is made up of loves of heaven, but an outreach into hellish communities if the ruling love is made up of loves of hell.

The reader may see above that spirits' and angels' every thought and affection has an outreach into communities. See the chapter on the wisdom of heaven's angels, and the chapter on heaven's form which determines friendships and communications there.

478. But the things mentioned so far appeal only to the thought of a rational person. To present these matters directly to sense perception, I should like to append some observed experiences to illustrate and reinforce the following points:

First: After death, a person is his love or intention.

Second: To eternity, a person stays the way he is as far as his intention or ruling love is concerned.

Third: a person who has a heavenly and spiritual love enters heaven; while a person who has a physical and worldly love without a heavenly and spiritual one enters hell.

Fourth: a person does not keep his faith if it does not come from a heavenly love.

Fifth: Love in act is what lasts; hence this is the person's life.

479. (i) *After death, a person is his love or intention.* This has been borne in on me by observed experience over and over again. The whole heaven is divided into communities on the basis of differences in the good that comes from love. Every single spirit who is raised into heaven and becomes an angel is taken to the community where his love is, and once he is there he is where he belongs [*apud se*], so to speak—as though he were at home, where he was born. An angel senses this, and makes close friends with others like himself.

When he leaves and goes somewhere else, there is a certain constant resistance. This is the effect of his longing to return to those who are like himself, which means to his own ruling love. This is how close friendships are formed in heaven.

The same holds true in hell, where people also form friendships on the basis of loves which are opposed to heavenly ones (on the matter of communities' making up heaven and also hell, and their being distinguished on the basis of differences in love, see above, nn. 41-50 and 200-212).

[2] We may establish that after death a person is his love from the fact also that there is a removal after death, a kind of carrying away, of the elements which do not make one with his ruling love. If a person is good, then all the things that are discordant or that disagree are removed and, so to speak, carried away. In this way he is installed in his own love. The same happens with a person who is evil (the difference being that true things are carried away from him, while false things are carried away from a good person), until finally each individual becomes his own love. This takes place when the spirit-person is brought through into the third state described below. Once this has happened, the

person constantly turns his face toward his love, keeping it always before his eyes wherever he turns (see above, nn. 123-124).

[3] Spirits without exception can be led anywhere as long as they are kept in their ruling love. They are unable to resist even though they know what is happening and think that they will resist. Attempts have often been made to see whether they could act at all contrary to that love, but to no avail. Their love is like a chain or rope fastened around them, so to speak, by which they can be pulled along, and which they cannot escape.

The same holds true for people in this world: their own love leads them too, and they are led by others by means of their own love. It is all the more true when they become spirits, because then they are not allowed to present the semblance of any other love, or to pretend a love that is not really theirs.

[4] All personal association in the other life evidences the fact that a person's spirit is his ruling love; for in fact, so far as anyone acts and talks in keeping with someone else's love, that person seems complete, with a fully expressive, cheerful, lively face. But so far as anyone acts and talks contrary to someone else's love, that person's face begins to change, to become hazy, and to fade from view. Eventually the whole person vanishes as though he had never been there. I have often been amazed that this is so, since nothing like it can occur in our world; but I have been told that something like this does happen to the spirit of a person, which is no longer within another person's view when it turns away from that other.

[5] I have been able to see that the spirit is its ruling love from another fact too, namely that every individual spirit grasps and claims as his own everything that fits in with his love, while casting off and disavowing everything that does

not fit in. Everyone's love is like a spongy or porous tree trunk, that soaks up the kinds of fluid that foster the growth of its foliage, and repels others. It is like animals of all sorts, that recognize their foods, and seek out those that agree with their natures and avoid the ones that disagree. Every particular love wants to be nourished by what is appropriate to it—an evil love by false things, and a good love by true things.

Several times, I have been enabled to see how good, simple folk wanted to educate evil people in matters of truth and goodness, and how these latter ran away from this education; and when they reached their own kind, they grasped the false elements that suited their love with an intense pleasure. I have also been enabled to see good spirits talking with each other about true things, which the good people present listened to eagerly, while the evil ones who were also present paid no attention whatever, just as though they did not hear anything.

Paths are visible in the spiritual world. Some lead to heaven, some to hell; one to one community, one to another. Good spirits travel only along paths that lead to heaven, to the community which is involved in the particular good that comes from their own love. They do not see paths leading in other directions. Evil spirits follow only paths that lead to hell, to the particular community there which is involved in the evil that comes from their own love. They do not see paths leading in other directions; and even if they do, they do not want to follow them.

Paths like this in the spiritual world are "real appearances" which correspond to true or false things, which is why "paths" in the Word have the same meaning.

These sample experiences reinforce the things already stated on the grounds of reason, namely that after death every person is his own love and his own intention. We say "intention" because everyone's actual intention is his love.

480. (ii) *To eternity, a person stays the way he is as far as his ruling love or intention is concerned,* which too I have had supported by a good deal of experience. I have been allowed to talk with some people who had lived two thousand years ago, people whose lives are described in histories and are therefore known. These people were found to be still the same, just like their descriptions, including the matter of the love which was the source and determining principle of their lives.

There were other people who lived seventeen centuries ago, known from historical sources, some who lived four centuries ago, some three, and so on, with whom I have been enabled to talk. I discovered that the same affection still reigned within them, the only difference being that their loves' pleasures had been changed into the kinds of thing that corresponded to them.

Angels said that the ruling love's life is never to all eternity changed for anyone because everyone is his own love. So changing this for a spirit would be taking away or extinguishing his life. Further, they told me why—namely that after death a person can no longer be re-formed by teaching the way he could in the world, because his lowest level, which is made up of natural insights and affections, is then stilled and is incapable of being opened because it is not spiritual (see above, n. 464). The more inward elements, which are proper to the person's mind or spirit [*animus*], rest on this level like a house on its foundation; and this is why a person stays to eternity the way his love's life was in the world.

Angels are quite amazed at man's ignorance of the fact that everyone's quality is the quality of his ruling love, and at the widespread belief in the possibility of salvation by direct mercy and by faith only, regardless of the quality of life. They are amazed at man's ignorance of the fact the

Divine mercy is indirect, that it involves being led by the Lord both in this world and thereafter to eternity, that people whose lives are not involved in evil are the ones who are led out of this mercy. Man does not even know that faith is an affection for what is true, which comes out of a heavenly love, which is from the Lord.

481. (iii) *A person who has a heavenly and spiritual love enters heaven; while a person who has a physical and worldly love without a heavenly and spiritual one enters hell.* All the people I have seen raised into heaven or cast into hell have made it possible for me to be sure of this. The people who were raised into heaven derived their life from a heavenly and spiritual love, while the people who were cast into hell derived their life from a physical and worldly love.

Heavenly love is loving what is good, honest, and fair because it is good, honest and fair, and doing it because of that love. So they have a life of goodness, honesty, and fairness, which is a heavenly life. The person who loves these things for their own sake and who does or lives them also loves the Lord supremely, because these things come from Him. He loves the neighbor as well, because these things are the neighbor whom he should love.

Physical love, in contrast, is loving what is good, honest and fair not for their own sakes but for the sake of oneself, because these are means for gaining fame, prestige, and profit. These people do not focus on the Lord and the neighbor within what is good and honest and fair, but on themselves and the world. They feel a pleasure in cheating; and any good, honest, or fair act that stems from cheating is actually evil, dishonest, and unfair—which is what they love within the acts.

[2] Since loves do define everyone's life in this way, everyone is examined as to quality as soon as he comes into

the world of spirits after death, and is connected with people who are involved in a love like his own. People who are involved in a heavenly love are connected with people in heaven, and people who are involved in a physical love are connected with people in hell.

Then too, after the first and second states have been completed, these two classes are separated so that they no longer see or recognize each other. Each individual becomes his own love, not only in regard to the more inward elements of his mind, but even in regard to the more outward matters that are proper to his face, body, and speech; for each person becomes an image of his love, even in outward things.

People who are physical loves look crude, dark, black, and misshapen; while people who are heavenly loves look lively bright, shining, and lovely. They are wholly unlike in spirit and in thought. People who are heavenly loves are also intelligent and wise; people who are physical loves are stolid and rather foolish.

[3] When one is enabled to examine the more inward and the more outward elements of people who are involved in a heavenly love, their more inward elements look like light—in some, like a flaming light—and their more outward elements appear in a variety of lovely colors like a rainbow. But the more inward elements of people who are involved in a physical love look like something black because they are closed—in some, like a dark fire. These last are people more deeply involved in malicious deceit. Their more outward elements appear in a color that is dirty, and depressing to look at. The more inward and more outward elements of the mind and spirit [*animus*] are presented to view in the spiritual world whenever it pleases the Lord.

[4] People who are involved in a physical love do not see anything in heaven's light. To them, heaven's light is gloom, while hell's light (which is like the light of burning

embers) is like a bright light to them. In heaven's light their more inward sight is actually darkened to the point that they become insane. Consequently, they flee from that light and hide in caves or caverns, more or less deep depending on the false things within them derived from their evils. It is quite the reverse with people who are involved in a heavenly love. The more deeply or highly they enter heaven's light, the more clearly they see everything, and the more beautiful everything is. To the same extent, they perceive things that are true more intelligently and more wisely.

[5] People who are involved in a physical love are wholly incapable of living in heaven's warmth, since heaven's warmth is heavenly love. They are however capable of living in hell's warmth, which is a love of cruelty toward other people who do not support them. The pleasures of this love are various kinds of contempt for others, of enmity, hatred, and revenge. When they are involved in these, they are involved in their own life, utterly ignorant of what its means to do something good to others on the basis of and for the sake of the good act itself—only of doing good on the basis of what is evil and for the sake of what is evil.

[6] People who are involved in a physical love cannot breathe in heaven either. If an evil spirit is taken there, he draws each breath like someone hard pressed in a struggle. But people who are involved in a heavenly love breathe more freely and live more fully the farther into heaven they are.

We can conclude from these considerations that a heavenly and spiritual love is heaven within a person because all the elements of heaven are engraved on such a love. Further, a physical and worldly love without a heavenly and spiritual one is hell within a person, because all the elements of hell are engraved on such loves.

We can see from these conclusions that a person who has

a heavenly and spiritual love enters heaven, while a person who has a physical and worldly love without a heavenly and spiritual one enters hell.

482. (iv) *A person does not keep his faith if it does not come from a heavenly love.* This has been made clear to me by so much experience that if I were to cite the things I have seen and heard on this subject, they would fill a book.

This I can affirm—that there neither is nor can be any faith whatever in people who are involved in a physical and worldly love apart from a heavenly and spiritual one; there is only knowledge, or any urge to regard something as true because it is useful to their love.

Several people who claimed involvement in faith were brought to people who were involved in faith. Once real communication was granted, they perceived that they had absolutely no faith. They even admitted later that simply believing what is true and believing the Word is not faith; rather it is loving what is true out of a heavenly love, and wanting to do it from a relatively inward affection.

I have also been shown that their urge to believe was only like the light in winter. Since there is no warmth in this light, everything on earth is dormant, fettered by the cold, and lies under the snow. So the moment heaven's light rays strike the light of this opportunistic faith within them, it is not merely extinguished, it actually becomes like a thick gloom in which no one can see himself. At the same time the more inward elements are so darkened that they understand nothing at all; and these people then become insane as a result of falsities.

For this reason, everything true is taken away from people like this, things which they have known from the Word and from the church's teaching, and have said were a part of their own faith. In their place, they soak up every falsehood that is in harmony with the evil nature of their lives. All of them are consigned to their own loves, and with them to the falsehoods that are in harmony. And since true things conflict with the falsehoods of the evil nature they are involved in, they bear a hatred toward these true things and turn away from them, thus throwing them away.

I can affirm, on the basis of all my experience of what pertains to heaven and to hell, that all the people who have confessed faith alone on the basis of doctrine but have been involved in evil as far as their lives are concerned, are in hell. I have seen many thousands of them cast there, on which topic see the booklet. *The Last Judgment and Babylon Destroyed*.

483. (v) *Love in act is what lasts; hence this is the person's life*. This follows as a logical conclusion both from the things now set forth from experience, and from the statements made about works and deeds above. Love in act is the work and the deed.

484. We need to realize that all works and deeds belong to moral and civic life, hence that they focus on what is honest and upright and then on what is just and fair. The honest and the upright belong to moral life, the just and the fair to civic life.

The love they come from is either heavenly or hellish. Works and deeds of moral and civic life are heavenly if they are done from a heavenly love; for things that are done from a heavenly love are done from the Lord, and all things that are done from the Lord are good. But deeds and works of moral and civic life are hellish if they are done from a hellish love; for things that are done from that love, which is a love of self and the world, are done from the person himself. And all the things that are done from the person himself are intrinsically evil. In fact man, seen in his own right, or man's own nature, is, only evil.

50.

AFTER DEATH, EVERYONE'S LIFE PLEASURES ARE CHANGED INTO THINGS THAT CORRESPOND TO THEM

485. In the last chapter, we showed that the ruling affection or dominant love in every person lasts to eternity. We need now to show that the pleasures of that affection or love are changed into things that correspond to them. By being changed ''into things that correspond,'' we mean ''into spiritual things that correspond to natural things.''

We may conclude that they are changed into spiritual things from the fact that a person is involved in a natural world as long as he is in his earthly body. Once he has left that body, he enters a spiritual world and puts on a spiritual body (on angels' being in a complete human form, likewise people after death, and on the spirituality of the bodies they put on, see above, nn. 73-77, and 453-460. On the nature of the correspondence of spiritual things with natural ones, *cf.* nn. 87-115).

486. All the pleasures a person has belong to his ruling love, for a person feels as pleasant only the things that he loves—particularly, then, what he loves above all else. It makes no difference whether you say ''his ruling love'' or ''what he loves above all.''

These pleasures are of different kinds—as many overall as there are ruling loves, or therefore men, spirits, and angels; for one person's ruling love is not exactly the same as any other's. This is why there is no way for one person's face to be just like another's, since the face is an image of the person's spirit [*animus*], and is in the spiritual world an image of an individual's ruling love.

The pleasures of individuals, taken singly, also display an infinite variety. There is no such thing as one of an individual's pleasures being exactly like, or the same as, another, whether one is following another or one happens at the same time as another. There is no such thing as one being the same as another.

Nevertheless, taken singly in a given individual, these pleasures go back to his one love, his ruling love; in fact, they make it up, and thus make one with it. In a similar way, all pleasures overall go back to one universally ruling love—in heaven, to a love for the Lord, and in hell to a love of self.

487. A knowledge of correspondences is the only source of knowledge about the nature and quality of the spiritual pleasures into which an individual's natural pleasures are changed after death. In general, this teaches that no natural entity exists without something spiritual corresponding to it; it also teaches in particular the nature and quality of the "something" that corresponds.

Consequently, a person who is involved in this knowledge is able to recognize and know what his state will be after death, if only he knows his love and what its quality is in respect to the universally ruling love—to which all loves go back, as stated just above. But knowing one's own ruling love is impossible for people involved in love of self, since they love whatever is theirs and call evil things good, and likewise call true the favorite falsities with which they reinforce their evil qualities. Even so, if they wanted to, they could know from others who are wise, because these people see what they themselves do not. But this does not happen with people who are so entranced with self-love that they find the teaching of wise people distasteful.

[2] People who are involved in a heavenly love do however accept instruction. They see the evil qualities into which they were born, even while they are caught up in them. They see them on the basis of truths; truths do in fact show up evil qualities.

A person can actually see what is evil and its falsity on the basis of what is true arising from what is good. But no one can see what is good and true on the basis of what is evil. This is because the falsities of evil are and correspond to darkness. So people who are involved in false things because of something evil are like blind people who do not see the things that are in the light, and they even hurry away from them like owls.

But things that are true because of what is good are and correspond to light (see above, nn. 126-134). So people who are involved in things that are true because of what is good are sighted and open-eyed; they see things proper to light and things proper to shade.

[3] I have been granted corroboration in these matters too through experience. The angels who are in the heavens both see and perceive the evil and false things that well up within them from time to time, likewise the evil and false things that engage spirits who are connected with the hells while in the world of spirits. The spirits themselves, however, are not able to see their own evil and false elements. They do not grasp what the good that comes from heavenly love is, what conscience is, what anything honest and fair is except for their own sakes, or what it is to be led by the Lord. They say that these things do not exist, that they are nothing.

We have mentioned these things to the end that the individual might examine himself, recognizing his love from his pleasures, and thereby, with enough information about correspondences, know the state of his life after death.

488. On the basis of a knowledge of correspondences,

it is definitely possible to know how the pleasures of an individual's life are changed after death into things that correspond to them. However, inasmuch as this knowledge has not been popularized yet, I should like to put that subject in a certain amount of light with some examples from experience.

All people who are involved in evil and who have reinforced themselves in false principles in opposition to the true elements of the church, especially the ones who have cast the Word aside, run away from heaven's light. They scurry into caverns that look terribly gloomy at their mouths and into openings in the rocks, and hide themselves there. This is because they have loved false things and hated true ones. Caverns like this correspond to false things, as do holes in the rocks and darkness; while light corresponds to true things. They find their delight in living in these places, and they find living in open fields unpleasant.

[2] People who found pleasure in secretive plotting and in working out stratagems in concealment behave in similar fashion. They are in these caverns too; and they go into rooms so dark that they cannot see each other, where they whisper into each other's ears in corners. This is what the delight of their love turns into.

As for people who have been diligent about data simply in order to sound learned, without developing a rational capacity by this means, who have derived pleasure from pride in matters of memory, they love sandy areas, choosing them over fields and cultivated lands. This is because sandy areas correspond to this kind of pursuit.

[3] People who have been involved in a knowledge of the doctrinal forms of their own and other churches without applying them to life choose rocky places for themselves, and live among piles of boulders. They avoid cultivated lands because they have a distaste for them.

Then there are people who have given nature and their own discretion credit for everything, who have used various devices to raise their prestige and to get rich. In the other life, they pursue magical arts which are misuses of Divine order. They sense in these the most pleasurable life.

[4] People who have devoted Divine truths to their own loves and who have rendered them false by so doing, love things that have to do with urine, because things that have to do with urine correspond to the pleasures of this kind of love.

People who have been disgustingly greedy live in hovels and love dirty things fit for pigs, and the kinds of reeking vapors that undigested foods in the stomach give off.

[5] As for people who have spent their lives wholly on pleasures, living in elegance and giving in to the palate and the belly, loving these as life's highest good, in the other life they love excrement and outhouses. They delight in things like this after death because their kind of pleasure is spiritual filth. They avoid places that are clean and free of filth because they find them distasteful.

[6] People who took their pleasures in acts of adultery spend their time in brothels where everything is filthy and foul. They love this, and avoid homes where there is chastity. The moment they reach such homes, they faint. Nothing is more pleasant to them than breaking up marriages.

People who have been eager for revenge, and who have thereby put on a cruel and vicious nature, love places that are full of corpses, and are to be found in hells like that.

Other people find other circumstances.

489. In contrast, the life pleasures of people who in the world have lived involved in a heavenly love, change into the kinds of corresponding things that exist in heaven. These things come into being from heaven's sun and from the light that comes from it, which light presents to view such things as have Divine elements hidden within them. Things which are seen from this light move the more inward reaches of angels, which belong to their minds, together with the more outward elements that belong to their bodies. And since a Divine light (which is the Divine-True coming forth from the Lord) flows into their minds, which have been opened by means of a heavenly love, it presents in the realm outside the kinds of thing that correspond to the pleasures of their love.

We have shown above that things visible to the eye in the heavens correspond to the more inward elements of angels, or to things proper to their faith and love and consequently to their intelligence and wisdom, this in the chapter dealing with representations and appearances in heaven (nn. 170-176), and in the chapter dealing with the wisdom of heaven's angels (nn. 265-275).

[2] Since we have already begun to corroborate this proposition by examples drawn from experience, in order to shed some light on what was said above on the basis of the reasons for things, I should like to bring into consideration something about the heavenly pleasures that natural pleasures turn into for people who have lived involved in a heavenly love in the world.

People who from a more inward affection, an affection for truth itself, have loved things at once true and Divine and have loved the Word, live in lofty places which look like mountains, where they are constantly in heaven's light. They do not know what the kind of darkness like night on earth is, and they also live in a climate of springtime. Before their sight, as it were, lie fields and crops and vineyards. In their houses, little things gleam as though they were made of gems; looking out their windows is like looking through pure crystal. These are their visual delights; but on a deeper level they are delights because of their correspondence with

Divine, heavenly things. For the true things they loved out of the Word correspond to crops, vineyards, gems, windows, and crystals.

[3] People who have promptly applied the church's doctrinal forms drawn from the Word directly to their lives, are in the inmost heaven, and are involved in the pleasures of wisdom more than others. They see Divine elements within particular objects. They do actually see the objects, but the corresponding Divine elements flow into their minds instantly and fill them with a blessedness that moves all their sensations. As a result, all things before them seem to laugh and frolic and live (on this subject, see above, n. 270).

[4] As for people who have loved knowledges and have developed their rational capacity with them, who have also furnished themselves with intelligence from this source, acknowledging the Divine at the same time, their pleasure in knowledges and their rational delight are in the other life turned into a spiritual delight involving insights into what is good and true. They live in gardens where they see beautifully laid out flower beds and lawns, all surrounded by rows of trees with gateways and walks. The trees and flowers alter from day to day. Their overall appearance offers pleasures to their minds, while the particular variations constantly renew them. Since these things correspond to Divine elements, and since these people are engaged in a knowledge of correspondences, they are always being filled with new insights, through which their spiritual rational ability is brought toward perfection. These things constitute their pleasures because gardens, flowerbeds, lawns, and trees correspond to knowledges, to insights and consequently to intelligence.

[5] As for people who have given the Divine credit for everything and have seen nature as relatively dead, simply submissive to spiritual things, and who have convinced

themselves of this view, they are in a heavenly light. All
the things they see before them derive a kind of translucence
from that light; and within that translucence they see countless hues of light which their inner sight seems to drink
directly in. They feel inward delights from this process. The
furnishings one sees in their houses are diamond-like, with
similar hues within them. I have been told that the walls of
their houses seem to be made of something crystalline and
therefore translucent, and that one can see within them
something like flowing forms representative of heavenly
matters, constantly changing; this because such a translucence corresponds to an understanding that has been enlightened by the Lord, with the shadows that arise from a
faith and love of natural things taken away. This is what
these phenomena are like, and there are countless others,
which people who have been in heaven describe by saying
that they have seen what no eye can ever see.

They also say that, from a perception of Divine elements
communicated to them through these sights, they have heard
what no ear can ever hear.

[6] Then there are people who have not behaved secretively, who have rather wanted everything they were thinking to be out in the open, as far as civic life allowed. Since
they have thought only what was honest and fair, based on
something Divine, they have radiant faces in heaven. As
a result of that radiance, the details of their affections and
thoughts can be seen in their faces as though they had taken
form, and the people themselves, in their speech and actions,
are like reflections of their affections. As a result, they are
more beloved than others. When they talk, their faces become a little dim, but after they finish talking, the very
things they have said are fully visible to the sight, all together in their faces. Since the things which occur around
them correspond to their more inward natures, they are all

in visible forms of such nature that other people perceive clearly what they portray and mean. Spirits who found pleasure in behaving secretively avoid coming anywhere near them; they seem to themselves to crawl away from them like snakes.

[7] People who have judged acts of adultery to be unspeakable and have lived involved in a chaste love of marriage, are more in the design and form of heaven than others. Consequently, they are in a total beauty and constantly in the bloom of youth. The pleasures of their love are indescribable and grow to eternity, for all the pleasures and joys of heaven flow into that love. This is because that love comes down from the Lord's bond with heaven and the church, or broadly speaking from the bond between what is good and what is true, this bond being heaven itself, both in general and in each individual angel in specific (see above, nn. 366-386). Their outward pleasures are of such nature that they cannot be described in human terminology.

But these things we have mentioned about the correspondences of pleasures for people involved in heavenly love are only a few.

490. We can know from these considerations that after death, everyone's pleasures are turned into things that correspond to them, with the same love lasting all the way to eternity. This applies, for example, to marriage love, love of what is fair, what is honest, what is good, and what is true, love of knowledges and insights, love of intelligence and wisdom, and others. The things that flow from such sources like brooks from a spring are pleasures which also endure, but are raised to a higher level when the transition is made from natural to spiritual matters.

51.

MAN'S FIRST STATE AFTER DEATH

491. There are three states a person passes through after his death before arriving in heaven or hell. The first state involves his more outward aspects, the second involves his more inward aspects, and the third is a state of preparation. The person passes through these states in the world of spirits.

There are however some people who do not pass through these states, being either taken up into heaven or cast into hell immediately after death. The people who are immediately taken up into heaven are the ones who have been regenerated and thus made ready for heaven in the world. People who have been regenerated and made ready in this way need only to cast off their soiled natural elements along with their bodies, and are immediately taken into heaven by angels. I have seen them taken up an hour after death.

In contrast, there are the people who have been vicious on the inside and seemingly good on the outside, who have therefore filled their malice with deceits and made use of goodness as a means to deception. They are cast into hell immediately. I have seen some people like this cast into hell right after death—one of the most deceptive went head first and feet up. Others go differently.

There are also people who are thrown into caves right after their death and so are kept away from people who are in the world of spirits. They are alternately let out and sent back in. These are people who have behaved viciously toward their neighbors under the guise of civil behavior.

But these two classes of people are small in comparison

to those who are kept in the world of spirit
for heaven or hell according to the Divine

492. As far as the first state is concerned, the state in volving a person's more outward aspects, he comes into this state immediately after death.

Every person has more outward and more inward aspects to his spirit. A spirit's more outward aspects are the means by which it adjusts the person's body in the world (especially his face, speech, and manner) for associating with other people. But the spirit's more inward aspects are the ones which belong to his own intention and resultant thought, which are seldom evident in the face, speech, or manner. From infancy, people get used to displaying friendliness and kindness and sincerity, and hiding what their own intentions think. So as a matter of habit they wear a moral and civic life in outward matters, no matter what they are like inwardly.

This habit is the source of man's virtual ignorance of what lies deeper within him, and also of his inattention to these matters.

493. A person's first state after death is like his state in the world, since at that point he is similarly involved in outward matters. He has much the same face, speech, and spirit, consequently he has much the same moral and civic life.

This is why he is then quite unaware that he is not still in the world, unless he pays attention to things that happen to him and to what he was told by angels when he was awakened—namely, that he is now a spirit (n. 450).

So the one life continues into the other, and death is only a crossing.

494. Because this is what a person's spirit is like just after his life in this world, at that time he is recognized by his friends and by his acquaintances from this world. Spirits n fact perceive this not just from his face and speech, but from the sphere of his life when they approach him as well.

Whenever an individual in the other life thinks about someone else, he sets the person's face before himself in his thought, together with many other things that belong to the person's life. When he does, the other person becomes present as though he were called and summoned.

This kind of thing happens in the spiritual world because thoughts are communicated there and because distances do not have the same attributes as they have in the natural world (see above, nn. 191-199). This is why everyone, on first arrival in the other life, is recognized by his friends, relatives, and acquaintances of one sort or another, and this is also why they talk with each other and then associate with each other along the lines of their friendships in the world.

I have often heard that people who arrived from the world were delighted to see their friends again, and that their friends were delighted in turn at their arrival. It is a frequent event for a married couple to meet and greet each other with great joy. They stay together for a longer or shorter period depending on the degree to which they had been happy living together in the world. But unless a true marriage love binds them (this love being a bonding of minds from a heavenly love), they separate after they have been together a while.

But if the partners' minds had been in conflict and more inwardly turned away from each other, they break into open enmity and sometimes fight with each other. Nevertheless, they are not separated until they arrive at the next state, which will be described shortly.

495. Granting, then, that the life of new spirits is rather like their life in the natural world, and that they know nothing about the condition of their life after death, about heaven, and about hell except what they have learned from the literal meaning of the Word and sermons based on it—for these reasons, once they have gotten over their surprise at being in a body and having all the senses they had in the world, at seeing the same kinds of thing, they become caught up in curiosity about what heaven and hell are like and where they are.

So they are taught by their friends about the state of eternal life, and are taken around to different places, into different companies. Some are taken to cities, to gardens and parks; most are taken to splendid places because this sort of place delights the outward nature they are involved in. Then they are intermittently led into thoughts they had during their physical life about the soul's state after death, heaven, and hell, until they resent their former utter ignorance of things like this, and resent the church's ignorance as well.

Almost all of them are eager to know whether they will get into heaven. Most of them believe that they will because they have led a moral and civic life in the world, without considering that evil and good people lead lives that are similar in outward aspects, do good works for other people in similar fashion, attend church in similar fashion, listen to sermons, and pray. They are wholly unaware that outward behavior and outward worship do not accomplish anything, but rather the inner elements from which the outward ones come.

Hardly one out of several thousand knows what inner elements are, or knows that they are where heaven and the church dwell within man. They are even less aware that the quality of outward acts is the quality of the intentions and thoughts they come from, and of the love and faith prompting those intentions and thoughts. Even if they are taught this, they do not grasp that thinking and intending are effective, only that speaking and doing are.

Most people who are entering the other life from Christendom nowadays are like this.

496. These people, though, are examined as to their quality by good spirits, which is done by various means. This is because in this first state evil people say just as many true things and do just as many good works as good people. The reason for this (mentioned above) is that they have lived just as morally in outward form, being involved in civil states under laws, gaining a reputation for fairness and honesty, turning people's heads, and so rising in prestige and getting rich.

The prime telltale mark of evil spirits as opposed to good ones is that the evil ones listen avidly to what is being said about outward matters and pay little attention to what is being said about inward matters, which are the true and good elements of the church and heaven. They do hear such things, but without attentiveness and joy. Another distinctive characteristic is that they repeatedly head for particular areas, and when they are left to their own devices travel along paths that leads to these areas. The quality of the love that is leading them can be discerned from the areas they head for and the paths they travel.

497. Then too, all the spirits who arrive from the world are put into a connection either with a particular community in heaven or with a particular community in hell; but this applies only to their more inward elements. These more inward elements, however, are not visible to anyone as long as the spirits are involved in more outward matters, since outward matters cover and hide inner ones especially with people who are involved in something evil on a more inward level. Later on, when they come into the second state, these more inward elements become very obvious, because at that point their more inward reaches are opened, and their more outward ones go to sleep.

498. For some people, this first state after death lasts a few days, for some a few months, for some a year. It rarely lasts more than a year for anyone. For given individuals, the difference depends on the harmony or discord of their more inward reaches with their more outward ones.

Actually, the more inward and more outward elements are going to act as one and correspond for every individual. No one in the spiritual world is allowed to think and intend one way while speaking and behaving another way. Everyone is going to be an image of his affection, or his love; so in more outward things he will have the same quality he has in more inward things. For this reason, a spirit's more outward elements are uncovered and set in order first, so that they can serve as a plane corresponding to more inward things.

52.

MAN'S SECOND STATE AFTER DEATH

499. A person's second state after death is called "the state of his more inward elements," because at that point he is brought into an involvement in the more inward things that belong to his mind, or his intention and thought, while the more outward things he was involved in during his first state go to sleep.

If anyone pays attention to a person's life and to what he says and does, he can recognize that there are relatively inward and outward aspects to everyone, or relatively inward and outward intentions and thoughts. This recognition is based on the following facts. If someone is involved in civic life, he thinks about other people as he has heard about and observed them either on the basis of their reputation or on the basis of conversations with them. But he still does not talk with them in keeping with what he thinks, and even though they are evil people, he still deals civilly with them. The truth of this is particularly recognizable in fakers and sycophants, who speak and act quite differently from the way they think and intend. It is also recognizable in hypocrites who talk about God, heaven, the salvation of souls, truths of the church, the good of their country, and the neighbor, as though they were speaking out of faith and love; while at heart they believe something else, and love themselves alone.

[2] On this basis, we can establish the existence of two "thoughts," one more outward and one more inward, with people speaking out of the more outward thought, while

feeling something else on the basis of the more inward thought. We can also establish that these two thoughts are separate, since people take precautions to prevent the more inward from flowing into the more outward and becoming somehow visible.

By creation, man's nature is such that his more inward thought acts as one with his more outward thought through the agency of correspondence. Further, it does so act as one in people who are involved in what is good, since they think only what is good and say only what is good. However, the more inward thought does not act as one with the more outward thought in people who are involved in what is evil, since they think what is evil and say what is good. For these latter people, the order is inverted, with what is good on the outside and what is evil on the inside for them. This is why the evil rules over the good and subordinates it to itself like a slave, so that it serves as a means of reaching goals that belong to their love.

Because this kind of goal is inherent in any good thing they say and do, we can see that "the good" in them is not good, but is stained by the evil, no matter how good it may look in outward form to people who have no knowledge of more inward things.

[3] It is different for people who are involved in what is good. The order is not inverted in them; rather, the good flows from their more inward thought into their more outward thought, flowing in this way into their speech and behavior.

This is the order into which man was created. In this way, his more inward reaches are in heaven, and are in the light that exists there. And since heaven's light is the Divine-True issuing from the Lord—since it is in fact the Lord in heaven (*cf.* nn. 126-140)—these people are led by the Lord.

We have mentioned these matters so that people might

know that every person has a more inward thought and a more outward thought, and that they are distinct from each other. When we say "thought," we mean intention as well, because thought comes from intention. In fact, no one can think without intention. From these considerations, we can see what a "state of a person's more outward things" is, and what a "state of a person's more inward things" is.

500. When we say "intention and thought," "intention" means affection and love as well, and also every delight and pleasure that belongs to affection and love, since these go back to intention as their subject. For if a person intends something, he loves it and feels it to be delightful and pleasant. Conversely, if a person loves something and feels it to be delightful and pleasant, he intends it.

Further, "thought" means everything that serves to reinforce his affection or love, for thought is nothing but the form of his intention, or a means by which something a person intends may come to light. This form is set up by various analytic rational processes which have their origin in the spiritual world and which are, strictly speaking, part of the person's spirit.

501. It is necessary to know that a person's whole quality is the quality of his more inward elements, and not the quality of his more outward ones apart from his more inward ones. This is because his more inward elements belong to his spirit, and a person's life is the life of his spirit; in fact, this is the source of his body's life. Also, this is why a person remains to eternity the same as the quality of his more inward elements.

Since, however, his more outward elements relate to his body, they are parted after death; and such elements as cling to his spirit go to sleep. They serve only as a field for his more inward elements, as we have shown above in our discussion of man's memory lasting after death.

We can see from this just what things are truly part of a person and what things are not; for evil people, all the elements that belong to the more outward thought that gives rise to their speech and the more outward intending that gives rise to their actions are not really part of them. Those things are part of them which belong to the more inward elements of their thought and intention.

502. Once the first state is over (the state of relatively outward concerns treated in the preceding chapter), the spirit-person is directed into a state of his more inward concerns, or a state of his more inward intention and consequent thought—the state he was involved in in the world when he was left to himself, when his thought was free and unbridled. He slips unconsciously into this state when (as he did in the world) he pulls in the thought nearest his speech, or the thought that gives rise to his speech, toward his more inward thought, and remains involved in this latter.

As a result, when the spirit-person is in this state he is involved in his very self and in his very own life. For thinking freely from his very own affection is a person's real life, and is the real person.

503. A spirit in this state is thinking on the basis of his very own intention, which means he is thinking from his very own affection or love. At this point, his thinking makes a unity with his intention—such a unity, in fact, that he hardly seems to be thinking at all, simply intending. It is almost the same when he talks; but there is the difference that he talks with a certain fear that the things his intention is thinking might come out naked. This is because his fear became part of his intention in the world because of the demands of civic life.

504. Absolutely everyone is directed into this state after death because it is the actual state of the spirit. The earlier state is the way the person was in his spirit when he was in company, which is not his proper state.

Several considerations enable us to conclude that this state of relatively outward concerns—the first state a person is in after death, discussed in the preceding chapter—is not his proper state. For example, spirits not only think but even speak from their affection, because it is the basis of their language, as we may conclude from the matters stated and presented in the chapter on angels' speech (nn. 234-245).

Then, too, the person thought in like fashion in the world when he was "within himself." For at that time he did not think on the basis of his physical language, he simply viewed these matters, seeing more things simultaneously, in a moment, than he could later articulate in half an hour.

Another phenomenon too enables us to see that a state of relatively outward concerns is not the proper state of a person or of his spirit. When he is among company in the world, his conversation is in keeping with the laws of moral and civic life. At such times, his more inward thinking controls the more outward, the way one person controls another, to keep it from going beyond the bounds of propriety and respectability.

We can also see this from the fact that when a person is thinking within himself, he is thinking how he may talk and behave to please people and to gain friendship, good will, and gratitude. He is doing this by incidental means—differently, then, than if it were occurring out of his own actual intention.

These considerations enable us to see that the state of relatively inward concerns into which a spirit is directed is his own proper state. So too it was the person's own proper state when he lived in the world.

505. Once a spirit is in the state proper to his more inward concerns, it is very obvious what kind of person he was intrinsically in the world. At this point, he is acting on the basis of what really belongs to him. If he was inwardly involved in something good in the world, he then behaves rationally and wisely—more wisely, in fact, than he did in the world, because he is released from his ties with a body and therefore from the things that darken and, so to speak, cloud things over.

On the other hand, if he was involved in something evil in the world, he then behaves senselessly and crazily—more crazily, in fact, than he did in the world, because he is in a freedom and is not repressed. When he lived in the world, he was sane in outward matters because he was using them to fabricate a rational person. So once these outward matters are taken away from him, his madnesses are unveiled.

An evil person who presents the appearance of a good person in outward things is comparable to a vase, outwardly gleaming and polished, covered with a veil, with all kinds of filth hidden inside, in keeping with the Lord's statement,

> You are like whitewashed sepulchres that look attractive on the outside, but inwardly are filled with the bones of the dead, and with all uncleanness.   (Matthew 23:27)

506. All people who have lived in the world involved in what is good, and who have acted out of conscience (these being the ones who have acknowledged something Divine and loved Divine truths, especially the ones who have applied them to their lives)—it seems to all such people, when they are brought into the state proper to their more inward concerns, as though they have been roused from sleep and come awake, or have come from darkness into light.

They are thinking on the basis of heaven's light, and therefore out of a deeper wisdom; they are acting on the basis of what is good and therefore out of a deeper affection. Heaven is flowing into their thoughts and affections with something more deeply blessed and pleasant, that they had not known about before. For they have a communication with heaven's angels. At this time too, they recognize the Lord, and are worshipping Him out of their very life; for they are involved in their very own life when they are in the state of their more inward elements, as we have just stated (n. 505). Further, they are recognizing and worshipping Him from their freedom, because their freedom is part of their deeper affection.

Then, too, they are withdrawing in this way from what is outwardly holy, and are entering what is inwardly holy, where actual, true worship takes place. This is what the state is like of people who have led a Christian life in accord with the commandments of the Word.

[2] Utterly opposite, however, is the state of people who have lived in the world involved in what is evil, having no conscience, and therefore denying what is Divine. For all people who live involved in what is evil, deep within themselves deny what is Divine, no matter how they think outwardly that they are not denying but acknowledging, because acknowledging the Divine and living evilly are opposites.

In the other life, once people like this come into the state of their more inward elements, when other people hear them talk and see them behave, they seem like simpletons. For because of their evil cravings, they break out into crimes, contempt for others, acts of derision and blasphemy, of hatred, in vengefulness; they contrive plots, some so shrewd and vicious that it is almost impossible to believe that anything like them exists inside any person. At this point, they are in fact in a state free to act according to the thoughts proper to their intention because they are parted from the relatively outward factors that repressed them and held them in check in the world. In short, they have lost rationality because in the world their rational ability had not dwelt in their more inward reaches, but in their more outward ones. Yet still they seem to themselves to be wiser than other people.

[3] Being like this, they are from time to time sent back briefly into the state of their more outward concerns while they are in this second state, sent too into their memory of what they did while they were in the state of their more inward concerns. Some of them are embarrassed then, and recognize that they were insane. Some of them are not embarrassed; some resent the fact that they are not allowed to be constantly in the state proper to their more outward concerns. But these last are shown what they would be like if they were constantly in this state, namely that they would secretly be working toward these same ends, misleading people of simple heart and faith by appearances of what is good, honest, and fair, with they themselves becoming utterly lost. For their more outward elements would eventually catch fire with the same blaze as their more inward ones, which would devour their whole life.

507. When spirits are in this second state, they come to look just the same as they were intrinsically in the world, and the things they had done and said privately are exposed. For since external factors are not controlling at this point, they say openly and try to do similar things without being afraid for their reputation as they were in the world. They are also then brought into many states of their evils, so that they may appear to angels and good spirits as they really are.

In this way, private things are disclosed and secret things uncovered, in keeping with the Lord's words,

> Nothing . . . is covered, which will not be uncovered, or hidden, that will not be recognized: . . . What you have said in the darkness will be heard in the light, and what you have spoken in the ear in closets will be preached on the rooftops.   (Luke 12:2,3)

And elsewhere,

> I tell . . . you, for every idle word people have spoken, they will give account in the day of judgment.   (Matthew 12:36)

508. No brief description can be given of what evil people are like in this state, since each individual is mad in accord with his own cravings, and these are all different. So I should like to cite just a few particular instances which will enable the reader to draw conclusions about the rest.

There are people who have loved themselves more than anything else, focusing on their own prestige in their duties and functions, fulfilling and enjoying useful tasks not for the sake of the tasks but for the sake of their own reputation, using them to make others think they are more important, being thus enchanted by a report of their own prestige. When these people are in the second state, they are more stupid than others; for to the extent that anyone loves himself, he is moved away from heaven, and to the extent that he moves away from heaven he moves away from wisdom.

[2] As for people who are involved in self-love and were also artful, and who climbed to positions of prestige by their stratagems, they make friends with the worst people. They learn magical skills, which are misuses of the Divine design, using them to harass and trouble everyone who does not show them respect. They concoct plots, they cherish hatreds, they are on fire with revenge, they long to vent their spleen on everyone who does not give in to them. They plunge into all these evils as far as the vicious mob supports them. Eventually, they mull over ways of climbing up to heaven, either to destroy it or to be worshipped there as gods. Their madness reaches even to this.

[3] Catholics of this sort are more insane than the rest. They actually have in mind that heaven and hell are in their power and that they can remit sins at will. They claim everything Divine for themselves and call themselves Christ. This conviction of theirs is of a kind that disturbs their minds when it flows in, and brings on a darkness to the point of pain. They are practically the same in either of the two states, though they lack rationality in the second. However,

their madness and their lot subsequent to this state are discussed in some detail in the booklet, *The Last Judgment
and Babylon Destroyed*.

[4] As for people who have given nature credit for creation
and have consequently denied the Divine at heart if not out
loud, and have therefore denied all elements of the church
and heaven, they make friends with people like themselves
in this condition, and give the title "God" to anyone who
is exceptionally clever, worshipping him with Divine respect. I have seen people like this gathered in worship of
a wizard and deliberating about nature and acting as senselessly as though they were animals in human form. There
were some people among them who had been of established
importance in the world, and some whom people in the
world had believed were learned and wise.

Then there are other types, who show different characteristics. [5] On the basis of these few examples, we can
draw our conclusions about the quality of people whose
minds' more inward reaches are closed off toward heaven,
as in the case with everyone who was not accepted some
inflow from heaven by recognizing something Divine and
by a life of faith.

Everyone can judge for himself what he would be like
(if he were this type of person) if he were allowed to behave
without fear for the law or for his life—without outward
bonds, which are fears of injury to his reputation or loss of
prestige and profit and their pleasures.

[6] In spite of all this, their madness is controlled by the
Lord to keep it from hurtling beyond the bounds of what
is useful; for some use comes even of every such person.
Good spirits see in them what evil is and what it is like,
and what a person is like if he is not led by the Lord.
Another useful function is the gathering of similar people
by them, and their separation from good people. Then there

is the use of getting rid of the good and true elements that the evil people have presented and simulated in outward matters, bringing them into the evils of their own life and the false elements of evil, and so getting them ready for hell.

[7] For no individual enters hell until he is engaged in his own evil and in the false things proper to evil. This is because no one there is allowed to have a divided mind, to think and say one thing while intending something else. Everyone who is evil there will think what is false there because of his evil, and will speak out of his evil's falsity. Both his thinking and his speech will come from his intention, and therefore out of his own proper love and its delight and pleasure, in the same way he thought in the world when he was in his spirit—that is, the way he thought within himself when he was thinking from his more inward affection.

The reason is that intention is the actual person, not thought except as it is derived from intention. Intention is a person's actual nature or bent. So being returned to one's own intention is being returned to his own nature or bent, and to his own life, because a person puts on a nature by means of his life. After death, the person keeps the kind of nature he has built up by his life in the world, which for evil people can no longer be corrected or changed by means of thinking or understanding what is true.

509. While evil spirits are in this second state, it is normal for them to be punished often and severely because they plunge into all kinds of evil. There are many kinds of punishment in the world of spirits, and there is no favoritism, whether the person was a king or a slave in the world.

Everything evil brings its own penalty with it. The two are bonded together. So the person who is involved in something evil is also involved in the penalty of the evil. Yet no one there suffers a penalty because of evil things he did in the world, but rather because of evil things he is doing currently.

Still, it comes down to the same thing whether you say he suffers penalties on account of the evil things he did in the world, or that he suffers penalties because of the evil things he is doing in the other life, because everyone returns after death to his own life, and therefore to similar evils. For the person is of the same quality as he was during his physical life (nn. 470-484).

The reason for this punishment is that the fear of punishment is the only means of controlling evil things in this condition. Encouragement no longer works; neither does teaching or fear of law and reputation, because the person's behavior now stems from his nature, which cannot be controlled or broken except by means of punishments.

Good spirits, though, are not punished at all, even if they did evil things in the world, because their evils do not come back. We may also know that their evils were of a different kind or nature. They did not in fact stem from a stance taken in opposition to what is true, not from any evil heart except what they had received from their parents by heredity. They were borne into this heart by blind enjoyment when they were involved in outward matters separated from inward ones.

510. Everyone arrives at the community where his spirit was in the world. In fact every person is, in his spirit, bonded to a particular heavenly or hellish community—an evil person to a hellish one, a good person to a heavenly one. (On the individual's return to his own community after death, see n. 458). His spirit is guided there step by step, and eventually gains entrance.

When an evil spirit is involved in the state of his more inward elements, he is turned by stages toward his own community. Eventually he is turned straight at it, before this state is completed. And once this state is completed, the evil spirit himself hurls himself into the hell where there are people like himself. Visually, this "hurling" looks like falling headlong, head down and feet up. The reason it looks like this is that the person is in an inverted order, having actually loved hellish things and spurned heavenly ones.

In the course of this second state, some evil individuals enter and leave the hells from time to time, but they do not seem to fall headlong as they do when they have been fully devastated.

While they are in the state proper to their more outward elements, they are shown the very community where they were in spirit while they were in the world. This happens in order to let them know that they were in hell even in their physical life. Still, they were not in the same state as the people in the hell itself, but in a state like that of the people who are in the world of spirits. We will discuss below how the state of these latter compares to that of people in hell.

511. A separation of evil spirits from good spirits occurs in the course of this second state; for during the first state they were together. The reason is that as long as a spirit is involved in his outward concerns, it is the same as it was in the world—the way an evil person is together with a good one there, and a good one with an evil one. It is different when he is brought into involvement in his more inward concerns, and left to his own nature or intention.

The separation of the good from the evil happens in various ways. Broadly, it happens by taking the evil ones around to those communities they were in touch with through their good thoughts and affections during their first state. In this way, they are taken to those communities which were persuaded by their outward appearance that they [these spirits] were not evil. Normally, they are taken on an extensive circuit, and everywhere are exposed as they really are to good spirits. On seeing them, the good spirits turn away; and as they turn away, the evil spirits who are being taken around also turn their faces away from the good ones toward the region where the hellish community is which is their destination.

Allow me not to mention other modes of separation—there are many of them.

53.

MAN'S THIRD STATE AFTER DEATH, WHICH IS A STATE OF INSTRUCTION FOR PEOPLE WHO ARE ENTERING HEAVEN

512. The third state of a person or of his spirit after death is a state of instruction. This state is for people who are entering heaven and becoming angels, but not for people who are entering hell, since they cannot be taught. As a result, their second state is also their third, concluding with their complete turning toward their own love, and therefore toward the hellish community that is involved in a like love.

When this has been accomplished, they intend and think from this love, and since the love is hellish, they intend nothing that is not evil and think nothing that is not false. These are their delights because they belong to their love. In consequence, they spurn anything good and true that they have adopted earlier because it was a useful tool for their love.

[2] Good people, however, are brought through the second state into a third, a state of their preparation for heaven by means of instruction. For no one can be prepared for heaven except by means of insights into what is true and good—only, that is, by means of instruction. This is because no one can know what is good and true on the spiritual level, or what is evil and false, unless he is taught. In the world, it is possible to know what is good and true on a civic and moral level, what is called fair and honest, because there are civil laws which teach what is false. There are also social contexts in which a person learns to live by moral

laws, all of which deal with what is honest and right. But what is good and true on the spiritual level—this is not learned from the world, but from heaven.

It is possible to know some things from the Word, and from church doctrine based on the Word. But still, these knowledges cannot flow into a person's life unless in the more inward reaches of his mind he is in heaven. A person is in heaven when he recognizes what is Divine and does what is fair and honest at the same time, behaving this way because it is commanded in the Word. This means behaving fairly and honestly for the sake of the Divine, and not for self and the world as goals.

[3] But no one can behave like this without first being taught, for example, that God exists, that heaven and hell exist, that there is a life after death, that God is to be loved above all, and the neighbor as oneself, that the contents of the Word are to be believed because the Word is Divine.

Unless a person realizes and recognizes these facts, he cannot think spiritually. Without thought about these matters, he cannot intend them; for if a person does not know something, he cannot think about it, and if he does not think about it, he cannot intend it.

When a person does intend these things, then, heaven flows in; that is, the Lord flows into the person's life through heaven. For He flows into intention, through that into thought, and through these into life, these two being the source of all a person's life.

We can see from these considerations, that there is no learning of what is good and true on the spiritual level from the world, but rather from heaven; and we can see that no one can be prepared for heaven except by being taught.

[4] The Lord teaches a person to the extent that He flows into his life. For to this extent, He kindles his intention with a love of knowing what is true and enlightens his thought

to know what is true. So far as this happens, the person's more inward reaches are opened, and heaven is grafted into them. Further what is Divine and heavenly flows in to this extent into the honest elements of his moral life and the fair elements of civic life within him and makes them spiritual, because the person, doing them for the sake of the Divine, is doing them from the Divine. In fact, the honest and fair things proper to moral and civic life, which a person does from this source, are themselves results of his spiritual life; and a result derives everything it is from its actuating cause, since the nature of the latter determines the nature of the former.

513. The work of instruction is done by angels of many communities, especially angels from the northern and southern regions because these angelic communities are involved in intelligence and wisdom stemming from insights into what is good and true.

The places where the instruction occurs are in the north, and are varied, arranged and set off according to the genera and species of their heavenly good qualities so that each and every individual can be taught as befits his own intrinsic character and his ability to receive. These places are spread out on all sides, to quite a distance.

To these places, the Lord brings the good spirits who are to be taught, after their second state in the world of spirits has been completed. This, however, does not apply to everyone, because people who have been taught in the world have already been prepared there for heaven by the Lord, and are brought into heaven by another route. Some are brought in immediately after death. Some are brought in after a brief stay with good spirits, where the cruder elements of their thoughts and affections are set aside, which they drew from matters of prestige and wealth in the world, which removal ourifies them. Some are desolated first, which takes place in the area under the soles of the feet called "the lower earth." Some people have harsh experiences there. They are the people who have settled themselves in false notions but have still led good lives. For settled false notions cling tenaciously; and true matters cannot be seen, and therefore cannot be accepted, until the false notions are shattered.

But we have discussed desolations and how they happen in *Arcana Coelestia*.

514. All the people who are in the places where teaching goes on live apart from each other. As far as their more inward elements are concerned, they are in fact connected with the communities of heaven which they are bound for. So since heaven's communities are arranged according to the heavenly form (see above, nn. 200-212), the places where teaching occurs are therefore arranged in the same way. As a result, when these places are examined from heaven, something like a heaven in smaller form is visible.

In length, these places stretch from east to west, in width, from south to north; but the width seems less than the length.

In general, the arrangements are as follows. People who have died in early childhood had been brought up to the age of early maturity in heaven are toward the front. People who are beyond their childhood state and the care of nurses are brought there by the Lord and taught.

Behind them are the areas where instruction is given to people who have died as adults, who were involved in an affection for what is true because of a goodness of life.

Then behind these are people devoted to the Mohammedan religion who lived a moral life in the world, recognizing one Divine Being and recognizing the Lord as the Essential Prophet. Once they withdraw from Mohammed, because he cannot help them, they approach the Lord, worship Him, and recognize what is Divine about Him; then they are taught in the Christian religion.

Behind these, more to the north, are places for the teaching of various heathen who have in the world lived good lives in keeping with their own religions. They have derived a kind of conscience from this; they have behaved fairly and rightly not because of their political laws but because of their religious laws, which they believed should be held holy and not dishonored by their deeds in any way. All of them are brought with ease to a recognition of the Lord once they have been taught, because at heart they have held that God is not invisible, but is visible in a Human form. There are more of these than there are of the others; the best of them come from Africa.

515. Not all people, however, are taught in the same way or by the same communities of heaven. The ones who have been brought up in heaven from early childhood are taught by angels of more inward heavens because they have not absorbed false notions from false elements of religion or polluted their spiritual life with dregs drawn from prestige and profit in the world.

Most people who have died as adults are taught by angels of the outmost heaven because these angels are better adapted to them than angels of the more inward heavens are, since these latter are involved in a deeper wisdom which these folk have not yet accepted.

Mohammedans are taught by angels who were once involved in that religion and have turned to Christianity; the heathen too are taught by their own angels.

516. All the teaching in these places is done on the basis of doctrine which comes from the Word—not from the Word apart from doctrine. Christians are taught on the basis of a heavenly doctrine that is in full accord with the Word's inner meaning. Other people, such as Mohammedans and heathen, are taught on the basis of doctrines suited to their level of comprehension, differing from the heavenly doctrine only in the fact that they teach spiritual life by means of a moral life consistent with the good tenets of their religion, the tenets on which they had based their life in the world.

517. Teaching in the heavens differs from teaching on earth in that the insights are not consigned to memory but to life. Spirits' memories are in their lives; in fact, they accept and absorb all the elements that harmonize with their lives, and they do not accept, let alone absorb, things which do not so harmonize. For spirits are affections, and are consequently in a human form that resembles their affections.

[2] Since this is their nature, an affection for what is true for the sake of life's useful activity is continually being breathed in. The Lord does provide that each individual loves the useful activities that fit his essential nature, this love being intensified by the individual's hope of becoming an angel. Now all the useful activities of heaven go back to a common use—for the sake of the Lord's kingdom, which is now their country; and all the individual, unique useful activities are effective the more closely and fully they focus on the common use. For this reason, the individual, unique useful activities—which are beyond counting—are good and heavenly. So an affection for what is true is bonded to an affection for useful activity within every individual, in such a way that they act as one. By this means, what is true is grafted onto useful activity so that the true things they learn are true things that belong to useful activity.

This is how angelic spirits are taught, and made ready for heaven.

[3] There are different ways in which a truth suited to a use is instilled, most of them unknown in this world. Most often, these means involve portrayals of useful activities which are presented in a thousand ways in the spiritual

world, with such delight and charm that they permeate the spirit, from the more inward elements belonging to the mind to the more outward elements belonging to the body, affecting in this way a person's whole being. Consequently the spirit virtually becomes his own useful activity, so when he enters his own community, having been introduced there by teaching, he is involved in his own life when he is involved in his own useful activity.

We can conclude from these considerations that insights, which are outward truths, do not effect anyone's entrance to heaven. This is done rather by the life itself, which is a life of useful activity, imparted by means of insights.

518. There were some spirits who in the world had, by thinking, convinced themselves that they were going to enter heaven and be accepted in preference to others because they were learned and knew a great deal from the Word and the doctrines of various churches. So they believed that they were wise, and were the ones meant by the people described as ''shining like the radiance of the firmament and like the stars.'' (Daniel 12:3). But they were examined to see whether their insights dwelt in their memories or in their lives.

Some were involved in a real affection for what is true, that is, for the sake of useful activities which, being distinct from physical and worldly concerns, are essentially spiritual uses. After they were taught, they were accepted into heaven. Then they were allowed to know what is radiant in heaven—the Divine-True which is heaven's light there, within the useful activity which is the field that receives the rays of light and changes them into different forms of radiance.

But then there were people whose insights dwelt only in their memories, leading to the acquisition of an ability to apply logic to matters of truth and to ''prove'' the propositions they had accepted as principles. Even though these principles were false, they saw them as true once they had "proved" them. Now these people were not involved in heaven's light at all, and yet were involved in a faith stemming from pride (often connected with this kind of intelligence) that they were more learned than others, and that they were therefore headed for heaven, and that angels would be their servants. So in order to get them out of their senseless faith, they were pushed up into the first or outmost heaven to bring them into a particular angelic community. But while they were in the process of entering, their eyes began to dim at the inflow of heaven's light, their discernment to be confused; and finally they began to gasp for breath like people who are near death. And when they felt heaven's warmth, which is heavenly love, they began to be tortured inside. Consequently they were cast back down. After that, they were taught that insights do not make an angel, but the actual life acquired by means of insights, since seen in their own right, insights are outside of heaven, while life by means of insights is inside heaven.

519. Once spirits have been prepared for heaven by teaching given in the places mentioned above (this takes a short time only, since the spirits are involved in spiritual concepts which take in many elements at the same time), they are dressed in angelic clothes, most of which are white, as though made of linen. So dressed, they are brought to a path that heads up toward heaven and are committed to angel guardians there. Then they are accepted by some other angels and introduced into communities, and there into many forms of happiness.

Each angel is then taken by the Lord to his own community. There are various paths by which this is done, sometimes roundabout. No angel knows the paths by which spirits are led; only the Lord does.

When they arrive at their communities, their more inward reaches are opened; and since these are in agreement with the more inward reaches of the angels who are in that community, they are recognized immediately and accepted with joy.

520. I should like to append something noteworthy about the paths which lead from these places to heaven, which the novitiate angels are led along.

There are eight paths, two from each region of teaching. One goes upward toward the east, the other toward the west. People who are entering the Lord's celestial kingdom are brought in by the eastern path, while people who are entering the spiritual kingdom are brought in by the western path.

The four paths that lead to the Lord's celestial kingdom seem decked out with olive trees and different kinds of fruit trees; while the ones that lead to the Lord's spiritual kingdom seem decked out with grapevines and laurels. This stems from correspondence, because grapevines and laurels correspond to affection for what is true and its uses; while olive and fruit trees correspond to affection for what is good and its uses.

54.

NO ONE ENTERS HEAVEN BY DIRECT MERCY

521. If people have not been taught about heaven, the way to heaven, and the life of heaven within man, they hold the opinion that acceptance into heaven is simply a matter of the mercy given to people who are involved in faith, for whom the Lord intercedes. So they think that admittance is simply out of grace, and therefore that no matter how many people it means, all can be saved out of good will. Some people actually think that this even applies to everyone in hell.

These people, however, do not know anything about man. They do not know that his quality is exactly like that of his life, which in turn is like that of his love—not only in respect to the more inward elements that belong to his intention and discernment, but even in respect to his more outward elements that belong to his body. They do not know that the physical form is only an outward form in which the more inward elements present themselves at work, with the result that the whole person is his love (see above, n. 363).

Nor do they know that the body does not live on its own, but lives from the spirit, the person's spirit being his actual affection and his spiritual body being nothing but his affection in a human form like the one in which it is visible after death (see above, nn. 453-460). As long as these facts are not known, a person can manage to believe that salvation is nothing but a Divine good will which is called ''mercy'' and ''grace.''

522. But let us first state what Divine mercy is. Divine mercy is a pure mercy toward the whole human race, to save it. Further, it is constant with each individual person and never withdraws from him; so everyone who can be saved is saved.

But the only way anyone can be saved is by Divine *means*, which means have been revealed by the Lord in the Word. Divine means are called Divine truths. They teach how a person is to live in order to be saved. Through them, the Lord leads the person to heaven, and through them He endows him with heaven's life. The Lord does this for everyone; but He cannot endow anyone with heaven's life unless the person refrains from what is evil, because what is evil forms an obstruction.

To the extent that a person does refrain from what is evil, then, the Lord does lead him, through His Divine means, out of pure mercy, from infancy to the end of his life in the world, and on into eternity. This is the Divine mercy we mean.

We can see from this that the Lord's mercy is a pure mercy but not a direct mercy—not, that is, one that would save all people out of good will, no matter how they had lived.

523. The Lord never does anything in violation of His design, because He Himself is the Design. The Divine-True issuing from the Lord is what constitutes the design, and Divine truths are the laws of the design. The Lord leads man according to these laws.

So saving a person out of direct mercy is contrary to the Divine design; and since it is contrary to the Divine design, it is contrary to what is Divine.

The Divine design is heaven within man. Man has perverted it within himself by a life contrary to the laws of the design, which are Divine truths. Man is led back into that design by the Lord out of pure mercy by means of the laws of the design. Insofar as he is led back, he accepts heaven into himself; and anyone who accepts heaven into himself enters heaven.

Once again, we can see from this that the Lord's mercy is a pure mercy, but not a direct mercy.

524. If people could be saved by direct mercy, then everyone would be saved, even people in hell. As a matter of fact, there would not be a hell, because the Lord is Mercy itself, Love itself, and Goodness itself. It would be an affront to His Divine to say that He could save everyone directly, and did not. The Word teaches the Lord wills the salvation of all and the damnation of none.

525. Quite a few people who enter the other life from Christendom bring with them an article of faith that people are saved out of direct mercy because they plead for it. On examination, though, it emerges that they believed that entrance to heaven was simply being let in, and that people who were let in were in heavenly joy. They had no idea whatever what heaven or what heavenly joy is.

So they were informed that heaven is not denied to anyone by the Lord—they could be let in if they wished, and could stay there as well. The ones who did wish it were let in; but at the first threshold, as a result of the breath of heavenly warmth (the love angels are involved in) and the inflow of heavenly light (Divine truth) they were gripped with such pain in the heart that they felt hellish torment in themselves instead of heavenly joy. Struck by this, they threw themselves out of heaven headfirst.

In this way, they were taught by living experience that heaven cannot be granted to anyone by direct mercy.

526. I have occasionally talked with angels about this, telling them that quite a few people in the world who live involved in what is evil and who also talk with others about heaven and eternal life, say only that entering heaven is simply being let in out of mercy alone. This is the belief especially of people who make faith the only means of salvation. For they, because of the fundamental premise of their religion, do not focus on life or on the deeds of love that constitute life; so they do not focus on other means by which the Lord endows man with heaven and makes him receptive of heavenly joy. And since they reject every real means, they are compelled by their fundamental premise to make it a law that man enters heaven out of mercy alone, believing that God the Father is stirred to this mercy by the intercession of the Son.

[2] The angels answered this by saying that they were aware that this dogma followed necessarily from the accepted fundamental premise of faith alone. Since this tenet is the head of the rest, and is one no light from heaven can flow into because it is not true, it is the source of the ignorance today's church is in—ignorance of the Lord, heaven, life after death, heavenly joy, the essence of love and charity, and in general of what is good and its bond with what is true —ignorance, therefore, about man's life, its source and its nature, which cannot in any way belong to a person as a result of thinking, but as a result of intention and resulting deeds, being a result of thinking to the extent that the thinking is derived from intention. This means that life results from faith only to the extent that faith is derived from love.

Angels are distressed that these people do not know that faith alone in a person is an impossibility, since faith without its source, love, is only knowledge. For some people, it is a persuasive something that simulates faith (see above, n. 482). Nothing persuasive is within a person's life; it is outside unless it fits together with his love.

[3] They went on to say that if people are involved in this kind of premise about the essential means of salvation

for man, they cannot help believing in direct mercy. This is because they do perceive, from a natural light and from visual evidence, that faith by itself does not constitute a person's life, since people who are leading an evil life can think and convince themselves of the same premise. This is why people believe that the evil can be saved just like the good, if only at the time of death they talk with assurance about intercession and mercy through intercession.

The angels kept insisting that they had not yet seen anyone who had lived evilly accepted into heaven out of direct mercy, no matter how much assurance or confidence (which "faith" is taken to mean in an obvious sense) he had talked with in the world.

[4] Asked whether Abraham, Isaac, Jacob, David, and the Apostles were accepted into heaven by direct mercy, they answered, "None of them," saying that each had been accepted according to his life in the world. They knew where these individuals were, and knew that they were not more highly valued than other people. The angels said that the reason they are mentioned with honor in the Word is that through them, the Lord is meant in the inner sense—through Abraham, Isaac, and Jacob, the Lord in respect to what is Divine and Divine-Human; through David, the Lord in respect to the Divine-Royal; and through the Apostles, the Lord in respect to things Divine and True. Further, the angels have no consciousness whatever of these people when someone is reading the Word, because names do not enter heaven. In their stead, they perceive the Lord, as just stated. For this reason, the people are nowhere mentioned in the Word which exists in heaven (described above, n. 259), that Word being the inner meaning of the Word that exists in this world.

527. I can testify from an abundance of experience that it is impossible to endow with heaven's life people who have lived a life opposed to heaven's life in the world.

There were some people who believed that they would readily accept Divine truths after death when they heard them from angels—that they would believe and would live differently, and that as a result they could be accepted into heaven. This has however been tried with any number of people—only people who were involved in this kind of belief, though—who were allowed the experience so that they could learn that repentance after death does not exist.

Some of the people with whom this was tried understood the truths and seemed to accept them. But the instant they turned back to their love's life, they rejected them; in fact, they spoke against them. Some others rejected them on the spot, unwilling to listen to them. Some wanted the love's life they had acquired in the world to be taken away from them, and an angelic life (or heaven's life) poured in in its place. Even this was done for them, by special permission; but when their love's life was taken from them, they lay like corpses, no longer in control of themselves.

From these and other kinds of experience, straightforward good folk are taught that there is no way to change anyone's life after death; by no stretch of the imagination can an evil life be rewritten into a good one, or a hellish life into an angelic one. This is because each individual spirit is from head to toe of the same quality as his love—his life, that is—and changing this into its opposite would mean the complete destruction of his spirit.

Angels insist that it is easier to change one owl into a dove or another owl into a bird of paradise than it is to change a hellish spirit into an angel of heaven. In the appropriate section above (nn. 470-484) we have shown that a person retains after death the quality his life had in the world.

We may conclude from these considerations that no one can be accepted into heaven by direct mercy.

55.

LEADING A HEAVEN-BOUND LIFE IS NOT AS HARD AS PEOPLE BELIEVE

528. Some people believe that it is hard to lead a heaven-bound life (which is called a spiritual life), because they have heard that a person needs to renounce the world, give up the appetites that are associated with the body and the flesh, and live like spiritual beings. They take this to mean nothing other than rejecting what is worldly—especially wealth and prestige—walking around in constant devout meditation on God, salvation, and eternal life, passing their lives in prayer and in reading the Word and devotional literature. They think that this is renouncing the world and living by the spirit instead of by the flesh.

But in abundance of experience and discussion with angels has enabled me to know that the situation is completely different from this. In fact, people who renounce the world and live by the spirit in this fashion build up a mournful life for themselves, one that is not receptive of heavenly joy; for everyone's life stays with him. On the contrary, if a person is to accept heaven's life, he must by all means live in the world, involved in its functions and dealings. Then through a moral and civic life he receives a spiritual life. This is the only way a spiritual life can be formed in a person, or his spirit be prepared for heaven.

For living an inward life and not an outward life at the same time, is like living in a house with no foundation, which gradually either settles or develops cracks and gaps, or totters until it collapses.

529. If we look at and examine man's life with rational acuity, we discover that it is threefold: there is a spiritual life, a moral life, and a civic life; and we find these lives distinct from each other. For there are people who live a civic life but not a moral or a spiritual one, and people who live a moral life but still not a spiritual one. Then there are people who live both a civic life and a moral life and a spiritual as well. These last are the ones who are leading heaven's life—the others are leading the world's life separated from heaven's life.

A first conclusion we can draw from this is that a spiritual life is not separated from a natural one, or from the world's life. Rather, they are bonded together like a soul with its body, and if they become separated it is, as just mentioned, like living in a house without a foundation.

A moral and civic life is the behavioral aspect of a spiritual life, since intending well is a matter of spiritual life and acting well is a matter of moral and civic life. If this latter is separated from the former, the spiritual life is made up of nothing but thinking and talking. The intention fades into the background because it has no grounding—and yet the intention is the actual spiritual part of the person.

530. The considerations about to be presented will make it possible to see that it is not so hard to lead a heaven-bound life as people believe it is.

Who can't live a civic and moral life? Everyone is introduced to it from the cradle and is acquainted with it from his life in the world. Everyone, good or bad, leads it as well, for who does not want to be called honest and fair?

Almost everyone practices honesty and fairness in outward matters, even to the point of seeming honest and fair at heart, or as though he were behaving out of real honesty and fairness. A spiritual person needs to live the same way—which he can do just as easily as a natural person—the only difference being that a spiritual person believes in what is Divine, and behaves honestly and fairly not just because it is in keeping with civil and moral laws, but because it is in keeping with Divine laws. For the person who is thinking about Divine matters while he is active is in touch with angels of heaven. To the extent that he is doing this, he is bonded to them, and in this way his inner person is opened, which, seen in its own right, is the spiritual person.

When someone is like this, he is adopted and led by the Lord without realizing it. Then anything honest and fair that he does as part of his moral and civic life is done from a spiritual source. Doing something honest and fair from a spiritual source is doing it out of what is genuinely honest and fair, or doing it from the heart.

[2] In outward form, his fairness and honesty look just like the fairness and honesty in a natural person—even like that in evil and hellish people; but in inward form they are wholly unlike. Evil people really behave fairly and honestly only for their own sakes and for the sake of the world. So if they were not afraid of laws and penalties, of losing reputation, prestige, money, and life, they would act with utter dishonesty and unfairness; since they do not fear God or any Divine law, there is no inner restraint to hold them back. So to the extent that they can, they cheat, tear down, and rob, because they enjoy it.

This nature of theirs shows up particularly in people of the same sort in the other life, when everyone's outward aspects are taken away and their inward aspects are opened up in which they will be living to eternity (see above, nn. 499-511). Since at this point these people do act without outward restraints (which are, as mentioned above, fears of the law and of losing reputation, prestige, money, and life), their behavior is senseless; they laugh at honesty and fairness.

[3] But people who have behaved honestly and fairly because of Divine laws behave wisely after their outward aspects have been removed and they are left to their inward ones, because they have a bond with angels of heaven who convey wisdom to them.

This enables us to conclude, to begin with, that a spiritual person can behave just like a natural person as far as civic and moral living are concerned, provided he has a bond with the Divine in respect to his inner person, or in respect to his intention and thought (see above, nn. 358-360).

531. The laws of spiritual life, the laws of civic life, and the laws of moral life are handed down to us in the ten precepts of the Decalogue. The laws of spiritual life are found in the first three precepts, the laws of civic life in the next four, and the laws of moral life in the last three.

A person who is simply natural lives by these precepts in the same way as a spiritual person does, in outward form. He worships the Divine in similar fashion, goes to church, listens to sermons, manages a pious face; he does not kill, commit adultery, steal, or bear false witness, he does not cheat his fellows out of their possessions. But he does this simply for himself and the world, for appearance' sake.

This same person is completely the opposite in his inward make-up to the way he looks outwardly. Since he denies the Divine in his heart, he is a hypocrite in his worship. When he is left to himself in thought, he ridicules the church's holy things in the belief that they are useful only as restraints for the unlettered masses.

[2] This is why he is completely cut off from heaven. As a result, since he is not a spiritual person, he is not a moral or a civic person either. For even though he does not kill, he still has a hatred for anyone who gets in his way, and a vengefulness flares from the hatred. So if civil laws and outer restraints did not block him, he would kill. Since he longs to do it, it follows that he is constantly killing.

Even though he does not commit adultery, still since he believes it is all right, he is always an adulterer. For as far as he can, as often as he is given leave, he does it. Likewise, even though he does not steal, since he longs for other people's possessions and thinks frauds and evil schemes are not contrary to general law, in his spirit he is always acting like a thief. It is the same with the precepts of moral life—not bearing false witness or coveting other people's possessions.

This is the nature of every person who denies what is Divine and who does not have any conscience that stems from a religion. Their nature shows up clearly in people of the same sort in the other life, when their outward aspects have been removed and they are let into their inward ones. At that time, being cut off from heaven, they act in unison with hell. So they make friends with people who are there.

[3] As for people who have at heart recognized what is Divine, who have focused on Divine laws in the deeds of their lives, and have lived by the first three precepts of the Decalogue as well as by the rest, things are different for them. When they are let into their inward aspects with their outer ones removed, they are wiser than they were in the world. When they come into their inward aspects, it is like coming from darkness into light, from ignorance into wisdom, and from a mournful life into a blessed one. This is because they are involved in what is Divine, and therefore in heaven.

We have presented these things to let people know what each type is like, in spite of the fact that both may lead the same kind of outward life.

532. Everyone might realize that thoughts have a motion and tendency in the direct of purpose, or where a person is headed. Thought is in fact the person's inner sight, which is set up like outward sight in that it turns and lingers where the person directs himself and heads.

So if the inner sight or thought is turned toward the world and lingers there, it follows that the thought becomes worldly. If it turned toward self and self-prestige, it becomes physical. But if it is turned toward heaven, it becomes heavenly. So too, if it is turned toward heaven it is lifted up; if it is turned toward self it is pulled away from heaven and plunged into what is physical; if it is turned toward the world it is bent away from heaven and scattered about on the things that lie before the eyes.

[2] It is a person's love that constitutes his purpose and focuses his inner sight or thought on its objects. So love of self focuses the inner sight on self and what belongs to self; love of the world focuses it on worldly matters; and love of heaven focuses it on heavenly matters. This enables us to evaluate the state of the inner elements of someone's mind once his love is identified. If a person loves heaven, his more inward elements are raised toward heaven and opened upward. If he loves the world and himself, his more inward elements are closed upward and opened downward. We can conclude from this that if the higher elements of the mind are closed upwards, the person is no longer able to see objects that have to do with heaven and the church—that for him, they are in darkness. Further, he will either deny or not understand things that are in darkness.

This is why people who love themselves and the world more than anything else deny Divine truths at heart, because for them the higher elements of the mind are closed. If they talk about Divine truths at all on the basis of memory, they still do not understand them. Too, they look at them the way they look at worldly and physical things. This being their nature, the only things they can reflect on are the things that come in through their physical senses, the only things they enjoy. These include many things which are foul, lewd, unholy, and criminal, which cannot be carried away because there occurs no inflow into their minds from heaven, their minds being closed upward, as just mentioned.

[3] A person's purpose, which focuses his inner sight or thought, is his intention. For the person purposes what he intends, and thinks what he purposes. So if he purposes heaven, his thought is focused on heaven, together with his whole mind, which then is in heaven. From that perspective he looks down on things that belong to the world, like someone on the roof of a house.

This is why a person whose more inward elements of mind have been opened can see evil and false elements which are in him, since these are below his spiritual mind. On the other hand, a person whose more inward elements have not been opened cannot see his evil and false elements because he is involved in them, not above them.

On this basis, we can determine the source of man's wisdom and the source of his madness. We can also determine what a person will be like after death once he is left to intend and think, then to behave and talk, in keeping with his more inward elements. Another reason for presenting these matters is to make it known what a person is like more inwardly, no matter how much he may resemble someone else outwardly.

533. We can now see that it is not so hard to lead a heaven-bound life as people think it is because it is simply a matter, when something gets in the way that the person knows is dishonest and unfair, something his spirit moves toward, of thinking that he should not do it because it is against the Divine precepts. If a person gets used to doing this, and by getting used to it gains a certain disposition, then little by little he is bonded to heaven. As this takes place, the higher reaches of his mind are opened; and as they are opened, he sees what things are dishonest and unfair; and as he sees them, they can be broken off. For no evil can be broken off until after it is seen.

This is a state a person can enter because of his freedom, for who cannot think this way, because of his freedom? And once this is begun, the Lord works out all good things for him, arranging things so that he not only sees evil elements but dislikes them, and eventually turns away from them. This is the meaning of the Lord's words,

My yoke is easy, and my burden light.

(Matthew 11:30)

But we need to realize that the difficulty of thinking this way and of resisting what is evil increases as a person does evil things intentionally. So far as he does, he gets used to them until he does not see them. Then he reaches a point where he loves them, and finds excuses for them out of the pleasure of his love, validates them by all kinds of deceptive notions, and calls them legal and good. But this happens with people who plunge heedlessly into evil matters in young adulthood and who, as they do, reject Divine things at heart.

534. Once I was shown a portrayal of the path that leads to heaven and the path that leads to hell. There was a broad path heading left or north. I could see many spirits following it; but in the distance there was a fairly large rock where the broad path ended. At the rock, two paths parted, one to the left and one to the other side to the right.

The path that headed left was narrow or constricted, leading through the west to the south and therefore into heaven's light. The path that headed right was broad and ample, leading down on a slant toward hell.

At first, everyone seemed to be following the same path, until they arrived at the large rock at the fork; but when people got there, they parted company. The good people kept turning left and entering the narrow path that led to heaven. But the evil people did not see the rock at the fork. They were falling over it, hurting themselves, and once they got up they were running along the path to the right that headed toward hell.

[2] Later on, the meaning of all this was explained to me. As for the first path, the broad one that both good and evil people were traveling together, conversing like friends because there was no apparent difference between them, it served to picture people who live alike, honestly and fairly, in outward matters, and who cannot be told apart at sight. As for the rock at the fork or corner, which the evil people were falling over, which they were then running away from along the path leading to hell, it served to picture Divine Truth, denied by people who focus on hell. In the highest meaning, this same rock served to indicate the Lord's Divine-Human. People who acknowledge what is true, though, and at the same time acknowledge the Lord's Divine, were being brought along the path that led to heaven.

Again, I could see from this that evil people and good people lead the same kind of life in outward matters, or take the same path—one as readily as the other. Yet the people who at heart acknowledge what is Divine (especially people within the church who acknowledge the Lord's Divine) are led to heaven; while the people who make no such acknowledgment are led to hell.

[3] The thoughts people have which come out of purpose or intention are pictured by paths in the other life. Paths are presented there with appearances exactly in keeping with thoughts springing from purpose; and every individual, too, travels by his thoughts that come out of purpose. This is why it is possible to tell what spirits and their thoughts are like from their paths. This also enables us to see what is meant by the Lord's word,

> Enter by the narrow gate, for wide is the gate and broad the path that leads to destruction, and many are the people who travel through it; . . . tight is the path and narrow the way that leads to life, and few are the people who find it.

(Matthew 7:13-14)

The path that leads to life is not narrow because it is hard, but because "few are the people who find it," as is said.

From the rock that was seen at the corner, where the broad, common path ended and the two paths were seen to lead in opposite directions, we can see what these words of the Lord indicate:

> Have you not read what is written? The stone which the builders rejected has become the head of the corner; anyone who falls on that stone will be shatttered.   (Matthew 21:42-44, Luke 20:17-18)

"The rock" indicates the Divine-True, and the "Rock of Israel," the Lord in respect to the Divine-Human. "The builders" are people from the church, "the head of the corner" is where the fork is, "falling" and "being shattered" are denying and dying.

535. I have been granted to talk with some people in the other life who retired from the world's affairs in order to live in a devout and holy manner, and with other people who had afflicted themselves in various ways because they believed that was renouncing the world and taming the lusts of the flesh. But many of them cannot associate with angels because they have in this way acquired a mournful life, and have retired from a life of charity which can only be led in the world; while angels' life is happy because of its blessedness, and is made up of serving good purposes which are works of charity. Besides, people who have led a life withdrawn from worldly matters burn with a sense of merit, and therefore constantly covet heaven. They think of heavenly joy as a reward, utterly unaware of what heavenly joy is. Once they are among angels and involved in their joy—which contains no sense of merit, and is made up of jobs and down-to-earth tasks, and a blessedness derived from the good they accomplish in this way—they are as surprised as people who are seeing something foreign to their faith. Since they are not receptive to that joy, they leave and associate with their own kind, people who were involved in the same kind of life in the world.

[2] But as for people who lived devout lives in outward form—always in churches praying, afflicting their souls, and thinking all the while about themselves as more worthy and honorable than other people, even thinking they would be thought of as saints after death—in the other life they are not in heaven because they have done this sort of thing for their own sakes. Since they have completely polluted things Divine and true with the self-love they have drowned them in, some of them are so crazy they think they are gods. So they are among their like in hell.

Some are wily and shrewd, and are in a hell of shrewd people. These are people who, by means of skills and wiles, manufactured outward appearances which led common people to believe a Divine holiness was within them.

[3] Many of Catholicism's saints are like this. I have been allowed to talk with some of them, when the quality of their life in the world—and afterwards—was clearly described.

We have presented these matters to let people know that a heaven-bound life is not a life withdrawn from the world but a life involved in the world, that a life of piety without a life of charity (which occurs only in this world) does not lead to heaven. Rather, it is a life of charity, a life of behaving honestly and fairly in every task, every transaction, every work, from a more inward source, hence a heavenly one. This source is present in that life when a person behaves honestly and fairly because it is in keeping with Divine laws.

This life is not hard. Rather, the life of piety withdrawn from a life of charity is hard. Yet this latter life leads away from heaven just as surely as people believe it leads to heaven.

PART III

HELL

56.

THE LORD GOVERNS THE HELLS

536. Earlier, in treating of heaven, it was everywhere demonstrated that the Lord is the God of heaven (specifically, nn. 2-6), with the whole government of the heavens belonging to the Lord. Granting that heaven has the same kind of relationship to hell (and hell to heaven) as two opposing entities that act against each other, with a balance resulting from their action and reaction, and with everything remaining in being within that balance, then for each and every thing to be kept in a balance, it is necessary that the person who rules one rule the other. For unless the Lord set bounds to the rebellions from hell and controlled the forms of madness that exist there, the balance would be destroyed, and with the balance everything would go.

537. At this point, though, let us first say something about the balance.

It is known that when two entities work against each other, and when one of them reacts and resists just as much as the other one acts and strives, neither of the two has effective power because each has the same force. Then either can be acted upon at will by a third entity because, there being no effective power because of their stand-off, the effective power of the third is in complete control, as easily as if there were no opposition.

[2] There is this kind of balance between heaven and hell. Not that it is the kind of balance that obtains between two

people of equal strength who are fighting each other—rather it is a spiritual balance, a balance of the false against the true and of the evil against the good. The false derived from the evil branches out of hell constantly; and the true derived from the good breathes out of heaven constantly.

This is the spiritual balance which puts man in a freedom for thinking and intending. For anything a person thinks and intends goes back either to something evil and the resultant false or to something good and the resultant true. [3] So when someone is involved in this balance, he is in a freedom to let in or accept what is evil and what is false from it out of hell, or to let in and accept what is good and what is true from it out of heaven.

Every individual is held in this balance by the Lord, since He governs both heaven and hell. In the appropriate chapter below, we will tell why man is held in freedom by means of this balance, why what is evil and false is not taken away from him by Divine power and what is good and true put into him.

538. Several times I have been granted to perceive the sphere of what is false resulting from what is evil, flowing out of hell. It was like a never-ending effort to destroy everything good and true, bonded to an anger and a kind of rage at the impossibility of doing so. Particularly, it was like an effort to annihilate and destroy the Lord's Divine, because He is the source of everything good and true.

But I have also perceived, out of heaven, a sphere of what is true resulting from what is good, which served to curb the rage of the effort welling up from hell, resulting in a balance.

Although this sphere perceived as flowing from heaven seemed to come from angels, I could tell that it came from the Lord alone. The reason it came from the Lord alone and not from angels was that every single angel in heaven recognizes that nothing good and true is from himself, but all from the Lord.

539. All the power in the spiritual world is a property of what is true resulting from what is good; what is false resulting from what is evil has no power whatever.

The reason all power is a property of what is true resulting from what is good, is that the actual Divine in heaven is the Divine-Good and the Divine-True, and all power belongs to the Divine. The reason what is false resulting from what is evil has no power whatever is that it all belongs to what is true resulting from what is good, and there is no trace of this in what is false resulting from what is evil.

This is why all power is in heaven and none in hell. Actually, every individual in heaven is involved in matters of truth resulting from what is good, and every individual in hell is involved in matters of falsity resulting from what is evil. For no one is let into heaven until he is involved in matters of truth resulting from what is good, nor is anyone cast into hell until he is involved in matters of falsity resulting from what is evil. We may see that this is true in the chapters that deal with the first, second, and third states of man after death (nn. 491-520); we may see that all power is a property of what is true resulting from what is good in the chapter on the power of heaven's angels (nn. 228-233).

540. This, then, is the balance between heaven and hell. The people who are in the world of spirits are involved in this balance because the world of spirits is halfway between heaven and hell. As a result, all people in the world are held in the same balance, since people in the world are governed by the Lord through spirits who are in the world of spirits (a subject which will be treated of in its own chapter below).

This kind of balance could not exist unless the Lord governed both heaven and hell and managed both of them. Otherwise, false things resulting from what is evil would become excessive and would influence the simple good folk who are at the boundaries of heaven, who can be misled more easily than angels. This would mean destruction of the balance, and with the balance, of freedom for man.

541. Hell is divided into communities the way heaven is—into the same number of communities as heaven, too, since each community in heaven has a community opposite to it in hell. But the communities in hell are distinguished by evil things and resultant false things because the communities in heaven are distinguished by good things and resultant true things.

We may know that every good element has an opposite evil element and every true thing an opposite false thing because nothing exists without a relationship to its opposite. Its nature and level are recognized because of this opposition, which is the source of all perception and sensation.

Because of this, the Lord provides that each community of heaven has its opposite number in a community of hell, and that there is a balance between them.

542. Since hell is divided into the same number of communities as heaven, there are as many hells as there are communities of heaven. For each particular community of heaven is a heaven in miniature (see above, nn. 51-58), and so each community of hell is a hell in miniature. Since overall there are three heavens, there are three hells as well. There is a lowest one opposite to the inmost or third heaven, an intermediate one opposite the intermediate or second heaven, and a higher one opposite to the outmost or first heaven.

543. Let us state briefly how the hells are governed by the Lord.

In general, the hells are ruled by a general impingement of the Divine-Good and the Divine-True out of the heavens, which serves to curb and control the general effort that flows

out of the hells. This is done also by a particular impingement from each individual heaven and each individual community of heaven.

In detail, the hells are governed through angels who are
enabled to inspect the hells and to control the frenzies and
riots there. Now and then, angels are sent there and calm
things down by their presence.

But in a broad sense, all the people who are in the hells
are governed by their fears. Some are governed through
fears grafted and then rooted in them in the world; but since
these fears are not enough and gradually ebb, they are ruled
by fears of penalties, which serve particularly to deter some
of them from doing evil things. There are many kinds of
punishment, milder or more severe depending on the evil
deeds.

For the most part, the more vicious ones are given authority over the others. They hold sway by means of their
cunning and their schemes, and are able to keep the rest in
compliance and slavery by means of punishments and the
resulting dread. These authorities dare not go beyond limits
set for them.

It is worth knowing that the fear of penalties is the only
means of controlling the ferocity and rages of the people
in the hells. No other means exist.

544. People in the world have believed that there is a
particular Devil who is at the head of the hells, that he was
created an angel of light, but that after instigating a revolt,
he was cast into hell with his mob. The reason people have
held this belief is that the Devil and Satan are mentioned
in the Word, as well as Lucifer, with the Word in these
instances being understood in its literal meaning. However,
"the Devil" and "Satan" there mean hell—"the Devil"
means the hell which is at the back, where the worst people
called evil genii live, and "Satan" means the hell which

is farther forward, where the people live who are not so evil, who are called evil spirits. "Lucifer" means the people who come from Babylon or Babylonia, the ones who stretch their sway into heaven.

We can see that there is no particular Devil to whom all the hells are subject from the fact that all the people in the hells (like all the people in the heavens) are from the human race (see nn. 311-317). There are myriads and myriads there, from the beginning of creation to the present day: and each individual is the particular kind of devil his opposition to the Divine in this world has made him (on these matters, see above, nn. 311-312).

57.

THE LORD DOES NOT CAST ANYONE INTO HELL; RATHER, THE PERSON HIMSELF DOES

545. Some people are persuaded that the Lord turns His face away from man, casts him away from Himself and into hell, and is angry with him, because of his evil. Some people are even persuaded that God punishes man and does evil to him. They support themselves in this notion with things from the literal meaning of the Word, where there are statements to that effect, not realizing that the Word's spiritual meaning (which unfolds the literal meaning) is completely different, or that the church's true doctrine (which comes from the Word's spiritual meaning) therefore teaches something different. This teaching is that God never turns His face away from man, never casts him away from Himself, does not cast anyone into hell or become angry.

Anyone whose mind is enlightened perceives this when he reads the Word, simply from the fact that God is the Good itself, Love itself, and Mercy itself, the Good itself being incapable of doing evil to anyone, Love itself and Mercy itself being incapable of casting a person away from themselves because this goes against the essential nature of mercy and love and therefore against the Divine itself.

In consequence, if people think with an enlightened mind, they perceive clearly when they read the Word that God never turns away from man. And since He does not turn away from him, he deals with him from Goodness, Love, and Mercy. That is, He wills what is good for him, He loves him, and He has mercy on him.

Such people also therefore see that the Word's literal meaning where things like this are stated is hiding within itself a spiritual meaning which is needed to explain statements in the literal meaning that are adapted to man's grasp and are in accord with his first and general concepts.

546. People in a state of enlightenment see further, that what is good and what is evil are two opposite things, as opposite as heaven and hell, and that everything good comes out of heaven, and everything evil from hell. They see that, since the Lord's Divine constitutes heaven (nn. 7-12), nothing but what is good flows in from the Lord for a person, and nothing but evil flows in from hell; so the Lord is constantly leading the individual away from what is evil and toward what is good, while hell is constantly leading the individual into what is evil.

If the individual were not in between these two influences, he would have no thought, no intention, and surely no freedom or choice. He possesses all these things as a result of the balance between what is good and what is evil. As a result, if the Lord were to turn away and the person be left to what is evil only, he would no longer be a person.

' We can see from these considerations that the Lord does flow into people with what is good—into an evil person just as much as into a good person. But there is this difference, that He is constantly leading an evil person away from what is evil, but leading a good person toward what is good. The reason for this difference lies within the individual, because he is the recipient.

547. This enables us to conclude that a person does what is evil because of hell and does what is good because of the Lord. But since the person believes that whatever he does he does on his own, when he does something evil it sticks to him as though it belonged to him. This is why the person, not in any way the Lord, is responsible for his own evil.

The evil within a person is hell within him, since it makes no difference whether you say "the evil" or "hell."

Now since the person is responsible for his own evil, it is he who leads himself into hell, not the Lord. Far from leading anyone into hell, the Lord frees people from hell to the extent that they do not intend their own evil and love to be involved in it.

A person's whole intention and love stay with him after death (nn. 470-484). If a person intends and loves what is evil in the world, he intends and loves the same evil in the other life, and will then no longer let himself be led away from it. This is why a person who is involved in what is evil is in contact with hell—is actually there as far as his spirit is concerned. And after death, his greatest craving is to be where his own evil is. Consequently, after death the person himself, not the Lord, casts himself into hell.

548. Let us describe how this happens. When a person enters the other life, he is at first welcomed by angels who do everything for him—talk with him about the Lord, heaven, and angelic life, and give him instruction in matters of truth and goodness. But if this person, now a spirit, is the kind who had in fact known these things in the world, but had denied them at heart or sneered at them, then after some conversation he craves and tries to get away. When the angels detect this they leave him.

After he has been with other people for a while, he eventually joins in with people who are involved in the same kind of evil as he (see above, nn. 445-452). When this takes place, the person turns away from the Lord, and turns his face toward the hell he had been bonded to in the world, where there are people involved in his own kind of love of what is evil.

This enables us to see that the Lord, through angels and through an inflow from heaven, leads every spirit toward Himself. But spirits who are involved in what is evil resist strenuously and virtually tear themselves away from the

Lord, with their evil—with hell, therefore—dragging them off like a rope. Because they are dragged off and because they follow along purposefully owing to their love of what is evil, we conclude that they cast themselves into hell out of their own freedom.

In the world, people cannot believe this because of their concept of hell. In fact, in the other life it looks exactly like this to the eyes of people who are outside of hell; but not to the people who are casting themselves into hell. They do enter of their own free will; and the ones who enter because of a burning love of what is evil look as though they were being thrown straight in, head first and feet up. It is because of this appearance that they seem to be cast down into hell by Divine power (on this subject, see further below, n. 574).

So now we can see from this that the Lord does not cast anyone into hell; each individual casts himself in, not only while he is living in the world, but after death, when he arrives among the spirits.

The reason why the Lord, out of His Divine Essence which is the Good, Love, and Mercy, cannot deal in the same way with every individual, is that evil things and consequent false things are in the way, not only dulling but even rejecting His Divine inflow.

The evil and consequent false elements are like black clouds that come between the sun and a person's eyes and cut off all its sunny and benign light, though all the while the sun keeps trying to break up the obstructing clouds. For the sun is behind them, working away, occasionally getting some shadowy light to the person's eye by various round-about routes.

It is like this in the spiritual world. There the sun is the Lord and Divine Love (nn. 116-140); there the light is the Divine-True (nn. 126-140). The black clouds are false elements resulting from what is evil; the eye there is the discernment. To the extent that anyone there is involved in false things resulting from what is evil, he has a cloud like this around him, black and thick in proportion to the degree of his evil.

We can see from this comparison that the Lord's presence is with everyone constantly, but is accepted in different ways.

550. Evil spirits in the world of spirits are punished severely so that through these punishments they may be scared off from doing evil things. This too seems to be done by the Lord. However, no part of the punishment is done by the Lord—it is done by the evil itself. For an evil thing and its punishment are so closely joined that they cannot be separated. In fact, the hellish mob has no greater craving or love than to inflict punishment and to torture. They do work evil and inflict punishment on anyone unprotected by the Lord. As a result, when something evil is done from an evil heart, since this rejects all of the Lord's safekeeping, hellish spirits rush into the person who has done this kind of evil thing, and punish him.

To some extent, we can illustrate this by means of evil deeds and their punishments in the world, where they are also closely joined together. Laws do set a penalty there for each evil deed; so the person who rushes into an evil deed rushes into its punishment as well. The only difference is that in the world an evil deed can be hidden, which cannot happen in the other life.

We may conclude from these considerations that the Lord does not do evil to anyone. This is much the way it is in the world, since neither the ruler nor the law is responsible for the punishment of the criminal because they are not responsible for the evil element within the evildoer.

58.

**ALL THE PEOPLE WHO ARE IN THE HELLS
ARE INVOLVED IN EVIL THINGS AND
CONSEQUENT FALSE THINGS AS A RESULT OF
THEIR LOVES OF THEMSELVES AND THE
WORLD**

551. All the people who are in the hells are involved in evil things and consequent false things; there is no one there who is involved in evil and in true things at the same time.

Many evil people in the world are familiar with spiritual truths, which are true elements of the church; they have in fact learned them from the cradle, later from sermons and from reading the Word, and later still have talked from this perspective. Some of them have even led other people to believe they were heartfelt Christians because they knew how to talk from the perspective of truths with feigned affection and to be honest in their behavior as though they were acting out of a spiritual faith.

But all such people whose inward thought was opposed to such truths, who simply because of civil laws refrained from the evil deeds that were in accord with their thinking, for the sake of reputation, prestige, and profit—all such people are evil at heart, and are involved in matters of truth and goodness only as far as their bodies are concerned, not as far as their spirits are concerned. As a result, when their outward aspects are taken away from them in the other life, and the inner aspects that pertained to their spirits are uncovered, they are wholly involved in evil and false things and not involved in any good and true things. It is clear that the good and true elements were settled in their memories only, exactly like data, and that they retrieved them when they talked and imitated good characteristics as though they resulted from spiritual love and faith.

When people like this are let loose into what lies within them (and therefore into their own evils), they cannot say true things any more, only false things, since they are talking on the basis of evil things. For it is impossible to say true things on the basis of evil ones, the spirit being nothing but his own evil at this point; and what is false comes out of what is evil.

Each individual spirit is reduced to this condition before he is cast into hell (see above, nn. 499-512). This is called "being devastated" in respect to good and true elements; and the devastation is nothing but being let loose into inner elements and therefore into what belongs to the spirit—or into the actual spirit (on these matters, see also n. 425 above).

552. When a person is like this after death, then he is not a "person-spirit" any more, the way he was in his first condition (see above, nn. 491-498), but really a spirit. For he is really a spirit when he is in a body and face which correspond to what lies within him, which belong to his mind [*animus*], being then in outward form a "type" or copy of what lies within him.

This is what a spirit is like after the first and second states have run their full course, as described above. So at that time people can tell when their eyes see him what he is like, not just from his face but even from his body, and especially from his speech and behavior. And since at this point he is "in himself," the only place he can be is where there are people like himself.

[2] There is in fact a sharing in all possible ways of affections and consequently of thoughts in the spiritual world. So a spirit is taken to people like himself, apparently on his own because it depends on his affection and its plea-

sure. Actually he even steers himself in that direction. For this is the way his life breathes, the way he freely draws his soul, which he cannot do when he is turning toward someone else.

It needs to be realized that in the spiritual world sharing with others depends on turning one's face. A person has constantly before his face the people who are involved in a love like this own, no matter where he turns his body (see above, n. 151).

[3] This is why all hellish spirits turn their backs to the Lord, and face the gloomy and dark things that occupy the place of the world's sun and moon, while all heaven's angels turn toward the Lord as heaven's sun and heaven's moon (see above, nn. 123, 143, 144, 151).

We can now conclude from these matters that all the people who are in the hells are involved in evil and consequent false things, and that they are turned toward their own loves as well.

553. When the spirits in the hells are examined in any of heaven's light, they appear in forms appropriate to their evil qualities. Each one is in fact a model of his evil quality because for each one the more inward and the more outward elements act in unison, with the more inward ones displaying themselves in the more outward ones, which are the face, the body, speech, and behavior. So it is possible to recognize the spirits' quality by looking them over carefully.

Broadly speaking, they are forms of contempt for other people and of kinds of menace for people who do not do them homage. There are various distinct kinds of hatred; there are various distinct kinds of vengefulness. Viciousness and cruelty show through them from their more inward parts; yet when other people praise them or do them homage or revere them, their faces compose themselves and something is visible like a happiness arising from pleasure.

[2] There is no brief way to describe the appearance of all these forms—no single one is actually just like any other. There is a general similarity only among people who are involved in a similar evil and are therefore in the same hellish community. A kind of similarity of individuals' faces does result there from this involvement, as if from a common background.

In general, their faces are frightful, lifeless as corpses. Some are black, some like fiery little torches, some swollen by pimples, distorted veins, and sores. Many have no visible face, but only something hairy or bony instead; with some, only the teeth stand out. Their bodies are grotesque, and their speech apparently arises from anger or hatred or revenge because each one talks out of his own false nature and has a voice quality that stems from his evil nature. In short, all of them are reflections of their own hells.

[3] I have not been allowed to see hell itself overall in its own form. I have been told that just as the whole heaven, taken as a whole, presents itself as a single Person (nn. 59-67), so the whole hell, taken as a whole presents itself as one devil; and further that it can be presented under the image of a single devil (see above, n. 544).

But I have quite often been allowed to see what kind of form particular hells or hellish communities have, since a monster may often be seen at their entrances (called the gates of hell) who pictures in a general way the form of the people within. At such times, the viciousness of their residents is pictured by things too frightful and disgusting to mention.

[4] It should however be realized that while hellish spirits look like this in heaven's light, they look like people to each other. This arises from the Lord's mercy, to prevent their filth from being for them the way it looks to angels. Still, this appearance is deceptive, for the moment any of

heaven's light is let in, their human forms change to bestial ones, forms of their own intrinsic qualities, as described above. For in heaven's light, everything looks the way it really is.

This is also why they run away from heaven's light and plunge into their own light, a light like that of glowing coals, from time to time like burning sulphur. However, this light turns into utter darkness when any ray of light flows in from heaven.

This is why the hells are described as being in gloom and darkness, and why the words "gloom" and "darkness" indicate false elements arising from what is evil, the kind that exist in hell.

554. I could see by examining the bestial forms of spirits in the hells (which, as mentioned, are all forms of contempt for other people and menace for people who do not show them respect or do them homage; and also forms of hatred and revenge against people who do not support them) that all of them, broadly speaking, are forms of self-love and love of the world. I could see, too, that all the evil elements, of which they are particular forms, derived from these two loves.

Further, I have been told from heaven and convinced by an abundance of experience that these two loves (love of self and love of the world) reign supreme in the hells and even constitute the hells—also that love for the Lord and love toward the neighbor reign supreme in the heavens and even constitute the heavens. Further, I have been told that the two loves that are hell's loves and the two loves that are heaven's loves are diametrically opposed to each other.

555. At first I wondered why it is that love of self and love of the world are so diabolical, why all the people involved in them are so horrible to look at. After all, in this world people pay little attention to love of self compared to the attention paid to that outward inflation of spirit called pride. Because this is obvious, people believe that it alone is love of self. Further, when love of self does not come out in the form of pride, people believe it is the fire of life that rouses a person to go his appointed rounds and perform his useful services. They believe that if a person did not see prestige and glory in such activities, his spirit would cool off.

They say, "Who ever did anything worthwhile, anything useful, anything worth mentioning, except for applause and prestige from other people, or in other people's minds? And what other source does this have than the fire of a love for glory and prestige—that is, then, a love of self?" This is why people in the world do not realize that love of self, seen in its own right, is the love that governs in hell and that constitutes hell within man.

Since this is how things stand, I should like to describe first what self-love is like, and then to describe how all evil and consequent false things flow from that love.

556. Self-love is willing well to oneself alone and not willing well to anyone else except for one's own sake—not the church, the country, or any human community. It also involves doing them good for the sole sake of one's own reputation, prestige, and glory. Unless the person sees these benefits in what he is doing for others, he says in his heart, "What difference does it make?" "Why should I?" "What's in it for me?" And he dismisses it.

We can see from this that a person who is involved in self-love does not love his church, his country, his community, or any useful functions—he loves only himself.

His pleasure is simply the pleasure of self-love. And since the pleasure that occurs as a result of love constitutes the person's life, his life is a life of self. A "life of self" is a life derived from the person's self image [*proprium*], and man's self-image, seen in its own right, is nothing but evil.

A person who loves himself does love people who belong to him as well—specifically, his children and relatives, and more broadly all the people who cooperate with him, whom he calls "his people." Loving these two groups of people is still loving himself, because he virtually sees them as being within himself, and himself as being within them. He also includes among the people he calls "his" all the people who praise him or respect him or wait on him.

557. We can determine the quality of self-love by comparing it to heavenly love. Heavenly love is loving what is useful for its own sake, or what is good for its own sake, these being what a person does for his church, for his country, for the human community, and for his fellow-citizen. This is actually loving God and loving the neighbor, since all useful functions and good deeds come from the Lord and are, fruther, the neighbor we are supposed to love.

But if someone loves these for his own sake, he loves them only as slaves who work for him. It follows that if a person is involved in self-love, he wants his church, country, human communities, and fellow citizens to work for him, not the other way around. He puts himself over them, and them under himself.

This is why a person is moving away from heaven to the extent that he is involved in self-love—because he is moving away from heavenly love.

558a. Beyond this, if someone is involved in a heavenly love (loving useful and good functions, moved by a heart-felt pleasure when he performs them for his church, country, human community, and fellow-citizen), he is being led by the Lord to the extent of his involvement because that is the love the Lord is involved in, the love that comes from Him. To the extent, though, that a person is involved in self-love (performing useful and good functions for his own sake), he is being led by himself. In the degree that anyone is being led by himself, he is not being led by the Lord. It also follows from this that the person moves away from the Divine and therefore also away from heaven to the extent that he loves himself. Being led by oneself is being led by one's self-image, and man's self-image is nothing but evil. It is actually his evil inheritance, which is loving self more than God and the world more than heaven.

A person is immersed in his self-image (and therefore in his evil hereditary elements) whenever he focuses on himself in the good things he does. This is because he is looking out of the good things at himself, not looking out of himself at the good things. So there occurs in the good things a reflection of himself rather than any reflection of the Divine.

I have become convinced of the truth of this too through experience. There are evil spirits whose homes are in the region halfway between the north and the west underneath the heavens, spirits with a practiced skill at leading upright spirits into absorption with their self-images and therefore into various kinds of evil. They accomplish this by leading the other spirits into thoughts about themselves—either blatantly, by means of praise and deference, or deviously by limiting their affections to themselves. To the extent that they achieve this, they turn the faces of the upright spirits away from heaven. To the same extent too, they darken their understanding and call evil elements out of their self-images.

558b. We can see from the respective sources and essential natures of the two loves that self-love is the opposite of love toward the neighbor.

In a person who is involved in self-love, a love of the neighbor begins from the self. He actually is saying, "Each individual is his own neighbor," and from himself as the center, his love moves out to all the people who unite with him with a decrease proportional to the degree of their bond with him, formed through their love. People outside this circle are considered worthless, and people who oppose this group and their evils are considered enemies no matter what they are really like—wise, honest, upright, or fair.

A spiritual love toward the neighbor, however, begins from the Lord and moves out from Him as the center to all people who are bonded to Him through love and faith—moving out, then, in proportion to the quality of the love and faith within them.

We can see from this that a love of the neighbor which starts from the person is the opposite of a love toward the neighbor which starts from the Lord. The first kind emerges from what is evil because it emerges from the person's self-image. The second kind emerges from what is good because it emerges from the Lord who is the Good itself. We can also see that a love of the neighbor which emerges from the individual and his self-image is physical, while a love toward the neighbor that emerges from the Lord is heavenly.

In short, self-love makes up the head of the person it occurs in, with heavenly love making up the feet he stands on. If the heavenly love does not serve him, it is something he tramples underfoot.

This is why people who are being cast into hell seem to be cast straight down into hell headfirst, with their feet up toward heaven (see above, n. 548).

559. Further, the nature of self-love is such that as its reins are loosened (that is, as outward restraints are removed, which are fears of the law and of legal penalties, of loss of reputation, profit, office, and life), it plunges forward all the way into a will to rule not just over all nations on earth, but even over all of heaven and the Divine Itself. It has no bound or limit whatever. This lies hidden in every individual who is involved in self-love, even though it is not visible to the world, where the restraints mentioned hold it in check.

No one can fail to see the truth of this in influential people and kings who do not have these reins and restraints, who plunge onward, conquering territories and kingdoms as long as it works for them, and aspiring to limitless power and glory.

We can see the truth of this even more clearly in today's Babylon, which stretches its sway into heaven, which has transferred all the Lord's Divine power to itself and constantly craves even more. It may be seen in the booklet *The Last Judgment and Babylon Destroyed* that people like this are completely against what is Divine and heaven, and in favor of hell after death, once they enter the other life.

560. Imagine some community made up of people who all loved themselves alone and loved others only as they joined them, and you will see that their love resembles nothing more than love among thieves. To the extent that they are working closely together, they embrace each other and call each other friends; but to the extent that they are not working closely together and refuse their leadership, they attack and butcher each other.

If their more inward reaches, or their spirits, are explored, one will see that they are full of hostile ill-will against each other, that at heart they scoff at everything fair and honest and at the Divine, which they cast aside as though it were nothing. We may reach this conclusion still more surely by examining their communities in the hells, which will be described below.

561. The more inward elements of the thoughts and affections of people who love themselves more than anything else, are turned towards themselves and the world, turned away therefore from the Lord and from heaven. This is why they are obsessed with every kind of evil and why the Divine cannot flow in. The moment it does flow in, it is plunged into thoughts about self, polluted, and filled with the evil elements that come from their self-images.

This is why all such people in the other life look backward, away from the Lord and toward the gloomy place which marks the location of the world's sun, directly opposite to heaven's sun which is the Lord (see above, n. 123). Further, "gloom" means what is evil, and "the world's sun" means self-love.

In general, the evil elements that belong to people who are involved in self-love are contempt for other people, envy, enmity against everyone who does not side with them, a consequent hostility, different kinds of hatred, vengefulness, craft, treachery, ruthlessness, and cruelty. As far as matters of religion are concerned, there is not just a contempt for the Divine, and for the Divine elements which are the true and good things of the church, there is an anger against these things. When a person becomes a spirit, this anger turns into hatred. At this point, the person not only cannot stand to hear these things, he is on fire with hatred against everyone who recognizes and worships what is Divine.

I talked with one man who had been influential in the world and who had too high a level of love for himself. When he heard the Divine simply named, or especially when he heard the Lord named, he was so stirred up with wrath from his hatred that he was ablaze with murder. When the restraints of his love were loosened, he also wanted to be the Devil himself in order to mount a ceaseless attack from his self-love against heaven. Many people who come from the Papal religion have the same craving when they discover in the other life that all the power belongs to the Lord and none to them.

563. Some particular spirits kept appearing to me in the western region toward the south, saying they had been appointed to positions of great importance in the world and that they deserved to be promoted over other people and to give them orders. They were examined by angels to find out what they were like inwardly, and it was found that they had not focused on useful service in their duties in the world, but on themselves. This meant that they had made themselves more important than useful service. But since they kept politicking and demanding urgently to be promoted over other people, they were allowed to join in with people who were conferring about quite important matters of business. But it became clear that they were unable to pay any attention to the business under consideration. They could not look deeply into the matters in their own right, and they did not speak on the basis of a thing's usefulness but on the basis of their self-image, desirous of acting preferentially to curry favor. Accordingly, they were dismissed from this task and left to look for jobs somewhere else.

So they moved farther into the western region, accepted here and there; but wherever they went, they were told that they were thinking only about themselves, and thinking about other things only in terms of themselves, which made them fatuous, just like sense-oriented, physical spirits. So wherever they came they were referred elsewhere. After a while they seemed to be reduced to poverty and to beg for charity.

I could also see from this that no matter how apparently wisely they might seem to talk in the world from the fire of their self-love, people who are involved in self-love do this only on the basis of memory, not from any light of reason. So in the other life, when no one is allowed to bring out matters of the natural memory, they are more fatuous than other people. This is because they have been separated from what is Divine.

564. There are two kinds of government. One is proper to love toward the neighbor, and one is self-love. Essentially, these two kinds of government are opposites.

A person who governs out of a love toward the neighbor

intends what is good to everyone. His greatest love is for useful service —doing things for other people (by "doing things for other people" we mean intending what is good to them and performing useful functions for church, nation, community, or fellow-citizen). This is his love and his heart's delight.

He is happy, too, to the extent that he is raised to positions above others, yet his happiness is not on account of the position but on account of the service, which he can then fulfill to a greater extent and on a higher level. This is what governmental control is like in the heavens.

[2] But a person who governs out of self-love does not intend what is good to anyone, only to himself. Any useful services he fulfills are for his own prestige and glory, which are the only things he finds useful. To him, working for others is a means to being worked for and respected, and to governing. He politiks for positions, not for the good he can do for country and church but to be in prominence and glory and therefore in his heart's delight.

[3] Everyone keeps his love of governing after his life in the world. People who have governed out of a love toward the neighbor are entrusted with the responsibility of governing in the heavens. Actually, they are not the ones who govern then; rather it is the useful services which they love; and when these govern, the Lord is governing.

But people who have governed out of self-love in the world are in hell after their life in the world, and are worthless slaves. I have seen influential people, who had governed out of self-love, cast among the most worthless folk—some of them among people who live in outhouses there.

565. Turning to love of the world, though, this love is not opposed to heavenly love to such an extent, because it does not have as many evils hidden within it.

Love of the world is wanting to channel other people's

wealth to oneself by any possible means, putting one's heart in riches, and letting the world lead one back and away from a spiritual love (which is a love toward the neighbor) and therefore away from heaven and from what is Divine.

There are, however, many varieties of this love. There is a love of wealth as a means to advancement in prestige, which is the sole object of the love. There is a love of prestige and high office as means toward amassing wealth. There is a love of wealth as a means toward various useful activities which give pleasure in the world. There is a love of wealth simply for wealth's sake—this is the kind of love avaricious people have. The list goes on and on.

The purporse behind wealth is called its use; and the purpose of use is the source of the love's quality. For a love has the same quality as the motivating goal—everything else, in fact, serves it as means.

59.

WHAT HELL-FIRE AND GNASHING OF TEETH ARE

566. To date, hardly anyone knows what the eternal fire and gnashing of teeth are which the Word attributes to people in hell. This is because people have thought about the Word's contents in material terms, unaware of its spiritual meaning. So some take "fire" to mean material fire, others torment in general, thus the pang of conscience. Others take it only as a phrase designed to touch people with terror in the face of things that are evil. Some people take "gnashing of teeth" to mean an actual gnashing, some only the kind of fear that is present when you hear teeth chatter this way.

But if a person is familiar with the Word's spiritual meaning, he is able to know what "eternal fire" and "gnashing of teeth" are. For every word, and every meaning of words in the Word has a spiritual meaning within it because the Word is spiritual at heart. What is spiritual can be conveyed to man only in natural terms because man is involved in a natural world and does his thinking in terms of the things that exist in it.

In the following sections, then, we shall describe the nature of the "eternal fire" and "gnashing of teeth" which come to involve the spirits of evil people after death, or which the spirits of those people, who are then in a spiritual world, undergo.

567. There are two sources of warmth. One is heaven's sun, which is the Lord, and the other is the world's sun. The warmth that comes from heaven's sun or the Lord is a spiritual warmth which essentially is love (see above, nn. 126-140); while the warmth that comes from the world's sun is a natural warmth that is not essentially love but does work for spiritual warmth or love as a recipient.

We can determine that love is essentially warmth from the fact that the spirit [*animus*] and consequently the body warm up because of love and in proportion to its level and quality. This happens to people in winter just as much as in summer, so it comes from a warming of the blood.

We can determine that the natural warmth that arises from the world's sun works for spiritual warmth as a recipient, from the fact that the body's warmth is revived and maintained as a result of the warmth of its spirit. We see this particularly in the effect of the warmth of spring and summer on all kinds of animals, which re-enter their yearly love-cycle at these seasons. [2] The natural warmth does not cause this to happen; it arranges their bodies to accept the warmth that is also flowing into them from the spiritual world. For the spiritual world flows into the natural one the way a cause flows into its effect.

Anyone who believes that natural warmth produces these loves is greatly misled. The inflow is an inflow of the spiritual world into the natural, not of the natural world into the spiritual; and all love, since it belongs to life itself, is spiritual. [3] So anyone who believes that anything happens in the natural world without a spiritual inflow is also misled. A natural phenomenon does not occur and exist except as a result of a spiritual phenomenon. The members of the vegetable kingdom, too, derive their powers to sprout from an inflow from the spiritual world. The natural warmth that comes in spring and summer times simply arranges the seeds in their own natural forms by swelling and opening them, so that the inflow from the spiritual world may play its role within them.

We have included this information to let it be known that there are two "warmths," a spiritual one and a natural one;

that spiritual warmth comes from heaven's sun and natural warmth from the world's sun; and that the inflow and resultant cooperation produce the results which are visible to our eyes in the world.

568. For people, spiritual warmth is the warmth of their life, because as already stated it is essentially love. This warmth is what is meant by "fire" in the Word—love for the Lord and love toward the neighbor by "heavenly fire" and self-love and love of the world by "hellish fire."

569. Hellish fire or love comes from the same source as heavenly fire or love—from heaven's sun, or the Lord. However, it is made hellish by the people who receive it. For all the inflow from the spiritual world varies depending on how it is received or depending on the forms into which it flows. There is no difference between this and the situation with the warmth and light that come from the world's sun. When warmth flows in from it into trees and flowering plants it brings about an enlivening and draws forth pleasing and sweet odors. But when the same warmth flows into fecal matter and dead flesh it brings about decay and draws forth rank and putrid stenches. In the same way, light from one and the same sun brings out beautiful and pleasing colors in one subject and ugly and unpleasant colors in another.

This situation is similar with the warmth and light that come from heaven's sun, which is love. When the warmth or love flows into good things—as it does with good people and spirits and with angels—it makes their good qualities bear fruit. But with evil people it has an opposite effect. In fact, the evil qualities either stifle or corrupt it. In the same way, when heaven's light flows into true elements from what is good, it grants intelligence and wisdom. But when it flows into false elements from what is evil, it is turned into forms of madness and various kinds of hallucination. In all cases, then, it depends on how it is received.

570. Since hellish fire is self-love and love of the world, it is every craving that belongs to those loves, the craving being an extention of love because a person constantly craves what he loves. It is also a pleasure, since when a person gets what he loves or craves, he perceives it as pleasant. This is the only source of heartfelt joy for man. So hellish fire is a craving and a pleasure that well up from these two loves as their sources. The evil elements are contempt for others, enmity and hostility toward people who do not support the individual in question. There is envy, hatred, and vengefulness, and there is viciousness and cruelty arising from them. As far as what is Divine is concerned, there is denial and consequent contempt, ridicule and blasphemy of the holy things that pertain to the church. After death, these attitudes are turned into anger and hatred at such things (see above, n. 562).

Further, since these evil elements constantly breathe the destruction and murder of people who are considered enemies, objects of flaring hatred and vengeance, the intent to destroy and murder is the delight of their life. To the extent that this is impossible, their delight is the intent to inflict harm, to wound, and to torture.

These are what "fire" means in the Word when it is talking about evil people and the hells. I should like to cite some such passages to strengthen the point.

Each one is a hypocrite and wicked, every mouth speaks folly;. . . because wickedness is blazing like a fire, devouring briars and thorns, setting the forest thickets on fire, and they rise up with rising smoke, . . . the people have become fuel for the fire, no man will spare his brother. (Isaiah 9:17-19)

I will set omens in heaven and in the earth—blood, and fire, and columns of smoke; the sun will be turned to darkness.

(Joel 2:30-31)

The earth will become burning pitch; it will not be quenched night or day, its smoke will rise forever. (Isaiah 34:9-10)

Behold . . . a day is coming that will burn like an oven, and all the proud people, all evildoers, will be straw, and the coming day will burn them.   (Malachi 4:1)

Babylon . . . has become the home of demons; . . . they were screaming when they saw the smoke of her burning; . . . the smoke rises up for ages and ages.   (Revelation 18:2, 18; 19:3)

He opened the pit of the abyss, where the smoke rises up from the pit like the smoke of a vast furnace, and the sun and the air were darkened by the smoke of the pit.   (Revelation 9:2)

From the mouths of the horses fire and smoke and brimstone came forth. A third of mankind was slaughtered by these, and by the fire, by the smoke, and by the brimstone.   (Revelation 9:17-18)

The person who worships the beast . . . will drink the wine of God's wrath prepared mixed with pure wine in the cup of His warth, and he will be tortured with fire and brimstone.   (Revelation 14:9-10)

The fourth angel emptied his vial on the sun, and it was allowed to scorch people with heat, so the people were seared in intense heat.   (Revelation 16:8-9)

They were thrown into the swamp that burns with fire and brimstone.   (Revelation 19:20; 20:14-15; 21:8)

Every tree that does not produce good fruit will be cut down and thrown into the fire.   (Matthew 3:10; Luke 3:9)

The Son of man will send His angels, who will collect all the obstacles out of His kingdom and all the people who do iniquity, and will despatch them into a forge of fire.

(Matthew 13:41, 42, 50)

[The King] will say . . . to the people on His left, "Go away from me, cursed ones, into the eternal fire made ready for the devil and his angels."   (Matthew 25:41)

[And they will be sent] into eternal fire . . . into a hell of fire, . . . where their worm will not die and their fire will not be quenched.

(Matthew 18:8-9, Mark 9:43-49)

The rich man in hell told Abraham that he was being tortured in flames.   (Luke 16:24)

In these passages and many others, "fire" means the craving proper to self-love and love of the world, while the resulting "smoke" means what is false as a result of something evil.

571. Since "hellish fire" does mean a craving to dc evil things that come from self-love and love of the world, and since all the people in the hells have this kind of craving (see the preceding chapter), when the hells are opened one can see something fiery, with smoke, the sort of thing one sees in great conflagrations. There is something fiery from the hells where self-love rules, and something flame-like from the hells where love of the world rules.

When they are closed, though, this fiery something is not visible. Instead, one can see something dark, thick with smoke. The fiery something is still burning inside it, as one can tell from the warmth that radiates from it, like the warmth from ruins after a conflagration—something like the warmth of a glowing stove, or at other times like that of a hot oven. When this warmth flows into someone it arouses cravings within him, arousing hatred and vengefulness in evil people and madness in sick people.

People involved in the loves we have mentioned possess this fire or this warmth because as far as their spirits are concerned, they are connected to appropriate hells even while they are living in the body.

It should however be noted that the people who are in the hells are not "in fire"—the fire is an appearance. They are not in fact conscious of any burning there, only of the same kind of warmth they felt before, in the world. The first is visible because of its correspondence, since love corresponds to fire. All the things that appear in the spiritual world appear according to their correspondences.

572. We should bear in mind that this hellish fire or warmth turns into an intense cold when warmth flows in from heaven. At such times, the people who are there start to shiver like people gripped by a cold fever, and are profoundly tormented. This is because they are completely opposed to what is Divine; and heaven's warmth, which is Divine love, quenches hell's warmth, which is self-love. In so doing it also quenches the fire of their life, resulting

in the cold described above which causes their shivering and torment. A gloom also occurs there at such times, resulting in folly and darkness. But this seldom happens—only when there is a need to quell rebellions that are mounting beyond proper bounds.

573. Because "hellish fire" means every craving to do what is evil that wells up from self-love, this same fire also means the kind of torment that exists in the hells. For the craving that arises from that love is a craving to injure other people who do not respect or do homage or offer worship. And the amount of anger they seize on from this source, with the amount of hatred and vengefulness they seize on from the anger, determines the intensity of their craving to vent their wrath on these people. When this kind of craving dwells in every member of a community where outward restraints are not in control (the outward restraints being fears of the law, of losing reputation, prestige, profit, and life), then everyone, out of his own evil, attacks his fellow, subdues him if he is strong enough and gets him under his control. He takes delight too in venting his wrath on people who do not give in to him.

This delight is totally yoked to a delight in giving orders, to the point that they occur at the same level of intensity. This is because a delight in doing harm dwells within enmity, envy, hatred, and vengefulness. These are the evil consequences of the love we are talking about, as we have already stated.

All the hells are this kind of community. So at heart, every individual in them nurses hatred against his fellow, and as a result of this hatred, breaks out into cruelty insofar as he is strong enough It is these bursts of cruelty and the resulting torments that are meant by hellish fire, for these are the results of cravings.

574. We have already explained (n. 548) that an evil

spirit casts himself willingly into hell; so now we may state briefly why this happens even when there are such torments in hell.

Every particular hell breathes out a sphere of the cravings its inhabitants are involved in. When this sphere is sensed by someone involved in the same craving, his heart is moved and he is filled with delight, since the craving and its delight constitute a single entity. In fact, whatever a person craves is delightful to him. This is why a spirit turns toward it and out of heartful delight craves to get to it. At this point, he still does not actually realize the kind of torment that exists there; but even people who do realize this still have a craving in that direction. Actually, no one in the spiritual world is able to resist his craving. This is because his craving belongs to his love, his love to his intention, and his intention to his nature; and there, everyone's behavior follows from his nature.

[2] When a spirit, then, comes willingly or out of his own freedom to his hell and enters it, he is received warmly at first and believes that he has arrived among friends. However, this lasts only a few hours. During this time, he is being examined to determine how clever he is and therefore how strong he is. Once this examination is finished, they begin to attack him in various ways, progressively more sharply and violently. This is achieved by leading him farther and more deeply into hell, for the farther and deeper one goes into hell, the more vicious the spirits.

[3] After these attacks, they begin to vent their wrath on him by punishments, which continue until he is reduced to slavery.

But since revolutionary movements are constantly arising there (for everyone there wants to be the greatest, and is on fire with hatred for the others), there are new uprisings. So one situation gives way to another. This means that the enslaved members are freed to lend their strength to some particular new devil in order to conquer others. Then the people who do not give in and obey the leader's whim are again tormented in different ways. This goes on and on.

These kinds of torments are the torments of hell called hellish fire.

575. Gnashing of teeth, however, is the constant clash and struggle of false elements with each other—particularly in people who are involved in false things—closely connected to a contempt for other people, to enmity, ridicule, derision, and blasphemy. These break out too as clawings of various sorts. In fact, everyone struggles on behalf of his own variety of falsehood, and calls it true.

Outside the hells, the clashes and struggles sound like the gnashing of teeth; and they do even change into gnashing of teeth when true elements flow in from heaven.

In these hells dwell all the people who accorded recognition to nature and denied what is Divine; the people who reinforced themselves in this opinion are in the deeper regions. Since these people are incapable of accepting any ray of light from heaven, and are incapable therefore of seeing anything within themselves, most of them are sense-oriented, physical people who believe nothing but what their eyes see and their hands touch. This is why for them all the deceptions of the senses are true, so that they clash.

This is the reason their clashes sound like the gnashing of teeth. For in the spiritual world, all false elements grind, and teeth correspond to the lowest elements of nature and also to the lowest elements in man, which are sense-oriented and physical things (on the occurrence of gnashing of teeth in the hells, see Matthew 8:12;13:42, 50; 22:13; 24:51; 25:30; Luke 13:28).

60.

THE MALICE AND UNSPEAKABLE ARTS OF HELLISH SPIRITS

576. Anyone who thinks deeply, and understands to some extent how his own mind works, can see and grasp the extent to which spirits surpass men. Within a minute, a person can actually turn over more things in his mind, sort them out, and draw conclusions from them, than he can express in speech or writing in half an hour. We can see from this how much more capable a person is when he is in his spirit—how much more when he becomes a spirit! For the spirit is what thinks; the body is the spirit's means of expressing what it thinks in speech or writing.

This is why the person who becomes an angel after death participates in intelligence and wisdom indescribable in comparison to the intelligence and wisdom he possessed in the world. In fact, while he lived in the world his spirit was bound by his body and was involved in the natural world by means of his body. So anything he thought about spiritually flowed into natural concepts which are relatively broad, crude, and vague. There are countless elements of spiritual thinking which these concepts do not accept, and which they enfold in thick clouds derived from a person's concerns in the world.

It is different when his spirit has been released from his body and has entered his own spiritual state. This happens when he crosses over from the natural world into the spiritual world which is proper to him. We can see from what has just been said that his state then, as far as his thoughts and affections are concerned, vastly surpasses his earlier condition.

This is why angels think indescribable, unutterable thoughts, the kind of thoughts that cannot enter a person's natural thoughts. Yet every single angel was born as a human being and lived as a human being, and during that space of time he seemed to himself no wiser than any other such being.

577. The malice and artfulness of hellish spirits is on the same level as wisdom and intelligence for angels. The situation is similar, since after a person's spirit is released from his body, it is involved either in its own "good" or its own "evil"—an angelic spirit in its own "good" and a hellish spirit in its own "evil." For every individual spirit is its own good or its own evil because it is its own love, just as we have already often said and explained.

So in the same way that an angelic spirit thinks, intends, speaks, and acts out of his own "good," a hellish spirit does the same things out of his own "evil." Thinking, intending, speaking, and acting out of what is really evil is doing these things out of the whole complex of elements involved in what is evil.

[2] It was different while he lived in the body. Then the evil part of the person's spirit was under the restraints that apply to every individual on account of law, profit, prestige, reputation, and fears of losing them. So the evil part of his spirit could not break out then and display itself in its own intrinsic quality. Particularly, too, the evil part of the person's spirit lay veiled over and wrapped up then by an outward uprightness, honesty and fairness and by an affection for what is good and true, which outward characteristics this kind of person presented in his speech and imitated for the world's sake. His evil part crouched so hidden and veiled by these things that even he himself scarcely knew that such malice and artfulness existed in his spirit, that he was intrinsically the kind of devil he was to become after death, when his spirit came into its own, and into its own nature.

[3] Then an absolutely incredible malice displays itself. There are thousands of things that erupt from this malice, among them some things such that they are beyond description in the vocabulary of any language. I have been allowed to know from abundant experience and to observe what they are like, because the Lord has allowed me to be in the spiritual world in respect to my spirit and in the natural world in respect to my body at the same time. I can bear solemn witness to the fact that they have so many forms of malice that scarcely one in a thousand can be described. I can also testify that unless the Lord protected individuals, they could never escape hell. For spirits from hell, as well as angels from heaven, are with every person (see above, nn. 292-293). Further, the Lord cannot protect individuals unless they accord recognition to what is Divine and live a life of faith and charity. Otherwise, they turn away from the Lord and turn toward hellish spirits, absorbing in this way similar forms of malice into their own spirits. [4] Even so, the person is constantly being led by the Lord away from his evil elements, which he is attaching to himself, virtually attracting, by his friendship with these spirits. If the Lord cannot lead him by means of the inner restraints of conscience (which he will not accept if he denies what is Divine), then He leads him by means of outward restraints (which as already stated are fears of the law and its penalties, and fears of losing profit and lacking prestige and reputation).

Actually, this kind of person can be led away from evil matters by the use of delights of his own love and his fear of this loss and lack; but he cannot be led into good spiritual matters. For to the extent that he is led into such matters, he contrives devices and deceits for imitating and feigning things that are good and honest and fair, his purpose being to convince people and thereby deceive them. These devices compound the evil element of his spirit and give it shape, making him as evil as he is in his own nature.

578. The worst people of all are the ones who have been involved in evil pursuits as a result of self-love, with an accompanying inward behavior stemming from deceit. This is because the deceit penetrates their thoughts and purposes too thoroughly and fills them with poison, destroying their whole spiritual life.

Many of these people are in hells toward the back, and are called "genii." There they find their delight in making themselves inconspicuous, flying around other people like ghosts, carrying concealed things which they spray around the way vipers spray venom. They are tormented more horribly than others. But people who have not been crafty and filled with vicious devices, though involved in evil matters because of their self-love, are also in hells toward the back, but not in such deep ones.

On the other hand, people who have been involved in evil pursuits because of their love of the world are in hells toward the front, and are called "spirits." They are not so evil—that is, they do not have as much hatred and vengefulness as people involved in evil pursuits out of self-love; nor do they have as much malice or craft. For this reason, their hells are milder.

579. I have been allowed to develop through experience a familiarity with the quality of individuals who are called "genii," as touches their malice.

Genii do not work on or flow into thoughts, but rather into affections. They watch these and smell them out the way dogs track wild animals in a forest. When they notice good affections, they promptly turn them into evil ones by leading and twisting them in an extraordinary way, using the other person's delights. They do this so furtively, with such vicious skill, that the other person does not notice a trace of it. They manage this by taking exquisite care that nothing reaches into the person's thought, for then they would become exposed. They station themselves under the back of a person's head.

In the world, these were people who guilefully ensnared other people's minds by using the pleasures of their affections and cravings to lead and sway them.

However, they are kept by the Lord away from any individual in whose case there is hope of reformation. They are actually the kind of being that has the ability not only to destroy people's consciences, but to stir up an individual's hereditary evil elements within them, elements which would otherwise rest concealed. To prevent the individual from being led into involvement with these evil elements, the Lord has arranged for these hells to be completely closed off. When a person who is this kind of "genius" arrives in the other life after death, he is instantly cast into their hell. When these individuals are examined for guile and craft, they look like vipers.

580. We can determine the nature of hellish spirits' malice by looking at their unspeakable arts. There are so many of these that it would take a book to list them, and a mass of books to describe them.

These skills are virtually unknown in the world. One kind has to be with the misuse of correspondences; another with the misuse of the lowest elements of the Divine design; a third with the communication and inflow of thoughts and affections, using transformations, investigations, other spirits beyond themselves, and emissaries. A fourth kind involves working with hallucinations, a fifth, projection beyond themselves so that they seem to be present where their bodies are not. A sixth kind involves impersonation, persuasion, and lies.

An evil spirit comes by its very nature into the use of

these skills when it has been released from its body. They are intrinsic to the nature of his evil, the evil he is involved in at that point. Hellish spirits torment each other with these skills in the hells.

Be that as it may, since all these skills are unknown in the world except the ones that use impersonation, persuasion, and lies, I do not want to describe them here in detail, both because they would not be understood and because they are unspeakable.

581. The reason torments in the hells are tolerated by the Lord is that this is the only way evil elements can be controlled and tamed. The only means of controlling and taming these elements and keeping the hellish mob under restraint is the fear of punishment—no other means exists. For if it were not for the fear of punishment and torment, what is evil would plunge into rages and the whole place would fall apart, as happens to earthly kingdoms where there is no law or punishment.

61.

THE APPEARANCE, LOCATION, AND ABUNDANCE OF HELLS

582. One can see in the spiritual world, the world where angels and spirits are, the same sorts of things that exist in the natural world where men are. They are so much alike that there is no difference in their outward look. One can see plains there, mountains, hills, and cliffs with valleys between them, one can see bodies of water and many other things that exist on this planet.

Nevertheless, all these things come from a spiritual source. So they are visible to the eyes of spirits and angels but not to the eyes of man, man being involved in a natural world. Spiritual beings see things which come from a spiritual source, and natural beings see things which come from a natural source.

As a result, man can never see with his own eyes things which are in a spiritual world unless he is enabled to be in the spirit, except when he becomes a spirit after death. Similarly, an angel or spirit is wholly unable to see anything in a natural world unless he is with a man who is being allowed to talk with him. Man's eyes are in fact adapted to receive the world's light, while the eyes of angels and spirits are adapted to receive the spiritual world's light. In each case, though, the eyes look just the same.

A natural person cannot understand that the spiritual world is like this. A sense-oriented person—one who does not believe anything unless he sees it with his own physical eyes and touches it with his hands—is even less able to understand. He believes especially the things he himself has selected from visual and tactile experience, and does his thinking on the basis of his selection; so his thinking is material and not spiritual.

Since there is this kind of resemblance between the spiritual world and the natural world, after death the individual scarcely notices that he is not in the world where he was born, the world he has left behind. This is why they call death only a transfer from one world to another like it (on the resemblance of the two worlds, see above in the treatment of representations and appearances in heaven, nn. 170-176).

583. In the spiritual world, the heavens are in the loftiest regions, the world of spirits in lowlier regions, and the hells beneath them both. The heavens are not visible to spirits in the world of spirits except when their more inward sight is opened. From time to time, though, they are seen as heavy clouds or as bright clouds. This is because heaven's angels are involved in a more inward state as far as their intelligence and wisdom are concerned, so that they are above the sight of people who are in the world of spirits.

Still, the spirits who are in the plains and valleys do see each other. True, when they are sorted out (which happens as they are granted entrance to their own more inward reaches) the evil spirits do not see the good ones. The good ones can still see the evil ones, but they turn away from them; and when spirits turn away, they become inconspicuous.

However, the hells are not visible because they are closed. Only the entrances are visible, which are called "the gates," when they are opened to let people in who are like others there. All the gates to the hells can be seen from the world of spirits, but none of them can be seen from heaven.

584. There are hells everywhere—under the mountains, the hills, the cliffs, under the plains and valleys. The openings or gates to the hells which are under mountains, hills, and cliffs look like crevices or clefts in the rocks. Some spread broad and ample, some are tight and narrow; most are jagged. All of them look dark and gloomy on close examination, but the hellish spirits who are in them are in the kind of light which burning torches give. Their eyes are adapted to receive this kind of light. This is because while they lived in the world they were in profound darkness as far as Divine truths were concerned, since they denied them, and were in a sort of light as far as false things were concerned, since they affirmed them. This is how their eyesight took the form it did. It is also why heaven's light is a profound darkness to them, so that when they leave their caves they do not see anything.

This has made it very clear indeed that a person enters heaven's light to the extent that he accords recognition to what is Divine, and reinforces within himself those things that are proper to heaven and the church. He enters hell's deep darkness to the extent that he denies what is Divine and reinforces within himself those things that oppose what is proper to heaven and the church.

585. The openings or gates to the hells which are under the plains and valleys are of various kinds in appearance. Some are like the ones that are under mountains, hills, and cliffs. Some are like caves and caverns, some like great holes and chasms, some like swamps, and some like stagnant ponds.

All of them are covered over, out of sight except when evil spirits are being cast in from the world of spirits. When they are visible, there breathes out something like smoky fire, the kind one sees in the air in great conflagrations, or something like a flame without smoke, or something like the soot from a hot forge, or something like a heavy or dense cloud.

I have heard that the hellish spirits do not see or feel these things because when they are involved in them it is like being in their own atmosphere and therefore in their life's delight. This is because these phenomena correspond to the evil and false matters they are involved in, the fire specifically corresponding to hatred and vengeance, the smoke and soot to false things that derive from them, the flame to the evils of self-love, and the heavy or dense cloud to consequent false things.

586. I have been allowed to examine the hells and see what they are like inside. For when it pleases the Lord, a spirit or angel who is above them can with his sight penetrate to the depths and survey what they are like with no coverings in the way. I too have been allowed to examine them in the same fashion.

Some hells give the visual appearance of caverns and caves in the rocks, leading inward and then on into the depths, obliquely or vertically. Some hells give the visual appearance of the kind of lairs and dens wild beasts live in, in forests. Some are like the kinds of hollowed vaults and passages we find in mines, with caves lower down.

Most of the hells are threefold. The higher parts within them look gloomy because the people there are involved in the false side of what is evil; while the lower parts look fiery because the people there are involved in the evil things themselves. Gloom in fact corresponds to the false side of what is evil, and fire to evil things themselves. For the deeper hells are where people live whose more inward behavior has arisen from what is evil, while the hells nearer the surface are where people live whose behavior has been more outward, which arises from the false side of the evil.

In some hells, one can see something like the rubble of homes or cities after a great fire, where hellish spirits live and hide. In milder hells one sees something like tumble-down huts, crowded together rather like a city, with sections and streets. Within the houses are hellish spirits, so there are constant brawls, hostilities, beatings, and clawings. There are robberies and hold-ups in the streets and districts.

In some hells there is nothing but brothels that look disgusting and are full of all kinds of filth and excrement. There are dense forests too, where hellish spirits roam about like wild beasts, and there are underground caves in them where they flee when others are after them. Then there are deserts where everything is barren and sandy, with jagged cliffs here and there with caverns in them, and even occasional huts. Into these desert places are cast the people from the hells who have gone through the very most, especially the ones who were more clever than others at working things out and scheming with their arts and deceits. Their final end is this kind of life.

587. Turning to the specific location of the hells, no one can know this, not even the angels in heaven—only the Lord knows. In general terms, though, their locations are known from the regions they are in. The hells are in fact divided into regions are way the heavens are; and in the spiritual world regions are marked off according to loves. All the regions in heaven start from the Lord as the sun, Who is the East. Since the hells are opposites to the heavens, their regions start from the opposite, that is from the West (in this connection, see the chapter on the four regions in heaven, nn. 141-153).

[2] This is why the hells in the western region are the worst and most terrifying of all—getting worse and more terrifying as they get farther from the East, step by step. These hells are where people live who were involved in self-love in the world, who consequently were involved in contempt for other people and in enmity toward people who did not support them, with a resultant hatred and vengefulness toward people who did not revere and honor them.

In the farthest reaches are people who belonged to the so-called Catholic religious persuasion, and who wanted in that context to be worshipped as gods, flaring up therefore with hatred and vengefulness at anyone who did not acknowledge their power over people's souls and over heaven.

These people have the same kind of spirit (that is, the same kind of hatred and vengefulness) against people who resist them now as they had in the world. Rage is their prime delight. However, this is turned back on themselves in the other life, since in their hells (which fill the western region) each one rages against every other who disparages his Divine power (but there is more on this topic in the booklet, *The Last Judgment and Babylon Destroyed*).

[3] There is no way of knowing how the hells in this region are arranged. We can know only that the most savage hells of this sort are on the side toward the northern region and the less savage toward the southern region. So the savagery of the hells declines from the northern part to the southern and step by step toward the East. On the eastern side live people who were proud and did not believe in what is Divine, but still were not involved in hatred or vengefulness, or deceit, to the same extent as the people who live deeper in the western region.

[4] At the present time there are no hells in the eastern region. The people who were there have been transferred into a western region toward the front.

There are many hells in the northern and southern regions. In them live the people who during their lives were involved in various kinds of evil—enmity, hostility, theft, robbery, fraud, greed, ruthlessness. The worst hells of this sort are in the northern region, the milder ones in the southern. Their ferocity increases as they are nearer the western region and declines toward the eastern as well as toward the southern.

Behind the hells in the western regions are dense forests

where vicious spirits roam about like wild beasts. There is something like this behind the hells of the northern region. Behind the hells in the southern region, though, are the deserts described just above. So much for the locations of the hells.

588. Turning to the abundance of the hells, there are as many hells as there are angelic communities in the heavens, because each angelic community has, by reason of opposition, a corresponding hellish community.

The reader may see in the chapters on the communities that make up the heavens (nn. 41-50) and the vastness of heaven (nn. 415-420) that the heavenly communities are beyond counting and are all set off according to the good elements of love. [2] It is the same with hellish communities, which are set off according to the evil elements opposite to the good ones. Each particular evil thing is subject to infinite diversity, just like each particular good thing.

People do not grasp the truth of this if they have only a simplistic concept of a particular element such as contempt, enmity, hatred, vengefulness, deceit, and the like. Let them realize, though, that every single one of these comprises so many distinct categories or details that a large book would be inadequate to list them. The hells are so precisely arranged according to the distinctions within each evil element that nothing could be more orderly and precise.

We can conclude from this that they are beyond counting—one near another, one far from another, according to the general, the more specific, and the detailed distinctions between evil elements.

[3] There are hells under the hells as well. Some communicate by passages, some by exhaltations, in precise dependence on the relationship between one genus and species of evil with others.

I have been enabled to know how numerous the hells are

on the basis of their presence underneath every mountain, hill, and cliff, every plain and valley, and their stretching far, wide, and deep. In brief, the whole heaven and the whole world of spirits are hollowed out, so the speak, and underneath them is an unbroken hell. So much for the abundance of the hells.

62.

THE BALANCE BETWEEN HEAVEN AND HELL

589. Everything needs to be in a balance if anything is to result. Without a balance, there is no "action and reaction," since the balance is between two forces, one acting and the other reacting. The state of rest that results from an equal agent and re-agent is called a balance.

In the natural world there is a balance in everything and in all details. Overall, there is a balance involving the actual atmospheres, with the lower ones reacting and resisting in proportion to the action and pressure of the higher ones. There is also a balance in the natural world between warmth and cold, light and shade, dry and moist; the halfway measure is the balance.

There is a balance as well involving all the members of the world's kingdoms, which are three in number—mineral, vegetable, and animal. For without a balance involving them nothing would occur or endure. Everywhere there is a kind of effort acting from one side and something reacting from the other.

[2] Every event, or every effect, occurs in a balance, or happens by means of one force acting and another force being acted upon. That is, one force, by acting, flows in, and the other accepts it and gives way appropriately. In the natural world, the thing that acts and the thing that reacts are called "force" and "inertia"; but in the spiritual world the thing that acts and the thing that reacts are called "life" and "intention." In that world, life is a living force, and intention is a living inertia, and the actual balance is called "a free state."

A spiritual balance or free state, then, arises and endures

between what is good acting from one side and what is evil reacting from the other side, or between what is evil acting from one side and what is good reacting from the other side.

[3] There is a balance between active good and reactive evil for good people, and between active evil and reactive good for evil people.

The reason the spiritual balance is between what is good and what is evil is that every element of man's life goes back to what is good and to what is evil, with his intention as their recipient.

There is also a balance between what is true and what is false, but this depends on the balance between what is good and what is evil. It is like the balance between light and shade, which are effective in members of the vegetable kingdom to the extent that warmth and cold are present in light and shade. We may conclude that light and shade by themselves have no effect, but only the warmth and cold they convey, by bearing in mind the similarity between light and shade in wintertime and in springtime.

The comparison between the true and the false on the one hand and light and shade on the other, derives from their correspondence. The true corresponds to light, the false to shade, and warmth to the good content of love. Then too, spiritual light is what is true, and spiritual shade is what is false, and spiritual warmth is the good content of love (in this connection, see the chapter on light and warmth in heaven, nn. 126-140).

590. There is a perpetual balance between heaven and hell. An effort to do what is evil breathes and rises incessantly from hell; an effort to do what is good breathes and descends incessantly from heaven.

The world of spirits is set in this balance—on its location halfway between heaven and hell, see above (nn. 421-431). The world of spirits is in this balance because after death man enters the world of spirits first and is kept there in the same kind of state he was in, in the world. This could not happen unless there were a perfect balance there. It is by this means that everyone is examined to find out what he is like, since people there are left in their freedom, of the same quality as the freedom they enjoyed in the world. The spiritual balance is a freedom for men and for spirits (as stated just above, n. 589).

Angels can tell what kind of freedom an individual has by a communication of affections and resultant thoughts. This becomes visible for angelic spirits in the paths they travel. The ones who are good spirits follow paths that lead toward heaven, while evil spirits follow paths that lead to hell. The paths are actually visible in that world. This is why in the Word, "paths" indicate true elements that lead to what is good, or in the opposite meaning false elements that lead to what is evil. This is why "going," "walking," and "traveling" in the Word indicate steps of life.

I have often been enabled to see these paths, and to see how spirits move and walk along them freely, following their affections and resultant thoughts.

591. The reason something evil is constantly breathing and rising from hell, and something good is constantly breathing and descending from heaven, is that every individual is encompassed by a spiritual sphere. This sphere flows out and radiates from the life of a person's affections and consequent thoughts. Since a life sphere like this flows out from every individual, it flows out from each heavenly community as well, and from each hellish community. As a result, it flows out from all of them combined—that is, from heaven as a whole and from hell as a whole.

The reason something good flows from heaven is that everyone there is involved in what is good; the reason something evil flows from hell is that everyone there is involved in what is evil.

All the "good" that flows from heaven comes from the Lord, since all the angels who are in the heavens are kept away from their self-images [*proprium*] and kept in the Lord's self-image, which is the Good itself. All the spirits who are in the hells, though, are involved in their own self-image. A person's self-image is nothing but evil; and since it is nothing but evil, it is hell.

On this basis, we can determine that the balance which angels in the heavens and spirits in the hells are kept in, is not like the balance found in the world of spirits. The balance for angels in the heavens is a matter of the extent to which they wanted to be involved in something good or lived involved in something good in the world—that is, how much they turned away from what is evil. On the other hand, the balance of spirits in hell is a matter of the extent to which they wanted to be involved in something evil in the world or lived involved in something evil in the world—that is, then, how opposed to the good they were in heart and in spirit.

592. If the Lord did not rule both the heavens and the hells, there would be no balance. If there were no balance, there would be no heaven or hell. In fact, everything in the universe—every single item—(everything in both the natural and the spiritual worlds, that is) results from a balance.

Any rational person can see the truth of this. Suppose an imbalance on one side with nothing to counter it on the other—would not both sides perish? This would happen in the spiritual world, if the good did not react against the evil and consistently keep its rebellion under control. If the only Divine did not accomplish this, heaven and hell would perish and the whole human race would perish with them. We use the phrase "if the only Divine did not accomplish this" because everyone's self-image is nothing but evil —angel's, spirit's, or man's (see above, n. 591). So there is no way for an angel or spirit to fight off the evil influences that constantly breathe from the hells, seeing that they themselves lean toward hell as a result of their own selfhood. We can see from this that if the Lord alone did not govern both the heavens and hells, no one could possibly have salvation.

Beyond this, all the hells cooperate because evil elements in the hells are organized the way good elements in the heavens are. Nothing but the Divine, which comes only from the Lord, can withstand all the hells, which are countless, and which act in concert against heaven and against all the individuals who are in heaven.

593. The balance between the heavens and the hells ebbs and flows in response to the number of people entering heaven and entering hell, which amounts to several thousand a day. No angel can know and perceive this, modify and adjust it precisely. Only the Lord can do this. For the Divine that emanates from the Lord is present everywhere, seeing just which way a given situation is leaning. An angel sees only what is near him, and does not see within himself even what is going on in his own community.

594. We can to some extent determine how everything in the heavens and the hells is so arranged that every particular element there is in a balance, if we recall some things mentioned and explained above about the heavens and the hells. We refer to the fact that all heaven's communities are very precisely arranged according to their good elements, their classes and sub-classes, while all the hells are similarly arranged according to their evil elements and their classes and sub-classes. We refer also to the fact that there is a community of hell underneath every community of heaven and inversely corresponding to it. A balance results from this inverse correspondence. In consequence, the Lord is constantly taking care that the hellish community underneath a given heavenly community does not get too strong. As one begins to get too strong, various measures are taken to confine it and bring it back to the proper proportional balance.

There are many such measures; we need mention only a few. Some of them involve a stronger presence of the Lord, some a closer communication or bonding of one community with others, some banishing excess hellish spirits to desert places, some transfer of various people from one hell to another, some the arranging of people in the hells (for which again various measures are used), some the hiding of particular hells under thicker and coarser covers, and then letting them down deeper. There are other measures taken, some even in the heavens overhead.

We have mentioned these things to help the reader see to some extent that only the Lord sees to it that there be a balance everywhere between what is good and what is evil, between heaven and hell therefore. For on this kind of balance rests the salvation of all the people in the heavens and on earth.

595. We need to realize that the hells are constantly attacking heaven and trying to destroy it, with the Lord constantly protecting it by keeping the people who are there away from their self-image and keeping them in the good that comes from Him. I have quite often been allowed to perceive the sphere that breathes out of the hells. In all respects, it is a sphere of efforts to destroy the Lord's Divine, and therefore heaven. From time to time, I have noticed outbursts of particular hells which were efforts to get loose and wreak destruction.

On the other hand, the heavens in no way attack the hells, since the Divine sphere that comes from the Lord is an unceasing effort to save everyone. Since the people who are in the hells cannot be saved (being all involved in what is evil and opposed to the Lord's Divine), the uprisings in the hells are mitigated as much as they can be, and the cruelties are confined so that they do not burst out against each other beyond proper bounds. This is done by countless methods that belong to Divine power.

596. There is a distinction between two kingdoms of heaven, a celestial kingdom and a spiritual kingdom (for further details, see above, nn. 20-28). In a similar fashion, there is a distinction between two kingdoms of hell. One of these is the opposite of the celestial kingdom, and the other the opposite of the spiritual kingdom.

The opposite of the celestial kingdom is in the western region, and the people who live there are called "genii." The opposite of the spiritual kingdom is in the northern and southern regions, and the people who live there are called "spirits."

All the people who live in the celestial kingdom are involved in a love for the Lord, and all the people in the opposite kingdom in the hells are involved in self-love. All the people who are in the spiritual kingdom are involved in a love toward the neighbor, while all the people in the opposite kingdom in the hells are involved in a love of the world.

This has enabled me to see that love for the Lord and self-love are opposites, as are love toward the neighbor and love of the world.

The Lord takes constant care that nothing should flow toward people in the spiritual kingdom out of the hells opposite to the celestial kingdom. For if this were to happen, the spiritual kingdom would be destroyed (for the reason, see above, nn. 578-9). These are the two overall balances that are constantly kept in good working order by the Lord.

63.

MAN IS IN A FREEDOM BY MEANS OF THE BALANCE BETWEEN HEAVEN AND HELL

597. We have just discussed the balance between heaven and hell, explaining that this is a balance between what is good, from heaven, and what is evil, from hell, being therefore a spiritual balance which essentially is a freedom.

The reason this spiritual balance is essentially a freedom is that it is between what is good and what is evil and between what is true and what is false. These are spiritual entities. So the abilities to intend either the good or the evil, and to choose one rather than the other, is the freedom which is our present topic.

This freedom is granted to every individual by the Lord, and is not in any manner taken away. It is something that by virtue of its origin belongs to the Lord and not to the individual, because it comes from the Lord. Yet it is given to the individual as a possession, along with his life, the purpose being his reformation and salvation. For without freedom, there can be no reformation or salvation.

Even a minimum of intuition based on reason will enable a person to see that it lies within the scope of an individual's freedom to think badly or well, honestly or dishonestly, fairly or unfairly, and further to speak and act well, honestly, and fairly. Yet because of spiritual, moral and civic laws, which keep restraints on the outer realm, this is not true of speaking and acting badly, dishonestly, and unfairly.

We can see from this that a person's spirit—the part of him that thinks and intends—is in a freedom. The same cannot be said for the outward part of a person—the part that speaks and acts—unless it follows the laws we have just mentioned.

598. The reason a person cannot be reformed unless he has some freedom is that he is born involved in all sorts of evil which need to be taken away if he is to be saved. They cannot be taken away unless he sees them within himself and identifies them, then wants not to do them, and finally turns away from them. Then for the first time they are taken away.

This cannot happen unless the individual is as much involved in what is good as he is in what is evil. It is possible, that is, to see evil things from an involvement in what is good, but not to see good things from involvement in what is evil.

A person learns from the cradle the spiritual "goods" which he can think, as a result of hearing the Word read and interpreted. He learns moral and civic "goods" from his life in the world.

[2] This is the primary reason for his need to be in freedom. Another reason is that nothing becomes part of a person unless it occurs as a result of some affection that belongs to his love. Other things may come into him, but they come no farther than his thinking —they do not enter his intention. Anything that does not enter right into a person's intention does not belong to him; for thinking draws its material from memory, while intention draws its material from the life itself.

Nothing is at all free that does not derive from intention—in other words, from an affection that belongs to love. In fact, a person does freely that which he intends or loves. This is why a person's freedom and the affection of his love or intention are the same thing. As a result, then, the individual has freedom so that he can be affected by what is true and good or love them, so that they become virtually parts of him.

[3] In short, anything that does not gain entrance when

someone is in freedom does not last, because it is not part of his love or intention. Anything that is not part of a person's love or intention is not part of his spirit. In fact, the essential reality [*esse*] of a person's spirit is his love or intention. We say "love or intention" because people do intend whatever they love.

This, then, is why the individual cannot be re-formed unless he is in some freedom.

599. It is to keep the individual in a freedom, so that he can be reformed, that in spirit he is bonded to heaven and to hell. There are spirits from hell and angels from heaven with every single person. The person is involved in his evil aspect by means of the spirits from hell, and in his good aspect from the Lord by means of the angels from heaven. In this way, he is in a spiritual balance—that is, in a freedom.

The reader may see in the chapter on heaven's bond with the human race (nn. 291-302) that angels from heaven and spirits from hell are attached to every single individual.

600. We do need to realize that a person's bond with heaven and with hell is not directly with them. It is indirect, through spirits who are in the world of spirits. These spirits are with the person; no one from hell itself or heaven itself is with him. The person is bonded with hell through evil spirits in the world of spirits, and with heaven through good spirits in that same world.

Since this is the way things are arranged, the world of spirits is midway between heaven and hell, and the actual balance occurs there The reader may see in the chapter on the world of spirits (nn. 421-431) that it is midway between heaven and hell. He may see that the actual balance between heaven and hell occurs there in the chapter previous to this (nn. 589-596). We can see from these considerations how it is that the individual has a freedom.

601. I should like to say something more about the spirits who are attached to people. A whole community can be in communication with another community or with another individual, anywhere, by means of a spirit sent forth from it. This spirit is called the group's "subject."

It is much the same with a person's bond with communities in heaven and with communities in hell, through spirits from the world of spirits who are attached to him.

602. In closing, we need to make some mention of the inborn notion of life after death, a notion which results from the inflow of heaven into man.

There were some very ordinary people who in the world had lived involved in what is good derived from faith. They were brought back into the same state they had been in in the world (this can be accomplished for anyone when the Lord grants it). I was then shown what kind of concept they had had of man's state after death.

They said that in the world some intelligent people had asked them what they thought about their souls after the end of life in the world. They said they did not know what the soul was. They went on to ask what they believed about their state after death; they said they believed they would live as spirits. They asked what kind of belief they had about "the spirit"; they said it was the person. They kept asking how they knew this; they kept saying that they knew it because it was so.

The intelligent people were amazed that these ordinary people had such faith when they themselves did not.

I could see from this that there is an instinctive idea of life after death in every individual who is involved in a bond with heaven. The only source of which instinctive idea is an inflow from heaven—more precisely, through heaven from the Lord—by means of spirits attached to the individual from the world of spirits. People have this if their freedom for thinking has not been quenched by acquired premises about the human soul, premises reinforced by various means, which state either that the soul is pure thought or that it is a vivified principle whose seat they look for in the body. In fact, the soul is nothing more than the person's life, and the spirit is the actual person. The earthly body he carries around in the world is simply a servant through which the spirit—the real person—acts suitably in a natural world.

603. The statements in this book about heaven, the world of spirits, and hell, will be obscure to people who find no delight in knowing spiritual truths; but they will be clear to people who do find this delight. This is particularly true for people involved in an affection for what is true for its own sake—that is, for people who love what is true because it is true. In fact anything that is loved brings light with it into the mind's concepts — especially when what is true is loved, for everything true is in the light.

Brief Descriptions of
THE THEOLOGICAL WRITINGS OF EMANUEL SWEDENBORG

(Not Available in Large Print)

These books may be ordered through your nearest bookstore or direct from—

SWEDENBORG FOUNDATION, INC.
139 East 23rd Street
New York, N. Y. 10010

Complete catalog and current price list sent free on request.

APOCALYPSE EXPLAINED, 6 Vols.

Presents the spiritual (symbolic) sense of the Book of Revelation up to chapter 19, verse 10, and many other parts of the Scriptures, especially the Psalms, the Prophets, and the Gospels. Extensive and practical doctrinal discussions are introduced.

APOCALYPSE REVEALED, 2 Vols.

A study which primarily concentrates on the exposition of the spiritual (symbolic) sense of the Book of Revelation. It is the work, therefore, to which the reader would turn first for the profound meaning in this dramatic book of the New Testament.

ARCANA COELESTIA (Heavenly Secrets), 12 Vols.

An exposition of the spiritual (symbolic) sense within the allegory and history of the books of Genesis and Exodus with numerous references to other parts of the Bible.

CONJUGIAL LOVE.

An ethical discussion of the relation of the sexes and a view of the enduring world of the spirit, of the nature and origin of true marriage love and of its indissoluble nature, of sexual irregularities and the avoidance of them. Also discusses the marriage of the Lord and the Church and its spiritual significance.

DIVINE LOVE AND WISDOM.

This book is an interpretation of the universe as a spiritual-natural or psycho-physical world. It treats of the activity of God's love and wisdom in the creation of this world and of the human being, who is similarly constituted.

DIVINE PROVIDENCE.

A profound philosophical work, revealing the law-abiding ways and merciful means by which God, in His immanence, cares for the individual and mankind.

FOUR DOCTRINES.

Swedenborg restates in this work four leading doctrines of the Christian religion: The Lord, The Sacred Scriptures, Life and Faith. These doctrines are drawn from, and substantiated by, numerous passages from the Divine Word, examined as a unified whole.

MARITAL LOVE, translated by Wm. F. Wunsch.

Another translation of *Conjugial Love* containing teachings regarding the home and marriage. It also deals with the true marriage and illicit loves, in the framework of morals and ethics.

MISCELLANEOUS THEOLOGICAL WORKS.

Bound together in this volume are the following treatises: *The New Jerusalem and Its Heavenly Doctrine; A Brief Exposition of the Doctrine of the New Church; The Nature of the Intercourse Between the Soul and the Body; On the White Horse Mentioned in the Apocalypse; On the Earths in the Universe; The Last Judg-*

ment (on a first Christian era); and *A Continuation Concerning the Last Judgment.*

POSTHUMOUS THEOLOGICAL WORKS, 2 Vols.

A number of the shorter posthumous works including extracts from Swedenborg's correspondence.

SPIRITUAL DIARY, 5 Vols.

A storehouse of spiritual facts, phenomena and principles which Swedenborg wrote during twenty years of his experiences in the spiritual realm.

THE SPIRITUAL LIFE, THE WORD OF GOD.

Extracts from Swedenborg's *The Apocalypse Explained,* make devotional reading on the spiritual or regenerating life, the significance of the Ten Commandments, our possible profanation of good and truth, and the power of God's Word.

TRUE CHRISTIAN RELIGION, 2 Vols.

Swedenborg's crowning work giving a complete exposition of doctrines for the New Christian Era. It is a powerful and massive presentation dealing with a broad spectrum of modern Christian concerns and draws upon more than nine hundred passages from all parts of the Bible.

OTHER TITLES:

THE BIBLE THAT WAS LOST AND IS FOUND, by John Bigelow.

Written for his family, this testimonial to Swedenborg as a revelator is a fascinating account of how one man discovered the true meaning of the Bible.

THE CEREBRUM, by Emanuel Swedenborg. 2 Vols.

The pursuit of the soul through anatomy with emphasis on the anatomy of the brain.

DICTIONARY OF BIBLE IMAGERY,
compiler Alice Spiers Sechrist.

Reveals symbolic meanings of thousands of words of the Bible.

DREAMS, HALLUCINATIONS, VISIONS, by Ernst Benz.

Explains the psychic and religious significance of these three types of phenomena.

THE ESSENTIAL SWEDENBORG, by Sig Synnestvedt.

Presents the basic elements of Swedenborg's thought.

GIST OF SWEDENBORG, by Smyth & Wunsch.

Topically arranged quotations from Swedenborg's works.

THE HUMAN MIND, by Hugo Lj. Odhner.

A collection of essays on the different degrees of the mind.

INSIGHTS INTO THE BEYOND, by Paul Zacharias.

An introductory guide to Swedenborg's most popular book, *Heaven and Hell.*

INTRODUCTION TO SWEDENBORG'S RELIGIOUS THOUGHT, by John H. Spalding.

A clear, comprehensive, and forcefully reasoned presentation of Swedenborg's teachings.

THE LANGUAGE OF PARABLE, by William L. Worcester.

This work takes commonly used expressions and traces them back to the letter of the Word presenting their spiritual sense.

MARRIAGE: IDEALS AND REALIZATIONS, by William F. Wunsch.

A compilation from several of Swedenborg's works on this subject.

MY RELIGION, by Helen Keller.

A beautifully written and inspiring account of the teachings of Swedenborg regarding the Divine which Miss Keller stated "...was a constant source of strength."

Also recorded for the blind and shut-in—set of 2 ten-inch records, 8⅓ rpm, dramatized by Lillian Gish. Also available in cassette tapes, and large print.

**NATURAL DEPTH IN MAN, by
Wilson Van Dusen**

A searcher's guide for exploring the secret spaces of our inner worlds.

**OUTLINES OF SWEDENBORG'S TEACHINGS, by
William F. Wunsch.**

A study guide dealing with a way of life of particular significance to those in quest of religious insights, emphasizing the Spiritual Life, the Word, and the Lord.

**THE PRESENCE OF OTHER WORLDS, by Wilson
Van Dusen.**

A fascinating account of Swedenborg's inner journey of the mind with spiritual and psychological findings.

**THE SERMON ON THE MOUNT, by Richard H.
Teed.**

An exposition of the acknowledged statement of the ideal religious life.

**SWEDENBORG, LIFE AND TEACHING, by George
Trobridge.**

The most widely read biography of the "Aristotle of the North."

TREMULATION, by Emanuel Swedenborg.

The beginning of the theory of motion.